EDMUN

HIS LIFE AND OPINIONS

EDMUND BURKE

HIS LIFE AND OPINIONS

STANLEY AYLING

CASSELL

Cassell Publishers Limited
Villiers House, 41/47 Strand
London WC2N 5JE

First published by John Murray (Publishers) Ltd
1988
This edition 1990

British Library Cataloguing in Publication Data
Ayling, Stanley, *1909-*
    Edmund Burke: his life and opinions.–2nd ed.
    1. Great Britain. Politics. Burke, Edmund,
    1729-1797
    I. Title
    941.073092

ISBN 0-304-34012-X

Printed and bound in Great Britain by
Mackays of Chatham

To the memory of my father,
Edward Stewart Ayling

Contents

Acknowledgements

National Gallery of Ireland 1; Countess of Fitzwilliam 2, 5; National Portrait Gallery 6, 8, 12, 14; Fitzwilliam Museum, Cambridge 7; The Victoria Memorial, Calcutta 11

Vignettes in text

A map of India will be found on p xi

Preface

IN THE Preface to his *Edmund Burke: Six Essays*, published nearly forty years ago, Professor Thomas W. Copeland, of the University of Massachusetts, recognising 'our present ignorance' concerning Burke, despite the abundant literature already devoted to him, reflected on how it was that he had 'eluded our curiosity' to the extent he had. A large part of the answer, of course, lay in the obstacle whose removal Professor Copeland himself was subsequently to preside over – the unavailability to scholars of that large collection of Burke's correspondence jealously guarded at Wentworth Woodhouse by the descendants of his friend and patron Earl Fitzwilliam.

The opening-up at last of this hoard, its transference to Sheffield City Library, and its eventual publication (together with all Burke's previously published letters, and many more held earlier in various hands) in that triumph of historical scholarship and transatlantic collaboration, the ten volumes (1958–78) of *The Correspondence of Edmund Burke*, for the first time made possible what Professor Copeland had been asking for in 1950, a new 'major study'. The present book is far from that – indeed the new major study was the annotated correspondence itself – but at least it has the advantage of being the first life of Burke to follow the publication of all his correspondence known to be still extant.

Heading any list of my acknowledgements therefore must be the late Thomas Copeland himself (the general editor), his chief associate editor the late John A. Woods of Leeds University, and the score or so of distinguished scholars and researchers who comprised their editorial and advisory committees. I would like also to add to their names those of Professor Ian Christie and Dr Paul Langford, for their encouragement when I was beginning work on this biography some years ago. Among others who have helped during its writing, I must especially thank Dr Malcolm Chapman, for much invaluable assistance of various sorts.

For Burke's writings and published speeches I have for the most part used and quoted from the Bohn six-volume edition of 1855. A complete modern edition, from the Clarendon Press, of *The Writings and Speeches of Edmund Burke* is currently in course of production, under the general editorship of Dr Langford. There have however been so far only two volumes published. My use hence of more than one printed source for the speeches and writings will explain some inconsistencies in my treatment of Burke's spelling, punctuation, and use of capital letters. Where the editors of the *Correspondence* or the new *Writings and Speeches* have reproduced Burke's own usages I have in general followed them. Where the Bohn edition is cited, I have necessarily followed its Victorian 'corrections'.

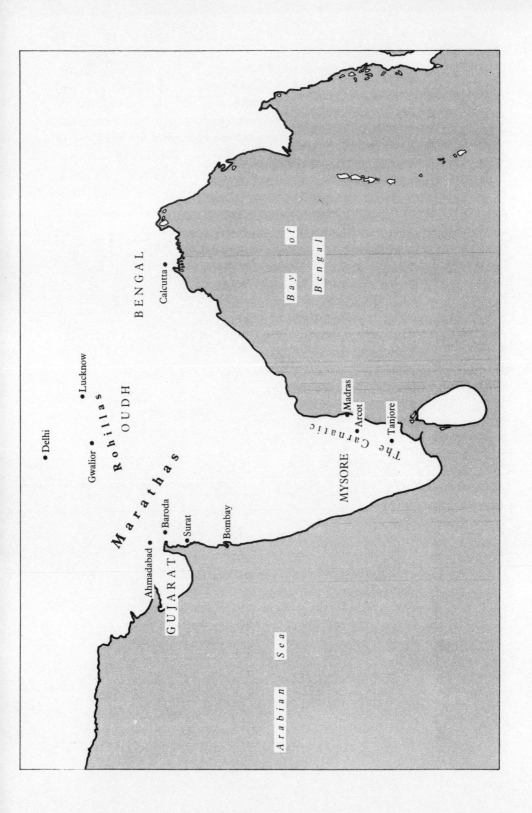

BENGAL

Calcutta •

Bay of Bengal

Lucknow •

Delhi •

OUDH

R o h i l l a s

Gwalior •

M a r a t h a s

Baroda •

Surat •

• Bombay

Ahmadabad •

GUJARAT

Madras
•
Arcot
• Tanjore

MYSORE

The Carnatic

Arabian Sea

Introduction

WRITING SOME ten years after Burke's death, Hazlitt declared that with him it had always been 'a test of the candour of anyone belonging to the opposite party whether he allowed Burke to be a great man'; but he had found few to pass that test. The others 'all seemed to be of opinion that he was a wild enthusiast, or a hollow sophist, who was to be answered by bits of facts, by smart logic, by shrewd questions, and idle songs. They looked upon him as a man of disordered intellects, because he reasoned in a style to which they had not been used, and which confounded their dim perceptions . . . They did not know whom they had to contend with.'[1] Hazlitt, politically radical, considered Burke to be not only 'a great man'; more specifically, he was a great *writer*. 'If there are greater prose writers than Burke', he wrote, 'they either lie out of my course of study, or are beyond my sphere of comprehension'. (Coleridge, De Quincey, Macaulay, Matthew Arnold, and Leslie Stephen all later expressed broadly the same opinion.)

A century or more afterwards, the socialist writer Harold Laski, from a political viewpoint even more radically opposed to Burke's than Hazlitt's, judged nevertheless that there was 'hardly a greater figure in the history of political thought in England'. Burke 'brought to the political philosophy of his generation a sense of its direction, a lofty vigour of purpose, and a full knowledge of its complexity, such as no other statesman ever possessed. His flashes of insight are things that go, as few men have ever gone, into the hidden deeps of political complexity'. How easy it was, Laski reflected, to show that Burke's 'picture of the British constitution was remote from the facts even when he wrote, or to argue that every change which he resisted was essential to the security of the next generation . . . Such criticism would be at almost every point just; and yet it would fail to touch the heart of Burke's position'.

Posterity no doubt has agreed to value Burke principally as a political philosopher, but he always (after coming to parliament rather late) saw himself less pretentiously as a practising politician, though one claiming scholarly standards and intellectual standing. He would certainly not have jibbed at being called a statesman; but our description of 'political philsopher' would have connoted for Burke too much of what he of all things despised – airy theorising and abstract metaphysics:

> Nothing universal can be rationally affirmed on any moral or on any political subject. Pure metaphysical abstraction does not belong to these matters. The lines of morality are not like the ideal lines of mathematics. They are broad and deep as well as long. They admit of exceptions. These exceptions and modifications are not made by the process of logic, but by the rules of prudence. Prudence is not only the first in rank of the virtues political and moral, but she is the director, the regulator, the standard of them all. Metaphysics cannot live without definition; but prudence is cautious how she defines.[2]

'A statesman', he wrote elsewhere, 'differs from a professor in an university':

> The latter has only the general view of society; the former, the statesman, has a number of circumstances to combine with those general ideas, and to take into his consideration. Circumstances are infinite, and infinitely combined; are variable and transient; he who does not take them into consideration is . . . stark mad – he is metaphysically mad. A statesman, judging contrary to the exigencies of the moment, may ruin his country for ever.[3]

No rational man governed himself 'by abstractions and universals'. Politics, on the other hand, for all its hurly-burly and intrigue, provided a calling whose worth and honour had no superior. When in July 1791 he thought that his *Appeal from the New to the Old Whigs* was being judged by one at least of its readers from too 'philosophical' a standpoint, he wrote to him: 'But surely you forget that I was throwing out reflexions upon a political event, and not reading a lecture upon theories and principles of government'.[4] And it was specifically to the Ireland of the 1780s that he was referring when he wrote to a friend there:

> I have no doubt that yourself and your connexions will always act the steady and honourable part that becomes you. I could wish indeed that some system existed to which such principles and conduct could be more usefully referred. But in that respect we must rest contented; for I believe, after all, that systems must arise out of events, rather than pre-exist and guide them as they happen; though the latter would be infinitely the most desirable.[5]

It must therefore be chiefly from Burke's reactions to current events and problems, in his innumerable speeches reported or published, in his controversial articles and pamphlets, and not least in his voluminous correspondence, that those 'flashes of insight' are to be discovered. No doubt from them a philosophy of history and politics and religion, of life itself, may be roughly assembled. Yet even his most famous work, the *Reflections on the Revolution in France*, is but intermittently a historico-philosophical treatise, and then only tangentially or parenthetically, the core of the book lying in his passionately hostile response to recent events in France and to the ignorant folly of those in Britain who welcomed them. Near to 'the heart of his position' is always the conviction that circumstances will alter cases; practicalities will govern decisions; one must always be wary of 'abstractions and universals'.

Thus, what naive folly it was to try governing by some abstract theory of rights, as the French revolutionaries and their English friends proposed, with the 'rights of man':

The rights of man are incapable of definition, but not impossible to be discerned . . . They are often in balance between differences of good; in compromise sometimes between good and evil, and sometimes between evil and evil. Political reason is a computing principle; adding, subtracting, multiplying and dividing, morally and not metaphysically or mathematically, true moral denominations.[6]

Indeed Burke's thought will seldom be altogether intelligible unless it is interpreted against the 'variable and transient' background either of contemporary public events or his personal and family circumstances. His condemnation for instance of democracy may be universally valid or it may not; but when it is preceded by a horrified account of the mob's doings at Versailles on 6 October 1789, how much sharper becomes the focus:

When popular authority is absolute and unrestrained the people have an infinitely greater, because a far better founded, confidence in their own power. They are themselves, in a great measure, their own instruments. They are nearer to their objects. Besides, they are less under responsibility to one of the greatest controlling powers on earth, the sense of fame and estimation. The share of infamy that is likely to fall to the lot of each individual in public acts is small indeed . . . Their own approbation of their own acts has to them the appearance of a public judgement in their favour. A perfect democracy is therefore the most shameless thing in the world.[7]

Again, an appreciation of Burke's liberal views on Ireland and its Catholics, and indeed on the whole question of religious toleration, is hardly separable from the realisation that he was an Irishman, the Protestant son of a Catholic mother, and the husband of a Catholic wife; his sister too was a Catholic. His shifting attitude to the removal of legal discrimination against Protestant Dissenters becomes comprehensible only when seen against the contemporary political background, in particular of the years 1784 and 1789. Then, the famous defence of political parties in his *Thoughts on the Present Discontents*, seen in its context – the factional struggles of the late 1760s – becomes less a thesis of general application than a testimonial to the virtues of one particular group, his own, led by Lord Rockingham; a mere extract from a party manifesto, not usually a place in which to look for 'universals'. The sharp contrast between his impassioned campaign against Warren Hastings and the East India Company during the 1780s and his violent championing earlier of the Company's chartered independence is not fully explicable without an understanding of the ways in which he and his brother and particularly his namesake and dearest friend William Burke became involved (over many years and often painfully and bitterly) in the financial and political affairs of the Company. Even that justly celebrated passage on the 'sacredness' of the state in his *Reflections*, though it may stand well enough on its own, must become doubly intelligible when its attendant circumstances are remembered: his fury at English support for the revolution in France, and his hatred of the 'literary cabal', those French *philosophes* who had scorned their native and religious traditions and bowed down at the false shrines of reason, the rights of man, and the ideas of Rousseau.

Perhaps even, when we read him on the subject of the social contract – that historico-philosophical bone which intellectuals of the 17th and 18th centuries never ceased to worry – it is not altogether irrelevant to remember that not only had he read and much disliked Rousseau's *Du Contrat Social* but had briefly known its author – or at least had had, as he said, 'good opportunities of knowing his proceedings almost from day to day'[8] – and thought him as odious as his theories: 'the great professor and founder of the *philosophy of vanity*'. As for the social contract, wrote Burke,

Society is indeed a contract . . . but the state ought not to be considered as nothing better than a partnership agreement in a trade of pepper and coffee, calico or tobacco, or some other such low concern, to be taken up for a little temporary interest, and to be dissolved by the fancy of the parties. It is to be looked on with reverence; because it is not a partnership in things subservient only to the gross animal existence of a temporary and perishable nature. It is a partnership in all science; a partnership in all art; a partnership in every virtue, and in all perfection. As the ends of such a partnership cannot be obtained in many generations, it becomes a partnership not only between those who are living but between those who are living, those who are dead, and those who are to be born.[9]

That numinous, ideal view of society and the state is something else that lies 'at the heart of his position'. Central to everything for which he argues was 'the wisdom of the forefathers', or perhaps we must say what he *took to be* that wisdom, for his analysis of it will frequently not stand scrutiny. Reform of abuses – what he liked to call 'renovation' or 'correction' – he admitted to be constantly necessary; and his views on many subjects were the reverse of conservative. But men may not build a future by turning their back on their past. They cannot choose where to build, for the very foundations were laid long ago, and any attempt to begin again from new ones allegedly stronger or more 'logical' is born of folly and foredoomed.

Burke perpetually evades attempts to categorise or pigeonhole him. If he is 'the father of English conservatism' he is also the man (of course no Tory but a Whig) who espoused such liberal reforms as relief for Dissenters and Catholics; mitigation of the laws permitting life imprisonment for debt; abolition of the slave trade; limitation of royal patronage and Court influence (what he called 'oeconomical reform') free, or at least freer, trade, notably with Ireland; and most persistently and passionately of all, if sometimes misguidedly, reform of the government and administration of British India in what he understood to be the interests of the Indians themselves – which, happily for his argument, he found largely identical with true British interests.

Again, if he is to be accepted as the most important of the writers in English ranged against the eighteenth-century 'enlightenment', that too needs qualification. Of his last decade, the 1790s, this is largely true; his *Reflections on the Revolution in France* and its successors bristle with hostility and contempt for those *philosophes*, Rousseau in particular, whose thinking had much influenced the revolutionaries recently come to power. But it was also Burke who held Montesquieu to be 'the greatest genius who has enlightened this age'. It is Burke whose convictions bear sometimes a close affinity even with those of the same Rousseau whom he so detested. Alike they insisted for instance on society's crucial need for a moral framework. Alike they were prepared to proscribe atheists, Rousseau even considering whether they should merit the death penalty, Burke the devout Anglican specifically exempting them from the toleration he thought should extend not only to all branches of Christianity, but also to other faiths.

Burke's literary beginnings indeed might well place him alongside his friend Adam Smith and the other writers of the *British* 'enlightenment'. His early books contain a characteristically eighteenth-century combination of rationalism and empiricism, though his devotion to Christianity and his trust in the benignity of Providence turned him sharply away from the scepticism of Bolingbroke and Hume. Adam Smith, and especially his *Theory of Moral Sentiments*, he deeply admired; and his own never-finished *Abridgement of English History* was largely inspired by his reading of, again, Montesquieu. Locke and particularly Montesquieu always retained his highest respect, though when during the turmoil of the French Revolution he is still found eulogising the perceptive wisdom of Montesquieu, we should remember that, by then, latterday *philosophes* were regarding Montesquieu as an outdated conservative. He had even, it was said, died a Christian.

Of the two books which first brought him acclaim, one, surprisingly, was an *imitation* of Bolingbroke, rather over-clever in its irony, so that many readers missed his intention, which had been to *counter* Bolingbroke's arguments. The other was a 'philosophical enquiry' into *Ideas of the Sublime and the Beautiful*, a book which met great favour both in England and in Germany, where Lessing and Kant acknowledged their indebtedness. Until he was in his middle thirties it remained the world of letters and the arts which Burke aspired to adorn. The man of affairs, the Whig politician, the enemy of 'abstractions and universals', the scourge of preaching radicals and democrat ideologues, was still in the future.

Seeming contradictions and necessary qualifications persist – for we have constantly to be reminded that this 'most profound of England's political thinkers' was strictly not English at all (proud though he was to call himself 'a true Englishman'),[10] but Irish born and bred and educated, with a pronounced Dublin accent to the end of his days.

CHAPTER
1

CHILDHOOD AND YOUTH

EDMUND BURKE was born on New Year's Day, 1729, in his father Richard's house on Arran Quay, Dublin, 'where Liffy rolls his dead dogs to the sea'.[1] Richard Burke, an attorney of the Irish Court of Exchequer, was a member of the Protestant Church of Ireland, but he had married a Catholic from County Cork, Mary Nagle. The Nagles were a family of some standing in their own parts, insofar as any Catholics in early Georgian times can be said to have had standing in a land where they were grossly discriminated against, forbidden to acquire freehold land other than by inheritance or hold land on a lease longer than thirty-one years, barred from trades, professions and education, from office great or small, from jury-service, the vote, the right to bear arms or even to own a horse. Some of this penal legislation was so severe as to be unenforceable, but its general effect was crushing, particularly upon the Catholic middle and upper classes among whom the Nagles stood. In sunnier times for them, one of their family had indeed, during the reign of James II, been Attorney-General in Dublin and Speaker of the Irish House of Commons.

If the marriage of Burke's father and mother (in 1724) had come only a few years later, Richard Burke himself would have been liable to be counted a papist by association, and hence disbarred from his legal practice unless he could have proved that he had converted his wife to Protestantism. But the relevant statute in the half-century-long sequence of anti-Catholic laws was not enacted until 1733, so the males of the Burke family were able to follow their careers, and face the world in general, as

1

properly and acceptably Protestant despite Mary Burke's Catholicism. All three sons of the marriage, Garrett, Edmund, and Richard,* were to be brought up in the established Church of Ireland. The one daughter, however, Burke's sister Juliana, though baptized in a parish church of the establishment, was reared in and remained in her mother's faith. Many years later, when she married a Catholic husband, she was however as a baptized Protestant actually obliged to have the wedding ceremony performed by a Protestant minister to avoid the risk of the union being declared invalid. That the marriage of Burke's parents was in this religious sense mixed was to be of the highest importance in influencing his adult opinions and sentiments, especially concerning those two linked issues never absent from the politics of his adult years, the Catholic question and the governing of Ireland.

It was among his mother's Catholic relatives at Ballyduff in County Cork that several years of his early boyhood were spent. Arran Quay, by Liffey-side and constantly liable to flooding, was deemed unhealthy for a child held to be delicate, so he was sent away at a tender age to Ballyduff, where until he was ten or eleven he attended the local village hedge-school. Strictly the law forbade these makeshift Catholic refuges of education yet was obliged in practice to countenance large numbers of them. At Ballyduff in fact the 'hedge' was a ruined castle, once a stronghold of the Nagles, and the school was conducted by one O'Halloran, whom Burke was to remember with something of the same affection Goldsmith preserved for a parallel figure, the rhymester–schoolmaster–Latinist Thomas Byrne.[2]

By the age of eleven Burke was back home and attending a school in Dublin; and a year later, together with his two brothers, he was sent away to board at Ballitore in County Kildare, where he was to remain until he was fifteen. The school at Ballitore was the creation of Abraham Shackleton,† a Yorkshire-born Quaker, who, left the youngest of six orphans, had begun at the age of twenty to teach himself Latin, had settled in Ireland and

*In this context, he is of course Richard Burke junior, but in the Burke literature he comes to be referred to generally as Richard Burke senior, since Edmund's own son was also named Richard, and so became Richard Burke junior.

†Shackleton was the great-great-great-grandfather of the polar explorer Sir Ernest Shackleton.

founded there a school – some fifteen years before Burke entered
it – which had by this time earned for itself golden opinions.[3]
Burke would always remember this Abraham Shackleton with
the utmost respect. In his forties, learning of his death, he wrote:
'I had a true honour and affection for that excellent man . . . He
was indeed a man of singular piety, rectitude, and virtue, and he
had along with these qualities a native elegance of manners
which nothing but good-nature and unaffected simplicity of
heart can give.'[4] 'Never were boys so carefully and well instructed, so well fed and taught'. Under Shackleton's eye – as
Burke related to the House of Commons in 1780 during a debate
on religious toleration following the Gordon Riots – he had read
the Bible morning, noon, and night and had 'ever been the better
man for it'.

The Ballitore School prospectus at its opening in 1726 had
informed the public that, 'being placed guardian over the morals
of the youth under his care', Mr Shackleton declined to teach
anything which was 'subversive of sound principles, particularly
those authors who recommend in seducing language the illusions
of love and the abominable trade of war'. But for £6 per quarter
he proposed 'to fit the youth for business and instruct them in
polite literature'. At Ballitore Burke found as fellow pupil and
soon as closest friend the schoolmaster's own son Richard, older
than Burke by two or three years. They were both natural
scholars, Burke (so Richard Shackleton said later) being 'particularly delighted with history and poetry', while making 'the
classics his diversion rather than his business'.[5] From these early
days and his middle teens a good many of Burke's poems and
verses, verse letters, fragments, and verse translations have survived. They are competent and conventional and unremarkable;
but as the juvenilia of one of the most accomplished of English
stylists they lend some support perhaps to the once well-accepted
theory that the disciplines of verse-writing build the surest road
to the writing of good prose.

At fifteen Burke left Ballitore's 'flowery meads' for Trinity
College Dublin: 'noise, smoak and Dublin town'. At this time
entry tests at Oxford and Cambridge were little more than social
formalities, but at Dublin plainly they were rather more exact-
ing. Burke's tutor-to-be, 'an exceeding good-humour'd cleanly
civil Fellow', first examined him on his Homer, Virgil, and

Horace, and 'was pleased to say . . . that I was a good scholar, understood the authors very well and seem'd to take pleasure in them'. A second Fellow then questioned him closely in the Odes, Sermons [Satires], and Epistles of Horace. 'To be short', he was then able to write to Richard Shackleton, 'I . . . am admitted. I cannot express nor have I the knack of doing it how much I am oblig'd to your Father for the extraordinary pains and care he has taken with me . . . and all I can do is to behave myself so as not to bring scandal upon him or his School . . . It is almost night . . . so I must conclude without more ado, all a one now.'[6] (This last the cry of the watchman on his rounds?)

The young undergraduate of fifteen was by no means lacking humour – indeed his early letters to his old schoolfellow are full of the light-hearted chatter and juvenile jocularity of friends sharing other friends and past experiences; but that he was a boy of fundamental, even precocious, seriousness is evident too. He learns that young Shackleton, at home in Ballitore, has taken up astronomy, and Burke, entering first a disclaimer of his own ignorance, praises 'the noble science'; and then exclaims:

. . . What grander idea can the mind of man form to itself than a prodigious, glorious, and firy globe hanging in the midst of an infinite and boundless space surrounded with bodies of whom our earth is scarcely any thing in comparison, moving their rounds about its body and held tight to their respective orbits by the attractive force inherent to it while they are suspended in the same space by the Creator's almighty arm! And then let us cast our eyes up to the spangled canopy of heaven, where innumerable luminaries at such an immense distance from us cover the face of the skies! All suns as great as that which illumines us, surrounded with earths perhaps no way inferior to the ball which we inhabit! and no part of the amazing whole unfilled! System running into system! and worlds bordering on worlds! Sun, earth, moon, stars be ye made, and they were made! the word of the Creator sufficient to create universe from nothing . . .[7]

Still only fifteen, he writes to Richard Shackleton:

I am too giddy; this is the bane of my life; it hurries me from my studies to trifles, and I am afraid it will hinder me from knowing anything thoroughly. I have a superficial knowledge of many things, but scarce the bottom of any . . . God gives me good resolve sometimes, and I lead a better life . . . and

then through the fickleness of my temper and too great confidence in myself, I fall into my old courses. . . . You see my
weakness dear Dick, and my failings; plead and pray for me:
we will pray for one another reciprocally . . .[8]

Elsewhere in the same letter the serious Christian and future
champion of the Established Church, but at the same time of
religious toleration, already appears. (Young Shackleton like his
father was a strict Quaker.)

We take different roads 'tis true . . . Far be it from me to
exclude from salvation such as believe not as I do; but indeed
it is a melancholy thing to consider the diversities of sects and
opinions amongst us. Men should not for a small matter com-
mit so great a crime as breaking the unity of the Church; and
I am sure if the spirit of humility, the greatest of Christian
virtues, was our guide, our sects and our religions would be
much fewer . . .[9]

These letters to Richard Shackleton, for much of the time our
only source for knowing of Burke's early years, fluctuate easily
between the trivia and ephemera proper to communication
between intimate friends, and such passages of considered earn-
estness as the above. At the same age of fifteen he must presumably have been reading Pope's recently published new edition of
The Dunciad, wherein the author's *bête noire* Colley Cibber,
dramatist, theatre manager, and poet laureate, was promoted to
be King of the Dunces, since one of the letters to Shackleton
ends, 'As you chuse to represent yourself as a considerable man
in the republick of Dullness I shall endeavour to exceed you by
being king of it and stiling myself C: Cibber Esqr Laur.' 'I spend
three hours almost every day in the public library', he writes two
years later in July 1746, 'where there is a fine collection of books
– the best way in the world of killing thought. As for other
studies, I am deep in metaphysics and poetry. I have read some
history. I am endeavouring to get a little into the accounts of this
our poor country'. Already his love of his homeland was mixed
with this sad sense of pity, always to remain.

Still working hard at his 'poetical scribbling' and translating of
Virgil's *Georgics*, in June 1746 he won a college scholarship which
would give him free 'commons', fifty shillingsworth of drink per
year, a parliamentary vote, certain small monetary advantages,
and the right to a room or share of a room in college. In

particular the term-time move away from Arran Quay after that Michaelmas came as a welcome relief. Life at home had not been very satisfactory. Although his relations with his mother were always close (he became very worried for her when she fell dangerously ill the month after he won his scholarship), with his father there was little rapport. Richard Burke mistrusted his son's literary and artistic tastes, wishing probably to see him qualifying for the law and joining the family practice. Indeed Burke while an undergraduate may well have done a certain amount of work in the paternal office. His father *as a lawyer* was first-class, he said; however as a father his humour was 'splenetic'. Richard Shackleton too described Richard Burke as 'a man of fretful temper', and Burke's college room-mate William Dennis said much the same: Burke 'must not stir out at night by any means, and if he stays at home there is some new subject for abuse'. His 'trouble' in fact was such that he often formed 'desperate resolutions'.[10] One of these may have been that he should emigrate to America, an idea that persisted with him over many years. Burke was at home on Arran Quay when it was hit by the great Dublin flood of 1746. As he told Richard Shackleton,

> No one perhaps has seen such a flood as we have now . . . Our cellars are drowned, not as before [towards the end of 1744], for that was but a trifle to this, for now the water comes up to the first floor of the house threatening us every minute with rising a great deal higher, the consequence of which would infallibly be the fall of the house. From our doors we watch the rise and fall of the waters as carefully as the Egyptians do the Nile, but for different reasons.
>
> It gives me pleasure to see nature in those great though terrible scenes. It fills the mind with grand ideas, and turns the soul in upon herself. This, with the sedentary life I lead, forced some reflections on me which perhaps otherwise would not have occurred.[11]

It is probable that he was already at this time incubating, if not actually writing, what turned out to be one of his first books, *Our Ideas of the Sublime and the Beautiful*, not published till 1756.

> I considered how little man is, yet in his mind, how great! He is Lord and Master of things, yet scarce can command anything. He is given a freedom of his will, but wherefore? Was it but to torment and perplex him the more? . . . Though I do lead a virtuous life, let it show me how low I am, and of

myself how weak; how far from an independent being; given
as a sheep into the hands of the Great Shepherd of all . . .[12]
He was still only seventeen, and this basic seriousness of disposition did not need to exclude less 'sedentary' relaxations and
pleasures, some of which he might well have thought foreign to
the severely inclined Shackleton, to whom he was writing in the
summer of 1746: 'I am here after a tedious journey and have,
join'd to that, so murder'd sleep with dancing these nights past
that I can hardly hold up my head (which you will doubtless say
I never did)'.[13]

By the end of his third year at Trinity he regarded himself as
given over to the *furor poeticus*, earlier studies centred successively
upon logic, metaphysics, and history having yielded place to a
'poeticall madness', in which he reckoned now to be 'far gone'.
Together with a handful of student friends in April 1747 he formally inaugurated a literary club, or 'Academy of Belles Lettres'
which had had some kind of informal existence for nearly two
years previously. It did not survive for many months, but when
twenty-three years later the Trinity College Historical Society
was founded – the senior university debating club in all Britain
and Ireland – it regarded Burke's club and the later historical
club of 1753 as its legitimate parents, and has done so ever since.
William Dennis was one of Burke's original fellow-members, as
too was Shackleton who, though based at Ballitore, attended
Trinity regularly, taking a course of Hebrew lectures there. It
was to Shackleton, years later, that Dennis reminisced, 'Though
the youthful vanity of writing first connected us, yet something
more than vanity keeps alive the remembrance'.[14]

During 1747–8 Burke and a small group of fellow students
produced a literary weekly, which they called *The Reformer*; it ran
for thirteen numbers. 'Few things have sold better', claimed
Burke; ' . . . the scribblers do us the honour to take notice of us'.
In this hopeful enterprise, launched against 'the Empire of
Dulness', loftily didactic editorial matter ('The poverty of this
kingdom can be no excuse for not encouraging men of genius')
went alongside verses such as the following 'proclamation',
typical of the conventional couplets which Burke at this time
turned out with effortless facility:

O yes! O yes! if any man can tell
Where Wit or Sense are fled, or where they dwell;

7

Let him stand forth, and if he love Mankind,
Say where th'illustrious fugitives to find . . .
Ye lawn-sleeved Levites! Deans! and Parsons sleek,
Who once a twelve-month preach, or once a week;
Ye well-taught Lawyers! who for sordid fee,
Will rail no less at Wit than Honesty . . .
Ye Play'rs who like parrots, jabber Wit,
Who speak the Words, but can't the Meaning hit . . .
Ye Students who to College do run,
Not to learn Wit or Wisdom, but to shun;
Say, if by clubbing each his blockhead's head
Any can tell me whither Wit is fled;
For a Reward, he who resolveth best
This doubt shall have the Brains of all the rest.[15]

From about the time of Richard Shackleton's first marriage in 1748 (his bride was to die young) the paths so long trodden in common, or at least in proximity, by him and Burke increasingly diverged, and one consequence of this, the correspondence petering out as it does, is that only the baldest account of Burke – and sometimes not even that – is discoverable between the time of his leaving Trinity at the age of nineteen and his first coming to prominence at Westminster at thirty-seven.

It is plain that long before he left Dublin for London in the spring of 1750 his prospects had been beckoning him London-wards. Since 1747 he had been clearly directed by his father towards a career in the law, and in April of that year was duly entered on the books of Middle Temple. Yet his ambitions always remained literary rather than legal, and as early as December 1747 he was seeing the possibility of making the best of the two worlds: 'I am told', he reports, 'that a man who writes can't miss here [in London] of getting some bread, and possibly good. I heard the other day of a gentleman who maintains himself in the study of the law by writing pamphlets in favour of the ministry'[16] This is the first whisper we hear from him of national, that is to say non-Irish, politics. Before this, and even for a time after-wards, for him politics meant chiefly, the politics of Trinity College, and the part played by Trinity undergraduates in the rowdy disturbances at Dublin's Smock Alley playhouse, where the indignant manager and victim was Sheridan's father – 'a pitiful fellow', Burke reckoned him.[17] However, during 1748–9 he vigorously involved himself in Dublin's long-standing 'Lucas controversy', which did spill over into 'patriot' versus 'courtier' politics, and into the question of Ireland's dependence on Britain and its subject status to George II. The apothecary and 'patriot' pamphleteer Charles Lucas had run into trouble by attacking not only the corruption rife in the Dublin corporation and the Irish parliament but also the hardships Britain inflicted on Irish woollen manufacture. Burke wrote seven anonymous pamphlets during this controversy, often eloquent, abounding in classical reference, but so carefully and weightily judicious that Burke scholars have quite failed to agree whether he was basically supporting Lucas or was contemptuous of him. That it was much likelier the latter is borne out by a comment in a letter he wrote twelve years later where he refers to Lucas's 'hackneyed pretences' and 'contemptible talents'. Medically as well as politically he came to regard Lucas as a mountebank; moreover by then (1761) he was in no doubt that he was 'somewhat out of humour with [Irish] patriotism'. Neither does anything anti-English emerge from these early *Letters* of Burke *to the Citizens of Dublin* or their companion *The Naked Truth*. 'Absolute independency would be fatal to this Kingdom', he wrote.[18] However, he thought he detected a threat by the Lord Chief Justice to restrict freedom of published opinion, and wrote, 'The bounds of the freedom and licentiousness of the press are delicate, nor can every hot-brained man determine them; [but] he who sets new limits to the press puts shackles on the arms of liberty and makes one great stride to her destruction'.[19]

CHAPTER 2

EARLY YEARS IN LONDON

BURKE TOOK his degree in February 1748, but it was over
two years later that he came to London and began keeping
his terms and eating his obligatory dinners at the Middle
Temple. He continued doing so at least until November 1755 and
possibly longer, sustained there of course by his father, who over
these years would spend some £1000 in preparing him to become
a barrister. But Burke did not take readily to legal studies; his
bent remained literary. Admittedly the law, as he said later (aiming then a shaft against the law-educated George Grenville) did
'more to quicken and invigorate the understanding than all the
other kinds of learning put together', but it did not proportion-
ately open and liberalise the mind.[1] In his second year of studying law, resignedly and wryly he was telling Richard Shackleton
that although law presented no difficulty either to those who
understood it or to those who never *would* understand it, yet 'for
all between these extremes, (God knows) they have a hard task of
it'. It looks as though he rated his prospects in the profession no
better than moderate; but at least, he said, he had this comfort,
'that tho' a middling poet cannot be endured there is some
quarter for a middling lawyer'.[2]

Writing this in the summer vacation, he was lodging then in
Monmouth, with his newly found companion and namesake
William Burke. This was to prove both the most and the least
rewarding friendship of his entire life; the most loyal, lasting,
and deeply felt; and yet the most chronically embarrassing.
Though the two Burkes would often be referred to as cousins,
there is no solid evidence of kinship; little beyond a remark by

Lord Verney, who later became William Burke's patron, money-lender, and fellow adventurer, that he thought the two men's fathers had been known to speak of one another as cousins. Edmund Burke himself, on oath during Chancery proceedings in 1783, made a statement to the same effect: 'he had no other occasion to believe they were of kindred'.[3] William, like Edmund, was a lawyer's son. He had been educated at Westminster School and Christ Church, Oxford, and was of much the same age as Edmund. The two soon became insepar-able – or, if briefly separated, would celebrate their mutual esteem, and sometimes bemoan each to each his poverty, in intimate exchanges of verse. A quarter of a century later Edmund spoke of William as 'a friend I have tenderly loved, highly valued and continually lived with in an union not to be expressed!'[4] Even Edmund's marriage (in 1757) would not separate them: William would then share the Burke family home.

Over most of his adult years, Burke's health was to be good, but as a boy and perhaps also now in his early twenties, he may well have suffered from more than the average number of bodily ailments. In particular we read of pain in a hip, which caused a slight oddity in his gait; it has been suggested that it was tuber-cular. (But even if this may have kept him away from youth's more active sports, it evidently had not stopped him from enjoy-ing dancing.) In his third year as a London law student, at a time when little can be discovered of him, we find him reporting that, being attacked by his 'old complaints', in early summer he had gone 'once more' to Bristol – most likely to that city's Hot Wells – and 'found the same benefit'.[5]

Any lack of health had not prevented him from pleasantly enough idling away his summer months in the west country with his now bosom friend William. Their 'adventures' in Monmouth during 1751 would, so Burke declared, 'almost compose a novel'; their presence and behaviour that summer seem to have mystified the inhabitants alike of 'town and adjacent country . . . The most innocent scheme they guessed was that of fortune hunting . . . and when they saw us quit the town without wives, then the lower sort sagaciously judg'd us spies to the French King'. Local reactions proved similar the following year, this time at Turleigh in Wiltshire, near Bradford-on-Avon:

My companion and I puzzle them . . . for this is a place of very great trade in making of fine cloaths, in which they employ a vast number of hands; the first conjecture that they made was that we were authors; for they could not fancy how any other sort of people could spend so much of their time at books, but finding that we received from time to time a good many letters, they concluded us merchants and so from inference they at last began to apprehend that we were spies from Spain . . . Our good old woman cries 'I believe that you be gentlemen, but I ask no questions'.[6]

To a certain Dr Christopher Nugent, of nearby Bath, an Irish Catholic, he wrote from Turleigh one of those fine-flowing, high-flown verse epistles on which he loved to exercise his pen. It must have been very soon after he first came to England that his ill-health had taken him to this doctor. Clearly he had for a time lodged as both guest and patient in Nugent's house; and he had conceived for him the keenest admiration.* Nor is it likely that he had failed to notice the excellent qualities of the Doctor's daughter, then aged sixteen. The 'he' of the following passage is Dr Nugent:

'Tis now two autumns since he chanc'd to find
A youth of body broke, infirm of mind.
He gave him all that man can ask or give,
Restor'd his life and taught him how to live;
But what and when and how this youth shall pay
Must be discuss'd upon a longer day.
Meantime ten thousand cares distract my life
And keep me always with myself at strife;
Too indolent on flying wealth to seize,
Of wealth too covetous to be at ease.[7]

This, amid all its facile poeticising, argues troubles serious enough, physical, mental, and already financial. Just how and where the subsequent years of his middle and late twenties were spent can only be surmised. By his own account in an isolated letter from 1757, his 'manner of life' had been 'chequered with various designs, sometimes in London, sometimes in remote parts of the country, sometimes in France'. By the time he was twenty-six he seems finally to have abandoned, to the great

*Montesquieu's *De l'Esprit des Lois* (1748) was translated into English by Thomas Nugent, a relation of the man who was to become Burke's father-in-law: a circumstance no doubt relevant to Burke's devotion to Montesquieu and immersion in his ideas.

disappointment of his father, any ambition – it had never been more than half-hearted – of becoming a lawyer. At twenty-eight he was ('shortly, please God') expecting to emigrate to America, but it may well have been an earlier proposal to try his luck abroad which had finally prompted his father to discontinue his allowance. 'Nothing', Burke then wrote to him, 'has this long time chagrind me so much as to find that the proposal of this matter has been disagreeable to you . . . I feel to the bottom of my soul for all you have this long time sufferd from your disorder and it grieves me deeply to think that at such a time your suffering should be at all encreased by anything which looks ill judgd in my conduct . . . In real truth in all my designs I shall have nothing more at heart than to shew my self to you and my Mother a dutiful affectionate and obliged son.'[8] Nothing came of these American plans, but that they were not altogether abandoned may be seen from what he was still thinking and writing as much as six years later.[9]

Although his designs were chiefly literary, he succeeded at this time in making contact with a number of prominent political figures, among them Lord Egmont and Lord Granville. He may have earned bread and butter by doing secretarial work for them. Probably also he wrote pamphlets for them, and even speeches. Politics too were involved in his principal literary effort about now, an extended essay which proved to be his first published work since his student days. It was an ironical pastiche directed against the anti-religious, or at least anti-Christian ideas, which Burke detested, of the recently deceased Lord Bolingbroke; and it was so artfully composed in Bolingbroke's own manner that some, including Warburton and Chesterfield, took it to be a genuine posthumous work of Bolingbroke himself. Burke called his little book *A Vindication of Natural Society*, or *A View of the Miseries and Evils arising to Mankind from Every Species of Artificial Society, in a Letter to Lord ****** by a late Noble Writer*. If the sceptic Bolingbroke had looked askance at 'superstition under the name of religion' and vindicated a purely 'natural' religion, Burke's elegant little squib pursued a parallel course with 'political society', and purported to argue that it was as immune to reasoned explanation as revealed religion. As a literary joke it was rather too clever and elaborate and mystifying. As a satirical polemic it missed fire by not being seen as a joke at all. Indeed when a second edition was printed nine years later, Burke thought it necessary to point out that his intentions had been ironical. It was not Burke, of course, but his contemporary Rousseau, his intellectual antithesis, for whom the irony was sober truth – that 'artificial' society *was* evil, representing a decline from a primitive state of nature.

Burke's *Vindication* earned him only twenty guineas,[10] and money was badly needed, for he wanted to get married. Jane Nugent, the doctor's daughter, was now nearly twenty-three. The two were as devoted to one another as, happily, they would always continue to be. A year or two earlier, when he had apparently not rated very highly his chances of winning her, he had written a starry-eyed eulogy of Jane Nugent which has survived, and whose reading might have proved embarrassing if we did not know that the outcome was to be so felicitous. 'Who can know her, and himself, and entertain much hope?' he had asked; 'who can see and know such a creature, and not love her to distraction?'

> Her stature is not tall. She is not made to be the admiration of everybody, but the happiness of one. She has all the delicacy that does not exclude firmness. She has all the softness that does not imply weakness . . . her voice is a low, soft music . . . To describe her body, describes her mind: one is the transcript of the other . . .[11]

They were married in 1757, and went to live beyond London's southern outskirts at Battersea, where in February 1758 a son was born and named Richard. In December of the same year, after the Burkes had moved to Wimpole Street, a second son was born. Like Burke's mother, his wife had been reared as a Catholic, but at her wedding and always afterwards she raised no difficulties in conforming to the Anglican rites. Can it be doubted that Burke's passionate championship later of religious toleration took strength from the fact that the two most intimate relationships of his life were with women born Catholic?

His next book, *A Philosophical Enquiry into the Origin of our Ideas of the Sublime and the Beautiful*, appeared in the year following the marriage, though it had been conceived and at least begun in his student days, and probably filled out gradually over the intervening years. It is a book of aesthetics; the sort of work that characteristically comes from a youthful, confident, ambitious intellect, ready to theorise on subjects whose psychological mystery and physical complexity might well keep older and more experienced minds at a respectful distance; the nature of beauty; 'the efficient cause of the sublime'; the relation of size, fitness, proportion, colour, etc. to beauty and sublimity; 'the difference between clearness and obscurity with regard to the passions'; sweetness, ugliness, variation; 'the physical causes of love'; 'how words influence the passions', and so on – in all some 75,000 stylishly presented words (with an 'introductory discourse concerning taste' added to a second edition). When this second edition appeared in 1759, Burke took the opportunity of sending an inscribed copy to his father, hoping that it might help to soften the parental displeasure over his abandonment of law studies. Within two years of this, Richard Burke died, leaving an estate worth some £6000. Burke's mother, though more than once reported as suffering from a 'severe nervous disorder', was to survive until 1770.

Burke's *The Sublime and the Beautiful* mixed much easily acceptable truth with plenty of highly subjective assertion; with not always convincingly supported generalisation (as that robustness and beauty go ill together); and with a good deal of pre-scientific science (as that beauty has its effect upon us by relaxing the body 'solids'). However, the book was very well received in England, achieved some influence in Germany, where it was to impress Lessing and Kant, and led the professor of moral philosophy at Glasgow, Adam Smith, to declare that the author of such a work deserved to have a university chair.

A fortnight before his wedding Burke had engaged with the Pall Mall firm of the brothers Robert and James Dodsley, publishers of *The Sublime and the Beautiful*, to write *An Abridgement of English History*, for which he was to be paid, in instalments, £300; it was to be finished by Christmas 1758. It was not; nor was it ever finished, though the poet Gray told Horace Walpole as late as 1762 that Burke was still working at it. It has been generally thought that he turned aside from it because of the resounding success of a rival *History of England*, David Hume's, which was completed in 1762. Well before that, the two men were 'very well acquainted'; and since Hume's celebrated work had been appearing, volume by volume, since 1754, this explanation seems on the face of it unsatisfactory. In any case before 1762 Burke had other irons in the fire. Whatever the reason, his interest in the *History* went cold.

In 1757 Robert and James Dodsley had published William Burke's *Account of the European Settlements in America*, in the writing and revision of which Burke had a share. Then, the next year, again for the Dodsleys, he undertook to edit the newly proposed *Annual Register*, a review of each preceding year's events, political, literary, social, artistic. With the first number appearing in 1758, it was to be thirty-two years before Burke finally relinquished his editor's chair. Over the first decade he worked single-handed, but understandably as parliament came to absorb more of his time and energy, and as the length and coverage of his *Register* expanded (and with it Burke's salary, from £100 to £300), editorial assistants had to be enlisted. The first and longest-serving of these was his Irish friend Thomas English, but in later years three younger men, Walker King and the brothers Richard and French Laurence, did much of the writing and editing. King and French Laurence were both men who, particularly in his last decade, became Burke's trusted friends and advisers, intimately involved in his many-sided concerns. On his death they were jointly to edit his *Works*. Both as a journal of factual record and as a repository of contemporary taste and opinion, the *Annual Register* (still appearing after 230 years), was destined to prove an enterprise of the most remarkable longevity.[12]

It was in the 1759 *Annual Register* that Burke was able to return compliments to Adam Smith. In it he reviewed, most favourably, Smith's *Theory of Moral Sentiments*: 'one of the most beautiful fabrics of moral theory that has perhaps ever appeared' – though in a letter introducing himself to the author he boldly mentioned 'a sort of fault' which he detected: 'You are in some few places . . . rather a little too diffuse'.[13] Of national politics Burke had as yet been able to have no more than a journalist's view, the observation of an intelligent outsider. He had made some advance in what he still saw as his true province, the world of letters. However, he disposed of little money and less influence, and success in that mid-Georgian world was hard to come by without the one or the other; it was undeniably better to have both. He strove assiduously therefore to cultivate friends of substance, intellectual, social, political.

One important political acquaintance he had already made was with the young member of parliament for Pontefract, William Gerard Hamilton, who in 1759 began employing him as secretary and personal assistant. It was in Hamilton's service that he would soon be making his first appearance, in a still very minor role, upon the political stage. He had hopes meanwhile of the influence of the celebrated bluestocking Elizabeth Montagu, who thought and had spoken highly of him; who had just helped to secure for William Burke an appointment as Secretary and Register of the West Indian island of Guadeloupe; and whose renewed favour Edmund was soliciting in the same year, 1759 – the elder Pitt's year of glory. Britain was at war with France but not yet with Spain, and Burke hoped that Mrs Montagu might be persuaded to support his application to be appointed consul at Madrid. 'It occurred to me', he suggested, 'that a letter from you to Miss Pitt [Pitt's sister] might be of great service to me . . . I thought too of the liberty of mentioning Mrs Boscawen' – wife of the admiral who had just won an important naval victory off the Portuguese coast. Nothing came of these feelers, or of a recommendation, made to Mr Secretary Pitt through Burke's friend Dr Markham, headmaster of Westminster School, via the good offices of the Duchess of Queensberry.[1]

In his capacity as personal assistant, Burke by the early 1760s was part of his time living in Hamilton's country house at Hampton in Middlesex, his wife and small children remaining in Wimpole Street, comfortably close to her father Dr Nugent, who by now had moved his practice from Bath to London. It was Hamilton whom Horace Walpole was visiting at Hampton in July 1761, to find Garrick there too,

> and a young Mr Burk, who wrote a book in the style of Lord Bolingbroke that was much admired. He is a sensible man, but has not worn off his authorism yet – and thinks there is nothing so charming as writers and to be one – he will know better one of these days . . . We walked in the great *allée*, and drank tea in the arbour of *treillage*; they talked of Shakespear and Booth, of Swift and my Lord Bath.[15]

Very shortly after this, Burke, with his wife and family, was back in Ireland for a stay which lasted the best part of a year. (He was there again, briefly, three years later.) On such occasions of course they would not fail to visit Ballitore, where Richard Shackleton had now succeeded his father as master, and where from the nursery window little Mary Shackleton always remembered seeing them once arrive, Burke 'leading in his wife, a pretty little woman with . . . beautiful unadorned auburn tresses'. The strictness of that Quaker household perhaps explains the child's associated memory recorded long after. Jane Burke, she said, dressed 'conformably with her husband's taste' – without a cap. But she promised to put one on, and appeared next morning 'with the first French night cap that was ever seen at Ballitore.' Young Mary Shackleton's expectations had been at first disappointed by Burke's own 'plain dress' – not nearly as fine as the postilion's, 'daubed with livery lace' – but the sight of his laced waistcoat had reconciled her somewhat.[16]

Hamilton had been appointed Chief Secretary to the Lord Lieutenant, Lord Halifax, so that Burke went with him to Dublin and took the opportunity of his stay to revive old connexions and friendships both there and in County Cork, where some of his maternal relatives were just then under suspicion (false, and based on forgery, Burke was sure) of aiding and abetting 'the clan of White Boys' currently involved in the latest chapter in the long story of Ireland's agrarian disorders.[17]

Burke had grown up mostly among the middle ranks of the Irish Protestant ascendancy, and his views on Ireland's woes – the wretchedness of the agrarian poor, the subjection of the Catholic majority written into the penal laws, the English discrimination against Irish trade and manufacture, Ireland's colonial status and the dependence of the Dublin parliament on the will of Westminster as it was handed down from Dublin Castle – would take time to develop towards the eloquent passion with which they were later expressed. At this earlier time his feelings about his native land and her problems are best seen through a long sequence of letters written by him in his thirties and forties to one of his closest Irish friends, Charles O'Hara of Nymphsfield in County Sligo, landowner, farmer, sportsman, and member of the Irish parliament. Throughout the 1760s these letters also keep O'Hara informed, often in fair though not always quite reliable detail, of developments and personalities on the political scene at Westminster. Burke, though private secretary to the Irish Chief Secretary, or, as he chose to put it, companion to his studies, was by no means required (either he or Hamilton) to spend all, or even most, of his time in Ireland. Indeed on his return from Dublin in 1762 he moved house in London to set himself up anew and more satisfactorily, this time in Queen Anne Street, Cavendish Square.

The immediate proposal for Ireland which Hamilton's superior the Lord Lieutenant was then suggesting, and Burke privately ridiculing (it was at a point when peace negotiations to end the Seven Years War were near to completion, and in fact the proposal fell through) was a scheme for maintaining an army even larger than before, 18,000 men, on the Irish establishment. 'We are assured', Burke wrote sardonically,

> that no measure can be more universally agreeable to, or more ardently desired by, the whole people of Ireland. For my part this same people of Ireland, their notions and their inclinations, have always been a riddle to me. Why they should love heavy taxation; why they should abhor a civil and covet a military establishment . . . I observed that the least pension or raised employment was far more odious and unpopular than ten times that military expence. The truth is this military servitude is what they have grown up under; and like all licentious, and wild, but corrupt people, they love a job better than a salary; it looks more like plunder . . .
>
> But I hate to think of Ireland, though my thoughts involuntarily take that turn, and whenever they do, meet only with objects of grief or indignation.[18]

Already Chief Secretary, Hamilton's further ambition was to secure the office of Chancellor of the Exchequer of Ireland, a sinecure. There was a feeling in Dublin's political circles that he was too clever by half and (so George Montagu told Walpole) 'treated the great people of Ireland with contempt',[19] but he managed to get his sinecure in the spring of 1763, and at the same time for his 'companion of studies' Burke a pension of £300 a year from the Irish Treasury. However, when Burke wrote expressing gratitude, he went out of his way to stress that a condition of his accepting would be that it was in no way to hamper his 'former freedom and independence'. Hamilton must realise that it was Burke's literary reputation that still came first with him, and he would need leisure to attend to it. (There was of course his *Annual Register* work for Dodsley, and besides he was still planning to complete his *Abridgement of English History*.) If this condition should be thought unreasonable, then Burke requested that Hamilton should 'get my Lord Halifax to postpone the pension, and afterwards to drop it'.

Burke did accept the pension, but Hamilton failed to keep his Secretary-ship. Halifax's successor Northumberland dismissed him, and Hamilton returned, still only thirty-five (the same age as Burke) to the House of Commons, where he was to remain for over thirty more years. But after 1765 he never spoke there again, always professing to hold that chamber and its members to be unworthy of his attention or respect.

Until February 1765 he was still proposing to retain Burke as his personal assistant. But then the earlier uneasiness between the two men grew into an open quarrel. Hamilton complained of Burke's 'unkindness' and 'want of friendship', while Burke rejected Hamilton's proposal for a permanent relationship, which he regarded as aiming to tie him to 'a settled servitude' intolerable to a 'gentleman, a freeman, a man of education, and one pretending to literature'. Would Hamilton have dared to bind his *footman* to such terms? Burke allowed that his friendship with Hamilton – now 'an infamous scoundrel' – had earlier been close and intimate; claimed that the 'eternal rupture' made was not of his seeking; alleged that the pension he had been granted, and now resigned, was thanks less to Hamilton's than to the late Irish Primate's goodwill; and further that in any case he had recently found Hamilton's conduct in public affairs 'extremely disgustful'[20] to him. When moved to resentment and anger Burke was never one to mince words. Three months after the quarrel he wrote to an Irish friend of Hamilton's:

> Six of the best years of my life he took from me every pursuit of literary reputation or of improvement of my fortune. In that time he made his own fortune (a very great one), and he has also taken to *himself* the very little one which I had made.* In all this time you may easily conceive how much I felt at seeing myself left behind by almost all my contemporaries.

A suggestion that he should become assistant to Charles Townshend, then Secretary at War, came to nothing. He also applied, unsuccessfully, for the post of London agent to a group of West Indian islands – that part of the world where already William Burke and Burke's brother Richard had both gone in search of fortune. In the spring of 1759 William Burke had been appointed Secretary and Register of the island of Guadeloupe, conquered from the French, and in the autumn Richard Burke followed William out. They both began pursuing their own

---

*Hamilton in fact did *not* keep 'to himself' Burke's pension. Later that year it was transferred to Robert Jephson.

profitable commercial transactions, William in particular incurring some displeasure from Guadeloupe's Governor, Campbell Dalrymple, for engaging in this private trade while still a government official.

Unluckily for William Burke, not all the British conquests were retained in the final peace settlement with France. Back in London in 1762, he pamphleteered vigorously against the feared sell-out. Alas, lamented his ally Edmund (though not correctly) 'our virtuous ministry intend to make a clear evacuation of all the French islands'. He was certain – one of the rare matters on which he was ever to agree with the elder Pitt – that it would be 'the most shameful peace that ever was made'. But William meanwhile was not letting the grass grow under his feet; he rarely did. Baulked in Guadeloupe, the richest of the islands that *was* returned to France, he set about cultivating powerful friends in England, Lord Verney and Henry Fox in particular. With Henry Fox's backing he applied successively, but unsuccessfully, for the governorship of Grenada, the governorship of Carolina, and the judgeship of the Admiralty in Grenada.

For his part Richard, after some prudent courting of important people by his brother Edmund and others, managed eventually to land the twin posts of Collector of Customs and Receiver of Revenues in Grenada – 'lucrative' indeed, Edmund was pleased to report, 'though in a remote and unhealthy climate, this is some drawback'.[21] Richard's appointments did indeed offer promise of substantial reward – but unhappily Burke's judgment in such matters was not always to be relied on. Wraxall's *Memoirs* has a story of how, one evening at Reynolds's, Burke was telling of the fortunes to be made in the West Indies, 'and in their praise he said so much that Mrs Harneck . . . resolved to lose no time in purchasing where such advantages would infallibly arise. She did so, and lost a large portion of her slender income.'[22]

Lord Verney was an Irish peer worth £10,000 a year and an influential Buckinghamshire landowner. In 1764 he did his best to manoeuvre his protégé William Burke into parliament as a member for Wendover in the Grenville interest, but in the end failed to gain approval for the arrangement from George Grenville himself – despite William Burke's emphatic self-testimonial: that he was to be relied on; that he would 'retain a proper sense of an obligation'; that he would maintain a 'steady adherence' to Grenville. Very soon after this came Edmund's break with Hamilton and his failure to gain any immediate alternative employment. By the summer of 1765 both Burkes, William and Edmund, were at a loose end. Their 'little budding hopes', as William wrote to O'Hara, were born one day and died the next.

Both Burkes: they were, of course, now that William's colonial adventures were at least temporarily at an end, living in the same house as members of one Burke family. Richard usually would be of it too, when in England, as he was again by October 1765, on six months' leave, 'in no very good state of health, and after a great deal of vexation from, but also after a great and perfect triumph over, his enemies, a set of the greatest villains that ever existed'.[23] That at least was Edmund's version of events; in Burkian quarrels detached judgments seldom appear. The Burkes shared house; Edmund and William shared letters; when William wrote to O'Hara, Edmund's contribution would go under the same cover; sometimes their paragraphs alternate. Thus when in July 1765 William tells O'Hara that he has heard that Lord John Cavendish has mentioned their names 'as fit men to be employed by Lord Rockingham', it is natural that it was *their* names. The Burkes were known to be plural.[24]

It was a time when Westminster politics were in a state of flux; even of crisis. George III, still in his twenties, had been on the throne for five frustrating years. Deprived in 1763 of his mentor and chief minister Lord Bute, he had had to suffer for two years the 'insolence' of his new administration, in particular of prime minister George Grenville and the Duke of Bedford; Bedford who was belligerently hostile, Grenville who nagged insufferably and endlessly.[25] By the summer of 1765, with the King straining every nerve to rid himself of his tormentors (and his nervous condition was already far from shock-proof), there had arrived, as Edmund put it, 'an immense stir and uncertainty of affairs'.[26] Just at this moment occurred the intervention which was to prove decisive for Burke's career. William Fitzherbert, a parliamentary supporter of the Marquis of Rockingham, spoke to his leader on Burke's behalf.

CHAPTER 3

WESTMINSTER AND BEACONSFIELD

O UT OF the political comings and goings, the confrontations and recriminations, of the summer of 1765 there emerged a new administration whose real though unofficial presiding head, until his early death, was the King's uncle the Duke of Cumberland, but whose first Lord of the Treasury and official chief minister was Lord Rockingham. Charles Watson Wentworth, 2nd Marquis of Rockingham (1730–82), was one of the wealthiest and most influential of the great Whig magnates. Though in his twenties he had been a courtier, he had in his make-up much of the old 'country' Whig ('country' as opposed to 'court'), with a stance of independence which had always been strong among the aristocracy of the northern counties where his power-base lay. Though he was undeniably a Whig, the King decided that at least he was a gentleman of honour, probity, and even modesty. He had no great reputation for ability, still less for intellect. Undoubtedly – although his health was chronically indifferent – he felt more at home with his horses at Newmarket or his local Yorkshire race-meetings than in the royal Closet or on the benches of the House of Lords, where in his early days as prime minister he felt obliged to apologise to the King for his timidity and reluctance to speak in debate.

Rockingham needed a knowledgeable and able private secretary, and on the recommendation of Lord John Cavendish and William Fitzherbert he appointed Burke, who entered upon his duties immediately. His post was unofficial, but from the first he received payments, some perhaps at first from the secret service account, some certainly and increasingly over the years from

Rockingham's private purse. For the fourteen or fifteen years after 1767-8 it seems probable that Rockingham paid him an annual salary.[1] Thus, fortuitously and simply was Edmund Burke placed in a position from which he would eventually become and be hailed by future generations as the chief founding father, polemical champion, political philosopher, and high priest of that group of Whigs who would come in course of time to be thought of, *tout court*, as *the Whigs*.

Rockingham's appointments to Secretary of State were the Duke of Grafton and General Henry Seymour Conway; Conway was also to be Leader of the House of Commons. His Under Secretary was to be William Burke, now member for one of the two Wendover seats controlled by Lord Verney, who unsurprisingly now transferred his allegiance from Grenville to Rockingham. Suddenly everything seemed to be going the Burkes' way. Perhaps William as a junior minister looked, of the two, to have come off the better, since Edmund was not yet even a member of parliament; but as right-hand man, as he soon became, to the prime minister – and moreover to a prime minister conscious of his own shortcomings and the need both of thoughtful advice and of moral and intellectual support – it was Edmund whose situation offered the higher promise.

And of course Edmund too had to be found a seat at Westminster. Lord Verney did not have a spare Wendover seat at his disposal, but William Burke was persuaded, apparently without difficulty, to vacate his in favour of Edmund. Meanwhile Verney would contrive matters at Great Bedwyn, near Marlborough (where, although he was not fully in control, he wielded influence through his burgage holdings), so that William might be returned there instead. This was all achieved without trouble by June 1766, and Burke never forgot the readiness of his friend to make way for him. Indeed he repeatedly trumpeted forth William's nobility and self-abnegation, even surely to the point of hyperbole when the limited extent of William's self-sacrifice is considered. Six years after these events, he is writing that William has pursued his friendship for him, Edmund,

> with such nobleness in all respects as has no example in these times, and would have dignified the best periods of history. Whenever I was in question, he has been not only ready,

but earnest even to annihilate himself. [And then, gilding this already remarkable lily:] Looking back to the course of my life I remember no one considerable benefit in the whole of it which I did not, mediately or immediately, derive from him.[2]

Nevertheless there is no doubting the sincerity, depth, or durability of Burke's feelings for his 'cousin', even when they led him, as they would soon, in directions whose respectability was, to say the least, questionable.

Returning Burke for the borough of Wendover presented of course no obstacles. 'This is only to tell you', he wrote to O'Hara on Christmas Eve, 1765, 'that yesterday I was elected for Wendover, got very drunk, and this day have an heavy cold'. In general Burke's habits, as Boswell confirms, were 'orderly and amiable', and drunkenness is certainly not a vice he is accused of, though Hester Thrale (Piozzi) also writes of an occasion when Burke, again with Lord Verney and after an election meeting, returned home drunk. She even recalled that it was Burke who was the first man she as a young woman had ever *seen* drunk, 'or heard talk obscaenely'. (Her sense of the social proprieties seems further to have been ruffled on a later occasion at the Burkes' country house, where she found that Jane Burke 'drinks as well as her husband, and . . . their blackamoor carries tea about with a cut finger wrapped in rags'.)

One of those present at the rowdy post-election drinking in 1765 was Lauchlin Macleane, a friend who, with William Burke, Lord Verney and others, would soon be playing his own part in those speculative ventures of which they entertained such intoxicating hopes. Christmas 1765 was a season when the name of the scandalous and witty Wilkes, the anti-establishment rabble-rouser of the previous two and a half years, was still loud in the land – which serves somewhat to elucidate Macleane's account of these Wendover celebrations (during the course of which he had just proposed a toast to his friend Wilkes with the company on their knees):

> . . . All the dishes were broken . . . ; in a few minutes the room was cleared of smoke and full of – Liberty, Wilkes and Liberty, Burke and Wilkes, Freedom and Wendover; empty bottles, broken glasses, rivers of wine, brooks of brandy, chairs overturned with the men that sat upon then, while others in rising from their knees fell under the table.[3]

It all sounds a little unBurkian. His own more sedate account sent to his Irish friend John Ridge under his newly won privilege as a member of parliament to frank letters, merely records: 'I was elected yesterday . . . I feel the effects of the drinking and exposure to a very nipping air this day. Will was with us, and has a sufficient headach also . . . Let my mother and Julia [his sister] know this piece of news.'[4]

His success in Parliament was immediate. 'Last night', wrote David Garrick on 18 January 1766, 'I had the honour and pleasure of enjoying your virgin eloquence! I most sincerely congratulate you upon it . . . I pronounce that you will answer the warmest wishes of your warmest friend'. Moreover, he pointed out, 'I am very nice and hard to please and where my friends are concern'd most hyper-critical'.[5]

Far from resting on his laurels after his maiden speech, Burke went near to wearing himself out over the next two months – indeed he did make himself ill – seizing every opportunity to contribute to the series of debates on the great question of the hour, Rockingham's proposed repeal of Grenville's Stamp Act of the previous year. To the displeasure and in some places the riotous fury of the Americans, this had sought to raise from them revenue contributing towards the expense of defending them from the French. A further effect of Grenville's ill-fated legislation had been to provoke American boycotts of British goods, which in turn had made it highly unpopular with those British merchants and manufacturers suffering as a consequence. The Stamp Act at least provided one issue where Rockingham and his new Commons lieutenant Burke might enjoy the broad general support of Pitt, still after his recent wartime triumphs viewed with much admiration by the public and with a mixture of distaste, amusement, bafflement, and awe by most of his fellow politicians. And it was particularly Pitt who now spoke in the strongest praise of the speeches of the member for Wendover – most kindly and generously, as Burke told O'Hara, 'twice or thrice in publick, and often in private conversations. Those who don't wish me well say I am abstracted and subtile; perhaps it is true . . . However, until I know better I intend to follow my own way.'[6]

At the core of Burke's arguments in these early speeches was the essential colonial and Rockingham-Whig objection to the

Stamp Act; Pitt's objection too. This was that, as long as man could remember, British intervention in American affairs had been solely for the purpose of regulating colonial trade in the interests of the mother country. Taxation to raise *revenue*, attempted by the Stamp Act, was a complete and unacceptable novelty.

One who did not consider her much respected friend Mr Burke too 'abstracted' or 'subtile' was Elizabeth Montagu. 'Mr Burke spoke divinely, yes divinely,' she rhapsodised to her fellow bluestocking Mrs Vesey. 'Don't misunderstand me and report that he spoke as well as mortal man could do, I tell you he spoke better.'[7] Praise as enthusiastic and, from the standing and weight of the donor, even more telling came from another friend, Samuel Johnson. Burke on his parliamentary debut, Johnson said, had 'gained more reputation than perhaps any man . . . before'; he had 'filled the town with wonder'. Burke was 'a great man by nature'.

It was Garrick who had first introduced Burke to Johnson some seven years before, and when Joshua Reynolds and Johnson started their celebrated literary-dining-conversation club in 1764 – 'The Club' – Burke and his father-in-law Dr Nugent were among the original nine members who met weekly at the Turk's Head in Soho. Johnson's admiration for Burke remained unstinting. His 'stream of mind', said Johnson, was perpetual. 'That fellow calls forth all my powers.' The diametrical opposition of their political views in no way affected their mutual respect. Johnson did not mind (he once said) Burke being the first man in the House of Commons because he was the first man everywhere; and again, replying to Boswell in praise of Burke's conversation:

> Yes, sir, if a man were to go by chance at the same time with Burke under a shed to shun a shower, he would say – 'This is an extraordinary man'. If Burke should go into a stable to see his horse drest, the ostler would say – 'We have had an extraordinary man here'.

This much-quoted eulogy appears in so many places, not all Boswellian, and in such differing forms (always leading however to the tribute to this 'extraordinary man') that one is left wondering whether it was Johnson himself who so frequently repeated it or Boswell who permitted himself the literary luxury of the constant variations. Both perhaps. Burke is sometimes imagined sheltering in a shed or a stable, or under a gateway, sometimes stepping aside to avoid a drove of oxen or even a 'shower of cannon bullets'. The chance companion may be an ostler or a thresher or – according to the *Quarterly Review* – even a barber's boy. Mrs Piozzi (Hester Thrale), adopting the shed version and acknowledging the observation's justice, then neatly turned it round to apply to Johnson himself.[8]

Johnson never presented bouquets lightly, and it certainly seems that of all the distinguished members of the famous Club Burke was the man he took to be his worthiest rival, in intellect and argument alike. Political argument must be included. Boswell does not much report it, but there is evidence that Johnson the Tory and Burke the Whig did battle not infrequently, and once very publicly. This occurred when Burke published his first great speech on American taxation in 1774, and almost immediately Johnson resolved to answer him and those who applauded his views. The outcome was the pro-government pamphlet *Taxation no Tyranny*. It appears that long before this, at what may have been their first meeting, over Christmas dinner at Garrick's in 1758, the twenty-nine-year old Burke had crossed swords with the much older and infinitely redoubtable Johnson, upon the subject prophetically enough of Bengal, and next morning Johnson remarked to Arthur Murphy (later the editor of his collected works), 'I suppose, Murphy, you are proud of your countryman: *cum talis sit, utinam noster esset*' ('if that is what he is like, I wish he was one of us').[9] On a later occasion Johnson told Boswell and Goldsmith, 'I love Burke's knowledge, his genius, his diffusion and affluence of conversation, but I would not talk to him of the Rockingham party'.[10] Sir Joshua Reynolds, according to his biographer Northcote, once asserted that Johnson even felt himself to rank *below* Burke.[11] However that might be, it is clear that the older man knew that he must be in fighting physical and mental trim when facing so tough an antagonist; and one day, when he was feeling ill, he admitted to the company, 'That fellow calls forth all my powers. Were I to see Burke now, it would kill me.'[12]

Success in the Commons for Rockingham's new aide was one thing; success for Rockingham's inexperienced new ministry quite another. (A ministry of boys, the King called it.) Its one significant achievement was the repeal of the Stamp Act, carried through with the vehement support of commercial interests outraged by the effect upon them of the American boycotts; and even with this Stamp Act repeal went a Declaratory Act, affirming the Westminster parliament's *right* to legislate for the colonies 'on all matters whatsoever'. But Rockingham was captain of a leaky ship. At first his government was kept afloat by the authoritative if unofficial helmsmanship of the King's uncle, the Duke of Cumberland, a personal friend of Rockingham; but he was to die within three months. Pitt, enigmatic, prickly, and uncooperative as always, held aloof, waiting for the administration's collapse and a situation in which the King would be obliged to invite the Great Commoner himself to form a new one on his own terms. In any case Rockingham's government was a coalition, as all governments of that era were, and his grew weaker and more divided as the months passed. Mid-Georgian ministries were coalitions in this sense: they were always a heterogeneous collection, first, of party groups and 'connexions'; second, of rain-or-shine independents open to ministerial offer from whatever quarter; and, third, of those other non-party men whom Burke would soon be prominent in attacking, as the enemy within, the 'court cabal' – 'King's Friends', members whose loyalty lay first and foremost to the monarch rather than to any chief minister or party faction; royal poison, as Burke came to think, injected into the virtuous veins of Whig party government.

Pitt's part in the repeal of the Stamp Act had been crucial. But already by April 1766 he was, by Burke's outraged account, 'abusing administration in the grossest and most unprovoked manner'[13] – he accused them in particular of seeking to destroy the militia. Soon after this, 'Pitt came down', Burke told O'Hara, 'and made a fine flaming patriotick speech, chiefly against any sort of personal connections; he means with any beside himself.'[14] Rockingham was by now using Burke as his spokesman in parleys to examine the prospects for a reconstructed and strengthened administration which must include Pitt. However, when Burke broached this ultra-delicate matter, he was treated to one of those lordly put-downs for which the great man had become notorious:. 'Mr Burke, I wonder you should make that proposition when I have given it under my hand in a letter to

Lord Rockingham that I will open myself upon that point to nobody but *to the King himself*.[15] Encounters like this can only have reinforced the resolution upon which Burke was already determined. He was and would remain Lord Rockingham's man; never Pitt's. He respected Rockingham; liked him, moreover. Despite all that generous early praise for the new member's speeches, Pitt he disliked and disapproved of; mistrusted his 'flaming patriotick' speeches; thought that he was much too devoted to 'rearing a pedestal to his statue'. When in a few months' time Pitt, no longer the Great Commoner but Earl of Chatham, was shuffling and reshuffling his new ministry (which first succeeded Rockingham's in July 1766) Burke would have had every prospect, had he so wished, of holding a place in it. Thenceforth he seldom refers to Chatham except in the language of disparagement, resentment, or sarcasm. He accuses him of pride and of expecting 'a very blind submission of men to him, without considering himself as having any reciprocal obligation to them'. He writes of the 'mysterious solemnity of the Great Oracle'; ridicules him as 'the Old Man of the Mountain', and when he dies, declares in relief that he has 'spit his last venom'.[16] By contrast, of Rockingham he would continue to speak in terms not merely of respectful friendship but (in view of Rockingham's modest pretensions to ability) even of eulogy not a little preposterous. Thus, in his celebrated speech on American taxation in April 1774 he would declare:

> I did see in that noble person such sound principles, such an enlargement of mind, such clear and sagacious sense, and such an unshaken fortitude, as have bound me . . . by an unviolable attachment to him.[17]

An additional and fortifying reason for choosing to stay outside Chatham's fold was financial: he saw before him very warming prospects of 'independency'. It had been over these first few months of his association with Rockingham that the Burkes – one needs always to think of them as plural, being in their considerably less affluent manner as much a 'connexion' as the Grenvilles or Bedfords or Gowers – launched themselves upon a highly ambitious and initially very successful speculation in East India stock.

Even before their sortie into this dangerous terrain of speculative finance, their monetary situation was impressively improved. Richard still held his 'very lucrative' posts of Collector of Customs and Receiver of Revenues in the island of Grenada. (Some however, including some of his masters in the Treasury, did consider that after breaking his leg while at home on leave he was contriving to delay its healing and his return for an unconscionable time.) William of course was receiving his ample junior minister's salary, and incidentally using what influence he possessed to help his friend Lauchlin Macleane into the post of Lieutenant Governor of St Vincent, a situation which offered pleasing 'prospects of private gain'.[18] (Reciprocally, Macleane would soon, with the super-gullible and reckless Lord Verney, be coadjutor in William Burke's grand raid into East India territory.) And Edmund, though his compilership of the *Annual Register* brought him only modest gain and his membership of Parliament none, was now getting, and would continue to get, monetary help – indeed, already probably a regular salary – from his wealthy employer Rockingham.

One of the minor luxuries which men so situated could afford was the ability to become, in however small a way, patrons of art. For Edmund in particular, author of *The Sublime and the Beautiful*, this seemed most apt. As early as 1763 he had taken under his wing a young Irish painter, James Barry, who came from the county of Burke's maternal forebears, Cork; brought him to London; introduced him to Reynolds and other leading painters; and generally acted as his artistic guide and mentor. Then, in 1765, the concerted Burkes decided to send Barry to France and Italy to advance his studies in the best schools. 'You see', William told him, 'it has pleased God to increase our store . . . The least contribution we can make is to . . . be useful to another friend of worth and merit.'

In the spring of 1765 Edmund was writing to this protégé in Paris with advice medical and aesthetical (Barry had been unwell):

. . . Singularity in diet is in general, I believe, unwholesome; your friend the doctor [Jane Burke's father] is in that way of thinking. I mention this as Macleane tells me you have been ill, by ordering your diet on a plan of your own. I shall be happy in hearing that you are thoroughly recovered . . . With regard to your studies . . . I do not choose to lecture to death. But to say all I can in a few words . . . Until you can draw beauty with the last degree of truth and precision, you will not consider yourself possessed of [the powers of a true artist] . . . My dear Barry, I repeat it again, leave off sketching . . . Whatever you do, finish it . . . Reynolds conceives extraordinary hopes of you . . . Let me entreat that you will go through a full course of anatomy, with the knife in your hand . . .[19]

Barry had been at the Palais Royal, and had made a copy which he presented to the Burkes of a painting by Le Sueur of Alexander the Great which he thought 'incomparably the first picture' he had ever seen. Reynolds had then paid Barry's copy the compliment of hanging it 'in his house for some time and returned it in a very fine frame; and it at present makes a capital ornament of our little dining room' [in Queen Anne Street]. Then followed much practical and theoretical advice from Burke to Barry, who was now in Rome – earnest and well-meaning advice, on greatness, on mediocrity, on style and perspective and composition, on 'contracting the circle of your studies', and again on anatomy: 'notwithstanding your natural repugnance to handling of carcasses, you ought to make the knife go with the pencil'.[20]

Until February 1767 William Burke remained (like his friend and fellow-speculator Macleane) an Under Secretary in Chatham's ministry, Secretary of State Conway, his superior, not having followed the main Rockingham contingent into opposition. Macleane was Under Secretary to the other Secretary of State, Chatham's disciple Lord Shelburne. Four months previously, William Burke as spokesman for all three Burkes had been explaining the happiness, and indeed the uprightness, of their political and financial position to O'Hara:

> Our fortunes are in a condition to second our views of independency, and our resolution of acting in our publick capacity with the same correctness as we have had the good fortune to observe in private life . . . All this, like the all before [getting into parliament] we owe to Lord Verney's wonderful goodness and friendship.

Like many others, he pointed out, they had foreseen a likely raising of the East India Company's dividend and consequently a steep rise in the stock value; but unlike most others and thanks to the excellent Lord Verney they had enjoyed the priceless advantage of ready money, with the ability to hold on to their stock quietly till the dividend was raised.

This Lord Verney could you know easily do and . . . he considered this an opportunity of making us independent, and actually paid down of his own above £9000 and engaged for above forty more for me. The dividend is come sooner than I expected, and . . . I have made £12000 at least.[21]

Protesting to O'Hara perhaps a shade too much, and with the timely reflection that such 'providential' good luck 'reminds us to endeavour to grow better men as we grow richer', he adds: 'It is our good fortune, you see, to have this advantage without even the imputation of stock jobbing'.*

As long as he continued to be employed under Chatham and Conway, Willam – much as he might have wished to – could hardly with any show of propriety vote against an inquiry into East Indian affairs now being proposed by Chatham, no friend of the Company. Edmund of course could, and he did. When shortly afterwards William (who, said Edmund, 'had stayed so long in Babylon') finally relinquished his ministerial office and joined his 'cousin' among the true-blue Rockinghams, Edmund was quite delighted: William would be 'an immense accession to the party'.[22]

In May 1767, with Chatham's health both physical and mental totally collapsed, the East India dividend was raised for the second time within eight months – to a handsome 12.5 per cent. This, recorded Horace Walpole, 'raised high resentment in the House of Commons', where 'Dempster and W. Burke . . . ventured to avow their share of the criminality'.[22] There were others beside the Burkes and George Dempster and Lord Verney who had speculated ambitiously and were eventually, when the bubble burst, to suffer heavy losses; among them were Henry Fox (Lord Holland) on behalf of his reckless son and heir Stephen; Sir George Colebrooke, one of the Company's chief spokesmen in the Commons; Lawrence Sulivan, Clive's old rival and enemy and an outstanding protagonist in the long struggle for control of the Company; Henry Vansittart, previously Governor of Bengal and now a wealthy 'nabob'; Lord Shelburne, Secretary of State for the Southern Department; and, of course, Shelburne's 'man of business', the army surgeon turned financial

---

*Most of the money came from Verney, but not all. For instance, £500 was borrowed by William and Edmund from Henry Fox, at 5 per cent; it appears that interest on this was not paid, nor was the capital ever repaid.

buccaneer Laughlin Macleane, generous-hearted but quite un-scrupulous. He was a close friend of John Wilkes and the three Burkes, and had been Edmund's contemporary at Trinity College Dublin. Another eventual victim attracted into his hopeful speculation – it seems by one of the Burkes – was Samuel Dyer, a fellow of Edmund's in the Literary Club. In the outcome, he lost disastrously, and apparently, upon his death in 1772, either William or Richard (the accounts differ) was discovered in his rooms rummaging for papers 'of great importance' in order to destroy them before Dyer's executors could lay hands upon them.[24]

Until the spring of 1769 prospects remained excellent. The Burkes could set about consolidating their advance: no longer mere Irish adventurers struggling for a foothold, but by this time established independent gentlemen. In the main it was William who acted as their 'man of business', and certainly he was the driving force behind their speculative ventures; but the three were still domestically, politically, and financially as inseparably one as the Trinity itself, sharing living quarters, ambitions, and a common family purse.

The Georgian gentleman was incomplete without his landed estate and country house. The Burkes therefore 1n 1768 made what Edmund called 'a push . . . to cast a little root in this country'[25] by buying Gregories, an imposing Palladian house near Beaconsfield in Buckinghamshire, standing with its dependent farmhouse in 600 acres of arable, pasture, and woodland. The cost, put baldly, was £20,000, no mean sum in 1768. Put differently, it was a millstone round Edmund's neck which hung there to the end of his days. Although in practice Gregories became the family home of all three Burkes, the purchase stood in Edmund's sole name, he being the only one of them married and with a direct heir. (A single child survived now, Richard, the second son Christopher having died.)

Thus Edmund, who in the East India stock adventures seems to have been a relatively silent and perhaps imperfectly comprehending partner, was to become in the ownership of Gregories the principal in law. The source or sources of his purchase money intrigued his contemporaries greatly, and many of his acquaintances shared Samuel Johnson's reaction to this 'push' made by a man known to be far from wealthy: *'non equidem invideo'*, quoted

Johnson; '*miror magis*' – the enterprise, that is, provoked astonishment rather than envy.[26] That much of the money came from loans or mortgages was assumed, and correctly. Indeed there is evidence from as late as 1801, four years after Burke's death, that a debt of £10,000 was still outstanding to one mortgagee, and £1200 to another. It is clear too that the ever-generous, fatally credulous, and almost unbelievably reckless Lord Verney lent Burke £6000 through the intermediacy of William Burke (unsecured moreover by any bond). This seems to have been to help Burke face a pressing financial and legal crisis immediately upon buying his estate – a situation which had arisen because, having as he thought satisfactorily finished with the purchase of Gregories and even taken up residence there, he found that the vendor then very precipitately and unhelpfully died, leaving the place still saddled with heavy debts upon his own mortgages. This in turn involved Burke with the costly defence in Chancery of the validity of his title, a predicament from which Verney's generosity helped him to escape but which fifteen years later, when Verney was facing bankruptcy, were to lay Burke open to his earlier benefactor's claims against him.[27]

In 1769, when the market took fright at news from India of Haidar Ali of Mysore ravaging the Carnatic and of a possible resurgence of French influence in the area, the price of East India stock suddenly fell by about 13 per cent – not in itself a spectacular collapse, but because of their adventurous borrowing and rash dealing in margins, the market 'bulls' quickly found themselves in perilously exposed positions. Laughlin Macleane alone lost the then very great sum of £90,000, and involved his late master Lord Shelburne in perhaps another £30,000. He was left owing over £6000 to William Burke, who himself owed very large sums to Lord Verney. In addition the wildly incautious speculations of Verney and William Burke on the Amsterdam market stranded them with a joint liability of £47,000. The losses of Richard Burke were no less crippling on the £29,000 of East India stock he had engaged for. Both Macleane and William Burke were to prove determined survivors, and eventually each of them would be struggling to revive his fortunes by seeking opportunity abroad in India, Macleane as 'commissary-general of musters' in Bengal,[28] William Burke (though not for another nine years yet) as agent to the Raja of Tanjore; but neither would ever succeed in freeing himself from his reputation for lack of scruples. Nor indeed would Richard Burke. He would soon be looking to change his luck, not like the other two in India but back once more in Grenada and neighbouring St Vincent. What he would never succeed in changing was *his* reputation either – that of unprincipled ne'er-do-well. In 1768, when Edmund and William were quietly re-elected for their respective pocket boroughs of Wendover and Great Bedwyn, Edmund tried to use such influence as he had with Rockingham's ally the Duke of Portland to find Richard a seat in one of the several decayed boroughs in Cornwall, but without success.

Edmund, never himself a stockholder, was probably unaware of the full nature or extent of the monies which his brother and 'cousin' had been gambling with. He sharply and quite properly denied personal involvement, while always upholding the other two's probity – ever more fiercely and unconvincingly as their questionable practices persisted. This became one of those matters upon which Burke's easily combustible emotions would quickly ignite. When, for instance, more than two years after the stock collapse, his old friend William Markham, now elevated from the headship of Westminster to the bishopric of Chester, wrote in harsh criticism of the behaviour of the Burke clan, the outraged response (to whose carefully considered and reconsidered composition each of the three contributed) became practically an apologia at booklet length, running in the surviving rough draft to some 33 pages of the Burke *Correspondence*.[21] It contains some of Edmund's most extravagant praise of his brother and his 'kinsman'. Happily the quarrel with Markham, despite the bitter initial animus, did not last.

Another friendship put at risk by Burke's money problems in 1769 was Garrick's, though it too survived. When Burke first moved into Gregories,* Garrick and his wife were among the first to be asked over for a few days' stay. Edmund and Jane longed 'most hugeously', they said, to welcome them – Edmund adding, in one of his seldom quite successful waggish turns, that if they

---

*The three Burkes, with of course Jane and her boy Richard, had already a few months earlier moved their London residence from Queen Anne Street (where however the 'family', in the person of Jane's father, Dr Nugent, remained) to superior and roomier quarters in Charles Street, St James's. Burke's practice was to live in his town house while Parliament was sitting, and at Gregories when it was not.

cared to bring their 'neighbour the Thames' with them it would be 'quite agreeable'. (Garrick's country villa, his 'sweet little – I am mad about it – inchanting place' was by the river at Hampton.) But there was no place for waggery in a brief to-the-point plea for help sent to Garrick just a year later:

> I make no apology for asking a favour from you, because you need make none to me for refusing it. I wish then, that you could let me have a thousand pounds upon my bond until this time twelvemonth. I shall at that time, possibly before, be able to discharge it, and will not fail to do so.

However, he did fail; and four years later was still having trouble in finding the money to pay, by instalments, arrears of interest.[30] Still chasing desperately needed money, but chasing in vain, Edmund and William Burke, with some help from O'Hara (the man on the spot), were over several years at this time pursuing in the Irish Court of Exchequer a £2160 will-of-the-wisp which they claimed was rightfully theirs from the estate of Sir Duke Gifford. This obscure case, originating as early as 1762, was still proceeding as late as 1773. In May 1770, on 'Gifford's business', Burke was begging O'Hara to 'see whether any contrivance can be made for a present supply of 12 or 1500£'. He was, he admitted, 'in the last degree of distress for money'.[31]

Two-thirds of Burke's Beaconsfield estate was arable land and pasture, and he lost no time in applying his intelligence towards getting a good return from his 400 acres, not least by making a study of the theories and practices of the leading agriculturists and 'improvers' of the day, the publications of Arthur Young in particular. By his third year at Beaconsfield he had begun a knowledgeable correspondence with Young, who decided that Gregories must be worth a visit and included mention of it later in his *Eastern Tour*.[32]

Burke's letters on farming – to his friend O'Hara and cousin Garrett Nagle in Ireland, as well as to Young – are often detailed and always full of his experiences and of advice, both given and asked – asked, often of Young; given, invariably, to the Irishmen: on the virtues of a 'cleaning' crop such as turnips or potatoes or beans, in preference to the outmoded year of fallow: on 'the grand enemy', turnip fly; on the 'Norfolk rotation' then being widely advocated; on the folding of ewes; on the excellence of clays for growing wheat; on deep ploughing; on the new 'Indian

37

corn', or maize, to be cut as green fodder ('my horses eat it'); on sowing peas in February, using one of the new drills, on well-dunged ground ('they will be off early enough to sow turnips'); these and a score of related matters. He plainly saw himself as something of a missionary spreading the gospel of the new farming to Ireland's backward acres. To O'Hara and Nagle he hammered away at the lesson that they must not expect a *cash* return from those fashionable turnips; the benefit would always come in the succeeding crop. If O'Hara had not enough dung for both turnips and potatoes, then he should abandon turnips, as being both more precarious and expensive. Potatoes, moreover, were excellent to prepare the land for wheat, but he must remember to dung liberally and hoe vigorously.[33]

Burke's farming (his 'only amusement', he called it) seems to have been generally profitable – in notable contrast to that of Arthur Young himself, whose successes were on the whole confined to his writings. After four years at Beaconsfield Burke was even reported to be thinking of breeding for the Turf; could this perhaps have been something to do with Lord Rockingham's devotion, addiction even, to the sport? (Rockingham, incidentally, had one of his fine bull calves transported over to County Cork for Burke's cousin Nagle.) Rallied on the racehorse-breeding rumour by O'Hara, Burke replied: 'My taste for breeding which has but just laid hold of me does not deserve a name so noble as that of *rage*; it is as yet only a *folly* and but a little one. To what size this infantile folly may grow if well nourished I know not . . .'[34]

CHAPTER
4

COURT, ARISTOCRACY, AND 'PRESENT DISCONTENTS'

T
HE THREE interrelated political topics dominating the years between the disintegration of the Rockingham ministry in 1766 and the King's promotion of Lord North to head the Treasury in 1770 were, first, the protracted furore over the Middlesex elections, when that 'chief of riot and disturbance' John Wilkes, outlawed since 1764, returned defiantly from his 'exile' and repeatedly managed to get himself elected to Parliament while as repeatedly Parliament voted to expel him – all this to the accompaniment of prolonged turmoil and some bloodshed in the streets of London; second, and partly in consequence, a spate of petitions emanating from the English counties and two angry 'remonstrances' from the City of London – these alike condemning parliamentary corruption, ministerial misgovernment and, if only implicitly, an alleged insidious growth in the exercise of the King's prerogative powers; and third, again closely connected to the foregoing, the anonymous *Letters* of 'Junius', those stylishly venomous attacks upon the government and its prime minister Grafton (who had been left in charge, though hardly in command, when his chief Lord Chatham had collapsed and deserted) and eventually upon the King himself. These were the principal events constituting 'the present discontents' which Burke was to give as the title of his first major political publication early in 1770.

Burke could hardly approve personally of Wilkes the impious libertine, or even politically of Wilkes the agitator and demagogue; but since Wilkes and he shared a common enemy in the 'courtiers', the group of royal nominees and 'King's friends' in whom Burke by now saw political evil personified, he was prepared to give Wilkes the benefit of most doubts, and even ready to extend it towards Wilkes's 'private character' – 'of which', he wrote, 'men are inclined to think much worse than it really deserves'. He thought Wilkes 'a lively agreeable man, but of no prudence and no principles'.[1] There was however a *political* objection even to Wilkes's dissoluteness: it held right-thinking men back from supporting those freeholders' petitions to the Crown which Burke was strenuously helping to organise, county by county, against the 'violent, arbitrary, and wicked' conduct of the King's ministers. Writing to O'Hara in October (and incidentally at the same begging him to 'hasten the money' he was hoping to extract from the Gifford estate) he described the York meeting in preparation for a Yorkshire petition: 'A considerable number of clergy were there: men of weight and character; and I was glad of it; because some people were willing to cast a stain of prophaneness upon our conduct, from our supposed patronage of Wilkes'.[2] When Wilkes's success in the prolonged election for Middlesex was for the third time rejected by the Commons and his defeated Court opponent was declared elected, Burke shared of course the general outrage of the parliamentary opposition; and in his pamphlet shortly to be published on *The Present Discontents* he declared that the peace of the nation had been 'shaken, to ruin one libeller, and to tear from the populace a single favourite'. Wilkes, he wrote, was persecuted 'not for the indecency of his publications or the impiety of his ransacked closet', but 'for the spirited dispositions which were blended with his vices; for his unconquerable firmness, for his resolute, indefatigable, strenuous resistance against oppression.'[3]

Throughout that year 1769, in concert with such other leaders among the 'Rockinghams' as William Dowdeswell and Sir George Savile, Burke worked hard at promoting county petitions, with especial energy of course in his own Buckinghamshire in association there with the powerful local landowners Lord Verney and Lord Temple. The freeholders' meeting at Aylesbury on 12 September, he reported to Lord Rockingham,

> proved beyond expectation . . . When we got into the Town Hall it was quite full; there were not fewer, I imagine than four hundred; many of them substantial people . . . Everything had been done to traverse us: the terrours of the House

of Commons were held over many; and the word was, the King will despise your petitions; and then what will you do? Will you go into rebellion, etc., etc.? The Tories in general staid away . . . But I take it the signature will be general. Above three hundred signed on the spot . . .[4]

Lord Temple's own account of this occasion praised Burke's 'manly eloquence'; the *Public Advertiser* reported the purity, eloquence, and 'Ciceronian' rhetoric of his hour-long speech; and William Burke wrote of it to O'Hara:

Among others Ned spoke, but with great modesty, declaring that the smallness of his property and the shortness of his time in the County made it a reluctant thing for him to speak, but . . . the fact is that everybody till he spoke was heard, well indeed, but patiently, but when he had done there was a thunder, and I who had kept myself in the crowd heard the fellows say, 'damn it, he has explained it', and they all understood their grievances quite plain.[5]

In this matter of petitioning the Crown, Rockingham needed persuading; needed even to be pushed; and although Horace Walpole would very soon be calling Burke 'Lord Rockingham's governor', the correspondence between the two men at this time, concerning both the petitioning and other matters, hardly bears Walpole out. It was not, for instance, until the M.P. for Knaresborough, Sir Anthony Abdy, at last lent his weight to Burke's, that Rockingham finally consented to support a Yorkshire petition. Indeed until the publication of his *Present Discontents* in 1770, with its unique contribution to his party's ideology and self-image, there is little to show that Burke's voice had more than modest influence in the counsels of the Rockinghamites. Dowdeswell, Savile, Lord John Cavendish, and the Dukes of Portland and of Richmond – and of course Rockingham himself – all carried more weight.[6]

From actual attendance at the York county meeting Burke asked Rockingham to excuse him. His talents would be more conveniently employed, he felt, down south in parleys with those other leaders of the opposition groups, and possible allies, Lord Temple and George Grenville (temporarily reunited with their unpredictable brother-in-law Lord Chatham) – but more particularly with something he now earnestly engaged upon: what would eventually be published as his 'thoughts' on the current troubles. Rockingham strongly encouraged him in this enterprise, and what was described as 'a good part' of Burke's sizable pamphlet was soon in his hands, and then was circulated for their comments among at least three other leaders of the Rockingham party – the Duke of Portland, William Dowdeswell (leader in the Commons), and Sir George Savile. By mid-December Burke became concerned when he had still not received back from Rockingham a report of their observations and criticisms, or even a judgment on the advisability of publication. Just before Christmas, however, Rockingham sent Burke's manuscript to Dowdeswell, together with instructions to him to contact Burke and to 'look over' with him the accompanying comments 'and some other particulars. I wish it was possible', he added, 'that this work could soon make its appearance. I am only fearful that my own delay must have made it difficult.'[7] However, by April 1770 *Thoughts on the Cause of the Present Discontents* was published.

It proved to be rather more than a political pamphlet: an extended essay rather, written with passion and decorum, qualities seldom found in concert. Its 75 pages proceed with measured eloquence. But of course it *was* a political pamphlet, and primarily so; it had an axe to grind; for all its grave periods and majestic political philosophising, it originated in the frustrations of the Rockingham administration of 1765–6 and remained a work of propaganda. Its main thrust was against the 'exhaustless well' of political corruption which proceeded from Court influence: 'The power of the crown, almost dead and rotten as Prerogative, has grown up anew, with much more strength, and far less odium, under the name of Influence.' To get rid of what Burke claimed to be the established constitutional system of government in Britain ('by men of great natural interest or great acquired consideration')

> and to secure to the court the unlimited and uncontrolled use of its own private favour, has for some years past been the great object of policy . . . By this operation, two systems of administration were to be formed; one which should be in the real secret and confidence; the other merely ostensible to perform the official and executory duties of government. The latter alone were to be responsible; whilst the real advisers,

who enjoyed all the power, were effectually removed from all the danger . . . A party under these leaders was to be formed in favour of the court against the ministry, [with] a large share in the emoluments of government. [Finally,] and that on which the success of the whole scheme ultimately depended, was to bring parliament to an acquiescence in this project . . . Thus parliament was to look on . . . while a cabal of the closet and the back-stair was substituted in place of a national administration.[4]

Such was Burke's Whigs-eye view of the politics of the first decade of the reign of George III: his cry of pain on behalf of the 'men of great natural interest or great acquired consideration' – and in particular of that group of them who under Rockingham, four years before, had so virtuously attempted to defeat the system; when he claimed, 'for the first time were men seen attached in office to every principle they had maintained in opposition'. However, Burke was at pains to stress that the evils he was diagnosing had not arisen (as many had alleged) simply from the special role assigned early in the reign to the Earl of Bute, the young King's mentor and favourite. 'It is the system, and not any individual person who acts in it, that is truly dangerous.' Nor did the individual person of George III himself come under attack or criticism from Burke, as it certainly had from 'Junius'. Burke preferred to regard the King sympathetically, as one deserving to be rescued from his self-styled friends:

What has the crown or the King profited by all this fine-wrought scheme? Is he more rich, or more splendid, or more powerful, or more at his ease, by so many labours and contrivances? Have they not beggared his exchequer, tarnished the splendour of his court, sunk his dignity, galled his feelings, discomposed the whole order and happiness of his private life?[9]

The central damaging allegation in the book, that there had over the preceding decade arisen a 'double cabinet', with one group of ministers thwarted by a second group composed of Court nominees conspiring against them and wielding secret levers of power, held unchallenged sway in the history books throughout the nineteenth and early twentieth centuries. The researches of the past sixty or seventy years have left very little of it standing. The 'corruption' and conspiracy of the decade 1760–1770 has turned out to be no more, if no less, than of the previous decade. The exercise of royal patronage, the king's share in the choice of ministers or appointment of placemen and sinecure-holders, the employment of secret service money as well as private money to influence elections – such practices had been and were to remain constant features of the Georgian political landscape. It is true that George III possessed strong views for or against this or that minister, and had no more intention than his predecessors of becoming a cipher; but if more acrimony than success attended his labours to find ministers with whom he could work harmoniously, he never resorted to 'secret cabals'. The theory of the Court conspiracy has for a long time now been consigned to mythology. Patently, however, Burke did believe it to be true. So did Rockingham himself and the other principal men in his party who went so carefully through Burke's book before publication. We may often find Burke to make historical errors or mistaken judgments, but in honesty he seldom falls short. He genuinely believed his story.

'I am no friend to aristocracy', claimed Burke in his *Present Discontents* – surprisingly and also misleadingly, for he added straight away, 'in the sense at least in which the word is usually understood', by which *he* clearly understood 'an aristocracy servile to the Crown'. What he did undoubtedly admire was an aristocracy of independent views, one associated with and ready to defend the rights of 'the people'. Indeed under a healthy political and social system the leading hereditary aristocrats and 'the people' ought to be parts of a harmonious whole. Burke only briefly and incidentally touches upon the function in that whole of 'the mere vulgar' (clearly the great majority), though he does write of their 'violence and instability; so that if you were to gratify them in their humour today, that very gratification would be a ground of their dissatisfaction on the next'. He never arrived at defining 'the people', but what he understood by that vague and emotive expression emerges very clearly. It was the duty and glory of 'the people', he wrote, allied with and led by an independent-minded aristocracy, to 'rescue themselves, their prince, and their posterity' from the evils of the 'court cabal' and the 'double cabinet', for it was they who together with the peers constituted 'the natural strength of the kingdom . . . the leading landed gentlemen, the opulent merchants and manufacturers, the substantial yeomanry . . .'[10]

Another and more famous statement from Burke on the proper role of the aristocracy occurs not in his *Present Discontents* but in the course of a long letter – more of an essay – written a year or two later to one of the highest-ranking aristocrats, the independently inclined but generally Rockingham Whig, 3rd Duke of Richmond:

> You people of great families and hereditary trusts and fortunes are not like such as I am, who whatever we may be by the rapidity of our growth and of the fruit we bear, flatter ourselves that while we creep on the ground we belly into melons that are exquisite for size and flavour, yet still we are but annual plants that perish with our season and leave no sort of traces behind us. You, if you are what you ought to be, are the great oaks that shade a country and perpetuate your benefit from generation to generation . . .

Plainly the emphasis for qualifying to be one of 'the people' in this political sense was upon ownership of property. It was not until very nearly the end of his life that Burke ever ventured to estimate the *number* who 'in any political view are to be called the people': he then put it at perhaps about 400,000.[11] But he always rejected the notion that representation should reflect a mere counting of heads. For Burke, Parliament properly represented, rather, a collection of the major 'interests' within the state. Moreover, as new interests arose, so they should be accommodated within the system:

> A great official, a great professional, a great military and naval interest, all necessarily comprehending many people of the first weight, ability, wealth, and spirit . . . must be let into the share of representation, else probably they may be inclined to destroy those institutions of which they are not permitted to partake.[12]

One of his clearest and most succinct declarations on this subject of aristocracy and the Whigs comes from a time in 1792, a little after his final break with Fox and those who followed Fox in praise of the French Revolution. Looking back to the days of Rockingham (long dead, but by then of almost sainted memory) he wrote, in sadness and in loathing of 'the new republican Frenchified Whiggism':

> The party with which I acted had, by the malevolent and the unthinking, been reproached, and by the wise and good always esteemed and confided in – as an aristocratick party.

Such I always understood it to be in the true sense of the word. I understood it to be a party, in its composition and in its principles, connected with the solid, permanent, long possessed property of the country; a party which, by a temper derived from that species of property and affording a security to it, was attached to the antient tried usages of the kingdom, a party therefore essentially constructed upon a ground plot of stability and independence; a party therefore equally removed from servile court compliances, and from popular levity, presumption, and precipitation.[13]

What Burke revered was an ideal aristocracy which never quite existed, as he well knew. However, the nation must make do with what it had got. What it must not do, indeed at this time had not even thought of doing, but what to his horror the French were soon actually to do, was to cut down the 'great oaks' in the mistaken belief that a proliferation of 'melons, annual plants that perish' with the season, would serve as well.

Certainly at this time, during the late 1760s and the 1770s, the showing of the 'great oaks' was far from what it 'ought to be'. Burke lamented to Rockingham: 'The court irreconcilable to you . . . the sober, large-acred part of the nation, whom you have most studied to please, and whom it is most reputable to please, either is indifferent about us, or of no considerable weight in the publick scale.' So much so indeed that for a time during 1772–3 the Rockingham Whigs seriously considered absenting themselves from parliament, in protest.

Burke, who saw such a poisonous well of corruption in Court influence, recognised no comparable evil in the immense wealth and arguably as 'corrupt' influence of the hereditary Whig magnates, the Rockinghams and Richmonds and Portlands whose servant and adviser, if never quite 'governor', he had now become. As Richard Pares once pointedly commented, 'Burke, who denounced every kind of placeman, saw nothing odd in accepting £30,000 from Lord Rockingham'.[14] The money which Burke thought it disgraceful to accept was public money or Court money. He himself sat for the undoubtedly corrupt borough of Wendover, which was to remain at the disposal of Lord Verney until Verney's funds, and hence that particular source of 'corruption', ran out in a few years' time. Towards such matters, and all those concerning the reform of parliament, Burke's attitude was to be consistently and conservatively pragmatical – *le mieux est l'ennemi du bien* – much as Chatham warned that in attempting to cut off dead limbs from the parliamentary tree, one must beware lest one killed the tree itself. In a letter written about this time to his old friend Richard Shackleton, Burke, first giving an opinion both against parliaments of shorter term and against voting by ballot, added a few lines which are of the essence of attitudes he would always retain: a wary conservatism, a mistrust of easy answers and starry eyes, a veneration for traditional forms and institutions. 'Nothing can be done', he pessimistically observed, 'by any alterations in forms. Indeed all that wise men ever aim at is to keep things from coming to the worst. Those who expect perfect reformations either deceive or are deceived miserably.'[15] In *The Present Discontents* Burke specifically declined to recommend remedies at all, even remedies for Court corruption: 'My aim', he wrote, 'is to bring this matter into more public discussion. Let the sagacity of others work upon it'.[16] In particular he rejected the two reforms being then most commonly proposed, a bill shortening the length of parliaments from seven to three years, and another disqualifying holders of 'places' (official positions whether civil, military, or naval) from membership of parliament. The question of a place bill, for instance, was 'not a thing to be trifled with; nor is it every well-meaning man that is fit to put his hands to it'. It would be better perhaps that place-holders 'should have a corrupt interest in the forms of the constitution than that they should have none at all . . . It is no inconsiderable part of wisdom, to know how much of an evil ought to be tolerated.' Indeed, Burke wished 'to give the reader some taste of the difficulties that attend all capital changes in the constitution'.[17]

During most of the first decade of his reign George III had been at loggerheads with the various parliamentary groups or connexions, support from some at least of whom was essential to the formation and continuance of government. Party, or connexion, Burke now asserted, had been deliberately and maliciously misrepresented and slandered by 'the court corps', including the Earl of Bute himself in 1766 (when Rockingham had headed the administration). 'That connexion and faction are equivalent terms is an opinion which has been carefully inculcated at all times by unconstitutional statesmen.' But the independent member was powerless against 'the subtle designs and united cabals of ambitious citizens. When bad men combine, the good must associate. Else they will fall, one by one.'[18] So Burke comes to his classic definition of what constitutes a political party, 'a body of men united for promoting by their joint endeavours the national interest, upon some particular principle in which they are all agreed'. To the objection that subscribing to such a body would involve the necessity of blindly following its opinion when in direct opposition to one's own, Burke countered: 'A man must be peculiarly unfortunate in the choice of his political company if he does not agree with them at least nine times in ten'.[19] 'This country will never be well-governed', he said on another occasion, 'until those who are connected by unanimity of sentiment hold the reins of power.'[20]

The Present Discontents was a success. Burke informed O'Hara that its reception had exceeded his expectations. Reporting in similar vein to Shackleton he added, significantly and a touch magisterially, 'It is the political creed of our party . . . Read it with some attention'. Even, so he said, the pamphlet's principal target, 'the courtiers', conceded it to be 'a piece of gentlemanlike hostility'. It was attacked however by a somewhat extreme radical group calling themselves 'Supporters of the Bill of Rights'. Like Wilkes and his supporters, this faction – to Burke's distaste and alarm – carried mob appeal, particularly in the City of London. Indeed, 'Wilkes trouble', and the further 'present discontents' associated with it, persisted through 1771. Released from jail and becoming a London alderman, Wilkes took a characteristically provocative part in the noisy quarrel which developed that year between the City of London and the House of Commons, originating in the House's attempt to prevent printers and journalists from breaching Commons privilege by reporting debates. At one stage the City authorities arrested the Commons messenger and committed him for trial. Then the Lord Mayor and Alderman Oliver were ordered to appear before the Commons to answer for a breach of privilege and, though only briefly, confined to the Tower of London. (Alderman Wilkes was not, being by now, as the King himself put it, beneath the notice of the House. 'Have nothing more to do', he advised, 'with that devil Wilkes'.)[21]

Rockingham, as an opposition leader, with Burke's unenthusiastic approval, thought it on the whole proper to pay the imprisoned Lord Mayor a courtesy visit, but throughout these ill-tempered constitutional exchanges and the accompanying bouts of political fisticuffs inside the Common Council of the City, the London streets were noisy with the disorders which Burke and his sober law-abiding fellow-Rockinghams could only deplore. 'You can scarcely conceive', he wrote to O'Hara, 'how nearly the Court and the Mob approach one another in their sentiments; only that in the one it is design, in the other folly . . . Between them, those I wish best to and think best of, are excluded from government and disabled in opposition.' As for Wilkes himself, his 'petulance and folly' put him beyond serious consideration; 'in the end' – and the judgment proved sound enough – 'he will jest and buffoon himself out of consequence'.[22]

Burke was by now a figure of accepted political importance. As such he was, as he put it, 'used to the most gross and virulent abuse daily repeated in the papers'. Abuse from known enemies, he claimed, passed him by. But in April 1770 an article in the *London Evening Post*, ostensibly neutral or merely informative, touched a nerve painfully, and his reaction to it admirably illustrates characteristics both of his private nature and of his public stance. When he had first been coming into parliamentary prominence, someone had asked Richard Shackleton, his oldest friend, to provide a written account of Burke's antecedents and family background. Shackleton obliged, though his sober version of the facts remained unpublished for four years. When the *Evening Post* eventually got hold of it and printed it, Burke, though he conceded that it contained 'ten thousand handsome things', took such fright at certain of its well-intentioned passages that he sat down immediately to tell Shackleton of his mortification.

Shackleton had described, first, Burke's mother as 'of a Popish family' and as 'practising the duties of the Romish religion with a decent privacy', and then Jane Burke, his wife, as 'a genteel, well-bred woman of the Roman faith'. The whole article, complained Burke, was

> evidently written by an intimate friend. It is full of anecdotes and particulars of my life. It therefore cuts deep. I am sure I have nothing in my family, my circumstances, or my conduct that an honest man ought to be ashamd of. But the more circumstances of all these which are brought out, the more materials are furnished for malice to work upon: and I assure

you that it will manufacture them to the utmost. Hitherto, much as I have been abused, my table and my bed were left sacred, but since it has so unfortunately happend, that my wife, a quiet woman, confined to her family cares and affections, has been dragged into a newspaper, I own I feel a little hurt. A rough publick man may be proof against all sorts of buffets, and he has no business to be a publick man if he be not so. But there is as natural and proper a delicacy in the other sex, which will not make it very pleasant to my wife to be the daily subject of Grubstreet, and newspaper invectives; and at present, in truth her health is little able to endure it.

(Jane Burke was in fact ill, with 'a slow fever', all that summer of 1770, and confined to her bed for over two months.)

Plainly even as late as 1770 it was still a serious embarrassment for a leading politician to have such close family association with Roman Catholicism. Burke also took strong exception to the *Evening Post*'s ventilation of his financial position and of the benefits he had received from political patrons or employers. These were matters where his pride and, as he felt, integrity were vitally involved:

Where you speak of my being made easy by patronage etc. I assure you, that if you allude to a small pension which I had for a time, and resigned upon an overstrained point of honour – I am to inform you that I got that from the patronage of no man living. It was indeed a defective performance of a bargain for full consideration. Nor have I had any advantage, except my seat in parliament, from the patronage of any man; whatever advantages I have had, have been from friends on my own level; As to those that are called great, I never paid them any court; perhaps, since I must say it, they have had as much benefit from my connection as I have had.

Even some of Shackleton's kindest words Burke thought would prove counter-productive:

Indeed what you have said of my modesty and moderation in debate will, I fear, take off not a little from the authority of the rest. It is but too well known, that I debate with great vehemence and asperity . . . Many of my adversaries . . . deserve not much quarter, and I give and receive but very little.

There was general agreement by this time among Commons members respecting Burke's debating abilities and on occasions high eloquence, but also on this 'vehemence and asperity'. 'There were high words in the House of Commons on Thursday', wrote Thomas Allan to Sir George Macartney in March 1770, 'between Mr Edmund Burke and Mr Rigby, exceeding gross on both sides, the former in better language, the latter very plain, said he was a scoundrel.'[23] Burke's temper was quite capable of being mightily roused over an apparently minor matter – the altercation with Rigby concerned a disputed Carmarthen election. It was over a similar election dispute the following month that Burke and Sir William Bagot were involved in hostile exchanges so excited that Burke's fellow Whig Lord John Cavendish thought it prudent to rise and 'intercept' him before matters proceeded beyond control. It was Cavendish again who with others managed to intervene a few years later when a quarrel between Burke and Wedderburn, the then Attorney General, seemed to be heading for a duel.[24] Some years later again, it was a much younger colleague, Sheridan, who is reported as having to 'pull down' Burke to his seat in order to calm dangerously troubled Commons waters.

In his long reply to Burke's complaint concerning the *Evening Post* article, poor Shackleton was 'covered with grief, shame and confusion'. His sketch of Burke's origins and early life had been given to a friend, who had passed it on to *his* friend, and so on, perhaps, to others. To have started this progress had admittedly been 'madness and folly . . . I was a blockhead to meddle in it'. But as for Burke's protests, 'If there had been any language of friendship in thy letter, it is only oil, to make the edge more keen'.

> Thou art grown a rough publick man, sure enough – I say I could bear even this from thee; . . . if the affair lay only between ourselves, there might be some time an end of it. But thy mention of my interfering in thy domestick connexions and dragging the partner of thy bed and the softener of thy busy scenes of life into a newspaper is wounding to the last degree . . . I do in the sincerest and most earnest manner beg forgiveness . . .[25]

Burke was right: his temper was indeed hasty. Yet a fundamental goodness of heart and loyalty to ties of kinship and old-established friendship were usually quick to reassert themselves. Now on getting Shackleton's letter he in his turn felt twinges of remorse, and replied by return of post. He had, he wrote, been 'weak and blameable', and his letter had been angry, cruel, and 'very improper'.

> As to my wife you needed to make no apology at all to her. She felt nothing but good wishes and friendship to you, and is by no means subject to those spurts of passion to which I am unfortunately but too subject . . . Adieu my dear Shackleton forgive one who if he is quick to offend is ready to atone, who . . . never can think of your early and continued friendship but as one of the chief blessings of his life . . . Have we no hope of seeing you here [at Beaconsfield] this summer?[26]

Shackleton did not come that year, but a few years later he did, and was apparently almost overwhelmed, both by Burke's great kindness and by the impressiveness of his estate:

> He had come from the House of Commons, and was ready with his family to receive me in London – the friendship, the freedom, the cordiality with which he and his embraced me was rather more than less what might be expected from long love. I could not well avoid coming with him to his country-residence – he left the important business of the nation . . . in order to have me with him a day or two here. Accordingly he and his wife and brother brought me here yesterday in his coach, his son accompanied us on horse-back . . . It is a most beautiful place, on a very large scale, the house, furniture, ornaments, conveniences, all in a grand style – six hundred acres of land, woods, pleasure grounds, gardens, green-house, etc. – for my part I stand astonished at the man and at his place of abode – a striking parallel may be drawn between them, they are sublime and beautiful indeed.[27]

From Mary Shackleton (Mrs Leadbeater) there comes a further touch to add to her father's picture of Gregories. At about a mile from the house, Burke, she writes, had a little 'tea-house', or as he called it 'root-house', roots of trees, moss, and so forth, with 'a retired view bounded principally by woods'. It had 'a little kitchen behind and an ice-house under it'.[28]

Another old friend from past Irish days, and the correspondent with whom Burke long maintained an exchange of news Irish and English, political and personal, was Charles O'Hara. Perhaps he too might be persuaded to visit again, and how better than to come for Christmas? 'My dear friend', he wrote, '. . . Oh do come over, if possibly you can, and let us walk one Christmas more on the pavement of our hall by the glimmering lamplight,

and try whether we can delude the cares of this life a little longer
– a little longer –'

The Church of England Burke regarded as an institution which
history had made an essential limb of the body of England:
organically intrinsic to it. 'In a Christian commonwealth', he
once wrote, 'the church and the state are one and the same thing,
being different integral parts of the same whole.' But his vehement loyalty to the established church by no means precluded
regard for other Christian persuasions, nonconformist or papist.
His mother and his wife both owning Catholic origins would
naturally have led him towards toleration in that direction; and
then too his much respected schoolmaster and the closest friend
of his young days had been Quakers. But likewise to all branches
of nonconformity he extended tolerance, and in that cause his
parliamentary vote was generally to be relied on. Only atheism –
'the conspiracy of atheism' – deserved to be crushed. 'The most
horrid and cruel blow that can be offered to civil society is
through atheism. The infidels are outlaws of the constitution . . .
of the human race. They are never, never to be supported, never
to be tolerated.'

Toleration, moreover, was to be sharply distinguished from
laxity. When certain Anglican clergy petitioned Parliament in
1772 to be relieved of subscribing to the Thirty-Nine Articles,
Burke found himself voting against most of his fellow Rockinghams who supported the petition; and when the subject arose
again in May 1774, Burke is reported as making 'a long and
masterly speech of upwards of an hour' against the proposals. It
was not reasonable, he argued, to expect the public to contribute
to the maintenance of a church without knowing what its clergy
believed.

Nor was it toleration of laxity, moral laxity in this case, which
prompted him in that same year to send eloquent pleas to
Secretary of State Suffolk and Attorney General Thurlow on
behalf of a lieutenant of the Royal Artillery who had been
sentenced to death for sodomy. Indeed Burke agreed that 'if the
crime be well and juridically ascertained the criminal deserves
his punishment' – he had absolutely no words in mitigation of
the *offence*, 'which admits no palliatives' – but since the evidence
of the thirteen-year-old victim was single, unsupported, and

suspect, and since testimony had been given for the officer's previously unblemished character, he considered that 'upon a public principle' this was a fit case for exercising the royal prerogative of mercy. His intervention bore fruit. The condemned man was spared, on condition that he quitted Britain for good.

This was not the only occasion on which Burke's name was to become associated with the fate of homosexual offenders. In 1780 when two men convicted of sodomy had actually been pelted to death in the pillory by a righteously vindictive mob, Burke raised the matter of this outrage and was predictably vilified in some virtuously inclined newspapers for his alleged homosexual sympathies – attacks which incensed him sufficiently for him to bring a suit of libel against the *Public Advertiser*. However, an apology being tendered, he did not proceed with the action.

CHAPTER
5

'THE LITTLE CIRCLE OF MY FAMILY'

EARLY IN 1773 Burke made a visit to France. It was suggested at the time, by Horace Walpole among others, that one at least of his motives for being abroad just then was a wish to be away from the Commons at a time when West Indian affairs were being debated there, and in particular hostilities against the Caribs of St Vincent, the island where Burke's brother was involved in ambitious land claims and, it was alleged, serious malpractices. But the motive which Burke himself offered concerned not his brother but his son, whose education would profit, he judged, by a stay in France. Richard Burke, junior, was now fourteen, and had been briefly at Westminster School. Just entered at Christ Church, Oxford, he had been granted a year's leave of absence before taking up study there. 'The boy deserves well of me', Burke told Rockingham, 'for he is not idle, and he has a good disposition . . . It is a good time to form his tongue to a foreign language. I feel, almost every day of my life, the inconvenience of wanting them.'

With him and his son Burke took Thomas King, a young clergyman acting as Richard's tutor. The party travelled via Dover and Calais (a two and a half hour crossing and a rough one – father and son both 'turned inside out'); thence to Paris, and then on the hundred miles to Auxerre ('two entire days on account of disasters which happened to our chaise'). At Auxerre Burke deposited Richard and his tutor before himself returning for a month's stay in Paris. Richard and King were left comfortably installed with the family of a 'gentleman' who was '*écuyer conseiller secrétaire du roi*'; and, so Burke took care to inform his no doubt anxious wife back home, he left them sitting down 'to Whist as regularly as if they had been of the family and perfectly at home'. 'Good night and God bless you, my dearest Jane, sleep well', he writes; 'Adieu, . . . may heaven preserve you to your son and your E.B.' During his Paris stay he would be writing home by every available post, characteristically addressing himself to *all* the Burke clan – 'my dearest Jane, my brother Richard, my William, my father [i.e. Jane's father], heaven protect you all'. To William and his brother he did not neglect to offer advice on the best tactics to employ in their 'great affair', Richard's struggle to secure his title – a dubious one – to land he had bought in the West Indian island of St Vincent.

From Paris he was earnestly liberal in advice also to his *two* 'dear children' at Auxerre: how to behave; how to be careful with money; what to study (French and Greek particularly) and what not to study 'until you hear from me' (geometry and logic). 'May God grant you every blessing. Remember him first, and last, and midst.'

It may indeed be that too many, for his liking, of the many distinguished French men and women whom he met during his month in Paris seemed to fail in that duty so to remember their God; and it is true that it was almost immediately upon return-ing home that he delivered in the Commons his first violent assault upon atheism and atheists. *Post hoc* certainly; *propter hoc* perhaps, though whether, as it has been argued, Burke's visit to Paris marked a turning-point in his life is open to question. He did meet some of the day's *savants* and *philosophes* at the salon of Mlle de l'Espinasse; and no doubt, there and at Mme du Deffand's and elsewhere, he did in his uncertain French defend Christian belief. Mme du Deffand's English confidant Horace Walpole gossiped rather unconvincingly that 'St Patrick himself did not make more converts',[1] but the lady herself, though she found Burke amiable, and gave him all the attentive respect a visitor of his distinction merited, admitted to the Duchess of Choiseul that he spoke French so badly that it was difficult for him to do himself justice in that tongue. He had certainly not needed a visit to France to take emphatic dislike to Rousseau, both to the man himself and to his ideas; he had had that ever since he had come across him in England seven years earlier. In any case Rousseau in 1773 was not on view in Paris. Neither was

Voltaire, in safe exile then beyond the Swiss border. Diderot however was, his great *Encyclopédie* just completed, and he was among those whom Burke did succeed in meeting.

At Versailles, together with other visitors and tourists he was able also to see Louis XV's court on one of its routine occasions of display; the old King himself, whose hand he was privileged to kiss; Mme du Barry, the current royal mistress, the modest refinement of whose dress and appearance almost persuaded him to tolerate the intrinsic 'vice' of her situation; the hapless Dauphin, who the following year was to succeed as Louis XVI; and most memorably of all, the young Dauphine Marie Antoinette, his sight of whom would one day, as he recalled it after the outbreak of revolution and her downfall, inspire the bitter reproach in one of the most memorable flights of his eloquent prose: 'Surely never lighted on this orb . . . a more delightful vision. I saw her just above the horizon, decorating and cheering the elevated sphere she just began to move in – glittering like the morning star, full of life and splendour and joy'.[2]

The elder Richard's 'great affair' – his attempt to recoup his East India losses by having his West Indies land bargain confirmed – rumbled slowly on and would continue doing so for a long time yet. The argument, in which Burke devotedly supported him, had by this time become intricately involved.

It was as long before as 1763 that the twenty-nine year old Richard Burke – he was nearly five years younger than Edmund – seeking for the second time to win a fortune in the West Indies, managed to get himself appointed Collector of Customs and then, after a struggle, Receiver General of Revenues for the island of Grenada, newly conquered from the French. 'Very lucrative', Edmund had commented, though he feared for his brother's health in the Grenadan climate.

Not taking up his post until 1764 (Richard was an impetuous fellow, but at the same time a master of tactical delay), he soon found himself in trouble with Grenada's governing authorities and returned home, officially on six months' leave, full of complaint for the wrongs he had suffered. The charges made against him by his enemies in the Grenadan government and assembly are not clear, but they concerned financial transactions, and possibly embezzlement. As ever, Burke rushed to his brother's defence, castigating the 'villainy', 'baseness', 'wickedness', of his opponents, those 'rascals'.[3] (This was in a letter to Garrick, who more than once over these years proved a good friend to both the Burke brothers.) Richard's only fault, declared Edmund, was 'over-sensibility', a trait not widely borne out by the judgment of most others who became acquainted with him: 'comic, humorous, bold', thought Fanny Burney, yet 'queer'; 'vulgar and fierce, rough and wild', said Boswell; and Hannah More – 'very bright, but a little coarse'. Goldsmith however clearly rather liked him:

> What spirits were his! what wit and what whim,
> Now breaking a jest, and now breaking a limb;
> Now wrangling and grumbling to keep up the ball,
> Now teazing and vexing, yet laughing at all!
> In short, so provoking a devil was Dick,
> That we wished him full ten minutes a day at Old Nick;
> But missing his mirth and agreeable vein,
> As often we wished to have Dick back again.[4]

Richard Burke's six months' leave was eventually stretched to about five years, during most of which time he lived in the Burke family home, but also visited Ireland with Edmund, made two trips to Paris (the second in the company of Joshua Reynolds), suffered a multiple fracture of a leg and periods of indifferent health, both of which he advanced as justifying his absenteeism; and, as we have seen, gambled ruinously in East India Stock.

On 2 November 1769 – a time when Burke was writing his *Present Discontents* – the Treasury ordered Richard to return to the West Indies. Not immediately complying, he was dismissed; then, petitioning, secured a temporary reprieve; again, delayed; was forced by threat of suspension and non-payment of salary to promise a return; but did not get back to Grenada until the late summer or autumn of 1770. Burke as an opponent of the administration was in no position to influence these moves, but he was sympathetic and apprehensive on his allegedly ill-used brother's behalf. He told Rockingham in November 1769:

> My brother is ordered to Granada [sic], though his leg is not yet in a condition . . . to conflict with that climate. If he goes, he goes I fear to his death. If he stays he loses his place, with the mortifying circumstance of accommodating an enemy. This is not pleasant to me.[5]

And to Shackleton the following August he wrote of 'poor Richard':

> His health was not very good, and the strength of his broken leg by no means thoroughly restored at his departure – but he was to look for no favour or indulgence from our present rulers; who even attempted to take his employment from him, but in this lesser as in many greater instances of their malignity they defeated their own purpose by the bungling method of the execution, and from shame they found themselves obliged to restore him to his offices, but under strict orders for departure, notwithstanding the testimony of the King's surgeon concerning the state of his leg.[6]

Almost as soon as he was back in Grenada, Richard snatched at what seemed an excellent opportunity to repair his fortunes, buying cheaply a large tract of land from the Caribs living in Grenada's neighbouring island, St Vincent. Again however he ran up against the island's government. Governor Melville, judging that Richard Burke and other speculators were taking an advantage of a disturbed situation to make a quick 'killing' at the expense of the native population and of the colonial authorities' own plans for land allocation, obtained from his masters at Westminster authority to invalidate the sale. Direct private bargains with the Caribs were not allowed to stand.

Richard Burke had made his purchase from the so-called 'Red' Caribs, that is from the indigenous non-negro natives. But he then met trouble from another quarter, when the Black Caribs (who were strictly not Carib at all, but descended from negro slaves) disputed the Red Caribs' right to dispose of their property and, in the words of Governor Melville's report, 'burnt down for a second time the houses and other work begun by Collector Burke and other intruders of the Crown lands'.[7] Petitioning to the Council of St Vincent proving fruitless, Richard was granted a further year's leave of absence. (This apparently followed a plea on his behalf from Garrick to the Treasury Secretary.) He left behind him a few vociferous supporters who 'stopp'd all public business for a time', but also strong official disapproval of this seemingly unscrupulous adventurer – one moreover who was now threatening 'tryal at law' unless he was given the rights and perquisites of the islands' Treasurership to add to his Collectorship and Receivership.[8]

Throughout 1771 and 1772 in London,* Richard Burke, with support from Edmund and William, continued to prosecute his two claims, to his lands and to his Treasurership. By July 1772 Edmund was hopeful that the Board of Trade would be deciding in Richard's favour, at least on the lands issue: 'Of the quiet and unmolested possession I do not despair', he wrote; 'but as it is an affair of magnitude, so it will be a work of time and patience'. A few months later he was pleased to note that a new ally and, it seems, financially interested partner in promoting Richard's enterprises – Charles James Fox – had become a Lord of the Treasury. Fox, only twenty-three, was still at that early stage of his career a supporter of North's government. His influence was, of course, soon to lose its value to the Burkes when he became too rebellious a junior minister for North (or the King) to stomach and was eventually dismissed, becoming thenceforth a member of the Opposition.†

The case of Richard Burke versus his enemies in the West Indies and Westminster was to achieve a remarkable longevity, lasting at least into the mid-1780s. In 1773 Lord North hoped to find a way of placating both Richard and another claimant upon governmental beneficence – General Robert Monckton, who was a ministerial supporter disappointed of being made Commander in Chief of the East India Company's army, and whom it would be convenient to sweeten by making him an offer of Crown lands in St Vincent. The ingenious North hoped that Monckton might be persuaded to accept this gift on the understanding that he agreed to sell back straight away, at a low price, part of his land to Richard Burke. Immediately Edmund,

*The Burkes' town house, their home during the months when Parliament was sitting, had been in Fludyer Street, Westminster, since they moved from Queen Anne Street in 1769. Early in 1772 they moved again, to Broad Sanctuary, Westminster, and remained there until 1779, when they went back to Charles Street, St James's Square. In February 1772 William Burke was writing to O'Hara: 'Ned is removed to the house Dr Markham once lived in, near the Abbey. It is convenient for the House of Commons, airy in itself and very roomy, Mrs B. has her two rooms, and Ned his study all upon the one floor. Richard is in lodgings.' In 1786 the Burkes moved again to Gerrard Street, Soho.

†The original occasion of Fox's fall from grace was his opposition to the act of 1772 forbidding members of the royal family to marry without the King's consent. Burke's own judgment on this measure was that it was 'little conformable to the spirit' of British law; it was 'bad as a regulation and worse as a precedent'.

fighting as hard as ever for, as he put it, 'the little circle of my family', was busy acquainting Rockingham with what was afoot, and proposing instead his own inverted version of the scheme: let *Richard* be granted the lands, on the understanding that *he* would then hand over a portion to Monckton. 'Here', he claimed, though the force of his reasoning is not immediately apparent, 'the whole transaction would be clear open, simple, and to be avowed to the world. In the other way, it would have all the air of a jobb.'[9] Nothing however came of North's idea of killing his two troublesome birds with one stone. Monckton did indeed get his 4000 St Vincent acres as compensation, but Richard Burke's claim was held over, considered again by the Treasury Board in 1774, and rejected by them in November 1775. Edmund, never prepared for one second to consider that Richard might have been guilty of any malpractice, remained obstinately hopeful on his behalf for a long time yet. In August 1776 he was telling his cousin Garrett Nagle in Ireland that Richard had had 'much wrong done to him', but the thing was 'not yet desperate'.[10] Much as in his *Present Discontents* theory to explain the 'conspiracy' between the Court and the 'secret' cabinet to defeat the true (that is, Rockinghamite) representatives of the people in 1765, so now, when he heard that the Red Caribs' land 'sold' to Richard had been transferred to the Blacks, he was perfectly able to persuade himself that this transaction and even the war with the Blacks that preceded it, were entirely 'the manufacture' of the Governor of Grenada and Commissioner Sir William Young – a conspiracy 'to oust my brother from his lands'.[11]

Sir William Young had been since 1764 Commissioner for the Sale of Ceded Lands in the West Indies. 'That man is active, specious, and plausible', Burke told O'Hara, 'and does not want friends in the Treasury. In order to divert pursuit from his own very great misconduct he will move heaven and earth to turn their thoughts against this purchase.' Blind though he always was to the questionable conduct of those near and dear to him, it may well be that Burke's tale of Young's 'misconduct' was not entirely prejudice and self-delusion. Young had failed to make payments due from him to the Treasury and had eventually to pledge his own West Indian estates to meet his liabilities; he resigned his Commissionership in 1774.[12]

To pursue for a while Richard Burke's progress, off the main

Edmund Burke track and down its own obstacle-strewn side-line: – He had by no means done with the West Indies yet, although it might have seemed so in December 1776, when he was suspended from office. However, eighteen months later he was restored to his post, though under direction that he pay the Crown the £2185 he owed. That sum, far from being paid, had soon swollen unconscionably, it seems, to £9586. It has been suggested, though never quite proved, that these were monies that had been 'borrowed' from the Crown to finance his attempted land purchase. In 1779 he once more faced suspension, though this time he contested it at law. Then when the Whigs (including of course his brother) came to office in 1782 he managed to get his so-called 'surcharge' officially 'relieved', and indeed for a time, thanks to his brother's influence, held the Treasury Secretaryship himself. The change of government in 1784 found him again ordered to pay his debts to the Crown on pain of prosecution, but somehow he succeeded in winning an indefinite reprieve, it must be conjectured thanks to the influence of friends and the championship of his brother.[13]

Malversation of funds was not the only misdemeanour popularly attributed to the younger Burke. He could observe a degree of casualness over his gambling debts not much esteemed by his fellow players. Once, after losing nearly £15,000 to two gentlemen at Brighton, he

> then declared he had but £2000 in the world *which he would pay to us* – but next morning when we talked the matter over by the seaside – he said he could not afford to pay anything at present, for he was going immediately to the Grenades, and that he must employ that sum for his equipment! and that he had the night before, at the time of playing, resolved in his own mind, let him lose what he might, never to pay more than £2000.

The promissory notes he gave for this sum seem never to have been honoured.[14]

CHAPTER
6

INDIA, IRELAND, AMERICA 1770–1774

IN THE early 1770s, before events in America came to perplex and dominate business at Westminster, it was largely the affairs of India and of Ireland which absorbed parliamentary attention, as they were persistently to do over the two centuries following. As an Irishman, Burke could hardly fail to have positive opinions on British policy towards his native land. India he never visited, and to begin with he had no claims to be expert in Indian affairs. Indeed the reverse: his association with his brother and William in their ruinous speculation in East India stock seems to have been rather that of a sleeping partner, probably a too trusting one. Soon, however, William Burke – the *closest* of all Edmund's friends, as he repeatedly insisted – would be away fortune-hunting again, this time as adviser to an Indian raja, in which capacity he would become immediately involved in the endemic Indian inter-princely strife and the perennial intrigue within the East India Company itself. Burke's private and family interest in these troubles would always intensify his concern with them and colour his judgments. By the next decade India would come intensely to absorb him, until the evils of the French Revolution eventually put even Warren Hastings and the scandals of Oudh in the shade. Obsessed maybe, warped probably in his sympathies by close personal and family ties, liable to serious misjudgments undoubtedly, Burke nevertheless would still come to be held, and justly, as one of the first important champions of the need for British government in India to have clean hands.

In Ireland too, naturally, Burke had ties and interests. He had a host of Irish relatives* and old friends. He had even in a small way become an Irish landowner – a situation in which he found himself awkwardly involved with the current laws restricting the inheritance and ownership of land by Catholics. There was an estate at Clogher in County Cork for which Burke's elder brother had earlier obtained a long lease from the (necessarily Protestant) landlord of the (Catholic) Nagles, and which he had then subleased for a term of 31 years – the longest period legally permissible – to his uncle Patrick Nagle. Then in 1765 Garrett Burke died and Burke took over his brother's lease. Thus as leasehold proprietor he had become landlord to his Catholic Uncle Patrick. He appointed a cousin, Garrett Nagle, to act as his agent, and continued to own the Clogher estate until 1790, when at last he succeeded in getting rid of it to another, an availably Protestant, Nagle.

1773 was the year of the Boston Tea Party, and soon the Irish Protestant governing class, taking its cue from America, would be simmering with revolt. But in 1773 the immediate Irish subject of dispute stemmed from an attempt by the Dublin parliament to repair Ireland's shaken finances by getting the Westminster and Dublin authorities to agree to a tax on absentee landlords. Now, as it happened, by owning the Clogher estate Burke had become an absentee landlord himself, but indeed one of such minor stature (compared for instance with such magnates as the Duke of Devonshire or the Earl of Bessborough, or of course Burke's own political chief Rockingham),† that there seems small reason here for imputing to him a bias arising from self-interest. In fact, in a contemporary list of Irish absentee owners his name does not appear at all – though it does in a later Dublin list of 1783, where his Clogher estate is valued at £500.

Later ages would have much to say on the evils of absentee landlordism, on the ground largely that it drained away the wealth of Ireland to be spent and enjoyed in England; but the political objections to taxing it in 1773 were powerful. Indeed Rockingham's own were so emphatic that once he even declared that any

---

*For instance, the biographer of Burke has to thread a path through *six* of his relations at this time or thereabouts named Garrett Nagle.

†From their Irish properties Bessborough drew £9000 a year, Devonshire and the Cavendishes £12,000, Sir George Savile £1500, and Rockingham £15,000.

minister proposing such a tax was worthy of impeachment. Without going quite as far as that, Burke was emphatic enough:

> There never surely was a scheme of such preposterous policy, nor that tends more . . . to the separation and derangement of the whole contexture of this Empire . . . I can never forget that I am an Irishman and I think I would shed my blood rather than see the limb I belong to oppressed and defrauded of its true nourishment . . . But —

Burke's conservatism never embraced the folly of 'whatever is, is right'; but it would always contend that those who proposed change must work hard to persuade a rational man that their innovations or reforms would not end in damage or absurdity. Fears of such an outcome always underlay his opposition to all measures of parliamentary reform other than those aimed specifically at reducing *Court* influence. Similarly he now judged that a tax on absentees must do more harm than good. It had not been thought through, and seemed to be based on illogicalities. In a lengthy letter which he sent to an Irish M.P., Sir Charles Bingham, we find not only a comprehensive statement of his position, but also some indications of how Burke understood the 'union' and 'contexture' of the British Empire – all the more significant in view of the looming crisis in America.

As for absenteeism, it was *unavoidable* that a great proportion of the money of every subordinate country would flow towards 'the metropolis'. It was *natural* that those directing the affairs of the Empire should reside at its heart and they ought not to be penalised for it. The suggested tax virtually declared that England was 'a foreign country'. It struck at the nation's power: 'in the end at the union of the whole Empire'. And suppose the idea to be extended: was there then to be a tax on an Englishman living at home but owning land in the West Indies or America? 'If he attempts to comply, he is likely to be more a citizen of the Atlantic Ocean and the Irish Sea than of any of these countries.' The matter was 'absurd and ridiculous'.[1]

According to Horace Walpole, it was Burke who drew up a protest submitted over the signatures of five of the most substantial absentee peers, including Rockingham; and finally opposition on both sides of the Irish Sea proved so strong that the measure, after being defeated in the Dublin parliament, was abandoned both by the Lord Lieutenant and (with some relief) by his masters at Westminster, Lord North and the King.[2]

During the two decades that followed the Seven Years War, successive English statesmen – Pitt the elder, North, Burke and Fox, Pitt the younger – grappled with the affairs of the East India Company: problems created by the widespread commercial activities and successful wars which had involved it in important political power-play and transformed it willy-nilly into a quasi-governmental force over large areas of the sub-continent. But as Horace Walpole remarked, it had proved easier to conquer the East than to know what to do with it.[3]

In the first century and a half of their operations in India, Englishmen had been essentially trading adventurers. In their four fortress-stations of Madras, Surat, Bombay, and Calcutta, they had been influential among local rulers but had not assumed any political authority with them. There was wide scope for the Company's servants to exploit private trade, sometimes on terms of special privilege from a complaisant ruler, himself hopeful of benefits to come. Business morality was easy-going, opportunities were immense, and it paid Englishman and Indian alike to cultivate good mutual relations. When they had made their fortune in India, Company servants often returned to spend it in England, buying up estates and perhaps a parliamentary borough, parading their wealth and enjoying their new social status, though often little accompanying public esteem. These were the 'nabobs', whose ostentation gave the stay-at-home English gentleman a sometimes exaggerated notion of the profits of the Company: the time came in the 1760s and 1770s when, although its servants had manifestly made fortunes, the Company itself, near bankruptcy, was seeking parliamentary rescue. At Westminster its 'interest' was always powerful, and its political patronage was second only to that of the Crown.

Clive, between 1757 and 1760, had won spectacular Indian triumphs: brilliant military victories and financial gains hardly less sensational – a million pounds for the Company, together with a half-million for the European inhabitants of Calcutta; £50,000 apiece for members of the Company's Council; nearly a quarter of a million for himself, plus an assignment of the Bengal land revenues worth £25,000 a year. But while he was back in

England between 1760 and 1765 the politicking, commercial rapacity, and occasional gross extortions of the Company and of its servants in their private capacity grew intolerable. When Clive returned, it was to find, in his own words, 'a scene of anarchy, confusion, bribery, corruption, and extortion'. He attempted reforms, but their failure sprang at least partly from his belief that Bengal could be governed by a division of power between the Company and the native ruler or Nawab – while the Company continued to pocket the Nawab's land revenues (*diwani*), whose value moreover Clive seriously overestimated.

It was amid an atmosphere of financial optimism after Clive's return to India in 1765 that the Company's shareholders in London, the Burkes among them, had managed to push the dividend up to an unrealistic and unwise 12.5 per cent. When prospects were still looking rosy, Burke had launched into the purchase of his Beaconsfield estate. Then, in 1769, had come the sudden stock depreciation which caught the exposed speculators napping, and left Edmund Burke seriously distressed, with both Richard and William near to ruin. For the succeeding quarter-century the affairs of India, and more particularly of the Company and its servants, would be constantly near the forefront of Burke's political attention. Indeed later during that period there were times when they would rouse him to passionate, even obsessive, concern. That this was genuine is difficult to contest; but likewise it is impossible to deny that his opinions upon Indian questions were always heavily influenced, and sometimes quite distorted, by partial or maliciously slanted views and judgments supplied to him by informants in or recently returned from India. Chief among these would be William Burke and Philip Francis.

Back finally in England, Clive was obliged to face examination by select parliamentary committee, and eventually a full-scale Commons attack, before each of which he made a hard-hitting defence, insisting that always and naturally the Company's servants had received 'presents' from the Indians; that his own had admittedly been very substantial; but that when he considered them he stood 'amazed at his own moderation'. William Burke, with Edmund's approval, spoke strongly for him in the Commons. Both men were happy to see him win the vote, and Edmund was convinced that after his 'fiery trial' Clive's reputation stood higher than ever. His attitude to the Clive affair stands indeed in remarkable contrast to the vendetta pursued later by him and his fellow Whigs against Warren Hastings.

Lord North acted in 1773 to 'regulate' British activity in India, the first statesman statutorily to acknowledge that the Company's independent status needed reconsideration, and that Westminster must involve itself in an oversight of the governing of its now very extensive Indian possessions – a first step down the road which led eventually to the suppression of the Company by the British government and Queen Victoria's assumption of the imperial crown. A trading company intent merely on profits and dividends could no longer be entrusted with unfettered rule of what had become a sizable empire. The state moreover had a right also to some share of the wealth that the Company was taking out of India.

To Burke this last was plain theft. 'We never denied Parliament's right to regulate but *do* their right to rob', he protested. 'They only attack the Company in order to transfer their wealth and influence to the Court.'[4] Next to the grand object of the destruction of Wilkes, he wrote, 'the leading object in the politicks of the Court is to seize upon the East India patronage of offices . . . To the attainment of their end mere despotick violence is not sufficient, or they would have attained it long ago.' And again, 'They have taken so much money from the East India Company by the composition for the Diwanna and by the tea agreement that they have fairly run the Company aground for cash.'[5] (The reference to the 'Diwanna' or *diwani* is to the annual payment of £400,000 by the Company to the state as a share of its acquisition of the revenues of Bengal, Bihar, and Orissa.) Rather more than a year later he was claiming that the Rockinghams were still trying to 'save something from the talons of despotism'.[6] At this stage of his opinions on India, always with Burke the enemy is not in faraway India itself or in the Company's headquarters in Leadenhall Street, but among those 'treacherous allies' on the opposition benches (Chatham, Shelburne and their group in particular) who failed to make common cause with the Rockinghams. But at least at this time, if Burke can hardly be acquitted of party prejudice, the accusation levelled against him that his opinions were dictated by direct financial interest seems invalid. The suggestion that it did stems third-hand from a passage in the memoirs of William Hickey,[7] who wrote that his father Joseph Hickey was told that Burke (or perhaps the combined Burke purse?) stood to win £80,000 in East India stock – a story that ought probably to have related not to 1773, where Hickey put it, but to a time four years earlier when the three Burkes were indeed extravagantly involved in such speculation. Nevertheless, the attitude taken by Burke and his fellow Rockinghams to North's 'regulation' of the East India Company appears both factious and ill-conceived, championing as they did a continuance of the Company's full independence.

During the years of the early 1770s, when the North administration was riding high, the Rockingham group became so oppressed by a sense of failure, indeed of impotence, that more than once they contemplated absenting themselves from parliamentary sittings. 'My dear Lord', wrote a 'monstrously vexed' Burke to Rockingham in March 1771, 'we are in our usual disarray . . . We shall bungle it worse than before . . . Nothing is concerted or composed.'[8] At one point the Duke of Richmond supported a proposal for non-attendance until ministers committed some 'crying injustice': 'then will be the time for us to stir'.[9] Rockingham himself proposed a 'partial secession' from Parliament during the session of 1772–3, a move opposed by Burke. He was willing to go along with it if others wanted it, but thought they would then run the risk of being forgotten by the public. Yet it *was* the public who plainly were the source of much of this Whig feeling of helplessness. 'The people without doors are cold and unconcerned in the contest which is carried on between us and the ministers', Burke told Dowdeswell. It was unfortunate, but 'the designs of the Court coincide exactly with the phrensy of the people'. In the 1774 general election, though Burke had a personal triumph at Bristol, the Rockingham party's strength in the Commons was reduced from 55 to 43.

In 1770 James de Lancey of New York, an old Etonian and an acquaintance of Lord Rockingham (whose passion for horse-racing he shared), had been chief mover in securing Burke's appointment to act as agent in London for the New York General Assembly. As a prominent member of the Whig party which had been primarily responsible for the repeal in 1766 of Grenville's hated Stamp Act, Burke was clearly one whose sympathies in general the New Yorkers might rely on – though it is true that only a year or so before getting the New York invitation he had been giving as his opinion that: 'America is more wild and absurd than ever'.[12] Once their paid agent, he was studiously faithful to his employers, keeping them minutely informed of those details of the Westminster scene relevant to the city and state of New York. Particularly important to them was the North government's Quebec Act of 1774, which angered them not only by extending the Canadian border southward and thus slamming the door on future American expansion westward, but also, as they saw it, by backing French-speaking Catholics to the disadvantage of the English-speaking Protestant colonies, New York in particular. Burke made no speech on the Quebec Bill – Horace Walpole imagined that that might be because of his alleged 'old Popery'[13] – but the account that he gave New York was a model of unbiased reporting. Even when, after the rebellious Bostonians had made their famous gesture of defiance against the East India Company's tea imports, North's government introduced punitive statutes against the port of Boston and the state of Massachusetts, Burke's reports from Westminster remained irreproachably factual and objective – even when from the opposition benches he was eloquently inveighing against the government measures. Moreover he took the trouble to stress that those like himself who spoke against penalising the port and merchants of Boston must not be thought in any way to be questioning British authority. 'All the true friends to the Colonies', he wrote to New York, '. . . have laid down and will lay down the proper subordination of America as a fundamental, incontrovertible maxim in the government of this Empire.' The Americans ought especially to mistrust British newspaper reports: 'They are rarely genuine; they are for the most part extremely misrepresented, often through ignorance, often through design; and very frequently the whole is a mere matter of invention'.[14]

Indeed it should not be thought that the Rockingham party, although they had pleased the American colonists by repealing the Stamp Act in 1766, had shown significant pro-American sympathies in the years immediately following. Burke's own *Present Discontents* of 1770 had at no point mentioned colonial grievances; Rockingham clearly feared that American agitation would soon be trying to undermine the whole system of trade and navigation; and as late as 1773 the clause in the East India Tea Export Act whch was shortly to provoke the Boston Tea Party went through without opposition from any of the leading Rockinghamites, Burke included.[15] But by this time Burke had become their chief spokesman on American affairs, and was convinced that nothing, no clinging on to Westminster's undoubted legal rights, nothing, nothing at all, would ever justify measures which would provoke colonial rebellion and what would be essentially a civil war between the British of Britain and the British of America.

On 19 April 1774, just four months after the Boston Tea Party – with Westminster in the midst of debates on the various punitive measures which stemmed from that incident and other rebellious American moves – Burke made the first of his two parliamentary speeches on America which may legitimately be called historic. 'They are the only English speeches', thought Leslie Stephen, 'which may still be read with more than an historical interest when the hearer and the speaker have long been turned to dust.'[16] The first of them came during a debate on the proposed repeal of the threepence per pound duty on tea, the only survivor of the original five 'Townshend duties' of 1767. Burke's speech, in the version later printed, occupies some sixty-five pages. It was argued passionately and exhaustively. Exhaustingly too; almost at the end he was obliged to break off and rest. Here the printed passage* reads:

> Reflect how you are to govern a people who think they ought to be free, and think they are not. Your scheme yields no revenue; it yields nothing but discontent, disorder, disobedience; and such is the state of America, that after wading up to your eyes in blood, you could only end just where you begun; that is, to tax where no revenue is to be found, to – My voice fails me; my inclination indeed carries me no farther – all is confusion beyond it.

The account continues with 'Well, Sir, I have recovered a little', and he proceeds to deliver a strong justification of the (Rockinghamite) Declaratory Act of 1766 which *declared* – that is,

*Burke told Boswell that he published this first famous speech on America too long after delivering it to be fully able to recall it unaided. He needed the help of Cavendish's notes made at the time. Burke 'foamed like Niagara' while Cavendish had contrived to 'bottle up' (*Boswell Papers*, vi. 132).

reaffirmed – the sovereign rights of Britain, whose Parliament 'as from the throne of heaven . . . superintends all the several inferior legislatures which ought to be subordinate to her'. Thus American independence was a thing not yet even to be dreamed of.

But 'every hour you continue on this ill-chosen ground [of seeking a revenue from a tea tax] your difficulties thicken on you'. Was the government afraid of a loss of dignity if it withdrew the tax? 'This dignity of yours is a terrible encumbrance to you, for it has of late been ever at war with your interest.' 'No man ever doubted that the commodity of tea could bear an imposition of three-pence. But no commodity will bear three-pence, or will bear a penny, when the general feelings of men are irritated, and two millions of people are resolved not to pay.'

Until the ill-judged Stamp Act of 1765, he argued – the first attempt to raise a revenue from America – Britain had gained hugely from her colonies and from her own wise policies of trade regulation: 'Whilst England pursued trade and forgot revenue . . . you acquired not only commerce, but you actually created the very objects of trade in America; and by that creation you raised the trade of this country at least four-fold. America had the compensation of your capital, which made her bear her servitude' – that is, the limitations imposed on her by British regulation of her trade and manufacture. In return she had the priceless boon of civil liberty, 'every characteristic mark of a free people in all her internal concerns'. She had both the 'image' and the substance of the British constitution, including the right to be taxed by *her own* representatives. But then, first George Grenville (the Stamp Act) and afterwards Charles Townshend (Chatham's Chancellor of the Exchequer – the Townshend duties) had interrupted this flow of mutual benefit.

Eloquent tributes to the qualities of these two men, Grenville and Townshend, and of Townshend's superior minister Chatham, preceded passages analysing the flaws in their make-up and the nature of their mistakes in fiscal policy. Consideration of Grenville, once a law student like himself, led him to question the value of dry legal studies in the training of a statesman, who must above all possess imagination. Praise of Townshend, 'this extraordinary man', led to the celebrated observation, 'To please universally was the object of his life; but to tax and to please, no more than to love and be wise, is not given to man'. A ringing eulogy of the prestigious Chatham – ringing, but not without a suggestion of double-take, for Burke could never love or trust Chatham – prefaced a mockingly humorous and much-quoted description of that great man's not-to-be-recommended method of choosing his subordinate ministers in 1766, including of course Townshend; an assemblage of men from any party or no party, this representing for Burke, the champion and idealiser of party, a clear recipe for governmental failure:

> He made an administration so checkered and speckled; he put together a piece of joinery, so crossly indented and whimsically dove-tailed; a cabinet so variously inlaid; such a piece of diversified mosaic; such a tesselated pavement without cement; here a bit of black stone, and there a bit of white; patriots and courtiers, king's friends and republicans; whigs and tories; treacherous friends and open enemies; that it was indeed a very curious show, but utterly unsafe to touch and unsure to stand on. The colleagues whom he had assorted at the same boards stared at each other and were obliged to ask, 'Sir, your name? – Sir, you have the advantage of me – Mr Such-a-one – I beg a thousand pardons' . . . Persons had a single office divided between them who had never spoke to each other in their lives until they found themselves, they knew not how, pigging together, heads and points, in the same truckle-bed.*

But this fun, however stylish, was not what long occupied his mind or his rhetoric. Soon he was again hammering away at his central message. It was one which was always at the heart of his politics. Beware of clever innovations, of 'metaphysical distinctions'; leave all that to 'the schools'. Return to what *worked*, to 'the good old mode', to what the practical wisdom of earlier generations had evolved:

> Again and again I say revert to your own principles – seek peace and ensure it – leave America . . . to tax herself. I am not here going into the distinctions of rights, nor attempting to mark the boundaries. I do not enter into these metaphysical distinctions; I hate the very sound of them. Leave the Americans as they anciently stood . . . They and we, and their and our ancestors, have been happy under that system . . . Be

*Lord North and George Cooke had been made *joint* paymasters in Chatham's ministry.

content to bind America by laws of trade; you have always done it. Let this be your reason for binding their trade. Do not burthen them by taxes; you were not used do so from the beginning. Let this be your reason for not taxing . . . Leave the rest to the schools . . . If intemperately, unwisely, fatally, you sophisticate and poison the very source of government by urging subtle deductions . . . from the unlimited and illimitable nature of supreme sovereignty, you will teach them by these means to call that sovereignty itself in question. When you drive them hard, the boar will surely turn upon the hunters. If that sovereignty and their freedom cannot be reconciled, they will cast your sovereignty in your face. Nobody will be argued into slavery.[17]

CHAPTER
7

BRISTOL AND AMERICA 1774–1779

AT THE general election in the autumn of this year 1774, Burke's previously secure position as member for Wendover was undermined. Lord Verney's finances were by now in so disastrous a predicament that he could no longer afford to award his seats at Wendover, Great Bedwyn, and Carmarthen to those who were unable to pay for them. Burke showed no resentment; indeed, how could he? 'We have infinite reason to be grateful', he told Rockingham, 'for the voluntary acts of friendship which are passed; none at all to murmur at the effects of the present urgent necessity.'[1] 'We' meant himself, William Burke, and a third, Joseph Bullock; and Burke stressed to Rockingham that William's needs ought to have priority, for was it not William's generosity in vacating Wendover which had first made Burke's own entry into the Commons possible? This was very fine and high-principled, replied Rockingham; nevertheless he was emphatic that 'both for Mr Wm Burke and all your family concerns, yourself being in Parliament is the principal thing necessary'.[2]

Fighting hard in William's cause, Burke exercised his eloquence upon another of the Whig magnates, the Duke of Portland, eulogising his 'friend and kinsman' in terms of the richest hyperbole, and it was probably thanks to Portland that William was enabled to stand for Haslemere in Surrey[3] – where however he proved unsuccessful. It was his defeat there which was to leave him dangerously exposed as a debtor, unprotected by a parliamentary member's immunity from prosecution. At this time judgments were entered against him in the Court of the King's

Bench for £6000, but his total indebtedness certainly exceeded, probably far exceeded, the £20,000 for which Lord Verney held bonds against him.[4]

Burke briefly considered standing for either Bristol or Westminster, but was then offered, and at first accepted, one of Rockingham's pocket boroughs in Yorkshire, Malton. But while he was away there, he received news from Bristol that one of the three prospective candidates was withdrawing. His Bristol friends were drumming up support for him, and he was told that his success would be 'certain'. Bristol was vitally concerned in the trade with the American colonies; its merchants were being hit by the colonials' commercial boycott, and Burke at this juncture seemed likely to be a suitable parliamentary spokesman for their interests. Before he himself was able to arrive in the town, his brother Richard hurried there to campaign for him, canvassing among others the old family friend Richard Shackleton in Ireland. Particularly as a Quaker, would he please write to reinforce support for Burke among the influential Quakers of Bristol, stressing that Burke's rumoured 'Popery' was rubbish: he was a true Protestant. Shackleton obliged. It was the first time Burke had had genuinely to contest an election, and this was one where the poll, in the manner of those times, dawdled on for weeks. The single government candidate was eventually defeated; elected were Burke and the American-born Bristol merchant Henry Cruger.

Prominent among the traders of Bristol were the Quaker porcelain-manufacturer Richard Champion, and John Noble, whose business lay in the fisheries off the coasts of Labrador and Newfoundland, just then suffering from the boycott ordered by American ports. Noble and Champion were both quickly on terms of the closest friendship with Burke; their wives also with Jane Burke. (Three years later, writing when the Champions had returned home after staying with the Burkes at Beaconsfield, Burke declared that his wife had 'not been so happy for a long time as she has been in Mrs Champion's company, who has made her pass a very happy summer'.)[5] Others of the Bristol bourgeoisie strongest in support were the Farr Brothers, Paul and Thomas, the banker Harford Lloyd (Mrs Champion was born Judith Lloyd), his cousin Joseph Harford, and Joseph Smith, a Presbyterian iron merchant in return for whose generous hospitality Burke commissioned Champion to make a presentation tea service 'only less famous than that which the Champions presented to the Burkes'.[6] The newly born sons of Smith and of Champion were each soon bearing the name of their godfather Edmund. Unable to be present however at the actual christening of little Edmund Burke Smith, Burke was writing in March 1775: 'The purpose of this is so whimsical that it breaks all the rules: I am to desire a Quaker [Champion] to be my proxy as godfather, at the christening of a Presbyterian!'

The burgesses of Bristol were far from being a united band, and division between opposing groups was immediately widened when Burke declined to have any part in a joint parade to celebrate the election victory, pleading pressure of parliamentary business: a rift apparently trivial, but indicative. It was not to be assumed that there would be any solidarity between Burke and Cruger – or, more importantly in the long run, between Burke and many of those who had elected him. Over the following months and years he did labour in the special interests of his constituents' businesses, particularly of those nearest in allegiance to him. For instance he worked hard at Westminster, though in the end unsuccessfully, to prevent Champion losing a vital patent battle with the rival firm of Wedgwood. (Champion's business was finally ruined.) But omens of trouble ahead at Bristol were there from the outset, even on the day when the poll closed in November 1774. In his speech then to the electors, he allowed that certainly their wishes and interests ought to carry weight with him; but, he said, contesting words which Cruger had just spoken,* the Bristol electors must remember that their wishes were not sovereign; that they should not count upon his subservience. *Mandate* was a word 'unknown to the laws of this land . . . You choose a member indeed; but when you have chosen him, he is not a member for Bristol, but he is a member of *parliament*'. There the interests he would represent were those of the nation, which were 'various, multiform, and intricate'.[7] Times have changed: if the *law* still does not recognise the word '*mandate*', political parties and candidates clearly do – even venerate it. Burke's speech to the Bristol electors remains a *locus classicus*, at least of British constitutional *theory*; but it did not endear him to

---

*'It has ever been my opinion that the electors have the right to instruct their members' (*Bristol Journal*, 5 November 1774).

those many of them who considered that their member's prime duty was to fight Bristol's corner.

Moreover, Bristol's interests themselves began to change as the hostilities in America developed and, with them, the attitude and temper of the city's merchants. With some success, especially in the trade in woollens and hardware, and especially in Poland and Russia, they found new outlets for their exports boycotted by America. Near to despair, Burke expected that ministers would soon be getting loyal addresses 'from those very merchants who last session harrassed them with petitions'. The war was actually becoming popular, and his constituents angered him by 'snuffing', as he put it, round the 'cadaver' of a lucrative war. Bristol was 'going headlong to the Devil, through the manoeuvres of the Court and the Tory party, but principally through the absurd and paltry behaviour of my foolish colleague', Henry Cruger.[8] When in 1777 the Bristol corporation made the government ministers, Lord Sandwich and Lord Suffolk, free-men of the city, Burke was disgusted.

Further to diminish his local reputation was the infrequency of his visits to his constituency. He had never had the need to 'nurse' Wendover, and now it was only when pressed that in each of the years 1775 and 1776 he made one rather short visit to Bristol. By the following year most even of his earlier backers would be restive enough for Champion to write warning him, and for Burke to respond by publishing his defence in the *Letter to the Sheriffs of Bristol*.[9] Already by that time he was aware that his constituents really wished him to be what he called their 'special agent' merely, and that at the next general election he would have to look elsewhere for a seat. That would become still more likely when in 1778 Burke, an Irishman and a man of principle, voted for a bill to remove some of the restraints imposed on Irish trade – on his judgment of the merits of the case, but contrary to the angry conviction of a majority of his former Bristol supporters that their hitherto protected interests would be damaged.

Burke's six-year tenure of his Bristol seat coincided with the decisive years of the struggle between the British government and the thirteen American colonies. It was as member for Wendover that he had given the first of his two celebrated discourses on America. The second came a year later, four months after his election by constituents of whom a fair proportion were losing money from the American boycott.

The speech began with a review of the economics of the struggle: a history of profits past, the fear of losses to come. Let members contemplate what they were in danger of losing: English exports to America alone in 1772 had risen to within a whistle of equalling the value of the entire export trade of England in 1704. Colonial trade in the 1770s represented one third of an ever-expanding total trade. In 1704 it had been only one-twelfth. (Later, Burke may have been surprised to learn that British trade with newly independent America actually continued to increase.)

However ominously American demands for independence were growing at this time – and the fourth of July 1776 was still sixteen months away – few in England were yet prepared to contemplate it. Certainly not Burke. 'All true friends to the Colonies', he wrote to the New York Assembly in this same year of 1774, 'the only *true* friends they have had or can ever have in England, have laid and will lay down the proper subordination of America as a fundamental, incontrovertible maxim in the government of this Empire.'[10] The idea of giving up the colonies, his speech continued, had 'met so slight a reception' that he would not dwell on it. 'It is nothing but a little sally of anger, like the frowardness of peevish children who, when they cannot get all they would have, are resolved to take nothing.' The aim must be conciliation, and he noted that North's government, even if its policies were 'indifferently suited' to that end, were at least agreed upon the principle. Britain as 'the superior power' must take the initiative, which inevitably implied concession. 'Magnanimity in politics is not seldom the truest wisdom; and a great empire and little minds go ill together.'

What in any case were the alternatives? Military force? No, force was 'but a feeble instrument for preserving a people so numerous, so active, so growing, so spirited as this, in a profitable and subordinate connexion with us'. Besides: 'The use of force alone is but *temporary*. It may subdue for a moment, but it does not remove the necessity of subduing again: and a nation is not governed which is perpetually to be conquered.' Or was it proposed to *prosecute* the Americans into obedience? How could one take legal action against 'the gravest public bodies, intrusted with magistracies of great authority and dignity, and charged with the safety of their fellow citizens'? For wise men this was 'not judicious; for sober men, not decent; for minds tinctured with humanity, not mild or merciful'. 'I do not know the method of drawing up an indictment against a whole people.'

Much of this long and eloquent speech – sixty pages, some 25,000 words, in the published version – consists of a closely argued analysis of the nature and the value to Britain of the American empire; of the reasons for the dangerous surge in the colonials' rebelliousness; of the why and wherefore of the spirit of liberty which informed and inspired them. For Burke no political problem was explicable except in terms of history. 'I put my foot in the tracks of our forefathers', he said, 'where I can neither wander nor stumble.'

> This fierce spirit of liberty is stronger in the English colonies probably than in any other people of the earth, and this from a great variety of powerful causes . . .
>
> First, the people of the colonies are descendants of Englishmen . . . They are therefore not only devoted to liberty, but to liberty according to English ideas and on English principles. Abstract liberty, like other mere abstractions, is not to be found. Leave that to the schools. Liberty inheres in some sensible object; and every nation has formed to itself some favourite point, which by way of eminence becomes the criterion of their happiness. It happened, you know, Sir, that the great contests for freedom in this country were from the earliest times chiefly upon the question of taxing . . . On this point of taxing, the ablest pens and most eloquent tongues have been exercised; the greatest spirits have acted and suffered . . . The colonies draw from you, as with their life-blood, these ideas and principles. Their love of liberty, as with you, is fixed and attached on this specific point of taxing. Liberty might be safe, or it might be endangered, in twenty other particulars, without their being much pleased or alarmed. Here they felt its pulse . . .

Under six heads Burke proceeded to analyse why it had come about that the Americans had now 'kindled the flame that is ready to consume us'. First, and most simply, it was because they were English. 'We cannot, I fear, falsify the pedigree of this people . . . Your speech would betray you. An Englishman is the unfittest person on earth to argue another Englishman into slavery.' Next, and consequently, their forms of self-government were popular and representative in the English tradition. Third, in the northern colonies the people were Protestants, and of a kind most adverse to submission of mind or opinion, for they were largely dissenters 'sprung up in direct opposition to all the ordinary powers of the world'. All Protestantism was a form of dissent, but American dissent was 'a refinement of the principle of resistance; . . . the dissidence of dissent'. Fourth, there were the southerners. They had 'a vast multitude of slaves. Where this is the case in any part of the world, those who are free are by far the most proud and jealous of their freedom . . . Such were all the ancient commonwealths; such were our Gothic ancestors; such in our day were the Poles, and such will be all masters of slaves who are not slaves themselves.' Fifth, American education laid special emphasis upon the law, and lawyers predominated among elected colonial representatives. Some were rendered docile by honours and emoluments, but the rest were largely hostile to government, 'stubborn, litigious, . . . acute, inquisitive, dexterous, prompt in attack, ready in defence, full of resources'. Sixth and last – 'the immutable conditions, the eternal law, of extensive and detached empires':

> In large bodies, the circulation of power must be less vigorous at the extremities. Nature has said it. The Turk cannot govern Egypt, and Arabia, and Curdistan, as he governs Thrace; nor has he the same domination in Crimea and Algiers which he has at Brusa or Smyrna. Despotism itself is obliged to truck and huckster. The Sultan gets such obedience as he can. He governs with a loose rein, that he may govern at all; and the whole of the force and vigour of his authority in his centre is derived from a prudent relaxation in all his borders. Spain, in her provinces, is perhaps not so well obeyed as you are in yours. She complies too; she submits; she watches times.

What then was to be done? On a repeal or amendment of the law regulating colonial trade, which colonists now were reported as resenting, he would offer no opinion; but the taxes imposed *to raise revenue* should be abolished immediately. Also for repeal should be the various punitive acts which had followed the Boston Tea Party and other lawless incidents. 'No way is open, but . . . to comply with the American spirit as necessary; or, if you please, to submit to it as a necessary evil . . . The question is, not whether you have the right to render your people miserable; but whether it is not your interest to make them happy.'[11]

The speech lasted some two and a half hours. Rockingham, listening throughout in the Commons gallery, sent Burke a note immediately he ended: 'I never felt' he said, 'a more complete satisfaction . . . the matter and the manner were equally perfect.'[12] But, impressive as it was, it had of course no chance whatever of convincing a parliamentary majority, or indeed, when the published version appeared a few months later, of converting public opinion. Even some of his friends wanted, at least, a little clarification. O'Hara, for instance, wondered whether Burke was not denying the British government's *right* to tax Americans, which surely had been specifically reasserted by the Rockingham Whigs' own Declaratory Act of nineteen years before. Burke's reply illustrates once again both the pragmatism and the historicism which lay at the root of his political thinking. Politics was not primarily about *rights*; it was about *practicabilities* and *usages* ('conventions real or understood'). How could O'Hara have imagined that Burke had tried *theoretically* to separate Britain's claim to tax America from her undoubted power to *legislate* for America?

> No bounds were ever set to the parliamentary power over the Colonies; for how could that have been but by *special convention*? No such convention has ever been; but the reason and nature of things, and the growth of the Colonies, ought to have taught Parliament to have set bounds to the exercise of its own power. I never ask what government may do in *theory*, except theory be the object. When one talks of *practice* they must act according to circumstances. If you think it worth your while to read the speech over again, you will find that principle to be the key to it.[13]

Throughout 1775 Burke saw the American situation accelerating towards ruin. It may well have been in part this which occasioned one or two spells of poor health, and certainly reduced him sometimes to a condition near to despair. His temperament was a long way removed from that of a Lord Rockingham who, though his physical health was poor by comparison, indeed chronically enfeebling, yet might alleviate his troubles without too much difficulty in the relaxations and pleasures of York races, say, or Newmarket's October meeting; different again from that of young Charles Fox whose natural buoyancy could make light of loss of office and keep him insouciantly afloat on a mountainous tide of debt.* Burke lived his politics more passionately and more all-absorbingly than Fox. He was incapable of private peace and contentment if the nation – 'the empire' – was in crisis.

By the summer, news had arrived of the bloody misadventure overtaking the redcoats at Bunker Hill. 'If we are beat, America is gone irrecoverably', he wrote; and although he still thought that British strength must finally prevail, military victory would mean disaster as surely as defeat: 'Our victories can only complete our ruin'.[14] In angry irony he told Champion, 'Things look gloomy. However they have a more cheerful aspect to those who know them better – for I am told by one who has lately seen Lord North that he has never seen him or anybody else in higher spirits.'[15]

He did allow himself a rest in the summer, at home on his Gregories estate or, as he now took to calling it, simply 'Beconsfield' or 'Beaconsfield' (or sometimes 'Butler's Court') since a neighbouring landowner had sued him over the right to be the lord of 'Gregory's Manor'. It was from Beaconsfield at the end of June that his brother Richard wrote to Richard Shackleton, 'After a very laborious winter . . . Edmund is come hither to enjoy some quiet and his only amusement, farming'.[16]

His despondency was deepened by the realisation that opposition to the government was weak; divided inside, and unpopular outside, Parliament. Some of the blame for this disunited opposition he was always ready to lay at the door of the other, non-Rockingham, Whig connexions, particularly his old bugbear Chatham and his followers. Even – or perhaps especially – when Chatham and Rockingham had early in 1775 begun exchanging visits (eventually unproductive) aimed at mutual understanding, Burke's suspicions of that unpredictable great man were as

*Fox had become a Rockinghamite colleague now, after his dismissal from the Lord North administration. His aunt Lady Sarah Lennox reported to her sister the Duchess of Leinster that 'last year' (1775) he 'left all his fine acquaintances and lived quite with Mr Burke etc., etc.' – adding however, from intimate knowledge of her much-loved Charles, that she did not expect the 'fit' to last long. She was, as it proved, wrong (*Correspondence of Emily Duchess of Leinster*, ii.204). Burke was soon telling his cousin Garrett Nagle that Fox was 'one of the pleasantest men in the world, as well as the greatest genius that perhaps this country has ever produced'.

strong as ever. 'Secure yourself against his manoeuvres', he warned Rockingham – for Chatham would remain a danger as long as he thought that the door of the royal Closet stood 'ajar to receive him. The least peep into that Closet intoxicates him.'[17] And how foolish it was of the Americans to place the trust they did in Chatham, the very man under whose premiership the so objectionable Townshend duties had been imposed; one who 'indeed never did a single service that I can recollect in the whole of his life'.[18]

But the Rockingham party itself hardly presented a vigorous posture in opposition. The Duke of Richmond seemed to embrace defeatism. England's meridian was past, he said. 'We must submit to our political as to our natural old age, weakness and infirmity'; and 'the good people of England will not much care whether America is lost or not till they feel the effects in their purses or in their bellies'.[19] Dowdeswell, the leader in the Commons, was dying. Lord John Cavendish, about to succeed him, saw politics as only one, perhaps not always the most important, among his pursuits. He should not be allowed, said Burke, to get away with the excuse of fox-hunting for irregular attendance at Westminster; permit him only 'a certain decent and reasonable portion' of it before he knuckled down. 'Anything more is intollerable.'[20] And Rockingham himself, leader in the Lords, was quite often away in his own 'kingdom' of Yorkshire, and moreover frequently unwell. Several of the party just now, and not for the first or the last time, were from a sense of their impotence counselling a policy of absenting themselves altogether from Westminster. Rockingham listened to them, and wavered; listened to the Duke of Richmond, to the Duke of Portland, to Sir George Savile; listened also to Burke, who, though he too sometimes flirted with this policy of non-attendance, came down usually against it. Rockingham was a civilised and honest man, modest, of unquestioned integrity, happiest when acting as *primus inter pares*; but Burke, much as he respected and genuinely admired him, was looking for more decisiveness. There is exasperation beneath the surface of his communications with Rockingham during 1775. In one letter particularly he fears that a parliamentary opposition which began by 'indicating a vigorous campaign' seemed likely to 'moulder into nothing'. He writes:

I passed rather a sleepless night; and I could not help rolling over in my mind our conversation at Richmond House. I cannot help continuing – however with the defference I owe, and most cheerfully pay, to your Lordship's judgment – very strongly in opinion that a plan of inaction, under our present circumstances, is not at all in our power, and indeed not at all to be adopted if it were. There are others in the world who will not be inactive because we are so . . . The question then is, whether your Lordship chooses to lead, or to be led . . .[21]

Apologising for his 'importunity', in August he was again urging Rockingham, with his 'great friends', to make 'one honest, hearty effort . . . to keep the poor, giddy, thoughtless people of our country from plunging into this impious war'. 'Indeed we are called to rouse ourselves, each in his post, by a sound of a trumpet almost as loud as that which must awaken the dead.' Against an opposition ill-prepared, unco-ordinated, or half-hearted, the government would be able to 'vote the war with every supply of domestick and foreign force . . . And then what is left for us but to spin out of our bowels, under the frown of the Court and the hisses of the people, the little, slender thread of a peevish and captious opposition, unworthy of our cause and ourselves?' Exactly what they might do however to restrain the Court and the government, Parliament and the nation, from plunging into war and calamity, he could not specify. In a fury of sadness, he had to admit that 'the puny voice of reason' was being drowned in the popular cry.[22]

On 11 October he attended the King's weekly levee and was able to present a petition from those Bristol merchants, the Champion camp, who opposed the use of force against the Americans. It had, reported the *Morning Chronicle*, 'a very gracious reception',[23] but of course no practical effect. Then the following month he made a third important speech in the Commons on policy towards America, going somewhat further than he had before in suggesting now a recognition of the all-American Congress's right at least to exist, if not to exercise lawful sovereignty. His last slight hope of preventing outright war rested in an attempt to persuade Richmond to persuade Rockingham to persuade the Irish Parliament to petition the Crown for permission to mediate and, if that were to come to nothing, to withhold grants and supplies for troops employed overseas. 'The least movement on the part of Ireland', he tried to convince O'Hara (in the last of his many letters to this old friend, who died in 1776) 'would have decided in favour of peace . . . Things are run so near, that without the four thousand men you so handsomely take from defence to lend to oppression, the war would in all human probability expire from want of fewel to feed it.'[25]

A few months later came the Declaration of Independence. It could only confirm his sense of defeat and despondency:

> We are deeply in blood . . . God knows how it will be. I do not know how to wish success to those whose victory is to seperate from us a large and noble part of our Empire. Still less do I wish success to injustice, oppression, and absurdity . . . No good can come of any event in this war to any virtuous interest. We have forgot or thrown away all our antient principles . . .[26]

Pro-American as his enemies were calling him, and especially his political enemies among the Bristol merchants, he could hardly be cheered to hear the news the following year of the surrender at Saratoga of the British army under General Burgoyne, an event seen in retrospect as decisive – militarily in America, diplomatically in Europe, since it provided the necessary encouragement for first France, eventually Spain, and finally Holland to involve themselves in war against Britain. Lord North turned once again, though without optimism, towards the proposals for conciliating the rebels, while some though not all of the Rockingham party now openly advocated recognising the colonies' independence. In the Commons in February 1778 Burke's eloquent indignation was turned against the British use of 'Indians' in the war (Horace Walpole called this 'the *chef d'oeuvre*' of Burke's orations),[27] and a few weeks later he and Charles Fox both supported a Commons motion, defeated of course, authorising peace commissioners to negotiate American independence. This was just three days after the moment of high theatre in the House of Lords when, in opposing a similar motion from the Duke of Richmond, the Earl of Chatham, unable to contemplate the surrender of Britain's 'fairest inheritance' – 'any state is better than despair . . . if we fall, let us fall like men' – suffered the seizure which led five weeks later to his death. Retailing to his friend Champion in Bristol the account of Chatham's dramatic collapse, and praising the 'great glory' earned in the debate by Richmond, Burke felt no need to summon words of sympathy for the fallen giant, this never-to-be-trusted ally: 'Lord Chatham fell upon the bosom of the Duke of Portland in an apoplectick fit, after he had spit his last venom'.[28] Later however Burke did inscribe a tribute to Chatham on the City of London's Guildhall memorial, and at the Westminster Abbey funeral he was one of the pall bearers.

Chatham's death left, at the head of the small group of Chathamite Whigs, the Earl of Shelburne, who next to Burke was probably the weightiest intellectual among the politicians of his day, but was as widely mistrusted as Chatham had been. Aloof, and generally thought to be over-subtle, intriguing and hardly less arrogant than Chatham himself, yet at the same time so ingratiating when seeking support that his insincerity seemed patent, he reaped severe unpopularity both from his inability to communicate satisfactorily with others, and from the suspicion which naturally attached itself to an aristocrat guilty of advanced thinking.* This being understood, it is still difficult fully to account for the universality of the dislike, even detestation, for 'the Jesuit of Berkeley Square'. His differences with Rockingham and Burke, though they were personal, were more than merely so. Burke had argued strongly for party government (though always with the unspoken proviso that it should be the right, that is the Rockingham, party) whereas Shelburne, like Chatham, believed that cabinets should be drawn from 'all the talents' regardless of party. Burke and most of the Rockinghams (though importantly neither Savile nor the Duke of Richmond) were suspicious of proposals for political reform affecting franchises, seats, or the duration of parliaments, although they enthusiastically embraced 'economical reform' – measures, that is, to curb Crown patronage and Court influence. Shelburne by contrast was much less impressed than Burke or Rockingham by the conspiracy theory which had been at the centre of their thinking since Burke's *Thoughts on the Present Discontents* – the allegation that

---

*On his Wiltshire estate at Bowood he patronised during the 1770s such radical intellectuals as the chemist and polymath Joseph Priestley, the philosopher and jurist Jeremy Bentham, and the unitarian minister and moralist Richard Price, the preacher who in a dozen years' time was to provide the spark to ignite Burke's *Reflections on the Revolution in France*.

bad governments were corruptly sustained in office only by the Court's conspiratorial manipulation of patronage. Thus paradoxically Rockinghamites came to mistrust Shelburne on two seemingly opposed counts: while advocating measures of parliamentary reform which George III was bound to resist, Shelburne at the same time contrived to appear less of an antiloyalist than Rockingham and his party, and hence eventually to prove more acceptable in the royal Closet.[29]

The inability of the Whig groups, or even the Rockinghams among themselves, to agree on opposition policy towards parliamentary reform or independence for America led to further years of Whig frustration. In 1779 – at a time when a French invasion appeared a strong enough possibility for the Champions to offer Jane Burke asylum in Bristol if staying at home with Edmund should be judged too risky[30] – there was much talk of instigating impeachment, or some other criminal process, against North and his leading ministers. There was 'abundant matter of impeachment against them jointly and severally', Burke wrote to Lady Rockingham, and he even prepared, though never proceeded with, articles of impeachment.[31] Nothing came, either, of inter-Whig discussions at this time concerning the chances of a coalition government if North's position should weaken still further and the King should throw him over, or (as North himself ever more fervently wished) allowed him to resign. In such circumstances Burke insisted – again it was to Lady Rockingham, a wife knowledgeably involved in her husband's political business – that whoever was offered the premiership, Rockingham or Grafton or Shelburne or Camden, the Whigs must unitedly insist on having their own admiral (Keppel or Howe) and their general (Conway) to conduct the war. At this stage, Admiral Keppel in particular was the especial hero of his fellow Rockinghams. After failing to beat the French off Ushant he had been accused of incompetence; had demanded a court-martial; been acquitted, to Burke's 'inexpressible joy';[32] and been subsequently fêted by Whig society with an enthusiasm even livelier than was likely to have arisen from his *defeating* the French. Keppel's portrait by Reynolds was soon hanging proudly in Burke's town house; Keppel presented it to him in gratitude for the 'anxious zeal and affection' Burke had shown him before and during the court martial.[33] For a short season it was a case of Keppel cockades in the London streets, and Keppel caps for Whig ladies at the opera. In a sense Keppel had indeed won a kind of victory, over not the French but the government, some leading members of which moreover had their houses attacked by pro-Keppel rioters, while Sandwich, First Lord, was even forced to make good an undignified escape from the mob through Admiralty gardens.

The French navy did not menace merely the Channel and southern England. A fleet under Admiral d'Estaing in 1779 left San Domingo and threatened the British position in Carolina. Being told of this at the same time that he learned of the French minister Necker's success in raising a large loan to finance the war, Burke observed bitterly that upon consideration this latter was rather the worse of these two items of news:

> It is to be done without any tax . . . This is very bad news. I dont know whether I should think that the very probable ruin of the American army [i.e. the British army in America] by Destaigns enterprise . . . is news of so ill a complexion. If nothing else can free us of that cursed American war, why let this do it – and the total failure of all our absurd designs may become the beginning of our salvation.[34]

It would be some years yet before the war ended and American independence came to be formally recognised, but after Saratoga and the intervention of France it looked increasingly that there would be no putting the clock back. The time for Burke to put forward constructive 'solutions' of the American question, however eloquent and imaginative they may have been, was gone by. Indeed his dream of a harmonious British empire linked rather than divided by the Atlantic, had been overtaken, decades back, by the daylight realities of economic self-interest, by the fading of sentimental and political ties, and by the three-thousand-mile oceanic divide.

CHAPTER
8

BRISTOL, IRISH TRADE, AND THE CATHOLICS

IT WAS the affairs of his native Ireland rather than of lost America which most closely occupied Burke's unsleeping attention over the latter years of the North administration –Ireland and its legacy of economic discrimination and religious intolerance. Although it never proved possible to operate all of them fully, the laws which had been passed in the aftermath of the Revolution of 1688 and the defeat of Catholicism which accompanied it still weighed heavily. They had perpetuated Ireland's division, Burke wrote, 'into distinct bodies, without common interest, sympathy, or connexion. One of these bodies was to possess *all* the franchises, *all* the property, *all* the education; the other was to be composed of drawers of water and cutters of turf for them.'[1] Some acts had specifically penalised Catholics; others more generally protected English commercial and manufacturing interests. Ireland was a conquered country and made to feel like one. By these penal laws, most of them enacted between 1702 and 1715, at least three Irishmen in every four had as Catholics been excluded from trades and professions, from public office and from juries, and been barred from buying freehold land. A Catholic eldest son could inherit his father's estate entire only if he turned Protestant; otherwise it was to be broken up between the family. Thus the Catholic squires remaining loyal to their religion were chopped into poverty and insignificance, and by 1780 about 4000 of them had been coerced into conforming to the established Church of Ireland. No Catholic might sit in the Dublin parliament or (after 1727) vote for it; neither could he legally attend school, keep a school, or send his children to be educated abroad: a good example of an unenforceably harsh law, for already by about the time of Burke's birth nearly 600 Catholic schools were estimated to be in existence. Somehow money was found for their maintenance and for that of about 3000 priests, as well as for the compulsory and detested tithes payable for the upkeep of the established Protestant church, whose membership has been variously put at between five and ten per cent of the population. Second to the Catholics in number were the Protestant Dissenters of the north-eastern counties, mainly Scots-Irish Presbyterians who like the Catholics were excluded from parliamentary membership or major public office, but were allowed freedom of worship.

Already by the 1760s the discriminatory legislation passed half a century before had been to some extent relaxed or, part of it, abandoned in practice if not in law, and by the 1770s there had arrived a new class of prospering Catholic merchants. But even these, as Burke pointed out, were men whose wealth was prohibited from being invested in land, and thence in the agricultural improvement the country needed. And they constituted only a very small minority of the Catholic population, who in general were 'reduced to beasts of burthen'.[2] This matter-of-fact observation (in a letter to Fox in 1777) arose merely *en passant*, his argument at that time being chiefly concerned with the folly of government policy towards America and the need for Ireland not to give assistance to it in any way. The basic injustices of the Irish situation were not just then their 'present business', but they prompted pertinent questions:

> Surely the state of Ireland ought for ever to teach parties moderation in their victories. People crushed by law have no hopes but for power. If laws are their enemies, they will be enemies to laws; and those who have much to hope and nothing to lose will always be dangerous more or less . . .[3]

Ireland's trade and industry, even more closely than America's, had long been regulated to suit English merchants and manufacturers – among them many of Burke's Bristol merchants. He had not so far opposed restrictions placed on colonial trade and industry in the interests of the home country, as his speeches on the American quarrel amply show. It would indeed have been surprising if he had, for such policies had general acceptance among European colonial powers of the time; but it would always prove difficult for Burke the Irishman to regard his native country merely as a British colony. He must feel for Ireland, he said, 'a dearness of instinct more than I can justify to reason'.[4]

Ireland had its own Protestant parliament in Dublin, but with limited powers: its legislation required the approval of the British Privy Council. The Westminster parliament moreover was empowered to make what laws it liked for Ireland, and executive authority lay wholly under the direction of the British-appointed Lord Lieutenant in Dublin Castle. Now however that the Americans had rebelled and, after Saratoga, looked likely to win, the Irish situation was transformed. Still needing Irish support in the war, and hoping at least to check any Irish inclination to follow the Americans' troublesome example, North's government took important steps to mollify Irish opinion and to placate those 'Patriots' among the Protestant Irish aristocracy and bourgeoisie who came close in their political attitudes to the Whigs in England. Two bills in 1778 proposed wide-ranging concessions to Ireland's trade, though before they could become law many compromises had to be made, with significant limitations set upon Irish rights of export. Among the complicated details of all this, Burke was tirelessly busy, both in the Westminster parliament and as adviser and liaison to the Dublin reformers.

When the merchants of Bristol however heard of what was not only on foot but also getting energetic support from their own elected member, their fear found angry voice. Some of them had already been hard hit by the disturbances in Anglo-American trade; now from Ireland worse threatened. Samuel Span, Master of the Society of Bristol Merchant Venturers, signalled to both Members for the city that it was 'greatly alarmed', and called for their 'strenuous opposition'.[5] Cruger was ready to comply; Burke was not. To Champion, still a loyal friend and supporter (though increasingly isolated and himself near to bankruptcy) he confided that he proposed to go his own way; the Bristol merchants would 'find the errors of theirs in the long run'.[6] But he also, in kindness, advised Champion 'not at this time to make yourself obnoxious by endeavouring to oppose what you cannot prevent. For Godsake lye by; and let the storm of this folly blow over you . . . God bless you.'[7] To another old Bristol friend, John Noble, to Joseph Harford the iron merchant, and to Samuel Span he set out his position at considerable length and took his stand:

After all, what are the matters we dispute with so much warmth? Do we in these resolutions *bestow* anything upon Ireland? Not a shilling. We only consent to *leave* to them, in two or three instances, the use of the natural faculties which God has given them, and to all mankind . . . Indeed, Sir, England and Ireland may flourish together. The world is large enough for us both. Let it be our care not to make ourselves too little for it.[8]

This was being written two years after the publication of Adam Smith's *Wealth of Nations*, and the views of Burke and Smith on liberalising trade were broadly similar:

I know [Burke wrote to the firm of Harford, Cowles and Company] that it is but too natural for us to see our own *certain* ruin in the *possible* prosperity of other people. It is hard to persuade us that every thing which is *got* by another is not *taken* from ourselves. Trade is not a limited thing; as if the objects of mutual demand and consumption could not stretch beyond the bounds of our jealousies . . . Ireland having received no *compensation*, directly or indirectly, for any restraints on their trade ought not in justice or common honesty be made subject to such restraints. I do not mean to impeach the right of the Parliament of Great Britain to make laws for the trade of Ireland. I only speak of what laws it is right for Parliament to make . . . I voted for these Bills which give you so much trouble. I voted for them, not as doing compleat justice to Ireland; but as being something less unjust than the general prohibition which has hitherto prevailed . . . Yet if the least step is taken towards doing common justice in the lightest articles for the most limited markets, a cry is raised as if we were going to be ruined by partiality to Ireland . . .[9]

When John Noble expressed anxiety about how this attitude might affect Burke's chances in the next election, he replied:

To represent Bristol is a capital object of my pride at present . . . If I should live to the next general election . . . I intend to offer myself again to your approbation. But . . . I do not desire to sit in Parliament for any other end than that of promoting the common happiness of all those who are in any degree subjected to our legislative authority, and in binding together in one common tie of civil interest and constitutional freedom every denomination of men amongst us . . . The principle I have stated to you I take to be Whig principles. If they are not I am no Whigg . . .[10]

That his ever-strenuous work for Ireland did not always escape even Irish criticism is shown in the political events and parliamentary sessions (both in Dublin and in Westminster) of the winter of 1779–80. In fact in January Henry Flood, then at the peak of his parliamentary influence, had to rise in Burke's defence during one of the Dublin debates, since Burke's silence the previous month at a sensitive point in the Westminster argument on Irish trade had come under attack. Consequently he was moved to write a detailed explanation and apologia, in a letter of some 8000 words intended for passing round among his Irish friends and allies. In the event, though not at his own instigation, it was printed, and has always appeared among his published works as *A Letter to Thomas Burgh, Esq.* (who was member for the Irish constituency of Athy). [11]

Burke's difficulties at this juncture had arisen because in the Westminster Commons a government bill aimed at ending more of the restrictions on Irish trade, having passed its early stages, was then bitterly resisted in the towns whose businesses it affected, Bristol of course among them – with the result that Lord North backed down. All this came at a critical time in the war with France and (still) the Americans, and the Irish saw their chance. Very soon they had at their disposal a citizen army of 40,000, the Irish Volunteers, ostensibly raised to resist a likely French invasion, actually putting the acutest pressure on the British government. 'Free trade or else –' became a cry impossible for North to ignore, and he backed away again, in the opposite direction. Repeal of the trade restrictions went through.

It was no wonder that Burke found his own position delicate. The *result* had turned out well – 'universal surrender' he called it – but the *means* by which the success had been gained, the organised threat of force, he was too good a parliamentarian to approve without demur. He did demur, but at the same time managed to find a theological, and indeed sophistical, analogy to allow approval: the volunteer army

> was not under the authority of the law, most certainly; but it derived from an authority still higher; and as they say of faith, that it is not contrary to reason, but is above it; so this army did not so much contradict the spirit of the law, as supersede it. [12]

In November 1779 the Dublin Catholic Committee, among

them Lord Kenmare and John Curry, who had been a friend of Burke's in his student days, signalled their gratitude for his 'distinguished zeal and patriotism' and his labours on behalf of Irish Catholics by voting him a reward of 500 guineas. But Burke, informed beforehand of their intentions, had already told Curry of the impossibility of his accepting such a gift, however 'kindly imagined'. Let them donate it instead to 'give some aid to places of education for your own youth at home': and over the next few weeks he outlined his own 'Plan of Education' for Irish Catholics, who under the penal laws were still denied their own schools and schoolmasters.

Throughout his political life Burke laboured with pen and voice and vote to mitigate the injustice of the laws discriminating against the Irish Catholics: *mitigate*, because his sharp sense of practicalities told him that *abolish* was not within immediate grasp. As always, day by day political controversy drew from him, in speeches and publications and private letters sometimes quite of pamphlet length, important declarations of moral and political principles. Thus: even if Protestants had formed a majority in Ireland, the Catholic code could not be justified, for majority consent was not enough in itself to give laws legitimate authority. All law ought to be based on two foundations: on general and public *utility*, and on *equity* which is 'grounded upon our common nature, and which Philo, with propriety and beauty, calls the mother of justice'.[13] On both counts the laws penalising Catholics failed the test. Utility? – 'Ireland, after almost a century of persecution, is at this hour full of penalties and full of Papists.' Equity? – 'Nothing is defensible which renders miserable millions of men coexistent with oneself.'[14] 'We are told that this is not a religious persecution', he said in a speech at Bristol in 1780; its abettors apparently 'disclaimed all severities on account of conscience':

> Very fine indeed! Then let it be so; they are not persecutors; they are only tyrants. With all my heart, I am perfectly in-different concerning the pretexts upon which we torment one another: or whether it be for the constitution of the church of England, or for the constitution of the state of England, that people choose to make their fellow-creatures wretched.[15]

Burke, steadfast in the Church of England, was no less so in the great cause of religious toleration; and not only within the many denominations of Christianity. It would for instance be absurdly misguided if the British in India attempted to affront or undermine Hinduism: 'We must not think to force [Hindus] into the narrow circle of our ideas; we must extend ours to take in their system of opinions and rites, and the necessities which result from both: all change on their part is absolutely impracticable . . . God forbid we should pass judgment upon people who framed their laws and institutions prior to our insect origin of yesterday.'[16]

Because religion was 'the basis of civil society' there was a strong case for denying toleration to atheists, but to atheists only. To everybody else

> I would give a full civil protection, in which I include an immunity from all disturbance of their public religious worship, and a power of teaching in schools as well as temples, to Jews, Mahometans, and even pagans; especially if they are already possessed of those advantages by long and prescriptive usage . . .[17]

The governing factor in admitting the right of a religion or branch of a religion to be considered 'established' must always be its historic pedigree: 'long and prescriptive usage'. An established religion was not 'believed because the laws have established it, but it is established because the leading part of a community have previously believed it to be true'.[18] Thus Presbyterianism was properly the established church of Scotland, as Anglicanism of England, and even North's government had judged it proper to admit Roman Catholicism as the established church of newly conquered Canada.[19] In a Christian society indeed, church and state ought not to be distinct and separable; they were 'integral parts of the same whole'.[20]

Ireland unhappily presented a special case, but the British ought to remember that Catholicism *had* formerly been the established religion. If Irish Catholics were judged to be doctrinally in error, to *inform* them was 'not only fair but charitable'; to *drive* them was 'a strain of the most manifest injustice'. The error was none of their forging: 'You punish them for acting on a principle which of all others is perhaps the most necessary for preserving society, an implicit admiration and adherence to the establishments of their forefathers'.

The Rockingham Whigs had said and done enough by 1780 to show themselves to be good friends to Irish Catholicism and religious toleration, but in the summer of that year they paid the price. It was a time when all over England associations were being formed, county by county, to petition for reform – principally for parliamentary reform, but a body formed by the fanatical and eccentric Lord George Gordon (the Protestant Association) was directed specifically at resisting any further removal of Catholic disabilities. It had been organised largely in protest against Sir George Savile's act repealing the statute of 1699 – a penal measure, declared Burke, devoid of 'common justice, common sense, or common honesty', which had deprived Catholics of the right to bequeath property, and had outlawed Catholic schooling and the saying of Mass.

The outcome of this Protestant backlash was the week-long London rioting of June 1780, when Catholic chapels and the houses of suspected Catholic sympathisers were fired or ransacked, Newgate's prisoners set free, distilleries raided, liquor looted; when drunken mobs rampaged through the streets until the army at last managed to gain control. From riot, alcohol, or gunfire that week some hundreds of lives were lost, perhaps as many as 450.

Rockingham's town house in Grosvenor Square had to be guarded by a combined force from the King's army and from a hastily enlisted emergency army of servants, tradesmen, and political friends. Fox was in the house with Rockingham, and eventually Savile joined them when his home had become likewise threatened. Devonshire House was another of the great London mansions put under siege and similarly defended. For four nights Burke kept watch at either Savile House or Rockingham House, and a few days after the disturbances sent Richard Shackleton an account of some of the week's adventures:

> . . . Yesterday our furniture was entirely replaced; and my wife, for the first time since the beginning of this strange tumult, lay at home. During that week of havock and destruction we were under the roof of my worthy and valuable friend*

---

*Burgoyne was home on parole after being captured at Saratoga. It was Burke who laboured devotedly, by means of a proposed prisoner-exchange, and through the good offices of Benjamin Franklin, to prevent Burgoyne having to be sent back into American hands. 'I apply', wrote Burke, 'not to the Ambassador of America, but to Doctor Franklin the philosopher; my friend, and the lover of his species.'

General Burgoine, who did everything that could be done to make her situation comfortable to her . . . On Monday sennight about nine o'clock I received undoubted intelligence that immediately after the destruction of Savile House mine was to suffer the same fate. I instantly came home . . . and I removed such papers as I thought of most importance. In about an hour after, sixteen soldiers, without my knowledge or desire, took possession of the house. Government . . . obligingly afforded the protection by means of which, under God, I think, the house was saved. The next day I had my books and furniture removed and the guard dismissed. I thought in the then scarcity of troops they might be better employd than in looking after my paltry remains. My wife being safely lodged, I spent part of the day in the street amid this wild assembly into whose hands I deliverd myself informing them who I was. Some of them were malignant and fanatical, but I think the far greater part . . . were rather dissolute and unruly than very illdisposd. I even found friends and well wishers amongst the blue Cockades. My friends had corne to persuade me to go out of town, representing (from their kindness to me) the danger to be much greater than it was. But I . . . resolved they should see that, for one, I was neither to be forced nor intimidated from the strait line of what was right; and I returned on foot quite through the multitude to the House, which was coverd by a strong body of horse and foot. I spoke my sentiments in such a way that I do not think I have ever on any occasion seemd to affect the house more forcibly.[21]

There was a general election in the autumn of that year, and Burke knew that he would have to face criticism and hostility from his constituents. He had offended on four counts particularly: first, excessive sympathy shown to the Americans, and corresponding failure to appreciate the severity of the disturbance to Bristol's prosperity; second, his favouring of Ireland rather than Bristol in the argument over liberalising trade; third, 'the business of the Roman Catholics'; and fourth, which Burke reckoned would weigh heaviest of all in a city of businessmen worried for the security of their credit, his support for a bill, introduced by Lord Beauchamp, which had sought to mitigate the severity – savagery, Burke called it – of the existing law punishing debt potentially with life imprisonment.

To justify his six-year parliamentary record, at Bristol Guildhall he delivered a powerful speech – over forty eloquent pages in the published version[22] – dealing with these four main issues. Among much on America, the following:

> We . . . plunged back again to war and blood; to desolate and be desolated, without measure, hope, or end. I am a royalist, I blushed for this degradation of the crown. I am a Whig, I blushed for the dishonour of parliament. I am a true Englishman. I felt to the quick for the disgrace of England. I am a man, I felt for the melancholy reverse of human affairs, in the fall of the first power in the world.[23]

On Irish trade, yes, he was 'an Irishman in the Irish business', and yes, he had become unpopular in England for it, and at one point, he reminded his audience, unpopular in Ireland too. 'What then? What obligation lay on me to be popular? I was bound to serve both kingdoms'. Had he failed to follow Bristol's *instructions*?[24] 'I did not obey your instructions: No. I conformed to the instructions of truth and nature, and maintained your interest, against your convictions.' He tore to shreds the 'mischievous, ludicrous, and shameful' statute of 1699, whose repeal by Savile's act he had vehemently supported. The 1699 act had in effect made the Irish Catholic 'a foreigner in his own land', and – in a reference to the recent Gordon riots – the English Reformation would remain incomplete until Protestants accepted that animosity to non-Protestants devalued their very Protestantism, creating 'to oppose Popery another Popery'.[25] As for life imprisonment for debt, it permitted intolerable wrong. Where was the justice in a system which allowed the aggrieved lender to be 'at once judge and party' and gave 'a private man' the ability 'to punish without mercy and without measure'? Here Burke went off at a tangent in praise of the tireless work then being done by John Howard 'to open the eyes and hearts of mankind':

> He has visited all Europe . . . to dive into the depths of dungeons; to plunge into the infection of hospitals; to survey the mansions of sorrow and pain; to take the gauge and dimensions of misery, depression, and contempt; to remember the forgotten, to atttend to the neglected, to visit the forsaken, and to compare and collate the distresses of all men in all countries. His plan is original; and it is as full of genius as it is of humanity. It was a voyage of discovery; a circumnavigation of charity.[26]

The whole speech reads now as one of his finest, but it was made to a gathering largely of his own supporters, and its effect upon his electoral chances must have been slight.

The circumstances of his eventual recognition of defeat were complex. His standing among members of the corporation and other leading citizens of Bristol was still high, higher in fact than when he was elected in 1774. But by 1780 *one* of his opponents, the Tory Brickdale, was reckoned to be a certain winner – which left the remaining seat to be disputed between Burke, a second Tory, and the other Whig, Henry Cruger, Burke's fellow sitting member, a man he disliked, despised, and had always found it impossible to work with. Each Whig had his rival group of supporters, but if Burke was backed by the 'principal merchants' and 'the better sort' (as he was sure he was), behind Cruger were many more whom Burke and his camp – which included his brother Richard, as usual – described as 'middling tradesmen' and 'lower' or 'common' voters.[27] Cruger had the bigger battalions. It would be impossible for *both* Whigs to win. Foreseeing defeat therefore, Burke 'declined the poll' and withdrew. In the event *neither* Whig was elected, though Cruger was to win his seat back in 1784.

The trials of canvassing, in foul weather moreover and with a heavy cold, had been distasteful and exhausting. 'I am sick, very sick', he wrote to Rockingham just before giving up the struggle, '– but in two minutes I must be one of the jolliest fellows in the world. They *expect* something of the kind here.' After it was all over, he was angrily resentful of Cruger and his friends and 'their successful endeavour to drive me from Bristol'.[28] Resentful, and depressed too. However sincerely he assured Lady Rockingham that he had arrived at a mood of post-poll 'serenity', he considered retiring from politics altogether, hinting as much to the Duke of Portland, who passed on to Rockingham news of this, to them, disturbing possibility. Rockingham was no doubt already contemplating an arrangement for providing the unsparing and unsparable Burke with a seat, persuading Lady Rockingham meanwhile to use her epistolary charm to salve Burke's wounds. Would he not pay them a visit to recruit his 'fatigued mind by a change of air and place'? Would he not bring his brother with him? This last was clever, and must have pleased Burke.

He confessed[29] that he was in a state of 'awkward indecision'. Apart from his Bristol misfortunes, there were important differences 'in views and plans of conduct' within the Rockingham party which worried him – differences not so much with Rockingham himself, but with colleagues of the highest 'parts and honour' such as Sir George Savile and the Duke of Richmond. Savile, for whom he had *immense* respect, wanted to provide seats for a hundred new knights of the shire to correct an imbalance in the parliamentary representation, while Richmond advocated annual general elections and universal male suffrage, and proposed sweeping away 'at one stroke all the privileges of freeholders, cities, and burroughs throughout the kingdom':

> Some of our capital men entertain thoughts so very different from mine, that if I come into Parliament, I must either fly in the face of the clearest lights of my own understanding and the firmest conviction of my own conscience, or I must oppose those for whom I have the highest value.

He had further grounds, other than political, for indecision and depression. His monetary affairs were in worse than their usual state of insecurity. William Burke, in Paris en route for India, conveyed his fears for Edmund to the Duke of Portland – in his own unique 'literary' vein, by turns pretentious, sycophantic, frenetic, and unctuous. Writing 'in some thing like an agony', he begged: 'For God sake dear Duke of Portland . . . contrive that the two [Beaconsfield] mortgages that harass him, if you cannot take them into your own, may be put into some friendly hands'. William plainly thought Rockingham remiss for failing to protect Edmund's interests, and ended ('forgive me, my dear dear Lord') with a plea to Portland – until such time as he, William, could replenish the Burke fortunes in India and effect a family rescue – to do something to enable Edmund 'quietly to end his days in some corner unnoticed and unheard of'. Portland had earlier been William's patron, and was still described by him as 'the one man whom greatness does not spoil'.[30]

Burke's complicated money difficulties would continue to torment him almost to the end of his life, but he was very soon to be reassured concerning his immediate future in parliament, for Rockingham could not afford to be without him. Rearranging the cards in his hand of boroughs, he contrived to have Burke returned for the constituency of Malton where, although there were some 300 burgage-holders having the right to vote, nobody ever seriously questioned Lord Rockingham's benevolent despotism, and where Burke could remain undisturbed by the presence of common voters and middling tradesmen or, most happily of all, of Henry Cruger.

CHAPTER
9

ECONOMICAL REFORM, TANJORE

IN THE Commons, Burke's first venture into the contentious arena of parliamentary reform, where his differences with those of his fellow Whigs who sought more radical change had become so troublesome to him, was made some months before his setback at Bristol. It was in the winter of 1779–80, when the ministry of Lord North still had two years of precarious life in it. Burke's plans of reform contained no tampering with ancient franchises or decayed boroughs, no making room for more county members, no flirting with the experiment of annual elections. He aimed instead to obviate waste (hence 'economical' reform) and to curb the improper or corrupt expenditure of public money. This meant reforming the royal household and the administration of the public accounts, and the abolition of at least some of the places which automatically conferred on their holders a parliamentary seat. Beyond economical reform he would not go. When the Savile proposals for annual parliaments and a hundred new county members came up for discussion in his Buckinghamshire 'petitioning' committee in 1780, he set down for his local chairman the grounds of his long-considered and fundamental opposition:

> I am growing old. [He was fifty-one.] I have from my very early youth been conversant in reading and thinking upon the subject of our laws and constitution, as well as upon those of other times and other countries. I have been for fifteen years a very laborious member of parliament; and in that time have had great opportunities of seeing with my own eyes the work-ing of the machine of government, and remarking where it

went smoothly and did its business, and where it checked in its movements, or where it damaged its work. I have also had and used the opportunities of conversing with men of the greatest wisdom and fullest experience in these matters; and I do declare to you most solemnly and most truly that on the result of all this reading, thinking, experience, and communication, I am not able to come to an immediate resolution in favour of a change of the ground-work of our constitution.[1]

He was never to abandon his belief that the right to a parliamentary vote sprang naturally from rights of property. Near the end of his life he would still be maintaining that there were only about 400,000 of the total population (of perhaps 10 million) whose property was sufficient for them to have a reasonable claim to vote. He could have no sympathy now with the Duke of Richmond's apparent wish 'to annihilate the [voting privileges of] freeholders'; and as for Savile's 'scheme of more frequent elections as a remedy for disorders', it was Burke's opinion that the disorders had 'a great part of their root in the elections themselves'. He would go so far as to admit that there might have to be '*some* remedy to the present state of the representation':

But it is an affair of great difficulty; and to be touched with great delicacy; and by an hand of great power. Power and delicacy do not often rule. But without great power . . . it *cannot* be done. By power I mean the *executive* power of the kingdom . . . In business of this sort, if administration does not concurr, they are able to defeat the scheme, even though it should be carried by a majority in parliament; and not only to defeat it, but to render it in a short time odious and contemptible.[2]

His resistance to changing 'the groundwork of our constitution' by reform of parliament would stay constant to the end of his days, and what he later watched happening over the Channel after the *ancien régime*'s 'groundwork' collapsed would merely confirm conclusions already solid. Towards the end of his life, Frances Crewe, the charming and celebrated Whig hostess, entertaining him among her company at Crewe Hall and elsewhere, amused herself by jotting down some of this elder statesman's table-talk, before she should forget it. On parliamentary reform the brief note reads:

Too dangerous an experiment to risque. Not any reform proposed yet that did not appear to him (Mr B–) highly hazardous. The least exceptionable that of Lord Chatham's 'adding fifty knights of the shire'; but this, as well as the rest already proposed, not to be thought of in such times as these, or perhaps ever.[3]

The Rockingham Whigs' proposal on strictly 'economical' reform enlisted an unusual degree of cooperation from other opposition groups. In fact, Burke's bill for 'the Better Security of the Independence of Parliament and the Economical Reformation of the Civil and other Establishments' went parallel with two others, one introduced by John Crewe, a Cheshire member, husband to Frances, for the disfranchisement of revenue officers, and one by Sir Philip Clerke, the member for Totnes, for the exclusion of government contractors from the House of Commons.

Economy *was* a concern of the economical reformers, but as a secondary aim only; their prime target ws the influence exerted by courtiers, court nominees, and the Crown itself. It should not be doubted that the motives of Burke and his allies were honest; but scepticism intervenes when the grounds of their attack and the credentials of their arguments are examined. The measure however of their persuasiveness, then in 1780 or in the history books for the next century and a half – even though the bills themselves could not in the end overcome government opposition – is seen when that landmark of a Commons motion, moved by Shelburne's follower Dunning, was actually *passed*: 'That the influence of the Crown has increased, is increasing, and ought to be diminished'. The thinking behind economical reform was close cousin to the conspiracy theory which had permeated Burke's *Present Discontents* ten years before. Court influence within the cabinet, it argued, together with royal and governmental influence over parliament, had corruptly and dangerously increased since the accession of George III.

Thirty-odd years ago Professor Ian Christie, on an expedition through the economical reformers' 'morass of unproven assumptions', examined two of them in particular. One: that the number of placemen in the Commons* had increased over those nineteen years. Two: that the executive power had added to the number of constituencies under its direct control. He discovered that the

*Members, that is, who held a position of remuneration from the Crown – ministers, court officials, civil servants, sinecurists, government contractors, pensioners, officers of the army and navy, etc.

number of placemen had, in total, *declined* by one fifth – 250 in 1761, fewer than 200 in 1780 – and, in the particular categories of sinecure-holders and court officials, had declined by one-third. The total of about 200 placemen for 1780, the year of Burke's bill, included about 50 government officials, 25 court officials, 30 sinecurists, 11 government contractors, 11 holders of secret service pensions, and 65 military and naval officers not included in the other categories. But the assumption of Burke and his fellow 'oeconomists' that placemen's voting was corrupt had no foundation:

> 'Influence' in the sense of corruption was of little account in the House of Commons in the later eighteenth century. In fact, that House was a far more unruly and independent body than its twentieth-century successor. The distribution of patronage doubtless helped to cement support for the government but . . . the more we come to know about individual members of the Commons in that period, the more we find them acting in accordance with their own judgement and conviction – and the placemen formed no exception to this general rule.[4]

Once reinstated in the Commons as member for Malton, Burke was soon as politically busy as ever. We read for a time no more of his considering retirement. Both the Richards, his brother and his son, were now intermittently engaged in work on the legal circuits, but in general the Burke 'family' – one might well say as usual – was lodged uncomfortably close to crisis. Edmund's Beaconsfield mortgages and loans weighed heavily; and William's latest adventure, undertaken in India with the clear objective of making big money and restoring the family fortunes, had run into one of those complicated internecine feuds which the eighteenth-century history of the East India Company is so full of – doubly internecine in this instance, in that one Indian ruler, backed by a camp within the Company, was confronted by, and from time to time at war with, another backed by an opposing camp.

In 1771 one of these protagonists, the Nawab of the Carnatic (with his capital at Arcot), a Muslim, attacked the neighbouring state of Tanjore. Bought off on this first occasion, two years later he struck again, with the support of Company troops, and deposed the Raja of Tanjore, a Hindu of Maratha origin. In 1776 however Lord Pigot, the Company's Governor in Madras (in domestic politics a follower of Rockingham) intervened on the Raja's behalf. It was at about this point that William Burke prepared to set out for India. He would go armed with a letter from Edmund to the influential Philip Francis – 'Junius', but by now a member of the Bengal Council – begging his help for this friend

> whom I have tenderly loved, highly valued, and continually lived with, in an union not to be expressed, quite since our boyish years . . . Bring him home with you an obliged person and at his ease, under the protection of your opulence . . . Let Bengal protect a spirit and rectitude which are no longer tolerated in England.[5]

However it was not to Bengal that William Burke went, but to Madras. News had reached London that there had been a coup against Pigot. He had been imprisoned by a majority of his own Madras Council, who were opposed to his pro-Tanjore policies and calculated that they stood to get a better deal, both for the Company and themselves, from support for the Nawab of Arcot. When William Burke left England it was with a letter of recommendation from Rockingham and with instructions from the Company in London that Pigot be released; but by the time he arrived, after distressing delays, Pigot had died in prison. Shortly after, William Burke became agent to the 'wronged' Raja of Tanjore; returned to England in that status in 1778; and the following year campaigned vigorously on Tanjore's behalf in public controversy with the Nawab of Arcot's London agents. In the composition of his pamphlet published in June 1779, *An Enquiry into the Policy of Making Conquests for the Mahometans*, William undoubtedly had some collaboration from Edmund, who had earlier published an article in his *Annual Register* condemning the joint Nawab–Company conquest of Tanjore in 1773 as 'cruel and unjust'.[6] For the next seven years, until his tremendous onslaught on the younger Pitt's government in 1785 for paying the Nawab of Arcot's debts, Edmund's views of the events in southern India derived in the main either from William directly or from information supplied by three members of the minority party on the Madras Council (Claud Russell, William Ross, Alexander Dalrymple) and filtered through William. But he also read everything he could find, historical or topical, on India, and gleaned news and views from every available source, until he probably came to know more about that vast country than anyone else who had never visited it. Bringing his powerful mind to bear on its problems and complexities, but always judging them from a distance (and no doubt often fed slanted opinions), he not surprisingly made many mistakes; sometimes major mistakes.

Probably he did idealise the highly fertile, densely populated little state of Tanjore, with its pious Hindu raja – Burke, tolerantly as he viewed Islam, never fell in love with it, as he *almost* did with Hinduism. Certainly he misunderstood and unduly vilified the Nawab of Arcot who, in fact, far from the 'man of wild and desperate ambition' that he alleged, was, it now appears, 'timid and irresolute'.[7] Burke sided emphatically with the threatened smaller states such as Tanjore, and with the other sovereign princes of the Carnatic who, he thought, left to themselves, would enjoy a prosperous self-sufficiency. The Company however at this time was interested less urgently in trade than in revenue, to provide it with the means of fighting its wars against Mysore and the Marathas. A majority in the Madras Council saw a unified Carnatic under a subservient Nawab as offering their best way forward. Until 1785 Burke was to continue fighting hard on Tanjore's behalf, and did manage temporarily to fend off attacks on the Raja's revenues. But independent Tanjore failed to flourish, and the move to unify the Carnatic gathered speed, not under a tyrannical all-conquering Nawab, but under the British. Before the end of the century Tanjore would be Company property.[1]

If Burke made mistakes over India, they were mistakes based on honest convictions; he was incapable of engaging in polemics without invoking moral principles. In the 1779 pamphlet on *Making Conquests for the Mahometans*, although it cannot be precisely determined which passages are by William Burke and which by Edmund, there can at least be little doubt who wrote the concluding lines:

It would provoke one's laughter, if it did not excite so much of our indignation, to see such an audacious attempt made to pervert our benevolent natural feelings . . . It is hoped, however, that the active partizans of oppression will do good at last; and, by officiously bringing those matters into discussion, will rouze the humanity of his Majesty, this nation, and the

Company, in favour of the unhappy nations, princes, and people, who are under our protection, and from whom we derive infinite benefit.[9]

By 1780, the year in which Edmund, rebuffed at Bristol, was returned for Malton, William, still deep in debt, was on his way back to India. That, however, by no means precluded him from canvassing his old patron the Duke of Portland to provide him with a seat in parliament. Or perhaps his previous patron Lord Verney – to whom he still owed some £20,000 – might oblige him. A request to Portland, made from Paris after he had set out, unhappily brought no result. William Burke, like Edmund, would have to wait a year or two for the Rockinghams to come into office.

Lord North was far from clinging to power. On the contrary, he repeatedly and wearily applied for royal permission to resign, but the King could see no way of putting together a satisfactory alternative ministry; that is, one which was resolute to pursue the American war, and would exclude Rockingham and his followers. As the King saw it in 1780, not altogether unreasonably, the war with the American rebels was *not* lost. 'Every account of their distresses', he wrote, 'shews us that they must sue for peace this summer if no great disaster befalls us.'[10] In May British forces under Clinton captured Charleston, with 7000 prisoners, and in August Cornwallis defeated Gates, the victor of Saratoga, in South Carolina. North soldiered on; but by the time in November 1781 that news was received in London of an undoubtedly 'great disaster', the British surrender at Yorktown, defeat appeared inevitable. North's Commons majorities dwindled towards vanishing point, until at last in February 1782 a Whig motion advocating the abandonment of the attempt to subdue the Americans by force passed by 234 votes to 215.

Facing defeat in America and the dispiriting prospect of perhaps having to accept a new ministry containing a strong element of Rockingham Whigs critical of him, George III for the first time contemplated for some days abdicating in favour of his son and heir. His mind, he told North, was 'truly tore to pieces'. His dislike of the Rockinghams moreover cannot fairly be dismissed as irrational or prejudiced. They had long alleged improper Court interference in government and parliament. Burke in particular, though from time to time he went out of his way to exempt the King personally from blame, had only recently made ringing attacks on the system of Crown finances and on the royal establishment. Not unnaturally George saw little to love among the Rockinghams, but it was not Burke or Rockingham himself or most of the other prominent men in the party who excited him to a pitch of *outrage*. That distinction belonged to Fox, now one of their chief men. To the King he was worse than objectionable; he was intolerable, politically and personally – devoid of principle and the purveyor of the sort of political rhetoric which the *Parliamentary History* reported as follows:

> There was one grand domestic evil, from which all our other evils, foreign and domestic, had sprung. The influence of the Crown. To the influence of the Crown we must attribute the loss of the army in Virginia; to the influence of the Crown we must attribute the loss of the thirteen provinces of America; for it was the influence of the Crown in the two Houses of Parliament that enabled his Majesty's ministers to persevere against the voice of reason, the voice of truth, the voice of the people.[11]

The King at first employed Lord Chancellor Thurlow to attempt the construction of a new administration 'upon a broad bottom'. Rockingham, however, his position reinforced after a meeting of his principal followers, proved uncompromising, and Burke was certainly among those counselling toughness. Two days after North announced that he was giving up, Burke, 'with the most affectionate attachment', wrote to Rockingham, whom the King at first refused to send for:

> Stand firm on your ground . . . I trust and hope that your Lordship will not let *one*, even but *one* branch of the State . . . out of your own hands, or those which you can entirely rely on. Otherwise depend upon it, all things will run to confusion and jobb, as hitherto they have done.[12]

And if there was an attempt to fashion a new ministry with Rockingham in some post other than the premiership, should not the whole body of his followers refuse to serve? The King was left with finally no alternative to accepting Rockingham's minimum terms: himself to have the Treasury; the exclusion of previously 'obnoxious' ministers; independence for America; and acceptance by George ('no veto') of Burke's Civil List Bill, together with the two other economical reform bills, Crewe's and Clerke's – 'oeconomy in every branch'.[13]

Even so, Rockingham was never in a position to achieve what Burke had advised him to hold out for. With hardly more than eighty followers in the Commons, he could not realistically claim to dictate the entire shape of the new arrangement. Perhaps to a degree he was outmanoeuvred and, numerically at least, Shelburne in fact managed to secure a cabinet majority. Rockingham became Prime Minister, Shelburne and Fox Secretaries of State. Thus from the start the ministry, if not as the King had wished broad-bottomed, was so to speak twin-bottomed. The King saw Shelburne as a counterpoise to Rockingham, and agreed to the distribution of patronage being shared equally between them. Having first used Shelburne as an intermediary during the government's formation, he continued afterwards to treat him as *persona grata* and a man easier to work with than Rockingham: practically as joint prime minister. However, the ministry once completed, the King cannot be seen as interfering substantially with its conduct of policy; he came even to accept, however reluctantly, Burke's 'economical' measures and the inevitability of American independence. But the mistrust felt by the Rockinghams for Shelburne, if not wholly justified, is at least understandable. Both Burke and Fox resented and even hated him, accusing him of opportunism, deviousness, and hypocrisy. Once a critic of the Court – after all, Dunning, of 'Dunning's resolution' deploring the alleged growth of Court influence, was a Shelburnite – in their eyes he had become the new Court favourite. 'He wants what *I* call principles', said Burke.

Burke knew that he was to have the office of Paymaster General of the Forces, which did not carry cabinet rank. That had been previously agreed. 'Take no thought of anything further for *me*', he wrote to Rockingham. 'You need stipulate nothing except for my poor lad.' For himself, he could readily 'consent to lie by' so long as, with his 'second rate pretensions', he was not to be put *below* 'others in that line'.[14]

He had every reason to be delighted with those of the new appointments affecting himself and his family. The Paymastership itself was worth £4000 a year, with the bonus of an official residence, although in Burke's proposed reforms the Paymaster's rewards from commissions and the private pocketing of interest earned on public balances – which over the decades had vastly enriched earlier holders of the office such as Robert Walpole and

Henry Fox and Burke's immediate predecessor Rigby – were scheduled for abolition. (In fact Burke would soon be able to claim with pride that he had saved the national exchequer £24,000 a year by removing the Paymaster's right to take for himself interest at 4 per cent on the balances, and a further £23,000 from other economies.) Burke's brother Richard was now appointed Secretary to the Treasury at a salary of £3000. The younger Richard, Burke's 'poor lad' – he was now twenty-four – and Richard Champion, his business ruined by the American war and Wedgwood's competition, were made Deputy Paymasters at £500 a year each. Another Burke connexion, Edmund Barrett, a distant cousin, was made Deputy Paymaster in the West Indies. Such appointments were entirely character-istic of the rewards for allies and relations customarily attendant upon eighteenth-century government shake-ups, and Burke himself and his immediate kin were not given to financial puritanism or eccentricities of self-denial. Indeed they were in no position to be. They might now look optimistically forward to years of Whig government as a highroad to solvency. In the general atmosphere of monetary relief Burke's recently widowed sister Julia (Mrs Juliana French, at that time of Loughrea in Galway) was not forgotten, though it does seem that at first she suspected she was going to be.[15] Jane Burke 'never wrote with more heartfelt satisfaction' to her 'dear, dear Sister' than at that moment, when 'we can be a comfort and a use to you'; and both Richards wrote kindly and reassuringly to her, her brother Richard sending 'for immediate use one hundred pounds English' and promising an easement of her rent situation.

Best of all perhaps, Edmund was now in a position to do some-thing substantial for William, belatedly back in India after his pro-Tanjore pamphleteering in London. His journey out, lasting fifteen months during 1780–81, had been traumatic: Paris–Marseilles–Naples–Famagusta (where he was shipwrecked) –Aleppo–Basra ('a dreadful unhealthy hole' where he was 'em-bargoed' by Company representatives of the opposing faction) and so down the Gulf to Muscat and eventually Bombay. In London all this time the Tanjore–Arcot imbroglio was still occasioning among the Directors in Leadenhall Street moves and counter-moves, instructions and revised instructions, in sum (Burke was indignantly sure) hostile to the Raja of Tanjore and therefore to William Burke. In Edmund's eyes the arch-villain of the piece was Laurence Sulivan, Deputy Chairman of the East India Company. 'Scarcely was Will Burke's back turned', he complained to Richard Champion, 'than Sullivan . . . began his old machinations for delivering Tanjour into the hands of his son'[1] – that is, of Stephen Sulivan, who was being backed to become, and 'very profitably', Resident in Tanjore. 'I have not slept a wink last night', Burke told the Duke of Portland in October 1780, 'from the agitation caused by this infernal piece of treachery'. As he saw it, the Raja of Tanjore was soon about to receive *two* letters – one from Lord North, borne by William Burke, acknowledging the fact that Tanjore was under British protection, and another, Sulivan's, 'with an arbitrary order to seize upon his revenues. This cannot be, while government is even a decent thing.'[17]

At about this point Haidar Ali, the Muslim ruler of Mysore, invaded the Carnatic and captured Arcot, which suddenly dwarfed the significance of the Tanjore–Arcot conflict. William Burke arrived at last back at Madras, but it was probably not until the autumn of 1782 that he received a letter from London written by Edmund just after he had kissed hands as Paymaster and been received into the Privy Council. It began, 'My dear, my ever dear friend, why were you not here to enjoy and to partake in this great, and I trust for the country, happy change', and continued:

> Be assured that in the Indian arrangements . . . you will not be forgotten, at least I hope not . . . Oh! my dearest, oldest, best friend, you are far off indeed! May God of his infinite mercy preserve you. Your enemies . . . are on the ground, suffering the punishment not of their villainy towards you, but of their other crimes, which are innumerable. I think the reign of Sullivan is over, the reign of Hastings is over . . .[18]

Until this time some of the duties of Paymaster in India had been performed by the Company's Commander in Chief, but Burke was able to demonstrate to his own and Rockingham's satisfaction that a new post was needed, of Deputy Paymaster, and it was to be William's, at £5 per day.

This second Rockingham ministry was destined to last hardly more than three months, but in that time it dealt with two matters of great consequence to Burke: economical reform and the legislative sovereignty of the Irish parliament.

In his Civil List Act, or Establishment Act, of 1782 the number of offices Burke abolished in the royal household and in civil administration totalled 134, more than forty of them, he claimed, 'considerable employments'.[19] Even so, this act was not so far-ranging as the economical reform bill he had introduced from the opposition benches in 1780. This earlier measure, eventually defeated almost in its entirety, had attempted the suppression of the subordinate exchequers and separate jurisdictions of Wales, Cornwall, Chester, and Lancaster, as well as proposing a thoroughgoing curtailment of the pension list and a radical pruning of appointments to the royal household. As for the anomalously surviving separate jurisdictions:

> Cross a brook, and you lose the King of England; but you have some comfort in coming again under his Majesty, though shorn of his beams and no more than the Prince of Wales. Go to the North, and you find him dwindled to a Duke of Lancaster; turn to the west of that north, and he pops upon you in the humble character of Earl of Chester. Travel a few miles on, . . . and the King surprises you again as Count Palatine of Lancaster. If you travel beyond Mount Edgecombe, you find him once more in his incognito, and he is Duke of Cornwall. So that . . . you are infinitely refreshed when you return to the sphere of his proper splendor, and behold your amiable Sovereign in his true, simple, undisguised, native character of Majesty.[20]

Such anomalies all provided, from the public purse, places and sinecures to bolster Court influence.

It was this same earlier bill which provided the occasion for a Commons performance generally allowed to be among his finest, full of destructive ridicule in attacking for instance the abuse of sinecures – as when he played with the exquisite possibility of the nation's affairs, indeed 'the system of Europe', becoming paralysed, frozen into inertia – because the turnspit in the King's kitchen *was a member of Parliament.* Had not the perquisites or fees of this obscure individual been the demonstrable cause of Lord Talbot's earlier failure to effect certain reforms in the royal household?

> On that rock his whole adventure split, – his whole scheme of oeconomy was dashed to pieces; his department became more expensive than ever; the Civil List debt accumulated. Why? Because the 'turnspit in the King's kitchen was a member of

parliament'. [Because of the inviolability of this sinecurist's rights] the King's domestic servants were all undone; his tradesmen remained unpaid and became bankrupt – because the turnspit of the King's kitchen was a member of parliament. His Majesty's slumbers were interrupted, his pillow was stuffed with thorns, and his peace of mind entirely broken – because the King's turnspit was a member of parliament. The judges were unpaid; the justice of the kingdom bent and gave way; the foreign ministers remained inactive and unprovided; the system of Europe was dissolved; the chain of our alliances was broken; all the wheels of government at home and abroad were stopped – because the King's turnspit was a member of Parliament. [21]

The hyperbole was enjoyable, even if in the end not enough votes were gathered in.

Burke's attitude towards sinecures was more than a little ambivalent. He was in fact far from objecting to them in principle; only when they led to 'corruption'. Some of them might be necessary and honourable, even those among them – indeed especially those – which were hereditary family possessions.

I would leave to the Crown [he said] the possibility of conferring some favours, which, whilst they are received as a reward, do not operate as corruption. When men receive obligations from the Crown through the pious hands of fathers . . . the dependencies which arise from thence are the obligations of gratitude and not the fetters of servility. Such ties originate in virtue, and they promote it.*

Among the offices he did succeed in getting rid of was the Third Secretaryship of State – this, the 'American' Secretaryship, was not an ancient survival but a dispensable novelty – and the eight Commissionerships of Trade and Plantations. When reminded that it was while employed at the Board of Trade that Gibbon was finding the leisure to write some of his *Decline and Fall of the Roman Empire*, he replied that while he might respect the Board as an academy of belles lettres, he considered it as an instrument

---

*Quoting this passage, Richard Pares, in his Ford Lectures of 1951–2, commented sharply: 'Since Burke was in Opposition in February 1780, one cannot say that these are merely the excuses of politicians in office who do not want to be turned out. They exhibit a far graver disease: that of treating waste and inefficiency as venial, indeed salutary, provided the politicians and their children have a freehold in them' (*King George III and the Politicians*, p. 127).

for promoting trade to be expensive and valueless. If it did house 'nightingales', he would like to release them to sing in freedom, not at the public charge.[23] (Gibbon retired to Lausanne and finished his book there.)

The King could hardly be expected to *like* the Civil List Act, but he studied it carefully, accepted its main provisions, and suggested several improvements – as for instance: 'The greatest savings that can be made in the household as to the number of useless places is in the department of the Chamberlain where no reform has yet been made'. And he was concerned also to protect the position of those place-holders 'who by services of twenty or thirty years are disabled from continuing . . . or have had any accident to disable them, and are not in circumstances to maintain themselves'.[24]

In general, though it made useful reforms, the measure in which the Rockinghams had invested so heavily was to prove a disappointment, for a variety of reasons. First and fundamentally, the influence of Crown and executive over parliament was neither as strong or as malign as they had supposed, so that economical reform produced few important and no startling changes; a more basic tidying up had to wait for the younger Pitt. Next, Burke had reckoned that, stripped of corruption, the Civil List would achieve solvency. He was wrong; it did not, but continued to pile up debt; his arrangements proved unrealistic. 'It is impossible to describe to you', Shelburne wrote to Grafton (if no doubt with more malice than fairness) shortly after Burke resigned, 'how provokingly my time is taken up with the non-sense of Mr Burke's bill. It was both framed and carried through without the least regard to *facts*.'[25] In one respect Burke's attempt to trim Crown influence may actually have strengthened it. By cutting the number of places open to members of parliament he enhanced the value of peerages, the creation of which remained wholly in the hands of the King, who did not hesitate later to make use of them.

The Rockingham and Shelburne groups found themselves able to work together on economical reform, but on the parallel issue of ridding parliament of abuses and archaisms in representation and the franchise, a united front would have been impossible. Apart from Burke and others, Rockingham himself, the prime minister, was hostile to the idea. It was not a member of the Whig government, but Chatham's son, the still very young Mr Pitt, who introduced a proposal for an enquiry into the state of representation in May 1782. Burke did not speak in this debate, but when John Sawbridge brought forward once again his more or less annual motion advocating more frequent general elections, he erupted – somewhat to the embarrassment of his friends and the astonishment of his enemies. Sheridan, now like Burke a junior minister, said that 'he acquitted himself with the most magnanimous indiscretion, attacked W. Pitt in a scream of passion, and swore Parliament was and always has been precisely what it ought to be'. Anyone who thought differently 'wanted to overturn the constitution'.[26]

If economical reform disappointed, the outcome of the crisis in Ireland gave as least some satisfaction, at least initially. The Dublin parliament, confident that the hard-pressed British were in no position to hold out against their demands, voted an Address to the King in April 1782 setting them out, and in May the Westminster House of Commons agreed unanimously to a resolution of Fox's for granting a key part of them, repeal of the Irish Declaratory Act of 1719. This, taken together with repeal of essential parts of the much earlier so-called Poynings Act, meant that the Irish parliament would no longer require British assent to its legislation. The other Irish demands – independence for the Irish judiciary, abolition of the right of appeal from Irish to English courts, limitation on the provisions of the Mutiny Act – were soon afterwards conceded by the new Lord Lieutenant, the Rockinghamite Duke of Portland. It was to him that Burke expressed his pleasure:

> Every thing asked or even hinted at from Ireland has been yielded in the fullest measure and with the compleatest unanimity. Fox handled this business incomparably well. Your time, I hope, will pass the better for what has been done . . . If things are prudently managed, Ireland will become a great country by degrees . . .

With or without prudent management, it was hardly enough. 'I am now', said the Irish leader Grattan, 'to address a free people.' But the new 'free' Irish parliament remained narrowly Protestant and as corruptible as before; the King-and-Government in London retained the control of honours and patronage, and the power of appointing all important offices of the executive; and, most vitally, several of the old penal laws continued in force. Ireland was far from becoming in Burke's sense 'a great country'. She would instead be heading soon towards atrocity and counter-atrocity, towards desperation and rebellion – and the extinction shortly afterwards of Grattan's 'free and independent' parliament by Pitt's Act of Union in 1800.

None of this could be foreseen in 1782. But the cautious phrasing of Burke's message to Portland hints well enough that he viewed the future less rosily than either the triumphant Protestant ascendancy in Dublin or their friends in the Westminster cabinet. Burke's support for the 1782 'settlement' was in fact lukewarm. He was of course not a member of the cabinet – it was Fox who had 'handled the business' – and he accepted only with misgiving the concessions to the Irish. The power of the ascendancy had been hardened, the 'popery laws' retained. Already America was as good as lost. What if Ireland were to follow? It was a possibility which so sound an imperialist as Burke must view with anxiety. Some of his old Irish friends and allies were to find him increasingly difficult to understand. When in 1785 Pitt attempted a further liberalisation of Irish trade, Burke took little part in the debates, and his vote was lined up with his party's in opposing the measures.

CHAPTER
10

SHELBURNE, COALITION, AND INDIA BILL
1782–1783

IT WAS a disaster for Burke when Rockingham died on 1 July 1782. At one blow he lost a close personal friend, an admired political chief, the proprietor of his parliamentary seat, and the long-term financial support which had made his political career possible.

The King made the obvious move and wasted no time in appointing Shelburne to be his new prime minister. Shelburne had been for some years Burke's *bête noire*; Fox's too, and in fact Fox, having failed to persuade the King that Portland, not Shelburne, ought to be prime minister, resigned next day. (Overruled in the cabinet over his wish speedily to advance towards acknowledging American independence, he had made up his mind to even before Rockingham's death.) Would Burke also resign? He could not bank on Rockingham's heir, Earl Fitzwilliam, continuing fully on Rockingham's generous lines, though Fitzwilliam was soon indicating that he wished to, and, before that, was sending a reassuring message: Rockingham's will had a fourth codicil, added two days before he died, which gave 'to Edmund Burke, Esquire all sums of money that are or may be due to me from him in any securities whatsoever . . . All such securities shall be delivered up to Mr Burke to be cancelled.'[1] A decision had to be made, and quickly. If it was to be resignation, then not only Burke's own future, but that of both the Richard Burkes, looked hazardous. It appears however that Burke was not in serious doubt. At a nine-hour meeting of the Rockingham party, peers and commoners, he spoke for two hours advising non-cooperation with Shelburne. It was 'the best speech he was ever heard to utter', in the opinion of Lord Carlisle. Still, although many junior holders of office resigned, only one other member of the cabinet departed with Fox. (This was the meeting where the Duke of Richmond, so it was reported, was sufficiently hurt by attacks upon him for opting to remain in his post 'that at length he burst into tears'.)²

Burke made his resignation speech in the Commons 'with considerable emotion' on 9 July and, tainted as it was by the intensity of his animus against Shelburne, it was some way from being 'the best he was ever heard to utter'. 'He called heaven and earth to witness', runs the Debrett parliamentary report, 'that he verily believed the present ministry would be fifty times worse than that of the noble lord who had lately been reprobated and removed' – Lord North, that is; and as for the new prime minister himself, rather extraordinarily and hardly in Burke's most felicitous vein: 'If Lord Shelburne be not a Catiline or a Borgia in morals, it must be ascribed to anything but his understanding'.³

There is evidence, at least some of it from sources reckoned to be friendly, that under the strain of misfortunes and apprehensions the fuse of Burke's always quick temper became at this time even shorter than usual. Horace Walpole hardly counts as friend, and his comments on Burke, though sometimes laudatory, are often not. In his *Last Journals*, in July 1782, he has this to say:

> The enthusiasm of [Burke's] luxuriant imagination presented every measure to him in the most vivid colours. In truth it had been supposed for above a year that his intellect and sensations had mutually overheated each other; his behaviour in the ensuing year did not remove this supposition.⁴

And some ten months later Boswell told Johnson that Burke had been 'represented as actually mad' – to which Johnson, who *does* have to be reckoned friendly, replied, 'If a man will appear extravagant as he does, and cry [*crier*, one presumes, not *pleurer*], can he wonder he is represented as mad?'⁵

These observations tally well enough with Sheridan's reference to 'magnanimous indiscretion' and Burke's 'scream of passion' when attacking Sawbridge's motion for shorter parliaments. Political passion there undoubtedly was; but always the strongest of his passions was for his family; and now, politically out in the cold (and again talking of possible retirement), the greatest of his worries seems to have been for his 'poor lad' Richard.

For one thing, Richard's health already was not good; and of course his official position and salary had disappeared with his father's. There was legal work on the northern circuit open to him, and Burke had managed to secure for him, on his resignation, a half-share (for life) of the receivership of land revenues for London and some of the south-eastern English counties. But the hoped-for 'something considerable to be a security for him and his mother' had not materialised. What was intended by that 'something' is uncertain, but it may well have been the reversion of the Clerkship of the Pells, a sinecure currently worth £3000 a year held for the preceding forty-odd years by Sir Edward Walpole, Horace's elder brother, now in his mid-seventies. Upon deciding to resign, Burke immediately sought an interview with Horace Walpole and tried to enlist his advocacy for a proposal to be made to his brother: that while enjoying the full income for the rest of his life and retaining also the right to nominate whom he pleased to have one-third of the sinecure's annual income after his death, he should agree to the transfer of the sinecure itself to Richard Burke, who on Sir Edward's death would also receive the remaining two-thirds income. Richard personally followed up by letter his father's proposal.

The reaction of Horace Walpole, himself of course a very wealthy multiple sinecurist – Sir Robert during his Paymastership and premiership had ensured his sons' futures more than well – was thoughtful but very cool. The jottings which he made of his ponderings happen to have survived. These are among them:

> Would any man alive do a deed that would shake the best security possible of his property, in order to have a third part of that property at his disposal after his death? Great delicacy in my proposing on account of Sir Edwd age. Is it creditable to Mr B. to propose. It must be known. I said I would not promise.[6]

And he quotes Richard as saying, 'My father always intended to get this for me – therefore the Clerk of Pells omitted'. Omitted, Richard must have meant, from Burke's economical reforms, because (according to Walpole's interpretation, which seems not unreasonable) Edmund had his eye on it for his son. Hence the acid amusement of the question posed and eventually printed in Walpole's *Last Journals*: 'Can one but smile at a reformer of abuses reserving the second greatest abuse for himself?'[7]

In justice to Burke it must be allowed that at no time did he advocate the complete abolition of sinecures; only of their corrupt use. Indeed in his important 1780 speech on economical reform he had gone out of his way to praise the giving of them as honourable rewards for honourable service, and moreover had justified their being inherited, again if in the first instance respectably won, along with other family property. Walpole's shaft falls therefore some way wide of its target, though it may well be thought that the distinction between worthy award and corrupt abuse might in practice prove altogether too subjective to be established.

Of the other members of the family circle, the elder Richard was again out in the cold, and Burke's sister Juliana over in Galway never received her £200 a year pension she had been led to hope for, despite the Duke of Portland's efforts for her. Superseded now as Lord Lieutenant, he tried his best, and was furious when the new Chief Secretary, 'in a manner as offensive as can well be conceived', refused to confirm the pension's award. The incoming Paymaster, however, the Shelburnite Colonel Barré, did agree to confirm William Burke in his post as Deputy Paymaster in India.

Also to suffer from the reversal in the Burkes' prospects (excluding William's – he like Micawber never lacked prospects) was their generous and improvident benefactor of earlier days, Lord Verney. He now claimed from Burke repayment of the £6000 which had been lent towards paying the mortgage on the Beaconsfield estate. This was quite separate from other claims which he had outstanding, one against Richard Burke senior earlier put at about £19,000, and another against William for £22,000. Unfortunately for Lord Verney, he held no bond for the £6000.

In February 1769 Chancery had ruled that Burke must pay off his remaining liabilities of £13,366 in the purchase of Gregories, and Burke claimed that within a week he had done so. How he raised the necessary money is unclear, the story of his borrowing at this time being difficult to interpret with certainty. It is known however that Mrs Caroline Williams and Admiral Saunders each lent a substantial sum. In his 1783 Chancery suit Verney testified that in March 1769 he had paid £6000 to *William* Burke's lawyer, and was promised but never received a mortgage on the estate as security. Burke's reply was that he had paid off his 1769 liabilities with 'the voluntary offer of another friend' (Admiral Saunders?) and that he had never *received* £6000 from Verney, though he knew that the money had been paid. Being without bond or security for his generous loan, Verney's claim against Burke failed. The £6000 was admittedly intended to assist the purchase of Gregories; what happened to it? At least it now seems that Burke should be exonerated from the charge, often made in the past, that by lying, he helped to ruin his one-time benefactor. Perhaps the most likely explanation for the money's disappearance is that it went down the drain in 1769 in company with the rest of William Burke's current assets in his disastrous East India speculation culminating in that year, and that in 1783 Burke was honestly incapable of accounting for it.[8]

Verney was very soon to accumulate misfortunes. Defeated in the 1784 Buckinghamshire election and no longer as a member of parliament protected from arrest for his disastrously swollen debts, he fled to France and remained there until after the outbreak of the revolution. It is a tribute perhaps to his popularity in the county and certainly to his powers of recovery that, coming home in 1790, he was returned again to parliament unopposed. He died next year, owing £115,731 5s 8d; his lawyers persisted for years in a vain pursuit of William Burke's elusive debts.

The ministry of Lord Shelburne – that 'wicked man' and 'liar', as Burke excitedly called him, 'and no less weak and stupid than false and hypocritical'[9] – was not destined for long life. There were now three main groupings in the House of Commons: the Fox party, as the Rockingham Whigs had now become, and the followers of Lord North and Lord Shelburne. These latter two each numbered about 130, the Foxites rather fewer. There were of course other smaller groups and many unattached members, but it became obvious by the winter of 1782–3 that decisive government would become impossible without a working arrangement between two of the main parties. In February the followers of North and of Fox united to defeat Shelburne on the articles of peace provisionally agreed with the Americans and with France and Spain. Early in March Burke was informing Richard Shackleton with modified jubilation, 'We have demolished the Earl of Shelburne'; *modified*, since he was by no means confident

of the ministerial outcome and, as he put it, afraid of 'the madness
of the people'. There followed six tense weeks of critical bargain-
ing – between King and party leaders, and between party and
party – during which the King strove by all means in his power to
avoid having to accept the detested Charles Fox as a leading
minister. At one point he contemplated abdication seriously
enough to compose a proclamation – a sombrely patriotic and
indeed moving document – announcing his decision to retire to
Hanover and leave the future prosperity of Great Britain in the
hands of his eldest son. Fox from his side reciprocated the King's
feelings; by now his contemptuous dislike amounted to a hatred
almost pathological. He was not joking when he referred to his
monarch as 'Satan'. When eventually George bowed to the inevitable, it was not to have Fox as prime minister. In that position he
agreed to accept the Duke of Portland, who was able to insist on
tough terms; but Portland in effect became only nominal head of
an administration dominated by its two Secretaries of State,
Charles Fox and Lord North. The King made little secret of his
intention of tolerating his new ministers – or at least 'this faction'
of Fox's followers – only as long as he was obliged to, hoping that
not many months would elapse 'before the Grenvilles, the Pitts,
and other men of abilities and character' would release him from
his discomfiture and humiliation – an outcome which was
precisely what he was very soon to bring about.

There is no reliable evidence that Burke played any part in the
establishment of this famous – so often and unreasonably called
'infamous' – coalition, but it brought him a very understandable
satisfaction, for once again he was to be Paymaster General, with
the two Richards back on the Treasury payroll, Richard senior
with a new fellow-Secretary, R. B. Sheridan. Richard Champion
was restored too; and again Jane Burke was able to write to her
sister-in-law in Galway county 'with news that will again make
you happy':

> Yesterday your brother Ned kissed the King's hand on being
> appointed Paymaster, and your brother Richard is again Sec-
> retary of the Treasury. You shall hear from us in a post or two,
> with something to enable you to go on. [*Seven months* later,
> Richard sent her a remittance for £54 3s 4d.][10]

However, within a week or two Burke was at the centre of a
political storm.

Two senior civil servants at the Pay Office, John Powell, cashier, and Charles Bembridge, accountant, were accused of surreptitiously tampering with the financial statement relating to the paymastership of Charles Fox's father Henry (Lord Holland), who in a long tenure of office ending in 1765 had made a notoriously vast fortune from Paymaster's perquisites. The two officials had 'improved' the appearance of accounts *after* they had been completed, rather as cosmetic attention might be paid to a corpse to conceal evidence of foul play. Burke during his first tenure of office had worked well with both men, who had performed (so he told each of them) to his 'perfect satisfaction'.[11] Even if not fully satisfied of their blamelessness, neither was he convinced of their guilt. Then, between Burke's two spells in the Office, Shelburne's Paymaster, Colonel Barré, dismissed both Powell and Bembridge and laid charges of fraud against them. Reappointed in 1783, Burke rashly reinstated them, on the grounds that they must be treated as innocent till proved otherwise.

On three occasions in May 1783 his action was debated in the Commons. On the first of these, when a member described the officials' reinstatement as 'a gross and daring insult to the public', Burke,

> rising in a violent fit of passion, exclaimed, 'It is a gross and daring –'; but he could proceed no farther, for Mr Sheridan by this time had pulled him down on his seat, from a motive of friendship, lest his heat should betray him into some intemperate expressions that might offend the House.[12]

Burke was nevertheless adamant: 'were the act undone he was convinced that he should do it again'; and two and a half weeks later, first apologising for his earlier loss of temper, he maintained his position. Then on the third occasion of debate, riding down many interruptions, he made a long defence of his conduct in the case:

> He took God to witness that in restoring Mr Powell and Mr Bembridge their office, he was activated solely by motives of justice. Before he took that step, he had weighed all the consequences of it and had passed many sleepless nights . . . He could not reconcile to his conscience to send men in many respects so meritorious, after so many years service, whatever their faults might be, to a trial, already pre-condemned and ruined . . .[13]

Powell resigned, and Burke, repeatedly pressed to accept the resignation which Bembridge proffered, at last reluctantly suspended him. Bembridge, found guilty, was heavily fined and sentenced to six months imprisonment. Powell committed suicide, which in the eyes alike of politicians and public confirmed his guilt also.

The aftertaste of all this was bitter. Opinions of Burke's capacity for sound judgment necessarily suffered; and he too late discovered that 'this fellow Bembridge' was 'a wild, precipitate, senseless, and now desperate wretch'. In 1784, after the prison term had been served, he was alarmed to discover that Richard Champion was in debt to Bembridge, who was now, being ignorant of Champion's address, trying to get Burke to forward letters to him. (By then Champion, no longer Deputy Paymaster and hard up, was preparing to emigrate to South Carolina.) Burke wrote to his son:

> I intend to write to [Bembridge] that as I am utterly ignorant of all transactions between him and Champion I shall not open his letters; and resolve to continue in the same ignorance, having been brought by my kindness to many people into more trouble than I can or will in future attempt to go through with.[14]

All this was a side issue, though a painful one. The principal business of the Fox–North coalition concerned the perennial problem of India and the East India Company. Indeed whether in office or out, Burke's political life during the 1780s – that is, during his fifties – was to be dominated by Indian difficulties and complexities and alleged scandals and attempted solutions. The problems, though aggravated by a series of complicated and expensive wars (notably against Mysore and the Marathas), were basically what had already been present for decades past, and what North's 'Regulating Act' of 1773 had only very partially succeeded in regulating. These were some of the chief of them: the extent of political control from Westminster necessary or desirable; the amount or proportion of Company revenue proper to be made over to the British Treasury; the gap between on one side the Company's military success and territorial expansion and on the other its bad financial performance; the division of interests and consequent in-fighting between Company factions, whether in London or in Madras and Bengal, and the extent to which it was proper for members of parliament to mirror these contending groups and lobby for them; the Company's trading monopoly, under its charter, and the question of its continuance; finally – what was to loom largest of all for Burke – the need for the British parliament to examine, and if necessary punish, the excesses of the Company's political power in India, and the opportunities open to its servants, high and low, for corrupt profiteering and self-enrichment at the expense of the native population.

Ever since becoming involved as a speculator during his late thirties, Burke's interest in Company matters had been close, if not always well-judged or consistently pursued. At first he had been strongly, even excitedly, on the side of the Company, against the state's interference and Lord North's in particular; and on Clive's side too against the grilling he received from parliament. The Company was 'a great, a glorious Company', capable if left to itself of setting up 'a system one of the most beautiful ever established in any place'. Once he even claimed to see divine Providence behind the splendid mansion-building of the 'Nabobs' returned home with their massive fortunes.[15]

After the Rockingham party's taking of sides in the Madras dispute and William Burke's adventures in Tanjore, Burke for the first time had enemies within the Company he could get his teeth into – notably Sulivan at this stage – and Burke had a terrier's teeth. His personal loyalty to William now converted mere intelligent interest into passionate concern. From about 1778 and what he saw as the Tanjore–Arcot scandal, he became ever more deeply involved in the affairs of India at every level, graduating eventually from the Madras Presidency and the Carnatic in the south, to the north, the Bengal Presidency and Warren Hastings the arch villain. For a decade or more he was to bring to bear on the subject of India and the Company the formidable resources of his penetrating mind, patient industry, and impressive command of intricate detail; high polemical and literary talents; and outstanding parliamentary rhetoric and eloquence. After it was all over and he was an old man, he was in no doubt, despite the taste of ashes then in his mouth, that it was this – and not, as most would expect him then to say, his crusade against the French Revolution – which represented the most important and valuable work of his life.

In January 1781 Burke made his first attempt to expose the
misdeeds of the man he was so loudly to thunder against four
years later in his parliamentry philippic on the Nawab of Arcot's
debts. Paul Benfield was a private merchant and banker who had
lent large sums both to the Nawab and to his enemy the Raja of
Tanjore, and indeed to anyone else in southern India able to pay
interest at 20 per cent or above. Benfield also *borrowed* widely, but
18 per cent was his top limit. Under the benefit of these arrangements his wealth accrued very satisfactorily until, when eventually in the late 1780s he left India, he was able to put himself
modestly at half a million; it was probably a good deal more.
(Back home, he was to become a government contractor and
loan negotiator – and die bankrupt.)

Burke's view of him in 1781 was that 'his coming into many
parts of India would fill the inhabitants with horror as much as
an irruption of Mahratta horse'; and his operations ought to be
investigated by the East India Company. When the Company
declined to act, Burke replied with a significant threat: Benfield's
dealings would be examined 'in some other place'.[16] That of
course meant parliament, and for the next three years Burke was
the driving force behind a Select Committee of the Commons
dedicated to the minute investigation of Indian affairs and composed predominantly of men sympathetic to his views. They produced altogether eleven reports, 'pretty large volumes', Burke
wrote,[17] 'some of which are *entirely* mine; and the materials of *all*
of which I have diligently perused and compared'. In particular
the Ninth Report,[18] a book in itself, presented a comprehensive
account of Britain's dealings with India in every aspect, mercan-
tile, financial, governmental.

Already by its first year but increasingly by its second, the
Select Committee had begun to look afield beyond the affairs of
Madras and the Carnatic towards the north and Bengal. Here a
new set of specialist informants began to carry influence with
Burke: principally Charles Rouse and General Richard Smith,
returned Company servants; to some extent the orientalist
William Jones; and most of all Philip Francis. Francis had served
six years on the Bengal Supreme Council under the Governor
General Warren Hastings; had opposed him, hated him, fought
a duel with him, determined to discredit him, and come back to
England looking for ways to promote two ambitions – to achieve

reforms in the government of India (many of these close to Burke's own ideas) and to gain revenge on Warren Hastings by ousting and *succeeding* him as Governor General. Hastings was already under criticism at Westminster. As early as May 1782 the Commons passed a resolution urging his recall. But Burke's explosive words of nearly a year later surely owe a good deal to the information Francis had been feeding him meanwhile. In the version given by the *Parliamentary History*: 'He pledged himself to God, to his country, to that House, and to the unfortunate and plundered inhabitants of India, that he would bring to justice, as far as in him lay, the greatest delinquent that India ever saw'.[19]

Early in 1783 a bill was coming before parliament which was the fruit of the deliberations of a second Commons group, the 'Secret Committee', a rival to Burke's but not always or necessarily hostile to it. This second committee had as its leading figures Henry Dundas, a specialist like Burke in Indian affairs and soon to be the younger Pitt's right-hand man, and Charles Jenkinson (as Earl of Liverpool a future prime minister). By now there was a fair degree of general parliamentary agreement that *some* redefinition of the East India Company's status and powers must be made, and that the government's hand must be strengthened. Dundas's bill was 'moderate, sensible, and workman-like'[20] and is indeed to be regarded as a blue-print of Pitt's East India Act of the next year which was broadly to dictate the relationship between Company and Westminster until well into the reign of Queen Victoria. But it never reached the statute book, for this was the point at which Shelburne's ministry fell and after a six weeks' hiatus the Fox–North coalition took over, a government which numbered among its members Burke, who had his own strong views on what needed to be done.

By September he was at work on what was to become known as 'Fox's India Bill'. Fox introduced it in the Commons and with Burke was a major spokesman for it; but Burke was the party's Indian expert, and in his hand there exists an endorsement to a letter 'from Mr Pigot' referring incontrovertibly to Pigot 'finishing' the bill 'from my drafts'.[21] Burke was however in a considerable quandary. It was generally agreed that the measure of domestic control over the Company's great powers must be increased; but the previously Rockingham, now Fox, party – and Burke in particular – had repeatedly and strenuously insisted that 'the power of the Crown' (that is, of the executive arm of government under the Crown) must be *reduced*. How could the powers of the Company be weakened without those of 'the Crown' being strengthened? To this difficulty, Fox and Burke now proposed a complicated, novel, and radical solution. The Company indeed was to surrender much of its power but not – or at least not at first – to the Crown; instead, to a body of seven commissioners, to be nominated in the bill, and to hold office for not less than three or more than five years. They were named in the bill and were all supporters of the Fox–North coalition. The bill also proposed to create nine assistant commissioners to supervise commercial policy and operations; these were to be chosen from those on the Company's Court of Directors broadly in line with the Select Committee. The principal commissioners who would succeed the original seven, four years or more ahead, *were* to be appointed by the Crown. Dundas and his Secret Committee would have aimed to check Company misdemeanours by increasing the authority of the Governor General; they would probably have replaced Hastings by General Cornwallis. Burke and Fox favoured the choice of Lord Macartney or William Eden, but proposed no strengthening of the Governor General's powers. Their answer to Company misrule was to lie with the Commission of Seven; and this was undoubtedly where the bill lay, and lies, open to basic criticism. It is difficult to see how subordinating the judgment of the Governor General to that of commissioners sitting in London thousands of miles and many months away could have improved administration or corrected abuses in India. Making just that point, Cornwallis (Governor General from 1786) declared, 'Mr Fox's plan would have ruined all'.[22]

This however was not the flaw in the bill which caused it to become so noisily controversial; nor was a second target of criticism, that it attacked chartered rights, and what would be next, the Bank of England? What produced the most excited anger and alarm was the transference of patronage from the Company to the predominantly Foxite Commission, seen as an act of theft, a naked attempt by the Fox party to strengthen its own power. It became easy for 'the public' (the inverted commas must continue to serve as a reminder) to view Fox, as in James Sayer's celebrated cartoon, in the person of 'Carlo Khan', the great potentate of 'Indostan', seated on an elephant bearing the face of Lord North which was being led along by a banner-bearing, trumpet-blowing Burke. In the ministers' defence it must be granted that only by securing their supporters firmly and for a time immovably in authority could they expect to see their honest hopes – and in Burke's case passion – for less corrupt and more humane government come to fruition. Sir Gilbert Elliot, Burke's friend and a member of the proposed Commission (and another future Governor General), put the balance between idealism and self-interest very fairly:

> There never was a measure taken so beneficial to so many millions of unhappy people as this one. This is one good reason for my liking a part in it. There are many lesser ones, amongst which a great deal of patronage and probably a handsome salary are two.[23]

Burke's major speech on the bill was made during its later stages through the Commons (where it passed with comfortable three-figure majorities) and nearly two months later appeared, no doubt somewhat revised and polished, as a pamphlet. Towards its end came what he described as 'a studied panegyric' of Charles Fox, the man with whose political fortunes his own were – it must have then seemed indissolubly – joined. It was an extended and remarkable tribute to a more than remarkable man, and if it leans in places towards hyperbole, or even towards the fulsome, there is no cause to doubt its sincerity:

> I must say then, that it will be a distinction honourable to the age, that the rescue of the greatest number of the human race that ever were so grievously oppressed, from the greatest tyranny that was ever exercised, has fallen to the lot of abilities and dispositions equal to the task; that it has fallen to one who has the enlargement to comprehend, the spirit to undertake, and the eloquence to support, so great a measure of hazardous benevolence . . . He well knows what snares are spread about his path, from personal animosity, from court intrigues, and possibly from popular delusion. But he has put to hazard his ease, his security, his interest, his power, even his darling popularity, for the benefit of a people he has never seen. This is the road that all heroes have trod before him . . . He is doing indeed a great good . . . Let him use his time . . . He is now on a great eminence, where the eyes of mankind are turned to him. He may live long, he may do

much. But here is the summit. He never can exceed what he does this day.[24]

In the body of the speech, the many criticisms of the bill were one by one considered and rejected. It and other proposed measures related to it were intended to form 'the Magna Charta of Hindostan . . . Whatever the great charter, the statute of tallage, the petition of right, and the declaration of right are to Great Britain, these bills are to the people of India.'[25] The Commons were then presented with a lengthy exposition of recent Indian history, with much erudite detail which must surely have baffled unlearned or inattentive members. The Company occupied the role of chief villain, and Governor-General Hastings was already a principal target of obloquy. We meet too, as if in a trailer for the main show to come later in Westminster Hall, the 'rapacious and licentious soldiery' and the scandalous mistreatment of the Begams of Oudh and their eunuchs. All those less than respectable aspects of the Company's historical and current record, commercial and governmental, are unsparingly examined and rhetorically castigated. 'I engage myself to you', he said, 'to make good these three positions':

> First, I say, . . . that there is not a *single* prince, state, or potentate, great or small, in India . . . whom [the Company] have not sold . . . Secondly, I say, that there is not a *single treaty* they have ever made, which they have not broken. – Thirdly, I say, there is not a single prince or state, who ever put any trust in the Company, who is not utterly ruined.[26]

Chapter and verse for this comprehensive denunciation follows at length. He then contrasts British 'internal government' in India with that of its previous invaders, 'Arabs, Tartars, and Persians', whose original irruptions were certainly more 'ferocious, bloody, and wasteful' than those of the British. But these 'Asiatic conquerors . . . made the country their own . . . Nature still had fair play; the sources of acquisition were not dried up, and therefore the trade, the manufactures, and the commerce of the country flourished.'

> The Tartar invasion was mischievous; but it is our protection that destroys India. It was their enmity, but it is our friendship. Our conquest there, after twenty years, is as crude as it was the first day. The natives scarcely know what it is to see the grey head of an Englishman. Young men (boys almost)

govern there, without society, and without sympathy with the natives . . . Animated with all the avarice of age and all the impetuosity of youth, they roll in one after another; wave after wave, and there is nothing before the eyes of the natives but an endless, hopeless prospect of new flights of birds of prey and passage, with appetites continually renewing for a food that is continually wasting. Every rupee of profit made by an Englishman is lost for ever to India.[27]

The India Bill sailed through the Commons easily, but it was to be Burke's and Fox's misfortune that the House of Commons could not yet dictate to the nation. Various counterpoises held its power in balance: public opinion, the House of Lords, the monarchy. With the public, and particularly the City of London, the bill was generally unpopular. In the House of Lords, a majority was far from certain – much would depend on the votes of the bishops. There remained the King, who felt he had accepted the Fox–North ministry only under duress.

Prompted at first by ex-Chancellor Thurlow, whose dismissal Fox had imprudently insisted on, and by Earl Temple; later, as the plot developed, given encouragement by the experienced old hand and ministerial adviser on India, John Robinson, and by Richard Atkinson, of the East India Company; by Dundas and Pitt; even by Fox's uncle the Duke of Richmond, once a Rockinghamite, always a maverick, and recently the despair of Burke – prompted, encouraged, and finally grasping the opportunity he had been waiting for ever since the hated coalition came to office eight months before, the King handed Earl Temple a written statement:

> His majesty allowed Earl Temple to say that whoever voted for the India Bill was not only not his friend, but would be considered by him as an enemy; and if these words were not strong enough, Earl Temple might use whatever words he might deem stronger and to the purpose.[28]

Twelve bishops out of twenty who voted sided with the King, and the Lords majorities for rejecting the bill ranged from eight to nineteen. Privately Fox spoke of the King's 'treachery'. He refused to resign. On 18 December therefore, seventeen days after Burke's big speech on the bill, Fox and North were required by the King's messenger to deliver up their seals of office. George chose not to receive them personally, since, he said, 'audiences

on such occasions must be unpleasant'.[29] Next morning the
twenty-four-year-old Pitt kissed hands as First Lord of the
Treasury, a position he would hold for nineteen of the following
twenty-two years, to within a few months of the death of Fox and
until long after the death of Burke. Burke would never hold office
again.

AWAY FROM POLITICS

SIR GILBERT Elliot, later Lord Minto – 'one of the best men I know', said Burke, 'and one of the ablest' – once wrote of him:

> Burke has now got such a train after him as would sink any-body but himself: – his son, who is quite *nauseated* by all man-kind; his brother, who is liked better than his son, but is rather oppressive with animal spirits and brogue; and his cousin Will Burke, who is just returned unexpectedly from India [this was in 1793], as much ruined as when he went many years ago, and who is a fresh charge on any prospects of power Burke may have.[1]

These were the three male members of his family circle in whom Burke found no blemish; towards whom his very genuine but always blinkered attachment often amused, sometimes amazed, his friends and enemies alike, as it has perpetually puzzled his biographers. But there it is: loves other than sexual may be as blind. Easiest to understand and sympathise with was the father's love for the son, the only son – little as the junior Richard seems to have been liked by the world in general. It would be an un-imaginative and churlish critic who wished to find fault with Burke over his very deep devotion to his son, the more so in view of the tragedy which finally crowned it. And perhaps the depre-ciation of young Richard Burke should not be carried too far or accepted too readily. Both Fanny Burney and the young Hannah More found him 'amiable', even if as Miss More decided 'not an adequate substitute for such a father'.

Richard senior, ebullient, caustic, unscrupulous – as in her early days Hannah More judged, 'very bright, but a little coarse' – was not without charm. A later estimate of hers, written on learning of his death, accords him wit and even eloquence. By then, Hannah the clever young bluestocking had been transformed into Miss More the philanthropic pious evangelical; so what, she asked, was all this 'without the one thing needful'?[2] If she meant, as presumably she did, godliness, certainly *that* no one would ever have held Richard Burke guilty of. Many however would have liked to find in him more common honesty. He was quarrelsome too, a trait he gladly owned up to: 'indolent', he admitted, 'in everything but a dispute'. Boswell found him on one occasion 'vulgar and fierce', and an another 'too rough and wild in his manner', concluding then that 'either he liked me worse than his brother did, or had less art to conceal his dislike'.[3]

Whether the world approved of them or no, it was always his immediate family, with its indispensable adjunct William, who lodged closest to Burke's heart. His wife Jane, happily, was closest of all: much too easy to overlook amid the acres of print devoted to Burke's masculine public world of politics and to his only slightly less man-dominated world of letters. Jane Burke, the doctor's daughter, was never required to attempt emulation in the social stratosphere with the great Whig hostesses and beauties like Mrs Crewe or Mrs Bouverie or Georgiana Devonshire, but neither politically nor domestically did she fail her husband. She was well esteemed by his political friends and their wives – Mrs Crewe indeed became one of her closest friends – and was a very capable mistress of London or Beaconsfield hospitality. Her dependable calm provided a necessary haven to which an often storm-battered Burke could count upon retreating; a solace; a tried companion. He once made a casual remark concerning *beds* and *bedrooms* which must surely relate to some truth close to their marriage. Separate beds for married couples, he declared, were a cardinal mistake. Sleeping apart, the husband would come to his wife's bed only for sexual enjoyment. In their double bed they were a truer pair, sharing not merely carnal pleasure, but a fuller and more rounded union.[4]

Boswell was pleased to observe the Burkes' 'conjugal affection'. It was at a time when Burke as Paymaster was under heavy pressure in the Commons and from the Press in the Bembridge-

Powell affair of 1783 – Powell had just committed suicide – and Boswell noted approvingly that Jane Burke showed no 'womanish extravagancies, but spoke of it with calm concern'.[5] When Burke 'discovered' the struggling poet Crabbe, it was Jane Burke who joined with her husband on Crabbe's behalf; took pleasure in entertaining him and his wife at Beaconsfield; and pressed for the success of his first public venture with *The Village*. For Fanny Burney too she shared Burke's affectionate enthusiasm, and Miss Burney in return spoke of the kindness and good sense of Mrs Burke. So too did Arthur Young the agriculturist. Even Hester Thrale, the wealthy brewer's wife, who privately and not for publication had some sour observations to make about Burke 'and his lady at Beaconsfield among dirt cobwebs pictures and statues', allowed that her party when visiting there 'was received with open arms; each scorned to contend who should be kindest'; and in *published* comments confined herself to praising 'the delightful society in which we spent some time at Beaconsfield'.[6]

Another of Hester Thrale's private remarks about her hostess tells us perhaps more about her own mentality and *milieu* than that of the Burkes; tells something also of the readiness of the Mrs Thrales of that time to associate the Burkes with Irish papistry – and how quick they could be to demote them socially on that account. 'The dirt cobwebs pictures and statues' at Beaconsfield, she wrote,

> would not have disgraced the city of Paris itself where misery and magnificence reign in all their splendour and in perfect amity. (Note, Irish Roman Catholics are always like the foreigners somehow, dirty and dressy with all their clothes hanging as if upon a peg.)[7]

It should be said that Mrs Thrale's voice in this Beaconsfield context, though interesting, is much at variance with that of other visitors there. Mrs Crewe, for instance, who was one of the most fashionable of the Whigs' great ladies and stood therefore several rungs above Mrs Thrale in the social ladder, does not have much to report of 'Mr Burke's table', but what she wrote sounds at least not disapproving. It 'was chiefly supplied by the produce of his farm – his provisions were plentiful – his taste delicate in cookery, which in his own house he chiefly confined to the English school; but he well approved of a more extensive scale [such as Mrs Crewe's perhaps?] being admitted into families of greater size and consequence.'[8]

Round Mrs Crewe's own table at Crewe Hall in Cheshire, at her Hampstead villa, or at Bath, the conversation ranged naturally enough upon much beside politics. On farming for instance: Mr Burke as gentleman farmer had thirty years of experience to share, a good deal of it chastening. Every farm held by a gentleman, he declared, ran at a loss broadly proportionate to its acreage, 'particularly if it be in tillage'. However, a gentleman's farm might 'be very innocently kept as an accommodation . . . for his own occupation and amusement . . . but then it is to be rated among his expenses . . . just like a pleasure ground or any improvement of that kind . . . It ought not to exceed 160 acres or thereabouts.' Gentlemen in general had too many duties to fulfil to be able to give sufficient attention to the 'minute oeconomy' which a profitable farm required.[9]

The conversation turning to pleasure grounds, the company may or may not have recalled that Mr Burke, nearly forty years before, had published a much-praised *Enquiry into the Sublime and the Beautiful*. His opinions on these considerable subjects proved still active. Mr Repton (the famous landscape gardener), he said, deserved much respect, which his 'late antagonists' did not. What affectation and presumption it was to claim that Nature should be viewed as chiefly 'pittoresque', or judged as though it were a work of art. He 'considered it as one of the many instances of the vanity of this age, that man should suppose he could improve all nature, and yet be so fastidious as to object to many good . . . ornaments of art.'[10]

'Oeconomy', political, agricultural, domestic, was ever 'a subject that Mr Burke was particularly happy in, because', wrote Mrs Crewe, 'he blended heart as much as mind in it'. The King's civil establishment, oak versus mahogany in furniture, the expense of horse-riding among the gentry, equally concerned this matter of oeconomy:

> Mr Burke thought that lounging rides on horseback had been of late one of the great checks to oeconomy in all families among the gentry. Very few younger brothers, said he, are able to keep two horses, and two must be kept when they are in the habit of riding every day, and . . . this expense incurs that of an additional servant besides necessary

riding accoutrements . . . which create endless bills and will run a man very fast into debts.[11]

Young men who 'could have no object but that of sauntering' on horseback would employ their time better if they made more use of their own limbs.

On this same subject of physical exercise and more particularly its place in education, Burke declined to distinguish any clean break between body and mind. Having first made the good Rousseau-an point that education must 'be considered an improvement to the heart as well as the mind', he would, he said,

> recommend bodily exercises not only as useful to the limbs but to the mind, which they render attentive to something: and as there are so few who will exercise their minds by the study of books, it is better they should employ it this way than let it get no energy or exercise at all; for all games are regular, and require some reflection or combination of thought.[12]

Unlike Tom Paine, his ideological antithesis, Burke never had among his published titles any work actually called *Common Sense* but, humanly fallible as he may often have been in the exercise of it, he nevertheless valued, indeed revered, that quality. Once, quite early in his career, already privately if tactfully critical of the Duke of Richmond's strongly individual views, he wrote warning the young Walker King, who was about to become a tutor at Goodwood and would one day become one of his closest friends and helpers. King should remind himself that with 'singular opinions' on matters of great and accepted importance – manners, life itself – *the chance undoubtedly was that they were wrong*.[13] Many years later, again round Mrs Crewe's dinner table, he pronounced in much the same vein: 'Common sense should be paid more respect to than uncommon sense, which can seldom improve the happiness of human life'.[14]

He went on to condemn what the slang of the time called 'quizzing'; what *he* called 'clumsy satire', for which perhaps the best modern equivalent might be the witless sneer of thoughtless denigration. Its effect was to level down, 'to produce equality of mind – quite dangerous to the understanding, which should early be taught respect for truth, even in trifles; subordination of mind being as necessary as subordination of rank'.

An egalitarianism of thought, as of society, was anathema. For Burke, class and rank were as demonstrably part of the natural order as gravity. Did such a conviction allow him to accept too easily the sufferings of the poor? It might well be argued so; and certainly he is on record as thinking that, for their main recompense for this life's buffetings, the poor must wait for a happier future in an eternal sense. But then this of course was a conviction shared by a majority of Christian believers in his day. Burke's capacity for sympathy and humaneness is hardly contestable, or his readiness with personal acts of kindness; but his humaneness could be tough and cold-eyed, some way from what is usually suggested by the word humanitarian. The same man who was outraged by the injustices inflicted on the Irish or Indian peasantry was yet ready to assert that much of what was said of the miseries of the English poor was fashionable humbug:

> Mr Burke disliked a sort of cant which was kept up and made a fashion of concerning the poor. Those who had known luxury and were reduced met with most of his compassion. The poor are not poor, said he, but men as we are, all born to be, and perhaps happiest for being, without more resource than their own hands, and common powers from nature.

A roughly contemporary parallel suggests itself – criticism levelled at the anti-slavery campaigners for being ignorant over the cruelties perpetrated against African blacks, yet unnoticing or neglectful of exploited child labour in the mines and mills at home. To such a kind of criticism Burke would not have been short of a reply: the Indian or Irish peasantry were indeed condemned to earthly poverty; but what incensed him was the grave *worsening* of their natural condition from British misgovernment and oppression.

It was through Mrs Crewe that, some time in his sixties, Burke was approached by Dudley North (Whig M.P. and a distant relative of Lord North) who, disturbed he said by many apparent inconsistencies in the Gospels, still wished to know how he was to become a Christian, a goal he had 'much at heart'. Burke first wanted to be sure that the request was in earnest, that North was not pulling his leg. Satisfied on this point,

> Observe, he repeated more than once, I consider a person who sets out on such enquiries as no way willing to be a Christian if he feels his mind bent on contention at every difficulty. There are many to be got over by the wisest of us . . . Whoever goes to the task of investigation must go with his heart inclined

to faith – he must forget jeers and jibing and quizzing at this very important moment [or in Mrs Crewe's engaging version, 'Geers and Gibing and Quizing'].

There were learned and pious books Mr North might read 'if he were ever in the habit of metaphysics' – Bishop Butler's *Analogy of Religion*, for instance, or Paley's recently published *View of the Evidences of Christianity*,

> but before a reader plunge into such deep studies, I would recommend more popular works such as may be found in Addison's Spectator . . . And Addison himself became a Christian, in the most enlarged sense of the word, by examining into his own nature and finding that there were chasms in his soul which could be filled only with religion.

Mr North apart, for the common man (and *a fortiori* perhaps for the common woman, though the eighteenth century saw no requirement to address itself specifically to her), metaphysics and books of divinity being irrelevant, the need was twofold. First, he should accept, however 'indistinctly', the belief which came as naturally to him as the basic human feeling of 'gratitude for all our blessings': *that there is a God.* Second, he ought to accept the voice of authority and the wisdom of the forefathers:

> The mass of mankind are made to be led by others. Habits and customs are their support, because it would be impossible that civil society could subsist long if we were all philosophers. Subordination therefore is necessary for the human mind. Men, long after they have left their state of nature, still require guides through life. Habits therefore are adopted for the multitude. Authority is enough for most of those who if they cannot think themselves, can be supported by habits and examples. [16]

With Burke's literary connections, there is a case for putting first, for influence and importance, his contact with the author and publisher Robert Dodsley. In his early twenties, still in chains to the law, he was quite unknown to the world. It was Dodsley who published all his early works, and it was probably round Dodsley's dinner table in the 1750s that he first met such literary figures as Bennet Langton and the Warton brothers, and leading men of the theatre like Murphy and Garrick. It was Dodsley too whose new venture in 1758 became the *Annual Register*, the year-by-year 'retrospections on men and things' whose editor, so

Burke and Fox, by Thomas Hickey

*William Burke,
by Reynolds*

Gregories, Beaconsfield, Bucks

*Mrs Edmund Burke,
by Reynolds*

*Richard Burke, Edmund's
son, by Reynolds*

The 4th Earl Fitzwilliam, an engraving by Grozer after Reynolds

The Unfinished portrait of Burke and Lord Rockingham, by Reynolds

William Pitt, by James Gillray

'Carlo Khan's Triumphal Entry into Leadenhall Street.' A caricature by James Sayers attacking Fox's India Bill transferring power from the East India Company whose headquarters were in Leadenhall Street. Fox is astride the elephant (Lord North) being led by Burke (1783).

SUBLIME ORATORY _____ A DISPLAY OF IT.

'Sublime Oratory.' Fox and Burke (in Jesuit's dress) fling mud at Warren Hastings (1786)

Warren Hastings and his wife, by Zoffany

Henry Dundas,
by Lawrence

'Smelling out a Rat,' by James Gillray. Dr Price, the Dissenting preacher whose sermon welcoming the French Revolution provoked the writing of the Reflections, *sees an apparition of Burke.*

Edmund Burke, a mezzotint by John Jones after Romney.

Dodsley wrote, would soon 'make a very great figure in the literary world'. Robert Dodsley died the year before Burke entered parliament, but the firm of Dodsley, under his brother James, would remain Burke's London publishers until very nearly the end of his life.[17]

No one is quite sure how much of the *Annual Register* Burke wrote or for how long he contributed to it, but until he was sixty he appears to have maintained general supervision and provided at least some of the articles; many of them probably for about the first eight years; fewer after 1766, though for a further twenty years or so he is thought to have written the book reviews and prefaces, employing as assistant editors at various times Tom English, Walker King (who became Rockingham's private secretary, and later an editor of Burke's correspondence), Richard Laurence, and his brother the lawyer French Laurence.[18]

As the young author of two books highly praised by the intelligentsia, Burke in the late 1750s became a likely catch for those talent-spotting ladies of the *bas bleu* who were becoming one of the fashionable phenomena of London society. Their avowed aim was to promote 'literary conversation as the chief pleasure of social life', and the talk of their cultivated drawing-rooms paralleled to some extent the intellectual fare provided by the mistresses of the great Parisian salons at the same time. Probably Mrs Montagu, 'the Queen of the Bluestockings', author of *The Genius and Learning of Shakespeare* and according to Fanny Burney 'our sex's glory', had discovered Burke even beore he published *The Sublime and the Beautiful*. Soon she was recommending him and it to the soirées of the recent translator of Epictetus, Elizabeth Carter, who found the young Irishman's force of mind to be as redoubtable as his powers of conversation. It followed naturally that during the 1760s and 1770s Burke was often to be found at the assemblies of these and others of the town's hostess-intellectuals – besides Mrs Montagu and Mrs Carter, the Irishwoman Mrs Vesey; Mrs Boscawen the admiral's wife; Mrs Chapone; Mrs Delany (once John Wesley's 'Aspasia'), Burke's 'fairest model of female excellence', who was remarkable, he said, for being able at the age of 88 'to blush like a girl', and Mrs Cholmondeley, another Irishwoman, the actress Peg Woffington's sister, who introduced Burke to the young Fanny Burney's novel *Evelina*. Fanny herself emerged more from the Streatham circle of the Thrales and Dr Johnson than from the world of the blue-stockings, though the two overlapped. 'Emerged'; one ought rather to say exploded. The book was a sensation, and Burke was among those bowled over by it, as the delighted Miss Burney herself recorded (repeated in fact five times) in her journal. 'Mr Burke dotes on it', she was told; 'he began it one morning at 7 o'clock, and could not leave it a moment; he sat up all night reading it. He says he has not seen such a book [since] he can't tell when.'[19]

Some four years later, Miss Burney met Burke personally for the first time (he was then fifty-three) and she immediately decided that she was 'quite desperately and outrageously in love with him'. 'Such spirit, such intelligence', she rhapsodised to Mrs Thrale, 'so much energy when serious, so much pleasantry when sportive, – so manly in his address, so animated in his conversation, – so eloquent in argument, so exhilarating in trifling.'[20] Fanny's second novel *Cecilia* pleased Burke no less than her first, and this time he tried to organise a sales strategy for her on different lines – not through booksellers but by subscription, especially through the intermediary of such fine ladies as Mrs Boscawen and Mrs Crewe and the Duchess of Devonshire. Thirteen years later, not for *Cecilia* but for her next novel *Camilla*, she did indeed adopt the subscription plan, and the Burkes subscribed with a £20 note. One book of hers, Burke then wrote, 'is certainly as good as a thousand others'.[21]

Burke's letter of appreciation for *Cecilia* in 1782 so entranced Miss Burney that she used it as preface to the novel's later editions. 'With great gratitude, respect, and esteem' he had written:

> . . . There are few, I believe I may say fairly there are none at all, that will not find themselves better informed concerning human nature, and their stock of information enriched by reading your Cecilia . . . let their experience in life and manners be what it may. The arrogance of age must submit to be taught by youth. You have crouded into a few small volumes an incredible variety of characters . . . though perhaps they are too numerous, – but I beg pardon; I fear it is quite in vain to preach oeconomy to those who are come young to excessive and sudden opulence. I might trespass on your delicacy if I should fill my letter to you with what I fill my

conversation to others . . . In an age distinguished by produc-
ing extraordinary women, I hardly dare to tell you where I
would place you among them – I respect your modesty . . .[22]

In the following year he was able to perform a useful kindness to
Fanny's father the musician and musical historian, Dr Charles
Burney – just in time before the axe fell on the Coalition: 'I had
yesterday the pleasure', he wrote, 'of voting you, my dear Sir, a
salary of fifty pounds a year as organist to Chelsea Hospital . . . I
am only sorry that it did not fall in my way to shew you a more
substantial mark of my high respect for you and Miss Burney.'
Fanny was moved: 'I could almost have cried', her *Diary* declares,
'when he said "This is my last act in office". He said it with so
manly a cheerfulness, in the midst of undisguised regret. What a
man he is.'[23]

The many new friends, literary, theatrical, and artistic, whom
Burke made in the seven or eight years following *The Sublime and
the Beautiful* and the first *Annual Register* were mostly inclined to
deplore his departure by 1765 into politics and the abandonment
of the Muses which it seemed to promise. The regrets expressed
by his literary friends, Oliver Goldsmith in particular, have
become almost too well known: how they rued the day he first met
Lord Rockingham; how he gave up to party what was meant for
mankind. Hannah More called him an 'apostate from social wit',
though afterwards it was less on that score than from her dislike of
his political views that her criticism sprang: 'I had a great deal of
chat with Mr Burke', she wrote after a party in the 1780s at Mrs
Vesey's; 'and so foolish and so good-humoured was he, and so like
the agreeable Mr Burke I once knew and admired, that I soon
forgot his malefactions, and how often I had been in a passion with
him for some of his speeches'. Even the disapproval of his malefactions evaporated however a little later, when she met him again,
this time 'very low in health and spirits', yet talking to her nevertheless 'with a kindness which revived my old affection for him'.[24]

Another who expressed a sadness for Burke's deserting liter-
ature and the arts for politics was the scholar-hostess Elizabeth
Carter. She had heard of his East India losses, and wrote to Mrs
Montagu:

I am sorry for the terrible stroke to Mr Burke's fortune. Indeed,
one has reason to be sorry, when he quitted the elegant and

amiable studies in which he was so well equipped to shine, and the tranquil pleasures of select society, for the turbulent schemes of ambition and the tricks of political life.

Like the salons of the bluestockings, 'The Club' – the celebrated literary club started by Reynolds, Johnson, and Burke and immediately joined by six more founder-members – existed to promote the exchange of good conversation. One of the original nine was Jane Burke's father, Dr Nugent, a man to whom Johnson in particular became very affectionately attached. (When Nugent died in 1775, Johnson wrote to Jane Burke a message of the kindest sympathy.)[25] The Club's membership gradually grew, until by the time of Burke's death fifty-four men in all had belonged at one time or another. But the attendance of relatively few of these was either regular or long-lasting; Reynolds, the principal founder, seems to have been the most constant. According to Boswell, Johnson was not 'over-diligent'; and Burke, after his election to parliament in 1765, was also a frequent absentee, often perhaps for longish consecutive stretches. During the decade 1773–1783, however, he seems often to have attended the monthly dinners. (The idea at first had been merely for weekly supper-meetings, to be held at the Turk's Head, Soho. By 1783, the meeting-place was at Prince's, in Dover Street.) He is recorded for instance on an occasion in 1773 as proposing for membership his Irish friend Vesey, and the following month he was certainly present at Boswell's election and first attendance; so too at Sheridan's four years later.

Goldsmith was one of the original nine. He and Burke had been contemporaries at Trinity College, Dublin, but they were probably not known to one another until a year or two before the Club's foundation. From then until Goldsmith's death they saw much of each other at the Club suppers or dinners, or sometimes at the St James's Coffee House round the corner from Burke's London house, at Reynolds's also or at his studio, or of course at Burke's own place in Charles Street. Burke, together with nearly everybody else who knew Goldsmith, was always ready to pull his infinitely pullable leg, or perhaps to exchange pleasantries (not always of the highest class) and puns (frequently execrable – Burke's were widely considered so); but none of this ran counter to Burke's serious and indeed enthusiastic admiration for Goldsmith's talents, both as pastoral poet (*The Traveller* and *The*

Deserted Village specifically) and as comic playwright. Garrick's rejection of Goldsmith's comedy *The Good-Natured Man* so disappointed Burke that he invited a group of friends to his house for a reading of the play, which was then successfully recommended to the Covent Garden playwright-manager George Colman the elder. When seven years later *She Stoops to Conquer* followed, Burke, with Reynolds and Johnson, was among the group of Goldsmith's close friends who dined together at the Shakespeare Tavern and then all together attended the first night.

Johnson, who once declared that, though Goldsmith 'wrote like an angel' he talked 'like poor Poll', was as dismissive of Burke's conversational *wit* as of Goldsmith's. Had not Burke a great deal of wit? asked Boswell. 'I do not think so, Sir', replied Johnson; 'he is indeed constantly attempting wit, but he fails.' Again, he once said that when Burke did *not descend to be merry*, his conversation was very superior indeed; it was 'the ebullition of his mind; he does not talk from a desire of distinction, but because his mind is full'. There was however 'no proportion between the powers which he shows in serious talk and in jocularity'.[26] Not everybody agreed, but it does seem very likely that as a humorist, and certainly as inventor of puns – though pleasure in attempting them never left him – Burke's success knew strict limits.

Horace Walpole's world was some distance away from that of the Club, and we should doubtless be as wary of accepting his judgments upon Burke's talk and his wit, or lack of it, as of taking too seriously his shallow and much too dismissive view of Johnson. Burke's was a more polished style of *writing* than Johnson's, he conceded, and his *public* speaking undoubtedly was 'luminous'; but in private he had too much 'bombast' and – the same complaint repeated – he pursued wit 'to puerility'.[27] Commonest of the objections however to Burke the conversationalist was to his excessive ardour and vehemence. The daughter of Sir John Hawkins, an early biographer of Johnson, explaining why her father withdrew from the Club, said she suspected 'that he was disgusted with Mr Burke's overbearing manners, and the monopoly of conversation which he assumed, reducing the other members – Johnson excepted – to silence'.[28] And Edmund Malone, a man devoted to Burke, admitted that his manner in conversation, were it not for the great superiority of his talents and knowledge, would be disagreeable. He seldom appears to pay any attention to what is said by the person or persons with whom he is conversing but, disregarding their remarks, urges on whatever rises in his mind . . .[29]

It would not do, said Malone, for Burke to replace the ever-admirable Reynolds as club host. Burke, like Johnson, 'by his eloquence and habitual exertions in company . . . would keep his guests too much under'.[30] When it was once put to Burke –naturally enough by Boswell – that there had been criticism of him (in fact from Bennet Langton) for his 'roughness in conversation', Burke did not contest the charge, but considered that it would be 'well, if when a man comes to die, he has nothing heavier upon his conscience that having been a little rough in his conversation'.[31]

For Johnson, much the older man, both for his 'transcendant talents' and his essential goodness, Burke had infinite respect. Their friendship lasted some twenty-five years, until Johnson's death in 1784. Over the sad months of his final decline, his closest friends, Burke among them, came frequently to sit and, as ever, *talk* with him. 'I am afraid, Sir', suggested Burke on one occasion, 'such a number of us may be oppressive to you.' Johnson: 'No, Sir, it is not so; and I must be in a wretched state indeed when your company would not be a delight to me.' Burke: 'My dear Sir, you have always been too good to me.' As he spoke, he controlled his emotion with difficulty, and then silently walked from the room.

At the Westminster Abbey funeral which soon followed, he was one of the pall-bearers, and soon afterwards joined the committee which planned and raised funds for a monument and memorial. The age knew that it had buried a great man, and the proliferation of post-mortem praise and appraisal brought from Burke later a comment which sounds a little less surprising and macabre when we recall that the great Boswell biography still lay a few more years ahead: 'How many maggots', he reflected (to Hannah More), 'have crawled out of that great body.'[32]

When finally in 1791 Boswell's massive *Life of Johnson* was ready for publication, he took care first to show it to Burke and gain his approbation. To Boswell the biographer Burke's imprimatur was enthusiastically given; for Boswell the man his approval had always been more guarded. By Johnson's account, at first he even doubted whether Boswell was worthy of admission to the Club[33] – although, once he was in, doubts disappeared. Indeed, Burke conceded, he had so much good humour it was 'scarce a virtue'. He even came to reckon Boswell 'much the most agreeable man he ever saw'. The two men met irregularly, but fairly often during the 1770s, Boswell the tireless celebrity-hunter studiously paying calls at Charles Street or meeting Burke at Reynolds's or in the company of other mutual friends. Their conversational exchanges (though they 'talked of religion . . . on several occasions')[34] seem generally to have tended towards friendly banter, including political banter – Boswell like Johnson was a Tory – with much word-play and punning, but little of the tough thrust and counter-thrust which Johnson so loved and admired. At a serious level Boswell is often self-depicted as the earnest seeker after truth, the willing collector of the intellectual crumbs falling from Burke's richly stored table.

Perhaps in these early days Boswell added to his admiration of Burke a touch of envy. Burke seemed to have so much which he longed to have himself. Although no man could 'hope for continual happiness in life', he wrote, yet he suspected (this was in 1775) 'that Edmund Burke does; he has so much knowledge, so much animation, and the consciousness of so much fame'.[35] And at another time, in his role as Scottish lawyer he noted, after a day in which things in court had gone well, 'I was in such a frame of mind as to think myself an Edmund Burke'.[36] Some years later after an evening at Reynolds's with Burke in 1787, with Boswell as usual priming the pump, Reynolds as usual mostly listening, and Burke 'talking a variety of knowledge ten times more than I have recollected', Boswell's *Journal* notes, 'I felt my own emptiness sadly'.[37]

After his father died and he became laird of Auchinleck, Boswell entertained hopes of 'place': a political position in London perhaps, or possibly a parliamentary seat, or more particularly, after the resignation of Sir James Dunbar, the post of Judge Advocate in Scotland. Understandably enough, he hoped that Burke, as a friend who was likely one day, perhaps soon, to be a government minister, might be instrumental in securing him an appointment. Knowing it would be prudent to keep in touch, he had as early as 1778 begun from Edinburgh what he hoped would be a continuing correspondence with this friend 'of superior knowledge, abilities and genius'. Back in London in 1781 he called on Burke immediately, met him again socially several times, and finally in March 1782, immediately before Burke became Paymaster General for the first time, wrote him a long letter appealing for the exercise of his influence. Again a month later he wrote specifically requesting Burke's 'interest' to obtain for him the post of Judge Advocate. Burke eventually replied: 'Don't censure me too harshly for not answering your very kind and obliging letter. I protest I had not time for it. Alas! in that letter you much overrate my power of serving my friends'.[38] He did in fact approach General Conway on Boswell's behalf, and 'conversed also with Mr Fox on the subject'; without success however; Boswell failed to become Judge Advocate.

He persevered nevertheless in keeping in touch with the now out-of-office Burke, twice writing to invite himself to Beaconsfield in the summer of 1782. For various reasons this visit proved impossible to arrange, though he did come in the following April and was very cordially received. Devoid now of influence and unable therefore to help, Burke advised Boswell to try 'the present Minister' instead. This was Shelburne, whose name was always liable to call forth a burst of Burke's bitterest bile: 'he, who is neither Whigg nor Tory, can have no objection to you for your principles, upon any other account than that they are principles'.[39]

In fact Boswell turned not to Shelburne but to Dundas and various others; with no greater success. When in August 1783 the post, not this time of Judge but of Lord Advocate, was due to be filled, Boswell approached Burke again. 'I ought not to neglect such an opportunity', he wrote. Then, 'were I to be brought into Parliament', he threw in, 'I hope I might perhaps be of some service'. Failing either of these two openings, was there perhaps a chance of something else, and would Burke please be good enough to recommend him to the Duke of Portland? If Burke was astonished at the scope of these requests, his reply – 'kind and candid' said Boswell – concealed the fact capably and politely. He had been ill; he would do what Boswell asked; but he apprehended a want of success.

In November 1783 Burke was appointed Lord Rector of

Glasgow University; it was 'the greatest honour he ever had in his life', he said in his speech at the installation ceremony five months later. Boswell was by this time anxious over the state of his relations with Burke – not unreasonably perhaps, in view of the fact that he had just published a pamphlet attacking the India Bill, *and sent Burke a copy.* He now hurried to Glasgow, met Burke's servant on the stairs of the inn where he was staying, and asked him to deliver a letter to his master. He had apparently requested three times previously to be told when Burke would be coming to Scotland, but had had no reply. Now his message read: '. . . I am grateful for your kindness. I love your virtues. I admire your talents . . . I intreat I may have the honour to see you at Auchinleck. But if you have aught against me . . . pray tell me frankly' – whereupon Burke immediately sought him out, embraced him, and demanded, 'What has made you so mad of late? As to quarrelling with you, that cannot happen.'[40]

But Boswell was not fully convinced; his apprehensions persisted. The next year, following the death of Johnson, he published his account of the celebrated tour they had made years before to the Hebrides, and again he sent Burke a complimentary copy, this time of the book's second edition which had been prepared with the assistance of Edmond Malone. Was there, though, a passage in it to which Burke might take exception? – for the book contained mention again of Johnson's lack of regard for Burke's wit and humour – even though a prodigiously long footnote by Boswell and Malone had been appended to contest Johnson's opinion, and to forestall or mitigate Burke's umbrage. But what came back to Boswell was a long and delightful letter mixing amused friendliness with the most urbane irony. He was extremely obliged to Malone and Boswell for their

> solicitude with regard to a point relating to me, about which I am myself not very anxious. The reputation for wit . . . is what I am certainly not entitled to; and, I think, I never aimed at. If I had been even so ambitious, I must shew myself as deficient in judgment as I am in wit, if I thought a title to pleasantry could be made out of argument. The feelings of every one you live with must decide without appeal. I am therefore in no sort disposed to bring a writ of errour on the judgment pronounced upon me. I admit the court to be competent; the

149

proceedings regular; and the reporter learned and exact . . . I shall be well content to pass down to a long posterity in Doctor Johnson's authentick judgment, and in your permanent record, as a dull fellow and a tiresome companion . . .

You see, my dear sir, that vanity always finds its consolation. But wisdom might draw a lesson even from this little circumstance . . . I ought not to take this publick reprimand amiss. My companions have a right to expect that, when my conversation is so little seasond, as it is, with wit, it should not . . . be so light and careless as it undoubtedly always has been, and is . . . I ought therefore to thank you for informing the world of this censure of our deceased friend, that I may regulate myself accordingly . . . I am with sincere respect and regard, My dear Sir, your most faithful and humble servant, Edm Burke, Beconsfield Jany 4. 1786.[41]

Boswell was somewhat, but only somewhat, reassured. He was still worrying two years later, professing himself 'very very uneasy' that there seemed to remain a coldness, especially, he wrote, 'when I recollect how much of your company I once enjoyed'. He pressed therefore for a meeting so that they could renew their friendship; and when, still busy with the Warren Hastings trial, Burke managed to find time to come to dinner with other guests at Boswell's, his host's journal recorded in relief: 'Had Edmund Burke at my table . . . He behaved wonderfully well'. It was like Boswell to add: 'I looked back to my first view of him as authour of the Sublime and Beautiful, and *felt* that I was now wonderfully up in the scale of literary and intellectual society'.[42]

For another five or six years they met as in the old days, fairly often. Boswell judged Burke to be over-violent in his political views – 'Irishly savage a little', he noted once, 'but full and flowing'; wrong about Warren Hastings; wrong to support Wilberforce in the anti-slave-trade campaign; and right in general about the French Revolution, where he reports Burke as telling him that the French had *almost* made him 'adopt your Tory principles'. Then came Boswell's great book, immediately following Burke's own on the revolution in France. Compliments were in order in both directions.

Ten years after her husband's death, Jane Burke, in acknowledging the receipt of George Crabbe's latest poem *The Parish Register,* wrote to him: '*Your friend* never lost sight of worth and abilities. He found them in you, and was happy in having it in his power to bring them forward.'[43] Crabbe himself much later, on a visit to Sir Walter Scott, is reported by Lockhart as praising, with tears in his eyes, Burke's kindness to him in his distressful early days.

At the age of twenty-six, failing in his attempt to become a doctor, he was desperate. He had left his native Suffolk fishing village of Aldborough by coasting vessel, carrying with him his total worldly assets – good health and intelligence, a few surgical instruments, a watch (soon to be pawned), some passages of verse, and five borrowed pounds. Arrived in London, his poems had no success, whether with magazines, printers, an attempted subscription list, or patrons. Of these last, Shelburne, Thurlow, and North all turned him down – though later on, to his credit, gruff old Thurlow (*after* Crabbe had been 'discovered' by Burke) handed him a sealed envelope with £100 in it.

At last with pauperism and imprisonment for debt threatening, he fixed (by his own account) 'upon Edmund Burke, one of the first Englishmen, and in the capacity and energy of his mind one of the greatest of human beings'.[44] He sent therefore a 'proposal' or sample of his current poetry to Charles Street, together with a dignified account of himself and his unfortunate history, an apology for his presumption, and a promise to call at the house the next day and learn his fate. Burke was both moved and impressed. After Crabbe had spent the night between hope and despair walking up and down Westminster Bridge, he called at Burke's door, was given food, drink, money to pay his rent, a little more for immediate needs, an encouraging criticism of those of his verses Burke had read, and an undertaking to give them all further study. He did better. He showed them to influential friends, Johnson and James Dodsley among them. He told Reynolds that this struggling young poet had 'the mind and feelings of a gentleman'.[45] He saw to it that the *Annual Register* published some of Crabbe's verses. He himself acted as literary adviser, encouraging Crabbe to submit 'a large quantity of miscellaneous compositions' to him, some of which indeed he condemned, though always looking for opportunities to praise.

After three months, while Crabbe lodged in Bishopsgate Street at his mentor's expense, Burke took Crabbe's poem *The Library* to Dodsley who, though he would not buy it, agreed to print it for 200 subscribers, push the sale, and make over any profit to Crabbe. At the end of the parliamentary session Mr and Mrs Burke carried off their poet to Beaconsfield for a month's stay as their honoured guest, Burke just before he left for the country taking care in a letter to William Eden, Irish Chief Secretary, to enclose a copy of *The Library* hot from the press, by 'a young man of Suffolk I think shews a talent for poetry'.[46]

Burke had developed plans for him. Even though he had no degree, he had a little Latin left over from schooling, and could learn more. Why should he not study to take orders? Burke therefore through intermediaries approached the bishops of St David's and of Norwich, who proved however at first very wary of admitting by such unorthodox procedures even one so warmly recommended. To begin with, Crabbe had to be content with being ordained deacon. Fortunately Burke happened to learn then that the Duke of Rutland's domestic chaplain was retiring. Why should Crabbe not succeed to his place? Meanwhile he continued to press his protégé's worth upon London literary and artistic friends. Finally the Bishop of Norwich relented, and the Duke of Rutland proved helpful, so that it was as the recently ordained *Reverend* George Crabbe that the poet was able to write to his benefactor from Belvoir Castle in May 1782:

> It is my duty to inform you that his Grace appointed me his domestic chaplain on Sunday last, and to thank you for this as well as every other advantage I have obtained since I had the happiness to know you. I hope so to conduct myself that you may never repent your recommendation . . .[47]

As a young 'man of letters' in the 1750s Burke had attempted, for Robert Dodsley, a history of England, which however ended at Magna Carta and remained unpublished until fifteen years after his death. But history was always central to his thought. A nation's manners and morals, its religious and political institutions, its social structure, were all *prescribed* by its past. Men might – and ought to – adjust, correct, renovate, ameliorate; but it was not within their power (without inviting ruin) to trifle with their history, to destroy the fabric, in order to rebuild radically. It was usage, longevity, *history*, which bestowed title and gave authority. The outlines of the 'script' were already written. Thus for instance the British constitution's 'sole authority' was that it had 'existed time out of mind'. 'Your king, your lords, your judges, your juries grand and little, are all prescriptive.'[48] It was this 'prescription' which gave to society order and stability.

No longer writing history, he never stopped reading it. In a sense, history was our master; yet he knew enough to know how little even the most learned could be sure of. The Scot, William Robertson, was the historian of his day whom he most admired, and the *Annual Register* – which probably means Burke himself – had favourably reviewed two of his earlier books. Then when he sent Burke a copy of his *History of America*, Burke responded with a long letter of thanks and the warmest praise, in the course of which he wrote (10th June 1777):

> . . . The part which I read with the greatest pleasure is the discussion on the manners and characters of the inhabitants of that new world [of Spanish America]. I have always thought with you that we possess at this time very great advantages towards the knowledge of human nature. We need no longer go to history to have it in all its periods and stages. History, from its comparative youth, is a poor instructor . . . But now the great map of mankind is unravelled at once, and there is no state or gradation of barbarism, and no mode of refinement which we have not at the same instant under our review; – the very different civility of Europe and of China; – the barbarism of Persia and Abyssinia; – the erratic manners of Tartary and Arabia; – the savage state of North America and New Zealand: – Indeed, you . . . have drawn new resources for philosophy . . . Adieu, Sir! Continue to instruct the world; and – whilst we carry on a poor unequal conflict with the passions and prejudices of our day, perhaps with no better weapons than other passions and prejudices of our own – convey wisdom to future generations.

Robertson, it seems to follow, had written a splendid history, but he had done more – given to it the insights of anthropology.

Towards that other Scottish historian, the philosopher David Hume, Burke was respectful but less enthusiastic. Hume had read *The Sublime and the Beautiful* – 'a very pretty treatise', he thought – and it was he who first introduced Burke to Adam Smith's *Theory of Moral Sentiments*. The two men became well acquainted but never close friends. Burke reviewed Hume's *History of England* favourably in the *Annual Register*, but found fault later with what he had written about Ireland, regretting to Malone that Hume did not give himself 'a great deal of trouble in examining records, etc.'[49]

Gibbon too was an acquaintance rather than a friend of any intimacy. He was a fellow member both of the Club and of parliament – even briefly at one time, during the Fox–North coalition, on the same side of the House. Being a Northite (in parliamentary terms a very silent one) in no way prevented him from admiring Burke the speaker: 'I can never forget', he wrote of the 1780 speech on economical reform, 'the delight with which that diffusive and ingenious orator was heard by all sides of the House'.[50] As for the famous Gibbon style, Burke did not like it. It was 'affected, mere frippery and tinsel', he said to Reynolds.[51] It took the French Revolution to bring the two men, and their opinions, closer together. The *Decline and Fall* complete at last, and Gibbon prepared now to admit that he had once in the notorious fifth chapter 'treated the primitive church with some freedom', he was almost as alarmed as Burke was at what he saw happening in France. He regarded the *Reflections* as 'a most admirable medicine against the French disease', and begged 'leave to subscribe my assent to Mr Burke's creed. I admire his eloquence, I approve his politics, I adore his chivalry, and I can almost excuse his reverence for church establishments'.[52]

'Almost'; and perhaps Gibbon was no more than *almost* penitent over his stylish fun at the early Christians' expense. But something he wrote at this time shows well enough that he was as aware as Burke declared himself to be, at much the same time over Mrs Crewe's dinner table, of the dangers of 'quizzing'. Facile derision was not for retailing to the vulgar: 'I have sometimes thought [wrote Gibbon] of writing a dialogue of the dead in which Lucian, Erasmus, and Voltaire should mutually acknowledge the danger of exposing an *old* superstition to the contempt of the blind and fanatic multitude.'[53]

His immediate family and the unique William Burke apart, of all Burke's friendships the most important to him was that with Joshua Reynolds. It was long-lived, lasting some thirty-four years; starting almost certainly when Reynolds, his mind already busy with artistic theory and the principles of aesthetics, first read *The Sublime and the Beautiful*. When ten years later he began his famous series of discourses before the newly founded Royal

Academy of Art, their admirable literary style led some to think that he must have had more than a little help from some writer of distinction. Was it perhaps his friend Johnson or, rather more likely, Burke? Horace Walpole for one favoured Burke, 'a more polished writer than Johnson'. Indeed as late as 1810, the *Hibernian Magazine* was still repeating an opinion held by many until about that time (one recalls that Burke was once very widely thought to have written also the Letters of 'Junius') that Burke *wrote* Reynolds's *Discourses*. Malone, who was well acquainted with both men, knew better and had, years before, denied the story. There was no doubt, he wrote, that some of Reynolds's lectures 'were submitted to Dr Johnson, and some to Mr Burke, for their examination and revision; and probably each of those sponsors suggested to their author some minute verbal improvements'.[54] Malone himself, it was later discovered, had performed for the author a similar service. It is only in Reynolds's seventh discourse, 'On Taste', that verbal similarities (or at one place *identity* of phraseology with an extra chapter in the second edition of *The Sublime and the Beautiful*, also 'On Taste') would convincingly argue a connection between the two closer than might come from the frequent discussions which Burke and Reynolds were constantly enjoying.

During the year in which Burke was putting the final touches to *The Sublime and the Beautiful*, Reynolds gave 677 sittings, and for the next thirty-four years – just the period of his friendship with Burke – he was almost universally accepted (though not by his monarch, who preferred others) as the nation's leading painter. He was undeniably the most fashionable. Everybody that was anybody sat to him, but few can have sat more *often* than Burke; eight times between 1766 and 1786, with his wife and his son in addition sitting twice each. Such frequency appears less surprising when we learn that Burke was often a morning visitor to Reynolds's studio, to talk, to discuss pictures, books, plays, affairs in general, or sometimes just to watch him at work. Once even, he is recorded as vigorously pressing Reynolds to remove a 'blemish' from his 'Death of Cardinal Beaufort' – Burke objecting to a representation in it of the devil. Sir Joshua, we read, replied: 'Having placed the devil there, there he should remain'.[55]

James Barry and George Romney were two other prominent artists who did portraits of Burke, the admirable Romney coming as a gift from the Duke of Richmond. Barry, the once penniless young Irishman, had first been brought by the Burkes to England and then sent abroad at their expense for six years to learn the painter's trade at the best continental schools. From Burke's correspondence it is clear that in his capacity of artistic mentor he never tired of holding Reynolds up to Barry as an example, sometimes advising him in the very phrases used in the *Discourses*. When therefore Barry, returning to England from his artistic apprenticeship in Italy, published to the world his dislike of portrait painters in general, and of Joshua Reynolds in particular, Burke not unnaturally felt that he was biting the hands that had fed him, and a coldness ensued.

Burke's own houses were full of paintings, and at Beaconsfield of statues too. Some of these 'pictures and marbles', so Burke declared, were from the previous owner's collection, and he had been obliged to 'take them with the house' when he first went there in 1767; but he was always adding to them. Sixteen years later, when a somewhat astonished Boswell visited, he found that among a great deal else they included seven Poussins, a Titian, and several Reynolds portraits, including those of the Burke family and of the Whig hero Admiral Keppel, always reckoned one of Reynolds's finest.[56]

Mutual visits in London were frequent, and quite often Reynolds came also to Beaconsfield. It was there, for instance, in the summer of 1781 that Burke introduced him to his recent discovery, Crabbe. According to the Burke protégé of earlier days, Barry, at the same time as *he* was being supported by Burke in Italy, Reynolds was coming to *Burke*'s aid at Beaconsfield.[57] Whatever the precise details of this, certainly the relatively affluent Reynolds lent Burke a good deal of money at various times, and took care in his will to cancel an outstanding debt of £2000 (just as Rockingham had done ten years before) – as well as setting aside a further £2000 for Burke's use as one of his executors. By that will, Burke was also made guardian of Sir Joshua's niece Miss Palmer, and a miniature of Oliver Cromwell by Samuel Cooper was bequeathed to Burke's son. Reynolds had been a good friend to both the Richards, senior and junior (he once spent a Paris holiday with Richard senior), and indeed to Jane Burke too – in fact to all the ever-plural Burkes, including apparently some of those outside the immediate family circle.

More than once he seems to have entertained at his country villa at Hampton in Middlesex a sizeable family assemblage. Hazlitt relates how he was told (by Northcote, Sir Joshua's biographer) that Miss Reynolds, who kept house for her brother, 'used to complain that whenever any of Burke's poor Irish relations came over, they were all poured in upon them for dinner; but Sir Joshua never took any notice, but bore it all with great patience and tranquillity'.[58]

When Reynolds was dying, in January 1792, Burke wrote to his son, who was away in Ireland:

> Our poor friend Sir Joshua declines daily. For some time past he has kept to his bed. His legs, and all his body, swell extremely. He takes great doses of laudanum . . . Nothing can equal the tranquillity with which he views his end. He congratulates himself on it as a happy conclusion of a happy life. He spoke of you in a style which was affecting . . .[59]

Within a few weeks the death of Reynolds came with this closest of friends at his bedside. An hour or two later, still in the same room, Burke wrote an obituary for the newspapers, and then set about making arrangements for the funeral at St Paul's, before which Reynolds's body was to lie in state at the Royal Academy. Emotion choking his voice cut short the speech Burke was making there, in honour of his friend, before the assembled academicians.

In December 1784, just a year after the downfall of the Coalition, and as it happens on the very day that Johnson died, a letter of Burke's was keeping warm a friendship older even than those he had enjoyed with Reynolds and Johnson. In the preceding summer Richard Shackleton, the son of his old Quaker schoolmaster, and his daughter Mary, now a young woman, had come over from Ireland on a visit to the Burkes at Beaconsfield. Returned home then to Ballitore, Mary (or Molly) Shackleton, who had plainly fallen in love with her hosts, their house, and its surroundings, showed her father a poem she had written about them, and Shackleton with understandable pride and pleasure had posted it for his old friend's perusal.

> I was gratified [he wrote] in finding that my honest lass inherited the attachment of her parents, and judged so well of what is excellent. – I send them to thee – if they do not please

157

thee, they will probably please thy wife – so throw them to her. – Thy wife exprest a desire to have copies of some other verses of my daughter's, which Molly means to send her.[60]

Burke's reply, behind its ornate formality, is charm itself. The young lady had done him a great favour: her poem ('Beaconsfield') made 'us all a little the more fond of ourselves and our situation'. No, the lines were not, as she had too modestly suggested, commonplace; it was 'a sweet poem', and showed 'a mind full of observation and retentive of images in the highest degree'. If there were a few trifling blemishes, these were 'easily effaced . . . You will excuse this freedom. But in so fine a poem . . . you will naturally expect that I should wish for the perfection which I know you can give *your* work with a little more of *your* care . . .' Mary Shackleton's diary of six days later reads: 'Saw a letter on the chimney-piece – seized it – can it be?– it really is from Edmund Burke to me – do not forsake me, my little wits'. Both Burke's letter and the Beaconsfield poem itself were later included in the *Poems* (1808) of Mary (as she became) Leadbeater: a collection which included also a second of Mary's poems about the Burkes, 'On a Report of Edmund Burke's Death and of his son Having been Lost at Sea'. Happily both reports had been false, though for a time Burke had been seriously worried for Richard's safety. On receiving eventually a copy of the poem, Burke replied, in much the same cordial vein as before, ending at length with, 'My dear young friend, I am nearly worn out with the fatigue of reading, comparing, and extracting mountains of papers – Excuse me that I break off – God bless you, your Father and Mother, and all with you! Adieu – Cultivate the talents that are given you . . .'[61]

An obligation less pleasant to fulfil arose from responsibilities incurred through another Irish friendship of years past. Two of the Irishmen closest to Burke until the mid-1770s, if latterly by correspondence only, were Charles O'Hara and John Ridge. Both men died in 1776. O'Hara's son became an Irish M.P.; Ridge left three daughters, in whose support Burke had interested himself, managing eventually to secure for the eldest daughter (who was sickly and half-blind) a pension of £100 a year on the Irish establishment. When Charles O'Hara, junior, refused a request that he should become a trustee for this award, Burke himself was left with the responsibility, which became barely tolerable as ill-tempered dissensions within the far from penniless Ridge family redoubled – until in Burke's words there was 'nothing but confusion, ill blood, and mutual hatred'. At one point he was shocked to learn that his old friend's three daughters had ostentatiously taken to advertising their resentments by going from Loughrea to Dublin and there putting themselves on display in the streets as beggars.

His 'compassion' had been called upon by Sir John Blaquière, Irish Chief Secretary (through whom he had first obtained the pension), but Burke's extremely long, soberly conscientious, but basically tough letter of November 1784 in reply – one of several relating to the Ridge disputes – made it clear that he thought Blaquière was having his pity and indignation artificially worked upon. The Ridge family, taken as a whole – there was a rich uncle – was 'opulent'. Let them find a little good will and common sense:

> The picture you paint is truly affecting. Two young women 'both pretty and one of them even handsome, the younger leading the elder stone blind through the streets with elegant deportments but tattered rags seeking almost for bread'. It was indeed a shocking sight . . . How they came, an hundred miles from their home, to be exhibited in this manner in the streets of a vast dissolute capital I cannot conjecture . . . If all the young women of middling condition in Ireland, who have but two hundred and fifty pounds for their fortunes were to be justified as appearing as beggars in the streets of Dublin, you wou'd have the most crouded metropolis in the world with female vice and wretchedness . . .
>
> Now my dear Sir . . . I cannot in honour and conscience charge the result of what your indulgence is pleased to think I have a right to dispose of . . .

Burke's obvious impatience with the quarrelsome cantankerousness of these Ridges, with whose affairs he had become so unfortunately entangled, offers one instance of a sentiment about his fellow Irishmen he was coming increasingly to entertain. It applied politically too; legislative independence seemed to have improved nothing. All was still 'ferment', making him more and more 'fearful of intermeddling at all in the affairs of Ireland':

> For I find along with many virtues in my countrymen there is a jealousy, a soreness, and readiness to take offence, as if they were the most helpless and impotent of mankind, and yet a

violence . . . and a boistrousness in their resentment, as if they had been puffed up with the highest prosperity and power. They will not only be served, but it must be also in their own way and on their own principles and even in words and language that they like . . . which renders it very difficult for a plain unguarded man as I am to have anything to do with them or their affairs.[62]

CHAPTER
12

THE CAUSE OF INDIA

BURKE TO William Eden, 17 May 1784: 'My dear Sir, -
I am obliged to you for thinking of me in the midst of your
cabbage garden: I never have been called away from mine
with so much reluctance in my whole life. It is not pleasant to
play the captive part in a triumphal procession, especially when
the weather is hot and the ways dusty'.

It had been a wounding four or five months. The defeat of the
Fox–North coalition over the India bills and, a few months later,
the joint triumph of Pitt and the King at the general election left
the Foxite Whigs in a state of parliamentary impotence in which
they were destined to remain for the remainder of the 1780s.
More disastrous still were to be their fortunes in the decade
following, when the Whig party would suffer disintegration from
the effects in England of the revolution in France. If any of that
could have been foreseen in 1784, Burke's despondency must
have been deeper still. As it was, although his own position as
member for Malton, a pocket borough, was secure (while, all
around, 'Fox's martyrs' went to the chopping block), ahead he
could see only helplessness and defeat. He reckoned

the House of Commons something worse than extinguished.
We have been labouring for near twenty years to make it independent; and as soon as we had accomplished what we had in
view, we found that its independence led to its destruction.
The people did not like our work; and they joind the Court to
pull it down. The demolition is very complete . . . The
English nation . . . are perfectly aware of . . . what they have
done, and they by no means repent of it.[1]

And it is clear that the great matter which was usually to dominate and sometimes to monopolise his thought and activity at least for the next five or six years was more emphatically than ever at the forefront of his attention, for he immediately continues:

> A more frightful symptom, in my mind, than this, appears in the nation at present . . . That is that all the tyranny, robbery, and destruction of mankind practised by the Company and their servants in the East is popular and pleasing in this country; and that the Court and Ministry who evidently abet that iniquitous system are somewhat the better liked on that account.[2]

Burke was far from believing that the British should withdraw from India. 'There we are placed by the Sovereign Disposer', he told the Commons, 'and we must do the best we can. The situation of man is the preceptor of his duty.'[3] The East India trade, if properly conducted – and this of course included trade with China – ought to benefit both India and Britain. But it was the welfare of the Indians themselves that must always have priority: 'the prosperity of the natives must be previously secured before any profit from them whatever is attempted'.[4] On Indian affairs, and with Warren Hastings in particular, he may sometimes have been led astray by prejudice; have misjudged evidence; have failed to make allowance for the complexity of problems facing 'the man on the spot'; even have allowed honest indignation to degenerate into vindictive fury; but in such pronouncements and sentiments 'the heart of his position' on India is to be found, a heart whose beat was firm, and a position which is worthy surely of respect.

He had been manoeuvring for the attack on Warren Hastings and the Bengal administration ever since 1781, but before the main offensive was prepared, there was unfinished business still be be attended to in Southern India – going back to, or even beyond, William Burke's first association with the Raja of Tanjore, and then to the (originally rebellious) Madras Council's backing for the Nawab of the Carnatic – the 'Nabob of Arcot' – both against Tanjore and against the dangerous later incursions of Haidar Ali and his son Tipu Sultan, successive rulers of Mysore. Now in 1785 there arose the question of the settlement of the vast and complicated debts which the Nawab had incurred over the past eighteen years as ally, or client, or catspaw, or puppet of the Company – the description varied according to taste or judgment. His banking services throughout that period had been mainly in the hands of the man already well-established (along with Sulivan and Hastings) in the company of Burke's arch-villains in the Indian story – Paul Benfield.

The abortive Fox–Burke bills of 1783 had been quickly followed by the Pitt–Dundas India Act of 1784 which set the pattern of British administration in India for three-quarters of a century. In some of its provisions it was not dissimilar to the Whig measures defeated a few months earlier but, significantly, it did have the support of the East India Company, whereas the Fox–Burke bills had earned their vehement hostility. In the 1784 general election the Company had given Pitt useful support, and it was widely assumed that its reward would include a generous settlement of the debts owed by the Nawab of Arcot to Benfield and those associated with him in the Company at Madras. Benfield himself, as disposer of parliamentary boroughs (in fact three, and not as Burke alleged eight) had been active in the election on the government's side.

The question was, *how much* of the Nawab's debt was to be officially recognised? The Company's Court of Directors in London decided that every claim must be investigated before repayment; but, to Burke's fury, the Board of Control set up under the new act – its chairman was Dundas – overruled the Court of Directors and ordered payment to be made from the public funds without enquiry. On 28 February 1785 therefore, on a government motion for authorising the necessary directions, Burke rose to deliver what must rank as among the weightiest, as it is certainly among the fiercest, of his great parliamentary performances.

It was in several different senses a tremendous speech: tremendous first in length, for it lasted at least four and perhaps nearly five hours; tremendous in the power of its rhetoric and occasional ventures into irony, pathos, or vituperation; in its exposition of dense detail and command of complexities which must have either bewildered or bored – perhaps bewildered *and* bored – a majority of members; tremendous also in the overwhelming impression conveyed of a passion for justice, of a demand for recognition of the wrongs done to Indians, and for the forced *excretion* of 'those inexpugnable tape-worms which devour the nutriment and eat up the bowels of India'.[5]

Of course it was a Whig speech, a party speech, not entirely fair or without error. Modern scholarship,[6] and even some evidence supplied by near-contemporaries, can demonstrate easily enough that the case was overstated and in parts based on misunderstood information. The devastation of the Carnatic in the wars with Mysore was grievous, but not quite as complete as Burke so memorably painted it. His dismissal of all the debts incurred by the Nawab as 'fraudulent' sidestepped the generally acknowledged propositions that the relationship between the Nawab and the British Indian empire (in which Burke did strongly believe) had on the whole been of benefit to both, and that at least part of his debt needed to be recognised and liquidated. The white heat of Burke's loathing of Benfield, chief money-lender to the Nawab and arch-profiteer, led him too willingly to exaggerate the number of Pittite M.P.s 'made' by Benfield in the 1784 general election. And Benfield earlier, though he had pocketed very large sums (and was personally to make £580,000 now from this 1785 settlement), had not in India always succeeded in actually *receiving* quite the exorbitant rates of interest which agreements may have promised him, and which Burke angrily publicised. A good deal more in the same vein may be lodged against Burke's arguments and allegations; but what remains is impressive – its factual weight and intellectual command, its varied scope and driving sincerity.

One target of the strongest fire was Dundas, who had earlier been the chief figure in the *other* Commons committee on India, the 'Secret Committee', and was now Pitt's Indian expert. Dundas had been pressing the need for 'delicacy' – the full details of the proposed debt settlement, if revealed, would be damaging to the national interest. Burke's assault upon this, and upon Dundas himself, despite the polish and elegance of his final reference to Virgil's *Aeneid*,[7] was formerly considered rather too coarse to be freely quoted:

> He [Dundas] and delicacy are a rare and singular coalition. He thinks to divulge our Indian politics may be highly dangerous. He! the mover! the chairman! the reporter of the Committee of Secrecy! He that brought forth in the utmost detail . . . the most recondite parts of the politics, the military,

the revenues of the British empire in India [the six official reports of the Secret Committee]. With six great chopping bastards, each as lusty as an infant Hercules, this delicate creature blushes at the sight of his new bridegroom, assumes a virgin delicacy; or, to use a more fit as well as a more poetic comparison, the person so squeamish, so timid, so trembling lest the winds of heaven should visit too roughly, is . . . exposed like the sow of imperial augury, lying in the mud with all the prodigies of her fertility about her, as evidence of her delicate amours – [the appropriate lines of the *Aeneid* follow].[8]

But it was not Dundas or Pitt, it was Paul Benfield and his associate moneylenders who were the main objects of his indignation, the men who for years had been so profitably playing their game 'of utter perdition to the unhappy natives of India':

> The Nabob falls into an arrear to the Company. The Presidency presses for payment. The Nabob's answer is, I have no money. Good. But there are *soucars* [moneylenders] who will supply you on the mortgage of your territories. Then steps forward some Paul Benfield, and from his grateful compassion to the Nabob, and his filial regard to the Company, he unlocks the treasures of his virtuous industry; and for a consideration of 24 or 36 per cent on a mortgage of the territorial revenue, becomes security to the Company for the Nabob's arrear . . .[9]

By chicanery and the exploitation of inefficiency among the Nawab's servants, the British *soucars* had even been enabled to collect interest payments, 'divided as lawful spoil', without parting with any *cash* in their loan, so long as they continued to hold assignments of land ('tuncaws', *tankhahs*) as security for charges previously unpaid by the Nawab:

> Bond is paid by bond; arrear is turned into new arrear; usury engenders new usury; mutiny [by unpaid troops 'famished to feed English *soucars*'] – mutiny suspended in one quarter, starts up in another; until all the revenues and all the establishments are entangled into one inextricable knot of confusion . . . [Thus] inexperienced young Englishmen . . . are enabled at once to take provinces in mortgage, to make princes their debtors, and to become creditors to millions.[10]

The Company itself had 'for years kept up a shew of disinterestedness and moderation', while by the 'operation of everything false' it had become pander and bawd to this 'unbridled debauchery and licentiousness of usury and extortion'. Native rulers like the Nawab and the Raja of Tanjore were now, as potentates, 'extinguished'; kept as puppet independent sovereigns 'for the purpose of rapine and extortion'.[11]

It was true that, after 'the black cloud' of Haidar Ali's Mysore armies had burst over the stricken population of the Carnatic, something was done for them by *private* charity. The desolation had indeed been hideous:

> A storm of universal fire blasted every field, consumed every house, destroyed every temple. The miserable inhabitants flying from their flaming villages, in part were slaughtered; others . . . enveloped in a whirlwind of cavalry . . . swept into captivity . . . Those who were able to evade this tempest fled to the walled cities. But, escaping from fire, sword, and exile, they fell into the jaws of famine . . . For months together these creatures of sufferance . . . perished by an hundred a day in the streets of Madras; every day seventy at least . . . expired of famine in the granary of India . . . Extend your imagination a little further, and then suppose your ministers taking a survey of this scene of waste and desolation. What would be your thoughts if you should be informed that they were computing how much should be the amount of the excises, how much the customs, how much the land and malt tax, in order that they should charge . . . upon the relicks of the satiated vengeance of relentless enemies the whole of what England had yielded in the most exuberant seasons of peace and abundance? What would you call it? To call it tyranny, sublimed into madness, would be too faint an image; yet this very madness is the principle on which the ministers at your right hand have proceeded in their estimate of the revenues of the Carnatic when they were providing, not supply for the establishments of its protection, but rewards for the authors of its ruin.[12]

Central to Burke's onslaught upon the British treasury's proposal to pay off in full the Nawab's creditors was his claim that the debts were not honest debts at all. They were fraudulent. The money had never been lent in the expectation that the Nawab would have to repay from his own resources. It had been a case of collusion between the Nawab on one side, and Benfield and his associates on the other. The 'payment' had come, first, from the oppression of the Indian population, and now was to be completed, on the government's proposals, from the British public revenues.

Towards the end of this long philippic came a spirited attack on that *other* collusion – between 'the men of intrigue' in India and 'the minister of intrigue', Pitt, in England – in the management of the previous year's general election. There had been 'a studied display of power of their connecting link'. Every trust, every honour, every distinction had been heaped on Benfield:

He was at once made a director of the India Company; made an alderman of London . . . [and] to secure his services against all risque, he was brought in for a ministerial borough . . . You all remember that in the same virtuous cause, he submitted to keep a sort of public office or counting-house, where the whole business of the last general election was managed . . . It was managed upon Indian principles, and for an Indian interest. This was the golden cup of abominations; this was the chalice of the fornications of rapine, usury, and oppression . . . Here! you have it here before you . . . The claims of Benfield and his crew must be put above all enquiry.[13]

But, again, it was a speech from greatly outnumbered opposition benches; and when at last it ended, at 1 a.m., an outbreak of furious hostility exploded from the other side of the House. At least this time he had said all he wanted to say. Six months earlier, when attacking Hastings as 'the scourge of India' who was reducing the country to 'a howling desert', a similar outburst shouted him down, and the debate was stopped.[14] This marathon speech of February 1785 went meagrely reported – partly perhaps because reporters preferred to be abed by the small hours – and Burke immediately set about preparing his own printed version, over which he took great care, consulting, checking, no doubt also polishing, amplifying, and correcting. When it appeared, it contained *ten* appendices of a total length roughly equal to that of the speech itself.

If some part of Burke's information on southern India derived from William Burke, much came from different sources, and the two men's *opinions* could hardly be more at variance. William, micawbering along as always, ever travelling hopefully, but never arriving, was at this time as usual full of some finely wrought plan for self-enrichment and family rescue, the current scheme consisting of a modest proposal for making £150,000 for himself out of 'the remittance of the public debt', and somehow at the same time making £4000 a year 'clear' for family use in London.

The details of this abortive project seem as obscure as the letter containing them appears self-contradictory, since simultaneously William laments (to Richard junior) that his castles in the air are vanished – or at least such as remain are all for Richard – and yet that he has 'conceived new hopes' of ambitious dimensions. In piety he adds, 'the crop is in the hands of God'. Further, he stresses that neither Richard nor his father need fear that any-thing crooked is being planned: the money he will make 'in remittance' is 'as fair as the product of a man's own acres'.

Edmund's concern for the Indian natives appeared to William high-minded but misguided. 'For the soul of me', he told Richard, 'I cannot feel as much as your father does for the black primates'. He had seen in the newspapers that men thought that Edmund's opinions and prejudices were assimilated from William's own; but, 'O my God', he wrote, there was 'something sad and ridiculous' in *that*. On the contrary, 'his alarms for me are the only stay . . . that hangs on his mind, in that noble walk of his'. 'Do say for me to your father – that the abstract right of things in the East has scarcely an existence, all is usurpation and force.'[15]

Edmund meanwhile was worried for 'poor Will', who he feared might be deprived of his office without compensation if, as seemed likely, William's paymastership was merged with the Company's own at Madras. Moreover, since William still owed Lord Verney £20,000, if he returned home without funds he faced imprisonment for debt. Edmund therefore tried to prevent this disaster by enlisting the advocacy of influential people, or those of his own friends who might know such people. Adam Smith, for instance, knew Colonel Ross, secretary to the newly appointed Governor General Cornwallis, and obliged his old friend Burke by writing for Ross's perusal a truly handsome testimonial to the virtues of William Burke. Edmund had assured Smith that William had no enemies 'but such as are so, and some are so very bitterly' on account of his, Edmund's, con-duct.[16] Among these he did *not* count Dundas, who he thought had shown generosity.

It had indeed been officially put to Cornwallis that he should find some less wasteful and inconvenient way of paying the King's troops in India but, on his arrival there, he discovered that William Burke was reckoned 'a man of respectable character', and Cornwallis expressly stated later that he had wished to avoid any imputation of 'being inclined to act hardly' from political motives hostile to Burke. He did however take steps to ensure that William's financial plans came to nothing. Thus the grand project for making a fortune out of 'the remittance of the public debt' was foiled; but the position of paymaster remained, and Edmund's anxiety could abate.[17]

To an uncomfortable extent he felt at this time that, both in parliament and from the newspapes, he was under siege. The noisy Commons demonstrations against him during the Indian debates of 1784 and 1785 were not isolated phenomena, and his correspondence shows very clearly that there was, as he put it, much 'malice' against him, 'a cry against myself', 'a run against me'.[18] He was even provoked to claim damages for libel against Henry Woodfall of the *Public Advertiser*, which had printed two articles alleging that he had used public money for his own and his family's profit. This was the latest version of an old story – the conspiracy of self-seeking Irish adventurers to enrich themselves at the expense of the British public. Woodfall's wild exaggerations and allegations had been made against the *five* Burkes – Edmund, the two Richards, and the *two* 'cousins' William and John (this was John Bourke, a friend but no relation) who between them, according to the *Public Advertiser*, received £35,800 annually, against the £33,600 which went to 130 other members of parliament with an income from public sources. The libel was easily enough proved, though the damages awarded were only £100. Burke had claimed £5000.[19]

Some of these unpleasantnesses came no doubt in response to the vehemence of his own speeches. And this sometimes was undeniably a vehemence which, when interruptions from government supporters goaded him beyond bearing, ran out of control. One such time was in July 1784 when he moved for papers in an attempt to prove that a certain Almas Ali Khan had been murdered on Warren Hastings's orders. (Strictly speaking, he had not, but Hastings *had* enjoined the Company's Resident at Lucknow to secure the person of this Almas Ali Khan and bring him to justice, 'urging the Nabob on due conviction to punish him with death', and Burke had a copy of these secret instructions.) Provocation from the benches opposite led him to wander widely and wildly, prophesying divine punishment on England for her Indian barbarities.[20] Thurlow, the Lord Chancellor, who was neither easily moved by extravagant rhetoric nor himself given to mincing words, claimed this sort of outburst to be 'the ravings of a madman' which made him ashamed to live in such a country in such an age.[21]

Burke expected rough treatment from his political opponents; what worried him was that he now suffered sharp criticism from friends too. He suspected, and not without reason, that Fox was lukewarm in the campaign against Hastings, and there were others in the party who felt that his Indian indignation had become obsessive. Even William Windham, who together with Gilbert Elliot among the younger men of the party stood closest to Burke now on Indian affairs, admitted that his judgment in them was 'a standing topic of ridicule'.[22] When a close personal acquaintance, Joshua Reynolds's niece Mary Palmer, appeared to join the chorus of censure – at least to the extent of passing on to him hostile opinions sent to her from a friend in India – he was moved to justify himself to her in a revealing and disarming letter, more an apologia, of substantial length. It was by his *friends* that he needed to be understood. Indeed there is much to be said for the view that his decision to attempt the impeachment of Hastings was first undertaken, not in any expectation that it could succeed, but as an exercise in self-justification. 'Speaking for myself', he wrote to Philip Francis, 'my business is not to consider what will convict Mr Hastings (a thing we all know to be impracticable) but what will acquit and justify myself to those few persons and distant times which may take a concern in these affairs and the actors in them.' And why was conviction impracticable? – because 'we know that we bring before a bribed tribunal a prejudged cause'.[23]

To Miss Palmer in January 1786, along with an elucidation of what he had actually said in the complained-of Almas Ali Khan speech, he was writing:

> My dear Miss Palmer, how could you aplogize, and apologize to me too, for an act of good nature and kindness? I hear enough of my faults from my enemies; shall I not bear to hear them from my friends? . . . Tell your worthy correspondent, who is so good as to take an interest in me, that I am truly thankful, to him or her (whoever it may be) for their obliging sollicitude . . . The only favour I have to beg of my friends is

that they will form their judgments of me by what the records of Parliament, and not the fictions of newspapers, relate concerning me . . . [He refutes the notion that he was voicing a *party* view.] I have no party in this business, my dear Miss Palmer, but among a set of people who have none of your lilies and roses in their faces, but who are the images of the great Pattern as well as you or I. I know what I am doing, whether the white people like it or not. They hear, it seems, at Calcutta, that 'I am declined in popular favour'. That cannot be, for I never had any to lose . . . [This account] is written *thro* you, not *to* you; and I wish you to send it (blots and all, for I have written in a good deal of haste) to your Indian friend . . . My dearest Miss Palmer, God bless you; and send your friend home to you rich and innocent . . .[24]

During the summer recess of 1785 he took a short holiday from his Indian preoccupations, making a tour of the Scottish Highlands in the company of Windham, taking in the Lake District on their way home. Immediately before this, he and his wife had been entertaining at Beaconsfield a distinguished visitor from France, Mme de Genlis, who it seems turned out to be the sort of demanding guest whose departure is greeted with some relief.[25] A by-product of this visit, indirectly and strangely, was the form and manner in which, five years later, Burke's historic *Reflections on the Revolution in France* was given to the public. Mme de Genlis introduced to the Burkes a certain M. Depont, with whose eighteen-year-old son the family also became acquainted. Burke's onslaught of 1790 on the revolution and its English apologists was to be presented to the world as an extended *letter* to an unnamed young French friend. This was in fact Charles-Jean-François Depont.

The year after his Scottish expedition, Burke took a short holiday in Ireland. He had not been there for twenty years. Just before the main parliamentary attack on Hastings was due to begin, he decided – 'quite a sudden thought started by the fireside' – to take his son Richard over to Dublin 'to make him a little known there'. Unfortunately, Richard proved to be 'ill the whole time he was in Ireland' with a succession of colds, and moreover remained 'ailing' after his return.[26] They stayed three weeks, and had hoped to get to Loughrea to see Burke's sister Juliana, but had to end by each sending her instead a letter of apology. They did however manage to spend one night with the Shackletons, 'charming everybody' according to Mary Shackleton.[27] It proved to be the last time Burke saw his native land, and indeed he was never to see his sister again. She died at Loughrea in 1790.

Burke's conviction that the Hastings regime in India was evil predates his friendship with Philip Francis. He hardly *needed* the stimulus of Francis's hatred of Hastings and his cornucopia of hostile evidence; but certainly from the turn of the year 1781–2 when his close association with Francis began, his tone of attack took on a new missionary fervour.

None of the three principals in the story of the Hastings trial – Burke, Francis, and Hastings himself – should be seen in black and white. Even Francis, full as he was of grudges and personal animus, was more than a mere vengeful self-seeker. He was a man of cultivated intellect, with his own honestly critical view of the existing administration of Bengal and his own schemes for reform and improvement. But from the outset he had set the sights of his ambition upon supplanting Hastings as Governor-General. In the four-man Council set up under North's Regulating Act of 1773 he had led the opposition; had recorded eventually in an official minute that he found Hastings's public and private conduct 'void of truth and honour'; was consequently challenged to a duel and was wounded; and returned to England more than ready to furnish the enemies of Hastings with his highly partial version of events.

Warren Hastings had been in the Company's service in India since leaving Westminster School at the age of seventeen. He was without money when he began and, although in his early years he like most others dealt in private trade, at the end of thirty-five years in India he had not made a fortune which by the standard of the 'nabobs' would be thought substantial. Despite, during the early days of his governor-generalship, being constantly hampered and at times almost paralysed by the opposition of members of the Council – Francis in particular – he managed to reform the administration, judiciary, and finances of Bengal, and succeeded eventually not merely in maintaining British power and influence during a period of prolonged and intense crisis, but actually in extending them. Combining first with the ostensibly autonomous state of Oudh to defeat the threat to it from the Afghan tribesmen to its west, the Rohillas, he sustained Oudh afterwards as a buffer state, in effect a protectorate, against the powerful confederacy of the Marathas. Then the Company presidency in Bombay precipitated a complete rupture with the Marathas just at the most awkward of times when Britain was faced with French intervention in her war with the Americans. Hastings organised a remarkably successful sequence of operations to occupy France's remaining Indian possessions while at least temporarily holding in check the Marathas. Among much else, all this involved sending a Bengal force of some 6000 Indians under European officers across India to occupy Ahmadabad, overrun Gujarat, reach the western coast at Surat, and make an alliance, which proved long-lasting, with the Gaikwar of Baroda. Another expedition, into Central India, captured Gwalior. Then, when the armies of Haidar Ali of Mysore swept through the Carnatic almost to Madras, Hastings concentrated all available forces in a southward drive by land and sea to save the city.

These impressive military undertakings did not come cheap, and it was in certain of the measures he adopted to provide money for them by exactions from the treasuries of two quasi-independent princes, the Raja of Benares (Chait Singh) and the Nawab Wazir of Oudh, that some of the severest charges against him were to come. In the case of Oudh, the payment was forcibly extracted from the palace eunuchs of the Nawab Wazir's mother and grandmother, the soon-to-be-famous Begams (dowager princesses) of Oudh.

But Hastings was much more than an administrative reformer and organiser of victory. Like his enemies Francis and Burke, he was a man of wide scholarship and far-ranging intellectual curiosity; classically educated; a linguist, speaking Urdu and reading Persian, the official language of the Moghul Empire; the promoter of the first grammar of Bengali; a patron of Hindu and Sanskrit studies; creator of a botanical garden at Alipur – an Indian Kew – 'for curious and valuable exotics from all quarters', and one who was justifiably proud of his attachment to scientific studies. On his return to England this was one of the points on which he challenged his critics: had he not 'by public endowments, by personal attentions, and by the selection of men for appointments suited to their talents, given effectual encouragement' to the sciences?[28] Most important of all, *and exactly like Burke himself*, he thought it impracticable and undesirable to tamper with Indian laws, customs, religions, or institutions. Again as emphatically as Burke, he considered Hinduism – especially Hinduism, though this implied no hostility to Islam – worthy of something better than mere toleration. It deserved to be valued for itself. Europeans ought always to respect the virtues of non-European cultures.

This however was not the Hastings whom Burke recognised, or even knew. Burke's Hastings was 'the captain-general of iniquity'; a spiller of blood, a violator of Indian property rights and human dignities, an instigator of unnecessary wars; the man who had forced Chait Singh from his throne and committed impious outrage upon the princesses of Oudh; shown criminal extravagance by awarding contracts (in the opium trade for instance) on wasteful terms, and by paying inflated salaries; had himself accepted 'presents', not forgivably for services rendered, but culpably as bribes; and had for years been the complaisant chief of an institution whose corrupt servants' main concern had been to enrich themselves at India's expense.

Burke's first success in the moves towards impeachment lay in persuading *both* opposition groups, North's as well as Fox's, to adopt it as party policy. Then in February 1786, when the main assault began in the Commons, to his surprised satisfaction he found Pitt publicly prepared to allow, on some counts at least, that Hastings was 'censurable'. Over the next three months there were assembled for presentation to the House twenty-two 'high crimes and misdemeanours' to which Hastings would be invited to submit a reply.

When in May he began his defence, it was to a crowded Commons, but if members had come expecting fireworks they were disappointed. Hastings's answer to the accusations, though detailed, was ill-prepared, casual-sounding, and in places factually in error. His response for instance to the Begams of Oudh charge, perhaps the most crucial of all for him, had later to be revised and corrected. He had made a bad start. The hopes of the opposition rose further as it became apparent that important government supporters (Wilberforce for one) were disinclined to see Hastings escape scot-free. Many independent members too seemed of that same mind. When however on 18 May Burke formally presented the first of his twenty-two charges to the House – concerning the war with the Rohillas – he was defeated by 119 votes to 67. This came after Dundas, for the government, while admitting this war to have lacked justification, nevertheless insisted that Hastings had been 'the saviour of India'.[29]

An important vote came in June, on the charge relating to the treatment of Chait Singh, Raja of Benares. To a general raising of eyebrows, Pitt in the course of a weighty speech[30] declared that in trying to fine the Raja £500,000 Hastings had acted 'in a manner repugnant to principles, which ought not to give way to any motive of interest or policy whatever'. Such sentiments from such a leader were decisive, at least for this particular charge. It was clear too that Dundas was no longer hesitant. Indeed he proved positive and cooperative enough to be praised by Burke years later for being 'very fair and very earnest in this affair from the beginning'.[31]

The Benares vote gave Burke a majority of 40, but the campaign had little more than begun. As usual, the approach of summer signalled the close of the parliamentary session. It was not until the following January that the examination of witnesses and the debates on the charges were resumed, and then rather disastrously. His most important witness, the former Resident at Lucknow, Nathaniel Middleton, collapsed under sharp questioning from Sheridan, and left the Hastings case on the Begams charge looking in very poor shape. By the following month, after Sheridan had finished with it, it was quite in tatters. Sheridan's speech, a marathon virtuoso performance delighting the opposition, converting some waverers, impressing even the not easily impressed Pitt, ranks with the most brilliant and famous ever made in the House of Commons. The next day Pitt described the Begams charge as 'that of all others which bore the strongest marks of criminality', and by March he appeared to be no longer insisting that each of the twenty-two charges (there were eventually only twenty) must be separately heard and debated before the House moved forward. Despite this, however, he continued to delay the decisive vote for impeachment until after Sheridan and Francis had introduced further charges in April, by which time Hastings, now more energetic in his defence, had enlisted a corps of Commons sympathisers. Wilkes was one of them. But unfortunately for Hastings too many of these were 'East Indians', members Burke referred to acidly as 'the gentlemen of India', and too few independent or county members of any standing. The

House finally instructing Burke formally to inaugurate impeachment proceedings, Hastings was then arrested by the Serjeant-
at-Arms and released on bail of £40,000 pending trial before the
Lords.

Matters had to wait through another summer and autumn until
the new session began in December 1787. A committee of the
Commons was then appointed, which soon became the 'Committee of Managers' of the trial, with Burke as chairman, and
among the other eighteen members Fox, Sheridan, Windham,
Elliot, Grey, Burgoyne, Fitzpatrick, and Erskine. They had all
wished the name of Francis to be there too, but a mistrust (shared
by Pitt and Dundas) of his known bias against an old enemy produced an emphatic Commons vote against his inclusion – to
Burke's disappointment and indignation. A letter written by him
and signed by all the Managers fulsomely praised the talents and
qualities of Francis and requested his continued assistance.[32]

Hastings and the Committee of Managers both now set about
appointing counsel, and among the five chosen by the prosecution the names appear of two men very close to Burke, his
brother Richard and the young Dr French Laurence, who was
already a devoted admirer* and would one day become one of
Burke's literary executors. Richard Burke still held the Recorder-
ship of Bristol which he had acquired in 1783, but was fortunate
to be eligible for this new appointment, since in the autumn of
1787 he had had to take refuge from his creditors and spend the
winter in Brussels. His return was made possible by the generosity of an unnamed wealthy friend, almost certainly identifiable
as Earl Fitzwilliam. But whether Burke was wise to enlist him on
the prosecution payroll is surely doubtful – it inevitably
encouraged still more accusations of Burke family jobbery.

Another of Burke's supporters, Sir Gilbert Elliot, was over that
same winter, with Burke's encouragement and blessing, in
charge of the opposition's attempt to impeach Sir Elijah Impey,
for *his* 'high crimes and misdemeanours' while Chief Justice of

---

*An admirer certainly; but a comment which he made to Elliot is of interest,
concerning the difficulties of working with Burke to prepare a case: 'He does
so ride up and down, backwards and forwards, so trot, canter, and gallop
now on the high road, now on the turf and sometimes by a short cut, till he is
stuck in the mire or lost in a wood; that we are not in truth very far distant
from the place where we set out' (quoted Marshall, *The Impeachment of Warren
Hastings*, p. 69).

the Supreme Court in Bengal – in particular for the alleged judicial murder of Maharaja Nandakumar ('Nuncomar'), the minister once responsible for the finances of the Nawab of Bengal.

After Elliot's opening speech against Impey in December 1787, which was acclaimed almost as enthusiastically as Sheridan's on the Begams of Oudh, he wrote to his wife: 'The passage of my speech which was by far the most admired was a panegyric on Burke, which *you know* did come from the heart . . . I am told that Burke, during what I said of him, was affected so as to drop almost off his seat, and that he shrank down to half his size.'[33]

Since Burke believed Hastings to be guilty of connivance in the death sentence passed by the Supreme Court in 1775 – for a forgery alleged to have been committed six years before – it is not altogether clear why he did not include the Nandakumar 'murder' among his original twenty-two charges against Hastings. Nandakumar, an old hand at intrigue, was a long-established enemy of Hastings, who was indeed likely to have been not displeased to see him removed from the scene. That, however, in no way made Nandakumar innocent or Impey guilty; and Pitt and Dundas lost interest in the credibility of this separate Impey prosecution. The Commons rejected it in the end by 73 votes to 55, and any further allegations relating to Nandakumar were confined to the 'Presents' charge in the main prosecution against Hastings. (Hastings freely admitted that 'presents' had passed to him from the Nawab's treasury through the intermediacy of Nandakumar, but claimed that they represented what he engagingly called 'entertainment' – legitimate perquisites.)

Impeachment proceedings in Westminster Hall began at last on 13 February 1788. They were to last for more than seven years, although the number of days on which the court actually sat totalled no more than 149, and the length of each sitting seldom exceeded a few hours. For the year 1793, for instance, the average was below three hours; and until the following year the court never sat on three consecutive days.

The House of Lords thus in its capacity as a lawcourt drew from Burke arguments which seem initially to strengthen the case of those who have claimed that at the root of his political thought lay a belief in man's 'natural reason' and in a 'natural law' to which mere 'jurisprudence' – statute and common law alike – must be ultimately subservient. 'We have here' (in Westminster Hall), he told the Lords, 'the natural reason of men, the principles of honour . . . not the low principles of jurisprudence only';[34] and again:

> We are therefore a court which may eminently be called a court of honour – not a court of chicane. This is a court in which you judge principally from those principles which God has planted in the breasts of men, which education has improved and a high situation brings to perfection.[35]

This took the high ground, and sounded splendid; but on the record of earlier cases – against the Earl of Danby for instance in 1678, or Sacheverell during the reign of Queen Anne, or the Jacobite losers after the rebellions of 1715 and 1745 – the thesis looks fragile, since it is easily demonstrable that impeachment proceedings had in general been politically rather than judicially motivated. Probably such ringing declamations as these from Burke are best accepted as a fervent advocate's rhetoric rather than considered assertions of political doctrine. In any case Burke was always insisting that doctrine must never be so absolute that it conflicts with current practicalities.

One such immediate practical problem was the virtual certainty of a Lords' bias in favour of Hastings. This extended from the Lord Chancellor, Thurlow, and the Chief Justice, Kenyon, through all the bishops, to a comfortable majority of the lay peers likely to attend. As it turned out, only forty peers attended more than half of the sittings, and only twenty-nine eventually agreed to take part in the verdict.[36] The knowledge that the Managers were almost sure to lose on practically every charge meant, first, that it seemed to be in their interest to spin the trial out (which Burke was still trying to do at the very end in 1795), and second, that he and his fellow Managers were always conscious of addressing – and with maximum éclat and panache – the public rather than the peers. While he soon abandoned any solid hope of obtaining straightforward legal verdicts in his favour, he continued for years to think that he might convince 'the people' and thus justify himself to the world and to posterity.

The long period of preparation and the great interest already engendered by the Commons debates – Sheridan's brilliant performance in particular – ensured that the opening of the trial would provide a great occasion, a moment of high theatre. Tickets were eagerly sought, some changing hands at sensational prices. Fanny Burney had hers free from Queen Charlotte, to whom she was then Assistant Keeper of the Robes, and as she took her seat in the Great Chamberlain's box she was a-flutter with a mixture of excited expectation and warm indignation. The indignation arose from the strong sympathy she felt for Mr Hastings, whom she 'knew a little'. There he was now, immediately below her, a prisoner at the bar, first dropping to his knees in submission to the court, then by permission sitting. 'What an awful moment this for such a man':

> I shuddered, and drew involuntarily back, when, as the doors were flung open, I saw Mr Burke, as Head of the Committee, make his solemn entry. He held a scroll in his hand, and walked alone, his brow knit with corroding care and deep labouring thought – a brow how different to that which had proved so alluring to my warmest admiration when I first met him . . . How did I grieve to behold him now the cruel prosecutor (such to me he appeared) of an injured and innocent man.[37]

Miss Burney was present again on the second day of Burke's opening speech. He was still 'the great Edmund Burke' to her – 'great in defiance of all drawbacks':

> All I had heard of his eloquence, and all I had conceived of his great abilities, was more than answered by his performance. Nervous, clear, and striking was almost all that he uttered . . . When he narrated, he was easy, flowing, and natural: when he declaimed, energetic, warm, and brilliant . . . His satire had a poignancy of wit that made it as entertaining as it was penetrating; his allusions and quotations, as far as they were English and within my reach, were apt and ingenious; and the wild and sudden flights of his fancy, bursting forth from his creative imagination in language fluent, forcible, and varied, had a charm for my ear and my attention wholly new and perfectly irresistible.[38]

Irresistible he may have been, but when at the end Burke recognised her, and 'bowed with the most marked civility of manner', her curtsey 'was the most ungrateful, distant and cold; I could not do otherwise, so hurt I felt to see him the head of such a cause, so impossible I found it to utter one word of admiration'.[39]

Next it was for Fox and Grey to open the charge relating to the Raja of Benares. After that, the high point of the season – it is difficult to avoid the use of a theatrical or sporting vocabulary – was reached with Sheridan's second marathon performance on the Begams charge: a rhetorical triumph to be present at which some of the audience had to fight their way through a mêlée at the doors, while some bought their ticket at anything up to £50. The occasion gave Hastings 'a rooted contempt', as he understandably put it, for such of his countrymen who sought that kind of entertainment from his sufferings[40] – and it is true that the atmosphere in Westminster Hall during 'Sheridan's week' was reasonably akin to the one prevailing at the trial twelve years before of the notorious one-time Maid of Honour Elizabeth Chudleigh, Countess of Bristol and/or Duchess of Kingston. She had been found guilty by the Peers of bigamy, before a deliciously scandalised public gallery. In her case there had been an additionally enjoyable *frisson* coming from the knowledge that the statutory punishment was death. (It was not enforced.)

The 1788 season ended with Sheridan and the Begams, by which time only two of the twenty charges had been heard. During the ensuing recess there came another Westminster by-election, with Burke and his anti-Hastings ally Francis both canvassing actively for the Whig candidate Lord John Townshend. Among those possessing a vote was Dr Burney, who found himself in a difficulty, in those days of public voting. He did not feel that in conscience he could vote for Townshend, but had no wish to offend his friend and earlier modest benefactor Burke. He wrote therefore to explain; and both his need to write and Burke's response are entirely in character. 'You have little or no obligation to me', replied Burke, '. . . Therefore, my dear Sir, put your mind at ease . . . and be assured, that in the mind of one at least, there can be no trace left of an impression unfavourable to you.' In Fanny's hand there is a no less characteristic endorsement on this letter: 'Answer of Mr Burke . . . full of noble-minded ideas and elevated kindness'.[41]

He himself received a kindness – quite a substantial one – during that same summer. His physician, Dr Richard Brocklesby, who had been his contemporary at Trinity College Dublin, knowing well the constant condition of crisis in the Burke finances, had already made a will bequeathing him £1000; but now, advancing his generosity to this 'ornament of human kind' and 'very dear friend', he made the £1000 an immediate token of his 'sincere love and esteem'.[42]

A month or two afterwards Burke, his wife, his brother, and his cousin Edmund Nagle were on holiday together, enjoying what had now become the usual out-of-season break. Richard, junior, was not with them, but instead was trying to mend his health by taking a course of sea-bathing at Brighton. Burke and his party were touring and seeing the sights, which included 'Shakespeare scenery' at Stratford and the new manufactures in the Birmingham district. There they visited Matthew Boulton, who 'behaved very elegantly' and took them round his 'enchanted castle' – presumably the famous Soho manufactory. The weather denied them their proposed tour of William Shenstone's celebrated garden (The Leasowes) and the glories of Lord Lyttelton's neighbouring Hagley; but in late September they had arrived at their main destination, the fine Jacobean mansion of Crewe Hall in Cheshire, one of the more prestigious meeting-places of aristocratic Whig society. 'I am vastly pleased with this place', Burke wrote to his son. 'We build no such houses in our time.'[43]

It was the holiday season for royalty too. The King, with the Queen and Princesses, was taking the waters at Cheltenham, completing, it was thought, his recovery from certain spasmodic abdominal attacks he had been suffering earlier in the summer; attending the Three Choirs Festival at Worcester; being welcomed everywhere by big crowds. He returned to Windsor apparently cured, but in October the attacks began again, and they were now accompanied by agitation, 'flurry of spirits', hoarseness of voice, ungovernable volubility, sleeplessness, occasional delirium and, most alarming of all, mental confusion. Politicians were soon confronted with a crisis which for the next half-year would relegate the Warren Hastings impeachment to comparative unimportance. The King might recover or he might not, but for the time being he was certainly mad, and his condition posed acute constitutional problems. Was a Regent to be appointed and, if so, who? If the Prince of Wales, under what limitations, if any? And since the Prince of Wales was agreed to be the intimate associate of leading Whig politicians, had the wheel of fortune turned in the Whigs' favour at last?

CHAPTER
13

THE REGENCY CRISIS AND THE CONSTITUTION

FOX WAS away with Mrs Armistead in Italy when it first became clear that the King's illness (which accumulating evidence now decisively points to having been the rare blood disease, porphyria)[1] had carried him over the brink into mental derangement. It seemed at first that he might die, but in any case his capacity to continue effectively as sovereign, the 'third estate' of the realm, was at an end, perhaps temporarily, perhaps permanently. Of a sudden therefore, the prospects for the Whigs, who had been languishing or fretting on the opposition benches for fifteen of the last eighteen years, looked surprisingly rosy, since it was generally presumed that the Prince of Wales, *their* Prince of Wales, now of full age, must soon become either King or Regent, and that he would choose Whig ministers.

The friendly relations between the Prince and the followers of Fox did not however present an entirely clear-cut picture. For one thing, although the Prince was not without talents and virtues, he was not popular. His debts were mountainous; his dissipation notorious; his honesty and reliability suspect. The union he had made in 1785 with the twice-widowed twenty-nine-year-old Roman Catholic Maria Fitzherbert, though null and void under both the Act of Settlement and the Royal Marriages Act, had been a ceremony properly conducted according to the Anglican rite. Only a few days before its celebration, however, he had culpably misled his friend Fox, and led him into the most awkwardly false political position by telling him that reports of the marriage were malevolent and groundless. This had encouraged Fox publicly to deny its existence – an honest gaffe which Mrs Fitzherbert never, and the Prince of Wales only slowly and partially, forgave. The official, or nominal, head of the Fox party and leader of the Whig peers, the Duke of Portland, was another who had fallen out with the Prince – in his case over the issue of the more than princely debts parliament had been called upon to meet.

The Prince's popularity with the politically-minded public (Burke's 'the people') was to play a part also in the coming parliamentary struggle over the Regency question. Although Pitt and the leading ministerialists never allowed it to surface in their speeches, nevertheless it was always present to reassure them that they had plenty of support 'out of doors'. When one of their backbenchers, John Rolle, who had long made a speciality of the Fitzherbert affair and its attendant mischief, proved unable to resist the temptation to bring up the matter once again in the Commons, Pitt prudently refused him encouragement.

The fact that Fox was at many travelling-days' distance when news of the King's madness was first confirmed, allowed those Whigs who were on the spot at Westminster (notably Sheridan) to try their hand at counselling the Prince, carving a future Whig ministry and their own place in it out of the air, parleying (again Sheridan in particular) with any leading ministerialist deemed vulnerable to the promise of a post in the predominantly Whig government so confidently expected. Here the likeliest catch was Thurlow, the Lord Chancellor, who was known to be on poor personal terms with Pitt. With the Prince's approval, Sheridan was soon in busy negotiation with him, to the vexation and alarm of the 'shadow' Whig Chancellor, Lord Loughborough.

Burke had no love of these tactics, or any part in the jealous bickering which was soon making the Whig leaders a very unfraternal band of brothers. Sheridan and Burke, though in some eyes they shared the obloquy of being thought upstart Irish adventurers, never had much in common. Sheridan's personal triumph with his Begams speech had brought him no closer to Burke's deeply held views on India, and he was in fact already telling the Duchess of Devonshire, First Lady of the Whigs, that he was 'fearful of Burke's impetuosity' and 'heartily tired' of the impeachment. He wished Hastings 'would run away and Burke after him'.

In mid-November, mutual jealousies notwithstanding, the Whigs were confidently counting their chickens. There was no sign yet that the eggs were addled. By 28 November, a few days after Fox's return, the *Morning Post* was actually printing a list of some of the more important members of the imminently expected administration: Portland First Lord, Fox and Stormont Secretaries of State, Cavendish Chancellor of the Exchequer (*not* the young Charles Grey, who badly wanted the post), Sheridan Treasurer of the Navy (Sheridan and Grey were openly at loggerheads) – and Burke once again Paymaster of the Forces: *not* in the Cabinet.

Nobody, least of all Burke himself, expected him to be. From the beginning, in the days of Rockingham, he had never been thought of as Cabinet material: the brains and conscience maybe of the party; first among its pamphleteers and its orators (though even there too excitable and indiscreet to be deemed 'steady'); always the admired poor relation, the esteemed counsellor; but never one of the innermost circle when it came to distributing the top places. Confirmation of this special position assigned to Burke by the hierarchy, which he never openly questioned whatever his private resentment, emerges strikingly from an account given by Sir Gilbert Elliot of a conversation between himself, Charles Pelham, and the Duke of Portland – that 'virtuous, calm, steady character', as Burke described him[2] – in the middle of the Regency crisis. They were at the time still confident of being soon in office, and the Duke, one of Burke's greatest admirers and on excellent personal terms with him (Burke at Beaconsfield and Portland at Bulstrode were quite near neighbours), saw the need to do *something* for their impecunious friend, despite 'the many difficulties' which seemed to be in the way. What they agreed over dinner was that Burke ought to be rewarded, partly through his brother. Richard Burke should have the Treasury Secretaryship temporarily (at £3000 a year) until he could be found a £1000-a-year vacancy in customs and excise. Burke himself should have the Paymastership (at £4000); but since he could not expect to hold this for ever – or perhaps for very long – Portland proposed (so Elliot wrote to his wife):

> to grant him on the Irish establishment a pension of £2000 a year clear for his own life, and the other half to Mrs Burke for her life. This will make Burke completely happy, by leaving

his wife and son safe from want after his death, if they should survive him. The Duke's affectionate anxiety to accomplish this object, and his determination to set all clamour at defiance on this point of justice, was truly affecting . . .[3]

At this time Burke certainly would need all the comfort and support which he could get, and not only financially. His campaign against Hastings had already brought him hostile criticism, a good deal of it from within his own party, and during the winter of 1788–89 his standing was to be lower than at any other point in his public life. The extravagance of his rhetoric, his 'extremism', ill taste, madness even, were never more generally the object of attack and derision. Addington, a future prime minister and son to one of the royal doctors, giving his father an account of one of the Commons debates, wrote, 'Burke was violent almost to madness, and I believe his party may thank him for the diminution of their numbers'. Sir William Young saw him as 'folly personified, shaking his cap and bells under the laurels of genius'. Walpole's friend George Selwyn, wit and scandalmonger, wondered if it was right that the King should be in a strait waistcoat while such a man as Burke was at large. Four times in the series of debates which began on 10 December he was called to order for going beyond accepted parliamentary bounds, and several times had difficulty in continuing his speeches against laughter from the government benches.

Fox, hurrying home through France, and quite expecting to find the King dead upon his return, arrived back, physically exhausted, on 24 November. By the time that a conference to decide tactics was meeting at Carlton House – with the Prince of Wales and the Dukes of York, Portland, and Devonshire present, together with Sheridan and Grey, and Lords Stormont, North, and Loughborough (but not Burke) – Fox was too ill to attend, but not too ill to experience lively resentment at Sheridan's apparent attempt to take over effective leadership of the party. Sheridan in fact ever since the Mrs Fitzherbert affair had in some measure been supplanting Fox as the Whig closest to the Prince's ear. The advice he was giving him now had little to do with Burke's constitutionally principled, if less moderate, stance. Sheridan badly needed office and was ready for any deal that would advance the prospect. Over some of the period he and his wife were actually living with Mrs Fitzherbert, having recently been evicted from their own house from inability to pay the rent. The condition of Sheridan's finances was chronically close to catastrophe – closer even then Burke's.

The modicum of filial propriety which had been incumbent upon the Prince while he was still with his father at Windsor soon disappeared, and the newspapers were now able to report happy celebrations and junketings at Carlton House and Brooks's Club. Burke had some years before been elected a member at Brooks's, but in general he was a non-attender; it seems never paid his subscriptions; and certainly played no part in these premature jollities.

This did not mean that he was without strong views on the constitutional issue which he saw looming. Indeed not a Whig among them all had stronger convictions, or so passionate a certainty that they were constitutionally incontrovertible. His position was clear and uncompromising, and remained so throughout the crisis – to the point, his critics complained, of fanaticism. In a sense, he denied the existence of a problem at all. He had 'ever understood that our constitution was framed with so much circumspection and forethought that it wisely provided for every possible contingency, and that the exercise of the sovereign executive power could never be vacant.'[4]

In other words, the Prince's right to assume full powers as Regent immediately upon his father's lapse into madness was automatic and indefeasible. The Prince should have taken an immediate initiative, gone to Parliament, and announced his assumption, as Regent by hereditary right, of the executive powers of the Crown.[5] Searches into precedents, as Pitt was to propose (at least partly as a tactic of delay, hoping for the King to recover) would merely confuse, and were in any case irrelevant to their existing situation.

For Burke the British constitution had reached its pitch of perfection with the Revolution of 1688–9 and the subsequent Act of Settlement. Any search for precedents of earlier date might well lead parliament astray; and precedents selected tendentiously might arrive at some very strange conclusions.* No doubt

---

*An alleged precedent viewed most hopefully by ministerialists came from the reign of Henry VI, when a Regent *had* been appointed by Parliament. But in this case, as on somewhat parallel occasions during the reigns of Edward III and Richard II, there had been no Heir Apparent of full age.

there existed 'precedents of civil violence and the specious pretences of usurpers whilst their power was green and immature, ready to let others into a share of it'. Parliament however ought to be very cautious how it took 'every *event* in constitutional history as a *precedent in law*. If you do, I will be bold to say that there is not one kind of arrangement of your Throne, nor any one opinion concerning the right to it, that is not somewhere or other to be found in the records of this kingdom.' And he defied anyone to tell him of a precedent 'where the heir apparent was of full age and discretion, and fit to govern', as was the Prince of Wales.[6] Pitt's move to search for precedents he saw merely as a self-serving device, and the contention that Pitt had 'the people' on his side was a red herring: 'the disposition of the sovereign power is not in the will of the people'. The British monarchy must not be thought of as in any sense elective.

The extent to which he felt himself to be both unpopular with the public and a lonely figure within the party is emphasised by one of his Commons speeches in December. He was very ready, he said, 'to speak against the wishes of the people whenever they attempted to ruin themselves'. And as to whether his sentiments 'would be considered as favouring of Whig or of Tory principles, he was very indifferent . . . He gave himself no uneasiness to discover' what others thought of his wish for office, and 'he knew as little of the inside of [the Prince's] Carlton House as he did of [the King's] Buckingham House'.[7] This last was undoubtedly true. Burke always remained at a distance from the Carlton House circle, and – for all his uncompromising championing of the Prince's full hereditary rights – had as small a *personal* regard for him as had the Whigs' official leader Portland.

In the debates of early December Fox had been somewhat knocked off balance by Pitt. Explaining why the Prince had chosen to wait before taking up his powers – 'in deference to the constitution' – Fox nevertheless insisted that those powers were there by hereditary right, and no precedent could have relevance to the existing situation. Pitt then had the pleasure, as he put it, of 'unwhigging' Fox by demonstrating that it was Fox and the Whigs, those pretended enemies of crown prerogative, who now seemed to be standing for hereditary privilege, while the ministry wished declaration of a Regency to wait, first, upon a search among historical precedents, and subsequently upon a decision by the two Houses of Parliament. Was not *Fox*, in fact, committing 'treason to the constitution'? This was too much for Burke. First calling for moderation, he then launched into an extremely immoderate asssault upon Pitt. Were they to be charged with treason, he demanded, by one of the Prince's *competitors*?. Here, says the *Parliamentary History*, that most staid of records, 'there was a loud cry of order from the treasury side of the House'. Yes, said Burke – shouted perhaps? – he would repeat the charge. Was not Pitt setting himself up as *competitor* to the Prince?

The inference to be drawn from these angry words was plain. He saw Pitt seeking to maintain his own power, or at least a share of power, not by a *denial* of the Prince's claim to the Regency but by subjecting it to parliamentary investigation, probably to statutory limitations, and in any case to delay. Pitt was demanding

> that the representative of the kingly honours shall have no other power than the House of Commons shall think fit to allow him; that the constitution shall in fact be changed, be overturned and annihilated. For his own part, he was perfectly contented with the constitution as he found it; he wanted no alteration; but there were others who did, and who set little or no value on the wisdom, integrity and patriotism of our ancestors . . .[8]

Among the 'others' was, naturally enough, his old *bête noire* Shelburne, now Marquis of Lansdowne. Baldly enough Lansdowne stated what to Burke was flagrant constitutional heresy: the right of nominating the Regent rested 'in the people'; the Prince of Wales ought indeed to be chosen, 'not from any claim of right on his part . . . but from the unanimous voice of a nation of freemen' as expressed by votes in the two Houses.[9]

This line of argument, however repugnant to Burke, won the day with some ease, not only in both Houses of Parliament but equally 'out of doors' with a majority of the newspapers, pamphleteers, and politically aware public. During January, with the doctors differing widely on the King's chances of recovery, the leading Whigs were still bickering among themselves and elbowing one another for vantage in the expected disposition of new posts. Fox's health grew worse rather than better, and before the end of the month he had retired to Bath, some said more in dudgeon that in serious sickness, but entirely and unreasonably optimistic of the final outcome. Even when the King did later begin unmistakably to mend, Fox obstinately refused to believe it. 'As to the poor man, he is mad', he wrote to Mrs Armistead.

The parliamentary debates of January turned mainly on Pitt's proposal to set restrictions on the Prince's prerogative when or if he became Regent. These were to include a removal of power to grant 'any office, salary, or pension whatever in reversion', and of 'the care of his Majesty's royal person'. (This was to be committed to the Queen.) But probably the most important of the proposed limitations was a ban on the Regent's power to create peers. This might have proved crucial, since management of the Upper House by the creation of new peers was an accepted feature of Georgian governmental tactics. George III and Pitt made lavish use of it.

Burke refrained from further attacks in the Commons during January, though he was one of the members' committee early in the month examining the royal physicians, notably Dr Francis Willis (Pitt's man) and Dr Richard Warren (the Prince's) – two experts whose prognoses, predictably, were widely at variance. Away from the Commons he decided, most characteristically, to try instructing himself on the subject of insanity. This course of study included a visit to a madhouse for 300 people at Hoxton, in the charge of a Mrs Harrison. He inquired particularly, it seems, the proportion of patients aged fifty or over (George III was fifty) who recovered their sanity.[10] Visits to other madhouses followed. He also examined as far as he was able the historical evidence of madness among European royal houses. These and perhaps further researches were to prepare the background to his next month's speech, which, above all others which he made during the Regency crisis, reduced the Commons benches to a state of shocked or, with some, hilarious incredulity.

But before that, he sat down to compose a careful letter, of many pages, to the man who, with Elliot, stood now nearest to him in the party, William Windham. First he explains that he has been spending some of his time 'in retreat', partly for the benefit of his health, but partly too because the Regency affair had been getting on top of him: 'I begin to find that I was grown rather too anxious'. Had it not been for 'the India business', which bound him 'in point of honour', he would seriously think of retirement. Indeed, *had* seriously thought: 'I sincerely wish to withdraw myself from this scene for good and all'.[11]

A cool analysis of the events of the preceding two months follows, far distant from the heated atmosphere of his parliamentary speeches: an explanation of how Fox had rejected his original advice favouring an immediate strong initiative from the Prince; how, although there had been a few 'consultations upon particular measures', there had been 'none at all *de summa rerum*'; how the party ought to approach what at that point (late January) seemed a real possibility, a Fox–Pitt coalition; how Pitt now undoubtedly entertained an intention 'of addressing the Prince to keep him in power'; how he was 'wholly at a loss' to comprehend Sheridan's speeches; but how, if it was Sheridan who had the Prince's ear, then all that he, Burke, said was 'vain and useless'; how the Whigs ought to conduct themselves if they came finally to accept defeat – leave parliamentary attendance perhaps to a 'corps of observation' only, and concentrate on the battle 'out of doors'? If nobody had the spirit and integrity to get it into the Prince's head that there was 'a dreadful struggle' ahead,

> he is, and we are, ruined. He must marry into one of the sovereign houses of Europe. Till then he will be liable to every suspicion and to daily insult . . . No King in Europe who is not married, or has not been so: no Prince appears settled unless he puts himself into the situation of the father of a family.[12]

These last observations were particularly relevant to the Prince's reported intention, if he became Regent, of 'making Mrs Fitzherbert as happy as he could make her' but giving her no rank.

Throughout January the King's physical illness and mental balance pursued their perplexingly erratic courses, sometimes markedly improved, sometimes very bad indeed, with unhappy recourse to the strait waistcoat and the 'restraining chair'. Once he knelt and prayed that he might recover his sanity or die. Two days later he was well enough to remember that it was the Queen's birthday and asked for a new coat to receive her in. By the first week in February he was sufficiently recovered to take walks, practically on his own, in the gardens of Kew House – and on one of these had that chance encounter with Fanny Burney so memorably described by her; at first desperately alarming, but in the end reassuring and delightful.[13]

Pitt had played his cards well, but had also been very lucky.

The Regency Bill did not come up for its first reading until 5 February, just as the King was at last incontestably better, and in fact asking on 10 February to see the Lord Chancellor (still Thurlow, prudently reconciled in good time to staying with Pitt); since he had been ill for seventeen weeks, he said, and had much to inquire about.

It was at this time, during the debates of 5 to 11 February, that Burke made some of his most violent attacks on Pitt's proposed measures.[14] They would degrade the Prince of Wales. They insulted alike common sense and the House of Hanover. They would cause 'a total revolution in the splendour of the Crown'. By restricting the Prince's right to create peers they were 'shutting the door of the House of Lords against the people', and by putting it out of their power ever to correct their error they were making the House of Lords virtually 'independent and omnipotent'. Already much interrupted and called to order, on 11 February he gave the House some of the fruits of his recent researches; and it was generally then thought that he passed permissible limits of taste and judgment. Having explained to the House his recent reading and his visits to 'those dreadful mansions where these unfortunate beings are confined', and observed how 'horrible in the extreme' it would be if the King suffered a sudden relapse – a quite probable eventuality, he suggested – he proceeded to read out an extract from a volume by 'an author of great authority' whom he had recently been studying on the subject of lunacy:

> Some of these individuals, after a supposed recovery, had committed suicide, others had butchered their sons, others had done violence to themselves by hanging, shooting, drowning, throwing themselves out of windows, and by a variety of other ways . . . (Cries of Oh! Oh! . . . Order!).[15]

Two months later, Burke was still refusing, almost as stubbornly and sourly as Fox, to credit the fact that the King was indeed once more in command of himself. 'He is much and materially alterd', he wrote to Lord Charlemont on 4 April – which was no doubt true, but what followed was not: 'He is in the most complete subjection to those who are called his attendants but are in reality his keepers.'[16]

But by that time the Regency issue was dead, at least for the next dozen years. It had, however, by bringing Whig differences and rivalries to the surface, played its significant part in the old Rockingham party's disintegration which the next few years would see completed. Although it was to be conflict over attitudes to the French Revolution that precipitated the final split, already beforehand the continuing Hastings trial played its part too. It was not only Sheridan who was thoroughly tired of it. Fox and several others would have been glad to see Burke willing to give up; but for him that was out of the question. He was 'bound in honour'.

Sheridan now excused himself from proceeding with the 'presents' charge, though Burke had tried to persuade him – through Mrs Sheridan, to whom he wrote praising her husband's 'great and vigorous mind'. While willing to respect Burke as 'leader and general' in the matter, Sheridan nevertheless declared that he would best serve the cause, which he *professed* to have sincerely at heart, by *not* helping in its presentation.[17]

Burke himself therefore opened the presents charge, and ran into immediate trouble by asserting that Hastings had 'murdered' Nandakumar 'by the hand of Sir Elijah Impey'. Hastings thereupon petitioned the Commons for protection, and at the end of a four-day debate on the issue, a resolution was approved that Burke's words 'ought not to have been spoken'. Many years later, Grey said that on the strength of that virtual vote of censure Fox intended trying to halt the prosecution, but that on the vital morning he arrived late for a meeting of the Managers, who advised Burke to continue.[18] If Fox had only been punctual and pressed his point, the fateful Burke–Fox rift of 1791, it has been suggested, might well have occurred two years earlier, for Burke would certainly not have agreed to abandon the impeachment.[19] As he wrote to one of the Managers, Frederick Montagu, at precisely this time, 'Neither hope, nor fear, nor anger, nor weariness, nor discouragement of any kind, shall move me from this trust – nothing but an act of the House, formally taking away my commission, or totally cutting off the means of performing it.'[20]

CHAPTER
14

REVOLUTIONISTS, DISSENTERS, AND THE 'PARIS LETTER'

WHILE THE Hastings trial was being resumed in 1789 the French States-General was assembling for the first time in 165 years. That year's sessions in Westminster Hall ended for Burke in complete frustration. Meanwhile the sporadic rioting of the spring and early summer in provincial France (culminating in the *Grande Peur*) went largely unnoticed in England. What followed, however, another outbreak of what Burke called 'the old Parisian ferocity', made big news: the sensational July explosion of violence in Paris. The metaphor was already Burke's own. 'It is true', he wrote to the Irish Whig Charlemont, 'that this may be no more than a sudden explosion: if so, no indication can be taken from it. But if it should be character rather than accident, then that people are not fit for liberty.'[1] Soon he was no longer prepared to suspend judgment, congratulating Windham in late September on safe return from 'a country where the people, along with their political servitude, have thrown off the yoke of law and morals'. France by now had a 'National Assembly'; but, he wrote:

> It does not appear to me that the National Assembly have one jot more power than the King; whilst they lead or follow the popular voice in the subversion of all orders, distinctions, priveleges, impositions, tythes, and rents, they appear omnipotent; but I very much question whether they are in a condition to exercise any function of decided authority – or even whether they are possessed of any real deliberative capacity, or the exercise of free judgment in any point whatever: as there is a mob of their constituents ready to hang them if they should deviate into moderation . . .[2]

By mid-October, after the so-called 'march of the women' on Versailles, the kidnapping of the King and Queen, and Louis' unconditional surrender to the authority of the Assembly (then led by Mirabeau, five years earlier a guest at Beaconsfield), Burke, though not yet fully apprised of the French royal family's humiliation and danger, noted that 'the elements which compose human society' seemed to have dissolved,

> and a world of monsters to be produced in the place of it – where Mirabeau presides as the Grand Anarch; and the late Grand Monarch makes a figure as ridiculous as pitiable. I expect to hear . . . that he has chosen a corps of Paris Amazons for his bodyguard . . . Here, thank God, we are all in our senses.[3]

Alas, he did not long think so. There was much sympathy for the people of France, seen to be emulating the English example of a 'glorious revolution'; and this feeling was shared both by prominent members of Burke's own party and by those political radicals, many of them Dissenters, who belonged to the Revolution Society, a group meeting yearly on 4 November to celebrate the anniversary of the 1688 revolution. This year on that day, at Old Jewry in London, they gathered to hear from a Dissenting preacher, Dr Richard Price, (who had earlier been one of Shelburne's protégés) an address hailing with enthusiasm France's revolution and the exalted ideas alleged to be behind it. One month later this address, or sermon, generally accepted as the spark which fired Burke's dynamite, was published.

But, before that, the *Reflections* were beginning to take shape. In November, Burke had received a letter (written on the very day of Price's sermon) from the young Frenchman Charles Depont,* to whom he and his family had played host in England four years before. Well before Price's words were in print, Burke was composing a lengthy reply to 'young Picky Poky', as the Burkes among themselves mysteriously knew Depont. It was of modest proportions compared with those assumed eventually by the *Reflections*, but contained a good deal of matter central to the philosophy which that book would enshrine.

*Depont, or de Pont, but not Dupont, as he has sometimes been presented. Dupont confusingly enough was the name of the first, and not very successful, translator of Burke's *Reflections* into French: Pierre Gaëton Dupont. The first Paris edition, produced at lightning speed but not without 53 errata, sold 9000 copies within three months. A German translation soon followed.

Depont was by now a member of the *comité patriotique* of Metz and had already spoken in the National Assembly in Paris. He had asked Burke for an honest opinion of what was happening in France, hoping, he said, for a reassurance that Burke wished the revolution well and would recognise that Frenchmen would know how to distinguish between liberty and licence, between legitimate government and despotism. 'As you are pleased to think', Burke replied, 'that your splendid flame of liberty was first lighted up at my faint and glimmering taper, I thought you had a right to call upon me for my undisguised sentiments on whatever related to that subject . . . You hope, Sir, that I think the French deserving of liberty?'

I certainly do. I certainly think that all men who desire it, deserve it . . . It is our inheritance. It is the birthright of our species. We cannot forfeit our right to it, but by what forfeits our title to the privileges of our kind; I mean the abuse or oblivion of our national faculties, and a ferocious indocility which makes us prompt to wrong and violence, destroys our social nature, and transforms us into something little better than the description of wild beasts. To men so degraded, a state of strong constraint is a sort of necessary substitute for freedom; since, bad as it is, it may deliver them in some measure from the worst of all slavery, that is the despotism of their own blind and brutal passions . . . Of all the loose terms in the world liberty is the most indefinite . . . it is not solitary, unconnected, individual, selfish liberty . . . The liberty I mean is *social* freedom. It is that state of things in which liberty is secured by the equality of restraint . . . This kind of liberty is but another name for justice, ascertained by wise laws, and secured by well constructed institutions . . .

When therefore I shall learn that in France the citizen, by whatever description he is qualified, is in a perfect state of legal security with regard to his life, to his property, to the un-controlled disposal of his person, to the free use of his industry and his faculties; – When I hear that he is protected in the beneficial enjoyment of the estates to which, by the course of settled law, he was born, or is provided with a fair compensation for them; – that he is maintain'd in the full fruition of the advantages belonging to the state and condition of life in which he had lawfully engaged himself, or is supplied with a substantial, equitable equivalent; – When I am assured that a simple citizen may decently express his sentiments upon publick affairs without hazard to his life and safety, even tho' against a predominant and fashionable opinion; When I know all this of France, I shall be as well pleased as every one must be who has not forgot the general communion of mankind . . .

. . . I am not so narrow-minded as to be unable to conceive that the same object may be attain'd in many ways, and perhaps in ways very different from those which we have follow'd in this country . . . It is not my having long enjoyed a sober share of freedom under a qualified monarchy that shall render me incapable of admiring and praising your system of republicks . . .

But if . . . neither your great assemblies, nor your judicatures, nor your municipalities act and forbear to act in these particulars upon the principles and in the spirit that I have stated, I must delay my congratulations on your acquisition of liberty. You have made a revolution, but not a reformation. You may have subverted monarchy, but not recover'd freedom.[4]

Thus far on liberty; but in the pages that follow we see more of the *Reflections* in embryo. On the tolerability of imperfections, for instance, and the relationship between ends and means:

Let me add . . . that you ought not to be so fond of any political object as not to think the means of compassing it a serious consideration. No man is less disposed than I am to put you under the tuition of a petty pedantick scruple in the management of arduous affairs: all I recommend is, that whenever the sacrifice of any subordinate point of morality, or of honour, or even of common liberal sentiment and feeling is called for, one ought to be tolerably sure that the object is worth it. Nothing is good, but in proportion, and with reference . . .

A positively vicious and abusive government ought to be chang'd and if necessary by violence, if it cannot be . . . reformed: but when the question is concerning the more or the less *perfection* in the organization of a government, the allowance to *means* is not of so much latitude. There is, by the essential, fundamental constitution of things a radical infirmity in all human contrivances, and the weakness is often so attached to the very perfection of our political mechanism that some defect in it, something that stops short of its principle, something that controls, that mitigates, that moderates it, becomes a necessary corrective to the evils which the theoretick perfection would produce . . .

It is true that every defect is not, of course, such a corrective as I state; but supposing it is not, an imperfect good is still a good. The defect may be tolerable, and may be removed at some future time. In that case, prudence (in all things a virtue, in politicks the first of virtues) will lead us rather to acquiesce in some qualified plan that does not come up to the full perfection of the abstract idea, than to push for the more perfect, which cannot be attain'd without tearing to pieces the whole contexture of the commonwealth, and creating an heartache in a thousand worthy bosoms. In that case, combining the means and end, the less perfect is the more desirable.[5]

He begs Depont's pardon for the freedom with which he has written – 'I have been led further than I intended' – but does not end without some further characteristic reflections on the subject of moderation:

Believe me, Sir, in all changes in the state, moderation is a virtue not only amiable but powerful. It is a disposing, arranging, conciliating, cementing virtue. In the formation of new constitutions it is in its province: great powers reside in those who can make great changes. Their own moderation is their only check; and if this virtue is not paramount in their minds, their acts will taste more of their power than of their wisdom or their benevolence. It will be submitted to with grudging and reluctance; revenge will be smother'd and hoarded; and the duration of schemes made in that temper will be as precarious as their establishment was odious.[6]

Burke did not see a copy of Price's sermon until mid-January 1790, and probably did not plan a full-length book upon events in France much, if at all, before that date. He had been at Beaconsfield, enjoying a long stretch of what he called 'idleness complete' or, as Elliot put it, 'grazing . . . , enjoying your pasture and leisure'. When he was back in London, ready for the new parliamentary session on 21 January, the immediate subject requiring a decision from him, though it did have French revolutionary connections, was essentially domestic. Not for the first time parliament was due to vote on removing the civic disabilities of the Dissenters remaining under the terms of the previous century's Test and Corporation Acts. The operation of these was by this time largely theoretical, eighteenth-century practice having to a great extent connived at their non-enforcement, but naturally their existence was deeply resented.

197

All his life Burke had supported the cause of full toleration for Protestant dissent, as for Catholic, while consistently refusing to concede them parity with the Church of England, which he always maintained was an integral part of the state's structure. In parliament and out, he was known to be one of the staunchest champions of religious freedom.

For at least the past five years, however, some of the postures adopted by prominent Dissenters had been troubling him. These men had come out strongly against the Foxite Whigs in the 'massacre' of the 1784 election. Some of their publicists and pamphleteers had been campaigning also, not merely for the repeal of the old discriminatory legislation but actively against the Church of England. That Burke would not forgive. When a motion for repeal of certain clauses in the two acts had come before the Commons in May 1789, he had been cool in his support, and was not present when the vote was taken – and lost. Now, when a new attempt was being made and he was approached again, his response was hostile. A 'considerable party', he thought, was 'proceeding systematically to the destruction' of some essential parts of the constitution. He was not alone in this; among the Whigs, Portland and Cavendish agreed with him, although Fox, despite Dissenter attacks on him mainly for what was claimed to be his lack of moral probity, remained ready to vote for repeal. (Burke came warmly to Fox's defence over the personal nature of these attacks and noted afterwards with bitterness that Price's sermon itself contained a veiled attack on Fox's immorality.)[7]

Giving chapter and verse to account for his apparent change of position on the Test and Corporation Acts, Burke cited the publications of such leading Dissenters as Samuel Palmer, John Robinson, Joseph Priestley (another of Shelburne's protégés) and, of course now, Richard Price. These and others showed 'a warm, animated, and acrimonious hostility against the Church establishment' and clearly wished to subvert it. He would therefore withhold his support until they came to consider the Church of England as 'a jealous friend to be reconciled, and not an adversary that must be vanquished'. In the debate before the Commons vote was taken in March 1790, he offered however something of an olive branch, suggesting that the sacramental 'test' of the Test Act should be replaced by an oath renouncing any attack on the established church – and it was something very like this which came to be accepted in the eventual repeal of 1828.[8]

A few weeks before this debate and vote, coming home from the dinner party at which he had defended Fox's reputation against some censorious Dissenter fellow-guests, he had read Price's sermon, 'late as it was, before I went to bed', and it had concentrated his mind wonderfully. He started straight away on his *Reflections*, at which he was to work steadily for the next seven months.

Criticism from friends and political allies, his current occupation being public knowledge, led him into some pre-publication private controversies, in which he was able to expand and clarify his views. To one acquaintance, Thomas Mercer, who had written to express his shock at reading in the newspapers of Burke's opinions and activities, his lengthy reply reads like a series of addenda or footnotes to the *Reflections* then in progress.* For instance, one of the central pillars of Burke's temple of political principles was his doctrine of 'prescription': 'prescriptive rights . . . that grand title which supersedes all other title' – that right to enjoy property or privilege or honour hallowed by the passage of time. It is possible, he argued, that 'many estates about you' – he was writing to an *Irishman* from County Down – 'were originally obtained by arms, that is by violence . . . but it is an *old violence*, and that which might be wrong in the beginning is consecrated by time and becomes lawful.' Mercer had declared such prescriptive rights to be 'accumulations of ignorance and superstition'. Very well, replied Burke, 'I had rather remain in ignorance and superstition than be enlightened and purified out of the first principles of law and natural justice'. As for property rights, 'I will never suffer you, if I can help it, to be deprived of the well-earned fruits of your industry' – Mercer from poor beginnings had become rich – 'because others may want your fortune more than you do . . . Nor, on the contrary, if you . . . had come home insolvent, would I take from [Mercer's phrase] any "pampered and luxurious lord" in your neighbourhood one acre of his land, or one spoon from his sideboard, to compensate your losses.' 'The order of property which I find established in my country' ought to be *secure*.

*In his turn, Mercer published a ten-page reply to Burke's reply, printed eventually in the *Monthly Magazine* of 1802.

Mercer had welcomed the confiscation of Church property in France to provide the basis for an annual state stipend to priests of 2000 livres; but for Burke this was a 'spoliatory reformation', overturning 'the sacred principles of property' and tending to subvert both church and state:

My dear Captain Mercer . . . when you find me attempting to break into your house to take your plate, under any pretence whatsoever, but most of all under pretence of purity of religion and Christian charity shoot me for a robber and an hypocrite, as in that case I shall certainly be. The 'true Christian religion' never taught me any such practices, nor did the religion of my nature, nor any religion, nor any law.[9]

He was equally forthright on other topics of the hour – Despotism and Democracy; Autocratic Tyranny and Mob Tyranny. Mercer had written 'I had long considered you the determined enemy of tyranny and oppression'. So he was, Burke assured him, so he was; but proceeded thoughtfully:

The tyranny of the autocrat seldom attacks the poor, never in the first instance. They are not its proper prey. It falls on the wealthy and the great, whom by rendering objects of envy and otherwise obnoxious to the multitude, they may more easily destroy; and when they are destroyed that multitude which was led to that ill work . . . is itself undone for ever.

I hate tyranny . . . But I hate it most of all where most are concerned in it. The tyranny of a multitude is a multiplied tyranny. If, as society is constituted in these large countries of France and England, full of unequal property, I must make my choice (which God avert!) between the despotism of a single person or of the many, my election is made. As much injustice and tyranny has been practised in a few months by a French democracy as in all the arbitrary monarchies in Europe in the forty years of my observation.

When Burke received early proofs of that part of his 'Paris letter' already written, he showed a copy to Francis as the only friend, so he said, who would dare to give him advice – with gentle self-irony reflecting 'what a rough and menacing manner' he must have, to frighten the others off. When Francis returned his comments, they were so far from encouraging (though he apparently considered them largely 'sportive') that the two men's friendship never fully recovered. Francis judged the whole enterprise – this 'war of pamphlets with Doctor Price' – mistaken and lacking in dignity; it would only lead to a 'vile and disgraceful' public altercation. It contained moreover too many 'jibes and insinuations'; Burke would be doing himself a mischief.

The pages so frowned upon happened also to contain the passage on the French Queen which was to become so famous – Burke recalling his seeing her at Versailles all those years ago in her youthful beauty; but then:

> Oh, what a revolution! and what a heart must I have to con-template without emotion that elevation and that fall! . . . Little did I dream that I should have lived to see such disasters fallen upon her in a nation of gallant men, in a nation of men of honour, and of cavaliers. I thought ten thousand swords must have leapt from their scabbards to avenge even a look that threatened her with insult. But the age of chivalry is gone. That of sophisters, economists, and calculators has succeeded; and the glory of Europe is extinguished for ever.[10]

Francis found these eloquent cadences to contain 'foppery'; Burke was using expressions 'ridiculous in any but a lover'. If he considered Marie Antoinette a 'perfect female character' he should have based his observations not on her beauty but upon her virtue. (In fact, Burke was far indeed from thinking her perfect; already with strong reservations about her, increasingly he was to think the behaviour both of Marie Antoinette and of Louis XVI highly imprudent.) Francis went on to criticise Burke – if 'sportively', it did not seem so – for the looseness of his com-position; he wished he might be allowed to teach him how to write English.[11] Naturally Burke was hurt, though in his digni-fied reply he modestly did not choose to contest this last sally.[12] But the attack by Francis on the Marie Antoinette passage was answered with feeling:

> I tell you again that the recollection of the manner in which I saw the Queen of France in the year 1774 [actually 1773] and the contrast between that brilliancy, splendour, and beauty, with the prostrate homage of a nation to her, compared with the abominable scene of 1789 which I was describing did draw tears from me and wetted my paper. These tears came again into my eyes almost as often as I looked at the description . . . My friend, I tell you it is truth . . .[13]

This letter was sent to Francis enclosed in a considerably more reproachful one from Richard Burke junior. 'My father's opinions are never hastily adopted', he wrote, not troubling to conceal his indignation; 'they were the result of systematick meditation . . . Are you so little conversant with my father . . . to mistake the warmth of his manner for the heat of his mind? . . . I tell you, his folly is wiser than the wisdom of the common herd of able men.'

Just one year later – one year nearer to the guillotine – Marie Antoinette herself, 'through the means of Miss Wilkes', John Wilkes's daughter then in France, was shown the French translation of Burke's already almost elegiac reflections upon her fate. 'One of the Queen's bedchamber women', Burke was told, 'carried it to the Queen, who before she had read half the lines, she burst into a flood of tears, and was a long time before she was sufficiently composed to peruse the remainder.'[14]

'REFLECTIONS ON THE REVOLUTION IN FRANCE'

THE *Reflections on the Revolution in France* is a book covering a wide assortment of topics – English, French, political, religious, historical, economic, financial, military, social, philosophical; the diversity suggests Polonius introducing the Players in *Hamlet*. It is also a work written on several different levels; Polonius, we may remember, added, 'Seneca cannot be too heavy, nor Plautus too light'. On one level the *Reflections* might reasonably be judged 'light' in the sense that they contain knockabout controversy of the sort to be expected in a war of tracts or pamphlets; with no holds barred; with plenty of the 'jibes and insinuations' that Francis considered to be beneath Burke's dignity; and with a liberal deployment of insult for those deemed deserving of it – such as the 'little, shrivelled, meagre, hopping insects of the hour' for the radicals of the Revolution Society; or the 'swinish multitude' for the murderous Paris mobs; or the 'petulant, assuming, short-sighted coxcombs' of literary men and *philosophes* who had helped dig the pit which the French had fallen into.

Dr Price ('chanting his prophetic song') was a man much connected with such 'literary caballers and intriguing philosophers, with political theologians and theological politicians, both at home and abroad'. Even if he had been talking political sense from his pulpit, instead of his 'sort of porridge' of opinions, the pulpit was not the place to talk it from. 'Politics and the pulpit are terms that have little agreement. No sound ought to be heard in the church but the healing voice of Christian charity.'[1]

Much of the latter half of the *Reflections* consists of detailed criticism of the policies and contrivances of the (as he insisted) *Paris*-dominated National Assembly – the confiscation of church property; currency reform with the *assignats*; administrative reform with the *départements*; the treatment meted out to the royal family, to the nobility, to the monasteries, the army, the judiciary; in sum, the 'imbecility' of the 'puerile, pedantick system . . . they call a constitution'.[2] But the main substance of the book – though it avoids the abstract theorising Burke always condemned, and constantly argues from contemporary and historical *events* both French and English – does present, however incidentally or tangentially, and in however higgledy-piggledy shape, a considered philosophy of politics and society which may fairly be called essential mature Burke.

Burke's book was written in a passion, and at speed. It can hardly expect to emerge unscathed from a modern dispassionate critique. But as the author of one of the weightiest political tracts of recent centuries Burke here may well be allowed a free run, unchallenged yet by Tom Paine and the *Rights of Man*;* his English unassisted by Philip Francis; uninterrupted by the parliamentary cries of 'Oh! Oh!' and 'Order' to which he had recently been so continually subjected; unedited and un-corrected by modern scholars who without difficulty find mistakes and omissions in his analysis of the *ancien régime* in France or of English constitutional history, who point to his neglect of events immediately preceding the great eruption of 1789, to his failure to understand that it was the *révolte nobiliaire* of 1787–8 which first validated the appeal to violence, and above all to his apparent unawareness of the crucial nature of economic facts which set the conflagration alight – a succession of harvest failures, industrial depression, extremely severe unemploy-ment, half-starved country workers drifting into the towns, Paris especially, to swell the ranks of the disaffected urban mobs.

For the first thirty or so pages, the *Reflections on the Revolution in*

---

*It is amusing and ironical to find Tom Paine, ignorant of the nature of the book Burke was midway through writing, sending him from Paris a very long and optimistic account of the latest developments there. Burke had met and entertained Paine, 'the great American' as he called him, some years earlier, and had taken him over to Bulstrode to dine with the Duke of Portland. He and Paine later spent some days as fellow guests of Earl Fitzwilliam at Went-worth Woodhouse. The three men together visited the nearby Yorkshire ironworks where Paine's iron bridge project was in train.

France are concerned hardly with France at all, but with the dangers facing England, and with the _English_ revolution of 1688 which Dr Price and the Revolution Society were celebrating. Confessing his 'anxious apprehensions', Burke explains: 'Whenever our neighbour's house is on fire, it cannot be amiss for the engines to play a little on our own'.[3] And it was not Britain alone that was under threat: 'Many parts of Europe are in open disorder. In many others there is a hollow murmuring under the ground; a confused movement is felt, and threatens a general earthquake in the political world.'[4]

According to Dr Price, the Revolution of 1688 had given Englishmen 'the right to choose their own governors', and hence George III was 'almost the only lawful king in the world'. This Burke had little difficulty in dismissing as a 'gross error of fact', the British monarchy being demonstrably hereditary. The undisturbed succession of the crown moreover was a security for the liberty of the people, and 'a pledge of the stability and perpetuity of all the other members of our constitution'. If it were objected that in 1688, with the expulsion of James II and the accession of William and Mary, there had been a breach of the strict principle of hereditary succession, that was true. But 'an irregular, convulsive movement may be necessary to throw off an irregular, convulsive disease':

> Unquestionably, there was . . . a small and temporary deviation from the strict order . . . but it is against all genuine principles of jurisprudence to draw a principle from a law made in a special case . . . *Privilegium non transit in exemplum* . . . The gentlemen of the Society for Revolution . . . take the deviation from the principle for the principle . . . Do these theorists mean to attaint and disable backwards all the kings that have reigned before the Revolution and consequently to stain the throne of England with a continual usurpation? Do they mean to invalidate, annul, or to call into question, together with the titles of the whole line of our kings, that great body of statute law which passed under those whom they treat as usurpers? to annul laws of inestimable value to our liberties? . . . King James was a bad king with a good title, and not an usurper. The princes who succeeded according to [the Act of 1701] which settled the crown on the Electress Sophia and her descendants, being Protestants, came in as much by title of inheritance as King James did.[5]

Then Price's sermon had laid down that the people had a right to 'cashier' their rulers for 'misconduct'. But, said Burke,

> No government could stand a moment, if it could be blown down with anything so loose and indefinite as an opinion of *'misconduct'*. They who led at the Revolution grounded the virtual abdication of King James upon no such light and uncertain principle. They charged him with nothing less than a design, confirmed by a multitude of illegal overt acts, to subvert the Protestant church and state, and their *fundamental*, unquestionable laws and liberties . . . This was more than *misconduct*. A grave and overruling necessity obliged them to take the steps they took with infinite reluctance . . .[6]

Again, Price had declared that the reigning monarch was 'more properly the servant than the sovereign of his people'. In one sense, Burke agreed, this was obviously true,

> but it is not true that [kings] are, in the ordinary sense, by our constitution at least, anything like servants . . . The king of Great Britain obeys no other person . . . The law, which knows neither to flatter nor insult, calls this high magistrate, not our servant, as this humble divine calls him, but *'our sovereign lord the king'*; and we, on our parts, have learned to speak only the primitive language of the law, and not the confused jargon of their Babylonian pulpits.[7]

Then, they had heard from the pulpit at Old Jewry of 'the right to form a government for ourselves' – a right flatly denied by Burke; one having moreover 'little countenance from anything done at the Revolution':

> The Revolution was made to preserve our *ancient* constitution of government which is our only security for law and liberty . . . We wished at the period of the Revolution, and do now wish, to derive all we possess *as an inheritance from our forefathers*. Upon that body and stock of inheritance we have taken care not to inoculate any scion alien to the nature of the original plant. All the reformations we have hitherto made have proceeded upon the principle of reverence to antiquity . . .

Let Dr Price read the 1689 Declaration of Right, 'the cornerstone of our constitution'; he would not find his Old Jewry principles there. Let him go further back, to the 1628 Petition of Right, to 'Magna Charta, our oldest reformation'; he would find no talk of the rights of man. Rights and liberties were there regarded as a patrimony, or entailed inheritance from the forefathers:

> We have an inheritable crown; an inheritable peerage; and a
> House of Commons and a people inheriting privileges, fran-
> chises, and liberties from a long line of ancestors . . . A spirit
> of innovation is generally the result of a selfish temper and
> confined views. People will not look forward to posterity who
> never look backward to their ancestors.[8]

No new society could be successfully created by a 'decomposition
of the whole civil and political mass, for the purpose of originating a new civil order out of the first elements of society'. Yet
every state ought to possess 'the means of some change':

> Without such means it might even risk the loss of that part of
> the constitution which it wished the most religiously to pre-
> serve. The two principles of conservation and correction
> operated strongly at the two critical periods of the Restoration
> and the Revolution, when England found itself without a
> king. At both these periods the nation had lost the bond of
> union in their ancient edifice; they did not, however, dissolve
> the whole fabric. On the contrary, in both cases they
> regenerated the deficient part . . .[9]

The situation in France before the explosion of 1789 had also
been reformable:

> You might, if you pleased, have profited by our example, and
> have given to your recovered freedom a correspondent dignity.
> Your privileges, though discontinued, were not lost to
> memory. Your constitution, it is true, whilst you were out of
> possession, suffered waste and dilapidation; but you possessed
> in some parts the walls and, in all, the foundations of a noble
> and venerable castle. You might have repaired those walls; you
> might have built on those old foundations. Your constitution
> was suspended before it was perfected . . . But you chose to act
> as if you had never been moulded into civil society, and had
> everything to begin anew. You began ill, because you began by
> despising everything that belonged to you. You set up your
> trade without a capital . . . Respecting your forefathers, you
> would have been taught to respect yourselves. You would not
> have chosen to consider the French . . . as a nation of low-born
> servile wretches until the emancipating year of 1789 . . .

Although the monarchy in France had not been 'without vices',
Louis XVI was 'a mild and lawful monarch' against whom the
French had rebelled

> with more fury, outrage, and insult than ever any people has
> been known to rise against the most illegal usurper or the most

sanguinary tyrant. Their resistance was made to concession; their blow was aimed at a hand holding out graces, favours, and immunities . . .

I shall be led with difficulty to think [Louis XVI] deserves the cruel and insulting triumph of Paris and of Dr Price. I tremble for liberty, from such an example to kings. I tremble for the cause of humanity, in the unpunished outrages of the most wicked of mankind . . .[10]

When the States-General, soon to become the National Assembly, was summoned in 1789, the merging of the three orders of clergy, nobility, and commons (*tiers-état*) effectively into one had ensured the dominance of the 600-strong *tiers-état*, itself dominated and disproportioned, Burke insisted, by innumerable minor lawyers – 'country attornies, notaries, and the whole train of the ministers of municipal litigation, the fomentors and conductors of the petty war of village vexation'. Along with these were doctors, 'dealers in stocks and funds', and others such, 'men formed to be instruments, not controls'. In striking contrast to the British House of Commons, the *tiers-état* lacked any proper representation of 'the natural landed interest of the country'. Among the representatives of the clergy, moreover, there was a preponderance of 'mere country curates', men with little regard 'to the general security of property'.[11]

The Chancellor of France, at the opening of the [States General] said . . . that all occupations were honourable. If he meant only that no honest employment was disgraceful, he would not have gone beyond the truth. But in asserting that anything is honourable, we imply some distinction in its favour. The occupation of a hair-dresser, or of a working tallow-chandler cannot be a matter of honour . . . Such descriptions of men ought not to suffer oppression from the state, but the state suffers oppression if such as they . . . are permitted to rule. In this you think you are combating prejudice, but you are at war with nature . . .

. . . Do not imagine that I wish to confine authority and distinction to blood, and names, and titles. No, Sir, there is no qualification for government but virtue and wisdom . . . in whatever state, condition, profession, or trade. Woe to the country which . . . would condemn to obscurity everything formed to diffuse lustre and glory around a state! Woe to the country too, that, passing into the opposite extreme, considers a low education, a mean contracted view of things, a sordid, mercenary occupation as a preferable title to command! Everything ought to be open; but not indifferently to every man.

. . . Though hereditary wealth, and the rank which goes with it, are too much idolized by creeping sycophants . . . they are too rashly slighted in shallow speculation . . . Some decent, regulated pre-eminence, some preference (not exclusive appropriation) given to birth is neither unnatural, nor unjust, nor impolitic . . .

Nothing is a due and adequate representation of a state, that does not represent its ability as well as its property. But as ability is a vigorous and active principle, and as property is sluggish, inert, and timid, it never can be safe from the invasions of ability unless it be out of all proportion predominant in the representation . . . The characteristic essence of property . . . is to be *unequal*. The great masses [of property] therefore which excite envy and tempt rapacity must be put out of the possibility of danger . . . The plunder of the few would indeed give but a share inconceivably small in the distribution to the many. But the many are not capable of making this calculation; and those who lead them to rapine never intend this distribution . . .[12]

Nobility is a graceful ornament to the civil order. It is the Corinthian capital of polished society . . . It is indeed one sign of a liberal and benevolent mind to incline to it with some sort of partial propensity. He feels no ennobling principle in his own heart who wishes to level all the artificial institutions which have been adopted for giving a body to opinion, and permanence to fugitive esteem. It is a sour, malignant, envious disposition . . . that sees with joy the unmerited fall of what had long flourished in splendour and honour.[13]

As to 'equal rights' and 'the rights of man', yes, men did have *real* rights:

In denying [the revolutionists'] false claims of right, I do not mean to injure those which are real, and are such as their pretended rights would destroy . . . Men have a right to . . . justice, to the fruits of their industry, and to the means of making their industry fruitful. They have a right to the acquisitions of their parents; to the nourishment and improvement of their offspring; to instruction in life, and consolation in death . . . All men have equal rights, but not to equal things. He that has but five shillings in the partnership has as good a right to it as he that has five hundred pounds has to his larger proportion . . . ; and as to the share of power, authority, and direction which each individual ought to have in the management of the state, that I must deny to be amongst the direct, original rights of man in civil society . . . The pretended rights of these theorists are all extremes: and in proportion as they are metaphysically true, they are morally and politically false. The rights of man are in a sort of *middle*, incapable of definition, but not impossible to be discerned. The rights of men in governments . . . are often in balances between differences of good; in compromises sometimes between good and evil, and sometimes between evil and evil.

These metaphysic rights [claimed by the revolutionary theorists] entering into common life, like the rays of light which penetrate into a dense medium, are by the laws of nature refracted from their straight line. Indeed in the gross and complicated mass of human passions and concerns, the primitive rights of men undergo such a variety of refractions and reflections that it becomes absurd to talk of them as if they continued in the simplicity of their original direction. The nature of man is intricate; the objects of society are of the greatest possible complexity; and therefore no simple disposition or direction of power can be suitable either to man's nature or to the quality of his affairs.[14]

And of democracy:

It is said that twenty-four millions [the population of France] ought to prevail over two hundred thousand [the privileged orders]. True; if the constitution of a kingdom be a problem of arithmetic. This sort of discourse does very well with the lamp-post for its second; to men who *may* reason calmly it is ridiculous. The will of the many, and their interest, must very often differ; and great will be the difference when they make an evil choice.

. . . I do not know under what description to class the present ruling authority in France. It affects to be a pure democracy . . . I reprobate no form of government merely upon abstract principles. There may be situations in which the purely democratic form will become necessary. There may be some (very few, and very particularly circumstanced) where it would be clearly desirable. This I do not take to be the case of France, or of any other great country. Until now, we have seen no examples of considerable democracies. The ancients were better acquainted with them . . . I cannot help concurring with their opinion that an absolute democracy, no more than an absolute monarchy, is to be reckoned among the legitimate forms of government. They think it rather the corruption and degeneracy than the sound constitution of a republic. If I recollect rightly, Aristotle observes that a democracy has many striking ponts of resemblance with a tyranny. Of this, I am certain, that in a democracy the majority of the citizens is capable of exercising the most cruel oppressions upon the minority . . . and that oppression of the minority will extend to far greater numbers, and will be carried on with much greater fury, than can almost ever be apprehended from the dominion of a single sceptre . . .[15]

Of parliamentary representation and the franchise, a subject on which his views had always been unyieldingly conservative and traditionalist, he repeats with no hint of retreat:

I see that your example is held out to shame us. I know that we are supposed a dull, sluggish race, rendered passive by finding our situation tolerable, and prevented by a mediocrity of freedom from ever attaining to its full perfection. Your leaders in France began by affecting to admire, almost to adore, the British constitution; but as they advanced, they came to look at it with a sovereign contempt . . . I shall only say here, in justice to that old-fashioned constitution under which we have long prospered, that our representation has been found perfectly adequate to all the purposes for which a representation of the people can be devised or desired. I defy the enemies of our constitution to show the contrary.

. . . With you the elective assembly is the sovereign, and the sole sovereign . . . But with us it is totally different . . . With us the king and the lords are several and joint securities of each district, each province, each city. When did you hear in Great Britain of any province suffering from the inequality of its representation; what district from having no representation at all? . . . The very inequality of representation, which is so foolishly complained of, is perhaps the very thing which prevents us from thinking or acting as members for districts. Cornwall elects as many members as all Scotland. But is Cornwall better taken care of than Scotland?[16]

He constantly stresses how small a minority in England comprise the party for revolutionary change:

I hear it is sometimes given out in France that what is doing among you is after the example of England. [This is not true]

211

either in the act or in the spirit . . . The cabals here who take a sort of share in your transactions as yet consist of but a handful of people.

. . . Thanks to our sullen resistance to innovation, thanks to the cold sluggishness of our national character, we still bear the stamp of our forefathers . . . We are not the converts of Rousseau; we are not the disciples of Voltaire; Helvétius has made no progress among us. Atheists are not our preachers; madmen are not our lawgivers. We know that *we* have made no discoveries, and we think that no discoveries are to be made, in morality; nor many in the great principles of government, nor in the idea of liberty, which were understood long before we were born, altogether as well as they will be after the grave has heaped its mould upon our presumption, and the silent tomb shall have imposed its law on our pert loquacity. In England . . . we have not been drawn and trussed, in order that we may be filled like stuffed birds in a museum, with chaff and rags and paltry blurred shreds of paper about the rights of man . . . We fear God; we look up with awe to kings; with affection to parliaments; with duty to magistrates; with reverence to priests; and with respect to nobility. Why? Because when such ideas are brought before our minds, it is *natural* to be so affected; because all other feelings are false and spurious . . .

[Here in Britain] we are resolved to keep an established church, an established monarchy, an established aristocracy, and an established democracy, each in the degree it exists and in no greater . . .

We know, and what is better, we feel inwardly, that religion is the basis of all civil society, and the source of all good and all comfort . . .

The people of England, far from thinking a religious national establishment unlawful, hardly think it lawful to be without one. In France you are wholly mistaken if you do not believe us above all other things attached to it.[17]

Burke's defence both of established property and established religion leads him to denounce the 'nationalisation' of the priesthood in France, the confiscation of church property, and the destruction of monastic institutions. This last, he presumes, was on the grounds that monks were both idle and superstitious. But *were* monks idle?

> The monks are lazy. Be it so. Suppose them no otherwise employed than by singing in the choir. They are as usefully employed . . . as those who sing upon the stage. They are as usefully employed as if they worked from dawn to dark in the innumerable servile, degrading, unseemly, unmanly, and often most unwelcome and pestiferous occupations to which by the social economy so many wretches are inevitably doomed. If it were not generally pernicious to disturb the natural course of things . . . I should be infinitely more inclined forcibly to rescue them from their miserable industry than violently to disturb the tranquil repose of monastic quietude.

And what if monks were indeed superstitious? He 'did not mean to dispute' this.

> But is superstition the greatest of all possible vices? In its possible excess I think it becomes a very great evil; but superstition is the religion of feeble minds; and they must be tolerated in an intermixture of it, in some trifling or some enthusiastic shape or other, else you will deprive weak minds of a resource found necessary to the strongest.[18]

What he suspected the new masters of France really intended was the 'utter abolition, under any of its forms, of the Christian religion' – yet 'we hear these new teachers continually boasting of their spirit of toleration'.

> That those persons should tolerate all opinions, who think none to be of estimation, is a matter of small merit. Equal neglect is not impartial kindness . . . There are in England abundance of men who tolerate in the true spirit of toleration. They think the dogmas of religion, though in different degrees, are all of moment . . . They tolerate, not because they despise opinions, but because they respect justice.[19]

Inherent in all the follies and crimes being perpetrated in France was the revolutionist's obsession with *speed*. Some things indeed might be done quickly: 'rage and phrensy will pull down more in half an hour than prudence, deliberation, and foresight can build up in a hundred years'. 'You may object', he writes, 'that a process of [gradual reform] is slow . . . "Such a mode of reforming, possibly, might take up many years". Without question it might; and it ought.' The slowness of progress was often its best security:

> Where the great interests of mankind are concerned through a long succession of generations, that succession ought to be admitted into some share in the councils which are so deeply to

affect them. If justice requires this, the work itself requires the aid of more minds than one age can furnish. It is from this view of things that the best legislators have been often satisfied with the establishment of some sure, solid, and ruling principle in government . . . and having fixed the principle, they have left it afterwards to its own operation.

To proceed in this manner, that is, to proceed with a presiding principle and a prolific energy, is with me the criterion of profound wisdom. What your [French] politicians think the marks of a bold, hardy genius, are only proofs of a deplorable want of ability. By their violent haste and their defiance of the process of nature, they are delivered over blindly to every projector and adventurer, to every alchymist and empiric . . .[20]

Everyone must agree that 'we must learn from history'. But we ought to be careful. Without care, history 'may be used to vitiate our minds and to destroy our happiness':

In history a great volume is unrolled for our instruction, drawing the materials for future wisdom from the past errors and infirmities of mankind. It may, in the perversion, serve for a magazine . . . supplying the means of keeping alive, or reviving, dissensions and animosities, and adding fuel to civil fury. History consists, for the greater part, of the miseries brought upon the world by pride, ambition, avarice, revenge, lust, sedition, hypocrisy, ungoverned zeal, and all the train of disorderly appetites which shake the public . . . These vices are the *causes* . . . Religion, morals, laws, prerogatives, privileges, liberties, rights of men, are the *pretexts* . . . You would not cure [great public evils] by resolving that there should be no more monarchs, nor ministers of state, nor of the gospel; no interpreters of law; no general officers; no public councils. You might change the names. The things in some shape must remain. A certain *quantum* of power must always exist in the community, in some hands, under some appellation. Wise men will apply their remedies to vices, not to names; to the causes of evil which are permanent, not to the occasional organs by which they act, and the transitory modes in which they appear . . . Whilst you are discussing fashion, the fashion is gone by. The very same vice assumes a new body . . . it walks abroad, it continues its ravages, whilst you are gibbeting the carcase, or demolishing the tomb. You are terrifying yourself with ghosts and apparitions, whilst your house is the haunt of robbers . . .[21]

'SEE, THEY BARK AT ME!'

THE *Reflections* were published in November 1790 – still a
year or two away from the beginning of the Terror – and
sold 19,000 copies in the first six months. In France too
the book soon had substantial sales. Trinity College Dublin immediately voted Burke an honorary doctorate 'as the powerful
advocate of the constitution, as the friend of public order and
virtue . . . and for his transcendent talents and philanthropy'. At
Oxford the heads of houses, by seven votes to six, rejected a proposal to confer a like honour – which offended Burke sufficiently
to cause him, when in 1793 the heads of houses were persuaded
by Portland to change their minds, to turn the offer down.

Reaction among fellow Whigs to the *Reflections* was mixed.
Gilbert Elliot and those whom Burke called 'the old stamina of
the Whiggs', headed by the Duke of Portland, were among its
strong admirers. Devonshire and Cavendish wondered whether
he had 'gone too far', but broadly approved. Fitzwilliam wrote
that the book was 'almost universally' praised but offered no
opinion of his own. Fox told Devonshire's mistress and future
Duchess, Lady Elizabeth Foster, that he thought it 'the least
perfect' of Burke's writings. Sheridan could hardly be expected to
approve. Like Fox, he had welcomed the French Revolution
enthusiastically and had been the chief speaker at a big meeting
held at the Crown and Anchor Tavern in the Strand to celebrate
the first anniversary of the storming of the Bastille. He was
moreover on ill terms with Burke personally.

Philip Francis was not alone in considering that Burke's mis-
representation of some of the facts of French history endangered

the validity of his conclusions. When a similar criticism, albeit friendly, reached Burke from a certain François de Menonville, a deputy from Lorraine in the National Assembly, Burke promptly wrote him a long answer, published as a pamphlet early in 1791, which may stand as a sort of appendix to the *Reflections*; it might indeed be entitled *Reiterations*. Burke wrote:

> I am unalterably persuaded that the attempt to oppress, degrade, impoverish, confiscate, and extinguish the original gentlemen and landed property of a whole nation cannot be justified under any form it may assume.

Much of the latter part of the pamphlet is occupied with a bitter and contemptuous attack on Rousseau, the Assembly's 'canon of holy writ, their figure of perfection', their 'insane Socrates', with his 'deranged eccentric vanity'. Depont, the man to whom the *Reflections* were nominally addressed, also wrote a reply to them, as Menonville had done. Depont's was published in London as a pamphlet, at much the same time as Burke's own reply to Menonville. It was only a few weeks later, in March 1791, that there appeared the first part of what was to be the great counter-blast to Burke's book, Tom Paine's *Rights of Man*.

Probably sweetest to Burke among the chorus of comments upon his *Reflections* came in some words spoken by the King himself – spoken, and then repeated the next day through the Duke of Clarence as King's messenger, in case Mr Burke had not fully grasped at first hearing the full force of the royal thanks and praises. Recounting her heart-warming little story in a letter to Will Burke away in India, Jane Burke's pleasure on her husband's behalf is evident:

> On his coming to town for the winter . . . he went to the Levee with the Duke of Portland . . . When he said his say to the Duke, without waiting for Ned's coming up in his turn, the King went up to him, and after the usual questions of how long have you been in town and the weather, he said you have been very much employed of late . . . Ned said no, Sir, not more than usual – You have and very well employed too . . . You have been of *use to us all*, it is a general opinion . . . ; your Majesty's adopting it, Sir, will make the opinion general, said Ned . . . You know the tone at Court is a whisper, but the King said all this loud, so as to be heard by everyone at Court . . . The King was very much afraid that Mr Burke did not conceive how much he wished to thank him and that it made him

uneasy . . . Then you see, Mr Burke's duty was to write to the Duke of Clarence to say he did understand the King and that his labours were all overpaid by his Majesty's approbation etca etca – [1]

If the King approved, the Prince of Wales emphatically did not. He dismissed the *Reflections* as 'a farrago of nonsense'[2] – which, when it was reported to Burke, caused him offence and resentment, the more understandable in view of his recent uncompromising championing of the Prince's rights in a regency. Further disparaging comments by the Prince of Wales left Burke in no doubt that he was 'in disgrace at Carleton House'.[3]

Fox was at first careful not to advertise his dislike of the *Reflections* too publicly, being aware of their potential for widening the Whig divisions, personal and ideological, which the Regency débâcle had recently sharpened. Sheridan in particular, publicly loud in his approval of the revolution, was acknowledged for the time being as chief spokesman of the party's radical wing. Well before his book was finished, Burke and he were being, as Lady Jersey reported to the Duchess of Devonshire, 'perfectly Irish, for they are now on worse terms than ever'. And Fox's friend James Hare wrote, also to the Duchess, 'Burke continues quite implacable; his son . . . and every Irishman that has access to him encourages him to persist in his madness, I despair of a cure . . . Charles Fox says that when Burke had fairly got the start in absurdity, it proves very superior parts in Sheridan to have recovered the lost ground and made it a near race.'

Burke did what he could through his son, who in February 1790 had become Fitzwilliam's London agent, to enlist support in that vital quarter. Being Rockingham's heir and successor in itself gave Fitzwilliam a special status, both in the party generally and more particularly with the Burkes. He and Portland, the two grandest of the politically active Whig grandees, in an important sense 'headed' this essentially aristocratic party, Fox's pre-eminent position in the Commons notwithstanding. It was to Fitzwilliam that Richard Burke – surely expressing the sentiments of his father – now wrote a very long and unmistakably urgent letter, outspokenly hostile to Sheridan and obviously nervous that Fox's 'moderation' might prove very temporary:

You know the facility of Fox. You know that he is surrounded and in many ways govern'd by those who have not a hundredth part of his parts, no share in his judgment, and principles absolutely bad . . . If Fox engages in this, will you not also be committed; and he is not far from it.

And if Sheridan were not *'disclaimed'*, Fitzwilliam's silence would surely 'pass for acquiescence'.[4]

There was well-justified alarm that Fox would not long succeed in preserving a tactful silence over his French sympathies, and Burke had made it clear that *his* views were much too passionately held to be muzzled in the cause of party unity. Pitt, moreover, who was just then (in April 1791) in political difficulties himself – with Thurlow, with the King, and with issues of policy towards Russia – did all he could, by encouraging Burke's strong stand, to divert attention from his own problems. The Pittite press, too, notably the *Public Advertiser*, was busy promoting a Whig rift by the time-honoured device of spreading rumours that it had already happened.

On 15 April, in a debate on what action should be taken against Russia, Fox's discretion, after Pitt had accused him of being a republican at heart, finally snapped. The new constitution of France he now declared to be 'the most stupendous and glorious edifice of liberty which had been erected . . . in any time or country'.[5] At the end of his speech Burke rose 'in much visible emotion', intending a reply; but for the time being was silenced by loud cries of 'Question' and the Speaker's ruling. Five days later Fox came to Duke Street* to see him; insisted that his own views enjoyed majority support in the party; and virtually accused Burke of being Pitt's agent – 'encouraged to it by ministers . . . who had instigated him to bring on the subject of the French Revolution for the purpose of fixing on him [Fox] a predilection for republican principles'. This at least was what Portland *heard from Burke* that Fox had said (so he told Fitzwilliam); and if it was true, 'there seems to me', wrote Portland, 'an end of the party, or at least an end of my belonging to it'.[6] Two days later Parliament was prorogued and Fox went off to Newmarket for the races. This, and other circumstances, prevented Portland and Fitzwilliam from managing to see Fox, in order to counsel continued caution, before the reconvening of Parliament on 6 May.

*The Burkes moved from Gerrard Street to 6 Duke Street, St James's at Michaelmas 1790. They remained there until the summer of 1794; it was the last London house they rented.

It was generally well known that Burke would take the first opportunity to re-state his views on the Revolution and its British supporters. He was not to be deterred by the knowledge that the first business of the Commons concerned the committee stage of the Quebec Government Bill setting up a constitution for the colony of Canada. Directly the chairman opened proceedings he rose, and immediately steered his speech to a consideration of the rival merits of the British and American constitutions, and the hardly-to-be-rivalled demerits of the new constitution in France, the parent country of so many Canadians. Once launched thus upon the iniquities of the French National Assembly and the contrasting virtues of the British constitution, he was not to be silenced by any number of calls to order. These emanated largely from what he resentfully called Fox's 'light troops', the squadron of twenty or thirty, mostly young, members of parliament and of Brooks's to whom Fox was an object of adoration. At one point, heckled and baited by these young Foxites, but able even in his fury to dig down for the exactly proper lines from *King Lear*, he cried out, 'The little dogs and all, Tray, Blanche, and Sweetheart, see, they bark at me!' When he sat down, Fox spoke, criticising him for the irrelevance and impropriety of his speech and repeating, for the record, what he had earlier said, that he thought the French Revolution 'on the whole, one of the most glorious events in the history of mankind'.[7] Then 'Mr Burke', the *Parliamentary History* records, 'commenced his reply in a grave and governed tone of voice', but went on to complain that

a personal attack had been made upon him from a quarter he never could have expected, after a friendship and an intimacy of more than twenty-two years; and not only his public conduct, words, and writings had been alluded to in the severest terms, but confidential conversations and private opinions had been brought forward, with a view of proving that he had acted inconsistently . . . He had met with great unfairness from the right honourable gentleman . . . [who] brought down the whole strength and heavy artillery of his own judgment, eloquence, and abilities upon him to crush him . . . He would not be dismayed . . . and he would tell all the world that the constitution was in danger . . .[8]

Burke then refreshed the memory of the House with mention of earlier matters, where he and Fox had adopted opposing views –

the Royal Marriages Act, parliamentary reform, the Dissenters' bill; but none of these had marred their friendship. On the matter of the French Revolution, however –

Mr Fox here whispered that 'there was no loss of friends'. Mr Burke said Yes, there was a loss of friends – he knew the price of his conduct – he had done his duty at the price of his friend – their friendship was at an end . . .

Mr Fox rose to reply; but his mind was so much agitated and his heart so much affected by what had fallen from Mr Burke that it was some minutes before he could proceed. Tears trickled down his cheeks, and he strove in vain to give utterance to feelings that dignified and exalted his nature . . . [9]

When he had gained control, he appealed again for a continuance of friendship, but again too returned to the affairs of France and the happy disappearance there of 'a tyranny of the most horrid despotism'. The course he would pursue in future, he said, 'would be to keep out of his right honourable friend's way till time and reflection had fitted his right honourable friend to think differently upon the subject'. [10]

Burke spoke a third time, repeating his deeply felt arguments and convictions. Finally, he said he was 'sorry for the occurrence of that day. "Sufficient for the day was the evil thereof". Yet if the good were to many, he would willingly take the evil to himself. He sincerely hoped that no member of that House would ever barter the constitution of this country, the eternal jewel of their souls, for a wild and visionary system which could only lead to confusion and disorder.' [11]

John Therry, a distant cousin of Burke's, travelled home with him from the Commons that night, and Therry's son, 35 years later, remembered being told:

In the carriage, Mr Burke observed a stern and inflexible silence. [Arrived home] he threw up the windows of the apartment, flung open his coat and waistcoat, and in a paroxysm of passion, paced up and down the room, until nearly four o'clock in the morning . . . My father deemed it but consistent with his duty not to leave him until . . . he was disposed to retire to rest. [12]

Burke left the Commons chamber on 6 May a politically lonely man. He had received no support whatever from his party colleagues, and for the time being it was Fox who was in command. Continuing to shun in public too warm an embrace for

French republicanism, and studiously absenting himself from a fraternal visit to Paris by fellow Whigs in the summer of 1791, Fox succeeded for a time in appearing altogether more moderate and sensible than the extremist Burke. When on 11 May the continuing debate on the Quebec bill produced further pointed exchanges between the two men, Burke, having first 'spoke much at large . . . returned to his own situation . . . He had been excommunicated by his party and was too old to seek another'. Hurt and embittered, and still thinking of retiring, he nevertheless took refuge characteristically in ceaseless activity – corresponding at length with French aristocrats and *émigré* counter-revolutionaries; discussing the practicability of a war of intervention; writing for the promptest possible publication a 115-page defence of his conduct and opinions (*An Appeal from the New to the Old Whigs*); but still managing to combine all this with a summer's break at Margate, where Jane Burke was able to report that her 'severe and long-continued' rheumatism took 'some benefit' from the warm and cold bathing.[13]

One of the letters to France was addressed to the Marquis de Bouillé, the army commander of the loyal troops whose protection the French King and Queen were trying to escape to when they were caught that summer *en route* at Varennes. 'I have not lost my spirit or my principles', Burke wrote to him, 'and I have rather encreased my inward peace. I have spoken the sense of infinitely the majority of my countrymen.'[14] This last conviction may well have been reinforced, though by events distasteful to him, when so-called 'Crown and Altar' mobs began violently assaulting the property of such prominent friends of the Revolution as Joseph Priestley, the pioneer chemist who was also, like Dr Price, well known as a Dissenter radical. Even so, he could muster no sympathy for Priestley.

The *Appeal* begins with a protest against Fox's 6 May attack. This had been unfair as well as being wrong-headed, aiming to show Burke's inconsistency by quoting, out of context, passages from speeches made over the previous twenty-five years, which Burke regarded as an unworthy debater's trick. The Commons, he complained, had been treated to 'a sort of digest' of his sayings, 'even to such as were merely sportive and jocular'.[15] There then follows extensive quotation from the official report of the impeachment of Dr Sacheverell in Queen Anne's reign, to demonstrate the congruency of Burke's views of the constitution as cited in the *Reflections* with those of the 'old Whigs' as propounded by the managers prosecuting in that famous trial. He then discusses and controverts some of the more dangerous heresies and aberrations being embraced by his fellow Whigs and their radical allies: for instance, the notion that decisions taken by 'a majority of the people' must be paramount. He questions the very term 'people' in the sense in which Jacobins and democrats employed it:

> In a state of *rude* nature there is no such thing as a people. The idea of a people is the idea of a corporation . . . When men . . . break up the original compact or agreement which gives its corporate form and capacity to a state, they are no longer a people; they have no longer a corporate existence . . . they are a number of vague, loose individuals, and nothing more. With them all is to begin again . . . It is perfectly clear that out of a state of civil society [as currently in France], majority and minority are relations which can have no existence; and that in civil society [as in England] its own specific conventions determine what it is that constitutes the people, so as to make their act the significance of the general will: to come to particulars, it is equally clear that neither in France nor in England has the original or any subsequent compact of the state, expressed or implied, constituted *a majority of men, told by the head* to be the acting people of their several communities. And I see as little of policy or utility as there is of right, in laying down a principle that a majority of men told by the head are to be considered as the people, and that as such their will is to be law. [16]

So much for democracy by arithmetic; and once again he champions the concept of 'a true, natural aristocracy' as an 'essential, integrant part of any large body rightly constituted'. A 'state of civil society' *necessarily* generates such an aristocracy, 'the leading, guiding, and governing part' of such a social order.

> When great multitudes act together, under that discipline of nature, I recognise the PEOPLE . . . But when you disturb this harmony; when you break up this beautiful order . . . , when you separate the common sort of men from their proper chieftains, so as to form them into an adverse army, I no longer know that venerable object called the People in such a disbanded race of deserters and vagabonds. [17]

He again commends 'rational liberty', 'liberty blended into government, to harmonize with its forms and rules'; but the flame of liberty in England needed no foreign examples to re-kindle it. 'The example of our ancestors is abundantly sufficient . . . He that sets his house on fire because his fingers are frost-bitten can never be a fit instructor in the method of providing our habitations with a cheerful and salutary warmth.'[18]

Once again he returns to praise the genius of Montesquieu, who in an earlier day had so penetratingly demonstrated the virtues of the British constitution; and in honour of that same venerable structure, which 'common minds' were capable of understanding, he adds his own eulogy:

> The British constitution has not been struck out at an heat by a set of presumptuous men, like the assembly of pettifoggers run mad in Paris . . . It is the result of the thoughts of many minds, in many ages. It is not simple, no superficial thing, nor to be estimated by superficial understandings. An ignorant man, who is not fool enough to meddle with his clock, is how-ever sufficiently confident to think he can safely take to pieces and put together at his pleasure a moral machine of another guise, importance, and complexity, composed of far other wheels, and springs, and balances, and counter-acting and co-operating powers. Men little think how immorally they act in rashly meddling with what they do not understand . . .
>
> The Whigs of this day have before them, in this Appeal, their constitutional ancestors; they have the doctors of the modern school. They will choose for themselves. The author of the *Reflections* has chosen for himself . . .[19]

The sixth of May 1791 virtually marks the demise of the Whig party as Burke had understood it, or indeed as it might reasonably be argued he had *created* it: the party of Lord Rock-ingham (latterly Portland–Fox), solidly aristocratic; standing for individual liberties restrained by the requirement of good order – 'rational liberty'; for the mixed constitution as amended by the Revolution settlement of 1688–9 and the 1701 Act of Settlement; for a balance of power between Crown, Lords, and Commons, but with special attention to correcting an alleged growth in improper Court influence; for the established Church of England, but with toleration and respect for other denomi-nations; for all prescriptive and hereditary rights of title and property (including, at least with Burke and Rockingham and

Portland, electoral franchise as a form of property); with due regard for 'the people' and their political importance, but often connoting by that term only a minority, if a substantial minority, of the total population, and always regarding 'democratic' as a pejorative epithet.

Burke had little hope that his *Appeal* would be much heeded by his late friends, and regarded himself as 'excommunicated' by the party, essentially now an independent. Even the Duke of Portland, who had approved of the *Reflections* and only recently been saying privately that the adoption of pro-revolutionary sympathies could mean an end of his association with the Whigs, bemoaned Burke's 'calumniation' of his colleagues. Despite some 'excellent and admirable' passages in the book, much of it 'grieved him to the soul' by its divisiveness. If the author, he said, had wanted to injure and annihilate the remains of the old Whig party', he could have chosen no better means. These comments were not made to Burke, from whom Portland now judged he ought to keep his distance, but to Burke's young friend French Laurence. Until in 1794 he came at long last home to haven in Pitt's administration, Portland over these years was all perplexity, drift, and indecision. He loved Fox so well and admired him so uncritically that for a long time he simply could not bring himself to believe that so excellent a man's benign attitude towards dangerous revolutionaries would prove to be anything other than a brief flirtation; and, as Burke complained, he refused to accept that there was any danger of revolutionary doctrines prevailing in England.

For Fox, the toleration afforded him by Portland and other leading Whig magnates was vitally important. Dominant figure among the Whigs though he was, his position would have been shakier and perhaps untenable without it. Although disgust and indignation at events in France and then Britain's entry into the war would finally turn Portland and the conservative Whig leaders against him, throughout 1791 and 1792 Fox remained comfortably in control, both of his followers and of himself. He managed to hold the middle ground, protesting that he disapproved both of the *Reflections* of Burke and of Paine's *Rights of Man*, and abstaining in April 1792 from membership of the newly formed Association of the Friends of the People although the young men of his gambling and drinking entourage at

Brooks's joined almost to a man. Challenged on this point, he 'didn't like to discourage the young ones', Fox said.[20] And even these same young ones, in May of that year, saw fit to 'defer to Mr Fox's judgment' and repudiate republicanism by ceremoniously burning copies of the *Rights of Man*.[21]

There was however no serious doubting where Fox's true sympathies lay. The French Revolution had made his Whiggism at once uncomfortable and old-fashioned: uncomfortable because, in the end, the Revolution and the war would make his stance extremely difficult to sustain; old-fashioned because the main drive of his Whiggism had lost much of its relevance to the new situation. Fox at the outbreak of the French Revolution could not help seeing Louis XVI, *mutatis mutandis*, as a French George III, with the revolutionaries like the English Whigs fighting for 'liberty'. At the centre of Fox's politics (as earlier of Burke's) had always been mistrust of the Crown and Court influence. Indeed he more than mistrusted George III; he hated him, and could never forgive him his victories of 1783 and 1784. But public fears of Painites and republicans and the French were quickening the process which had begun even before the royal illness of 1788-9 and the French revolutionary violence. George III, not always a popular monarch in the early days, could now be honestly and patriotically toasted as 'the good old King', and the ugliest riots of the early 1790s were *against* the radical reformers. Fox would remain king at Brooks's, but his followers among 'the people' became a dwindling band. Essentially the clock of his Whiggism had stopped, and was showing 1784.

There is no doubt that in 1791, with Burke's unpopular *Appeal* just published, it was he who appeared to have lost the battle; most unhappily to have confirmed his friend Windham's rueful diagnosis (made in fact the previous year, after Windham read the *Reflections*): 'a man decried, persecuted and proscribed; not being much valued, even by his own party, and by half the nation considered as little better than an ingenious madman!'[22] Even Elliot, one of Burke's most faithful followers, thought his *Appeal* and his attitude to 'the French question' mistaken and ill-judged. Elliot was aware of how 'powerful and sovereign' over him had been the sway of Burke's mind in the past – even to the point, he admitted, of sometimes overthrowing his own better judgment. He was therefore nervous when he was once more invited to

Beaconsfield, knowing that he owed it to his own integrity to take his line and stick to it. After the visit however he felt 'much relieved'; Burke was 'full of kindness', and they exchanged their differing views in amity.[23]

Burke presented a copy of his latest pamphlet to the royal, if unofficial, patron of the Whigs, the Prince of Wales. He had heard – and with much resentment – that the Prince had earlier spoken slightingly of the *Reflections*, and hoped this time for a more favourable reaction. He was disappointed; his 'respectful and humble' covering letter was never even acknowledged. Privately it seems that the Prince spoke of the author's 'wildness', and at the same time 'animadverted much' on *young* Burke. For his part, young Burke animadverted no less, in a letter to his mother, against the incivility his father had met with from that quarter. The King, he wrote, appeared to have better manners than his son.[24] The King, in fact, had not only read the *Appeal* and approved of it, but at one of his regular levees went out of his way to compliment the author. As Burke told his son:

> I was at the Levee yesterday, as the rule is when the King sends you a civil message. Nothing could be more gracious than my reception. He told me that he did not think that any thing could be added to what I had first written [in the *Reflections*]. But he saw he was mistaken; that there was very much added, and new and important . . . He then asked me whether I had seen that scheme of absurdity the French constitution and what I thought of it. I told him I had seen all the flowers separately and did not like them better now that I had seen them tied up in one bouquet . . .

Although Fitzwilliam was less inclined than the rest of the party to condemn the *Appeal* and Burke's anti-revolutionary 'extremism' – indeed Burke was told that he had once praised the *Appeal* in the presence of 'a large publick company' – he too for the time being felt obliged to stand alongside Fox and the majority, and this increased the strain Burke was already feeling in his dependence on Fitzwilliam's wealth and generosity. Like his uncle Rockingham before him, Fitzwilliam had always made contributions to the chronically embarrassed Burke purse, sometimes directly, sometimes discreetly through a third party. The financial situation of the Burke family as it happened was even more than usually precarious at this time, as they had agreed to find £5,250 to pay to the Verney estate (Lord Verney had just died) as composition for William Burke's long-standing debt.[25] In view of William's possible return home from India, this matter became doubly pressing, since coming back as a debtor could well invite imprisonment. (In the event William did not arrive home till 1793, by which time his major indebtedness at least was settled, and the Burke finances, though still unhealthy, had benefited somewhat from the earnings of Burke's son, from further Fitzwilliam generosity, and from Joshua Reynolds's bequests.)

Even before the *Appeal* was published, Burke in June 1791 was writing to Fitzwilliam, handsomely acknowledging his 'unequalled friendship, . . . unbounded partiality and goodness', but nevertheless feeling 'compelled to decline' further money payments, in view of the gap that had opened between their opinions. Once again he stated at length his fear of the 'terrible contagion' of French levelling doctrines, 'the doctrines of Paine, Priestley, Price, etca, etca' – for which Brooks's had now apparently become 'a sort of academy'; and again he rehearsed his deep resentment at Fox's attempt in parliament to represent him as an apostate from his principles – and also at the hostility shown him by the Prince of Wales. 'I desire nothing now but to depart quietly into such retreat as Providence . . . shall allot for my declining hours. After all . . . I leave your party far richer in abilities than I found it.'[26]

There was never a hint of any break in so well established a friendship – which might show itself in many ways other than financial. Soon, for instance, Fitzwilliam was obligingly responding to Burke's request that his 'Colchian ram' at Beaconsfield should entertain 'half a score' of Fitzwilliam's 'best made and best woolled large ewe sheep and particularly those which have the largest tails. 'I will', he promised, 'send your lordship five back in lamb – and keep with your leave the other five as my perquisite.'[27] 'Never hesitate one instant', wrote Fitzwilliam in September 1791, 'to doubt my affection, esteem, and admiration.'

Before the end of the year, in the course of yet another long letter outlining his political position and repeating his fears for the party and the nation, Burke was once more thanking Fitzwilliam for some 'new mark' of his 'persevering and unconquerable friendship'. Fitzwilliam was apparently not going to let

Burke deny him the pleasure of supplying further assistance, and Burke's refusal to accept it must have been short-lived.[28] By now too Richard Burke junior as the Earl's agent was firmly incorporated within the Fitzwilliam interest. He had hoped that this employment might earn him one of Fitzwilliam's parliamentary seats (at Higham Ferrers) but that did not materialise.

CHAPTER
17

FRANCE AND IRELAND 1791–1793

IT WAS as his father's representative that Richard Burke now began to assume a certain importance, if only at the margin of events. Edmund's renewed talk of declining hours and retreat from the parliamentary scene, however honestly meant, was as misleading as it had been earlier. His *Reflections*, if it had broken his connection with the Westminster Whigs, had forged many links for him abroad and made him to a novel extent a figure of European significance. It was primarily to the Austrian and Prussian monarchies that the *émigré* French princes and nobles were looking to attempt a Bourbon restoration – the Austrian Emperor Leopold was Marie Antoinette's brother – but what of Britain, where the Pitt ministry and George III seemed agreed on a policy of caution and avoidance of war? Among leading British politicians Burke appeared to be the one man who advocated counter-revolution by all necessary means. Thus in the summer of 1791, while on holiday with his wife at Margate, he had been most conspiratorially approached – at first through a very odd and mysterious anonymous letter – by someone seeking an interview. The mysterious someone eventually materialised as none other than Charles-Alexandre de Calonne, formerly French Controller General of Finance, the minister who, having convened an Assembly of Notables in 1787, then failed to persuade them to agree to measures of necessary taxation, and was dismissed when the Notables disbanded. The following year he came to England, married a wealthy French widow, and set up house at Wimbledon, where Pitt and Dundas were among his neighbours. By this time he was acting as emissary for the leaders of the 'first emigration', Louis XVI's brother the Duke of Artois (the future Charles X) and the Prince de Condé, who had set up a headquarters at Coblenz and were soon joined there by the King's other brother the Count of Provence (the future Louis XVIII). Calonne, failing to persuade Pitt and Dundas to deviate from their policy of non-intervention, turned to Burke in the perhaps tenuous hope that he might bring some influence to bear on a British government towards which it was perceived that his old hostility had softened. With Dundas in particular, his old half-rival, half-associate in the Indian business, Burke's relations were now fully cordial,* and it was Dundas especially that he now tried to influence. In Britain, he wrote to Dundas, there was a party, he estimated of 'at least seven hundred thousand souls' (surely an exaggeration), a great proportion of them Dissenters, who wished to 'break down all barriers tending to seperate them from . . . the republican, atheistic faction of fanaticks in France', and 'to merge them all in one interest and one cause, which they call rights of man'. There was not perhaps an *immediate* danger; but 'our danger must be from our not looking beyond the moment'. The British constitution *was* in danger; and *it would be fought for, not in Britain but in France*. It was there that 'the cause of all monarchies, and of all republicks too constituted upon antient models', was on trial.[1]

Burke lost no time in establishing contact with the party of the Princes at Coblenz. It was done through his son, that 'dearest dearest son', 'dearest son and friend'[2] who, always the apple of his father's eye, was by now also his best-trusted personal assistant, to some extent his financial prop, and always his faithful and tireless champion. Richard, accompanied by his cousin Edmund Nagle (Captain, R.N., later Rear-Admiral), left for Coblenz on the first of August, less than a fortnight after Calonne had first made his mysterious approach to Burke at Margate, and while the last corrections to Burke's *Appeal* were still in the hands of the

*On 1 August 1791 Dundas wrote to the Governor-General of Bengal: 'The Burkes are now great favourites with us. [Burke] has made a noble stand against those who by adopting a line of panegyrick of the French Revolution have endeavoured to unhinge the principles of the body of the people of this country . . . If you can in any way befriend Mr Willm Burke I shall feel happy in your doing so.' The Governor-General's reply indicated that he thought William was preparing to leave India (quoted *Correspondence*, vi. 363n.).

printers. In that same month of August 1791 he wrote another appeal, much shorter but equally urgent – this one addressed directly to none other than the virtually imprisoned Queen of France herself. She would never be allowed to see it in full translation, though the substance of it – in cipher, the only available means of communication – certainly reached her. This was managed through friends in France of the Duke of Dorset, who until 1789 had been British ambassador to the French court. A letter addressed a few days earlier by Richard Burke to Louis XVI did get through. Its message was similar to his father's: 'You have nothing to hope for *from the interior of your dominions.* Nothing, nothing . . . It is *only* from abroad that relief can come; and *it is coming*.' Edmund was worried that the Queen, for whom he now had the deepest mistrust, was secretly negotiating with those relatively moderate revolutionaries such as Barnave, La Fayette, and the group known as the *Feuillants*, who seemed willing to accept a form of constitutional monarchy. Marie Antoinette for her part, and not without justification, at this stage professed to *fear* the successful outcome of the sort of counter-revolution being prepared by the Princes and Calonne, of whom she was suspicious. In conjunction with him the Princes might, she thought, place the King and herself under what she called 'a new slavery'.[3]

To Burke, 'moderate' revolutionaries were still revolutionaries – and traitors. 'Madam', he wrote, 'all is in your hands. The moment you begin to negotiate with traitors you lose your greatest strength. It is wholly in patience, firmness, silence, and refusal . . . If the King accepts their pretended constitution you are both of you undone for ever. The greatest powers in Europe are hurrying to your rescue.'[4]

It might be reasonably argued that Marie Antoinette's behaviour, her apparent willingness to compromise, was by no means as senseless as Burke considered it. It is difficult, given the circumstances of Paris in 1791, to make retrospective awards for relative wisdom. We find in any case that at this very time – Burke could not possibly have known – the Queen was sending secret letters to her brother the Austrian Emperor, denouncing the Assembly and all its works and calling for what Burke wanted – armed intervention as 'the only resource' for the French monarchy.

'That unfortunate woman is not to be cured of the spirit of court intrigue even by a prison', Burke wrote to his son, newly arrived at Coblenz, in the course of a very long letter of 12–18 August. A few days later the Austrian Emperor and the King of Prussia were making a joint proclamation (the 'Declaration of Pillnitz') boldly asserting that *all* the sovereigns of Europe ought to come to the aid of the French monarchy – yet plainly indicating that without such concerted action the *émigré* Princes at Coblenz and the beleaguered King and Queen in Paris must shift for themselves. 'The Emperor has betrayed us', wrote Marie Antoinette; and indeed the eyes of both the Austrians and the Prussians at that time were looking east rather than west. Nervous of the expansion of Catherine the Great's Russia, their minds were concentrated upon the need to secure the largest possible share in the continuing partitions of Poland. The Empress Catherine herself gave verbal support to the Bourbon cause and even sent subsidies to the *émigrés*; but she too was more interested in Polish spoils. At one point rather later, in November 1791, Burke, disappointed at her inaction in the French question, and knowing that she had read and praised his *Reflections*, took it upon himself to write her a letter pleading for co-operation. Before dispatching it, he showed it to the Foreign Secretary, William Grenville, who took it to the King. 'Much struck with the eloquence and force of the reasoning', the King agreed with Grenville nevertheless that no good would come of sending it; so Burke withdrew it.[5] He had promised the French Queen that the greatest powers of Europe were hurrying to her rescue. But now, with the major European powers, there was inaction from Austria, from Russia, from Prussia; inaction equally from the British government, which was broadly content to see the power of its old enemy across the Channel weakened by revolutionary confusion.

Hence the prognosis for Richard Burke's mission to Coblenz did not hold much cheer, though he worked hard and conscientiously there, corresponding indefatigably with his father back home, arranging for Calonne and the Princes to appoint an agent to represent them in England; not always winning golden opinions among the Coblenz camp – Calonne indeed came to mistrust him – but then the Coblenz camp itself was hardly a mutually trusting band of generous-hearted brothers. When, hoping to add his own weight to his father's in trying to influence British government policy, Richard wrote directly to Dundas, Dundas's reaction and comment are interesting. He showed the letter to the Foreign Secretary, with the suggestion that it should be seen by Pitt and the King; and then of Richard himself (whose constant misfortune was to be compared unfavourably with his father), he wrote, 'I do not think he wants talents; there are now and then strokes in [the letter] which mark his father's son'.[6]

The monarchs of Europe were not going to wage war on the French Revolution. What they none of them bargained for – though Burke had always warned that revolution and the pretended 'rights of man' were meant for export – was that the French Revolution would one day soon wage war on *them*. The Declaration of Pillnitz had little or no effect on the diplomatic or military scene outside France, but inside France it did have an effect. Its threat (though it was no more than a threat) to wage a war of intervention intensified the trend towards bellicosity among the French themselves, and within a month or two Brissot and the Gironde group in the Assembly were loudly advocating war. It would unite the nation, they thought, against the hereditary enemy Austria in particular, and it would internationalise the ideas of the revolution. Robespierre in the Jacobin club debates fought hard against the idea – 'nobody', he said, 'loves armed missionaries' – but Brissot, Dumouriez, and the war party were gradually gaining ground. By the spring of the following year 1792 they would be in control.

Richard returned from Coblenz before the end of September 1791. Soon there were *two rival* French royalist agents in London, Richard's man the Chevalier de la Bintinaye representing Calonne and the Princes, and an envoy from Louis and Marie Antoinette, the Baron de Breteuil, an intimate friend of the Queen and an old enemy of Calonne. Though both Burkes did their best to placate him, the Chevalier was soon making known his displeasure, both with the tepid nature of his reception in England and with Calonne's failure to keep him in funds. Then in October a further emissary from the Princes arrived, Count Dillon, who quickly found himself at odds with Bintinaye. After a meeting with the Burkes, Dillon, as instructed, reported back to Calonne. He was sure that in *Edmund* Burke the Princes could not 'have a better agent'. Of Richard however he was most disparaging, though much of what he wrote was doubtless a retailing of the opinion of others. Richard Burke, he reported,[7] pushed vanity and conceit (*suffisance*) to the point of impertinence, and was 'excessively presumptuous'. Perhaps Dillon need not be credited too readily. His was the sort of criticism often made of Richard, who seems to have over-compensated for a real lack of self-confidence by an apparently over-confident and dogmatic outward manner. (His 'natural timidity', someone later wrote of him, 'was in no small degree increased by his great inferiority to his father, of which no man was more conscious than himself'.) If it was possible to love one's only son to excess, Burke perhaps did; it is at least a failing easy to forgive. He certainly entertained high expectations of him. Richard was assiduous and conscientious – his letters are seldom short of sense, if often long of wind – and perhaps Burke was not so foolishly starry-eyed for his son as has generally been supposed. It is true that Richard had achieved nothing of importance in Coblenz, but who could realistically have expected it, given the European diplomatic situation at the time and the conflicting ambitions among the French royalists themselves? Soon he would be playing a modestly significant hand in the once more critical affairs of Ireland, where Burke had for some time envisaged a political future for him. Again he was to have little success – but who from London could ever hope, then or since, to 'succeed' in Ireland?

In 1790, a little before publication of Burke's *Reflections*, Thomas Hussey, a London-based Irish Catholic, had approached him with an eye to some initiative being taken to win further relief for Catholics, earlier acts of 1778 and 1782 having left important disabilities untouched, including denial of the right to vote. Hussey, knowing Burke's views, both on 'the French disease' and on the injustice of the remaining discriminatory laws, made the shrewd point that in Ireland the disease might be catching, and those infected by it might not for ever remain willing to submit peaceably to 'the lash of tyranny and oppression' – and if events should come to another war against France, some grant of further toleration must surely become irresistible.[9]

War seemed improbable in 1790; but Burke, his thoughts

heavily engaged by events in France, turned to his son as his mouthpiece and representative, encouraging him to begin negotiations with a newly reconstituted Catholic Committee in Dublin. A year later Richard was asked by Edward Byrne and John Keogh, both prosperous Catholic merchants, to become the Committee's agent in London; and immediately upon his return from Coblenz he accepted the invitation. 'The many obligations we are under', Byrne wrote, 'to the zeal and brilliant abilities of the father inspire us with the strongest reliance on the son'.[10] Apart from the approaches to a sympathetic but cautious Dundas (Home Secretary from 1791) and interviews with the Irish Chief Secretary Hobart and a non-committal Pitt, there for some time the matter rested, until at the turn of the year 1791–2 Richard crossed to Ireland and, constantly bombarded and forti- fied with counsel from his father, began his mission there. An immediate difficulty soon became apparent, the Catholic Com- mittee itself being seriously divided between the aristocratic party led by Lord Kenmare (whom Richard found to be 'a poor little creature')[11] and the more radically inclined wealthy merchants such as John Keogh.

From father to son and son to father there came now a volu- minous flow of correspondence on the Irish tactics which Richard was employing or ought to be employing. But simul- taneously Burke was now composing something rather more fundamental and wide-ranging. This was ostensibly a reply – it ran eventually to forty-seven printed pages[12] – to correspondence from his friend Sir Hercules Langrishe, member for Knock- topher in the Dublin parliament. As with the *Reflections* of two years earlier, this consideration in depth of the problems facing Ireland, and particularly facing the Catholic majority there, took the *form* of a private letter, but combined the substance of a polemical pamphlet with the weight of a historical dissertation. Again as with the *Reflections*, it was intended rather less for its addressee than for the general public, and received prompt publication – to the annoyance, soon expressed, of the Lord Lieutenant (Lord Westmorland) and his Chief Secretary, Robert Hobart.

The executive arm of government in Ireland – 'Dublin Castle' – in the persons particularly of these two men, for a while yet was to prove an insuperable obstacle to the measures of Catholic relief which Edmund and Richard Burke were working for. At Westminster, Pitt's Home Secretary, Dundas, for a time seemed to offer hope that some grant of a limited franchise might be acceded to; but the attitudes held at 'the Castle' continued to dominate, and already when Burke wrote to his son at the end of February his news was disappointing: 'When I came to town', he wrote, 'it was in vain that I attempted to see [Dundas]. At length an interview was obtained . . . He did not open a word of discourse about Ireland – I introduced it. He preserved a dead silence; and heard me like a man who wished an unpleasant conversation at an end.'[13]

In his letter to Sir Hercules Langrishe, Burke reminded him:

You hated the old system [of anti-Catholic laws] as early as I did. Your first juvenile lance was broken against that giant . . . You abhorred it, as I did, for its vicious perfection. For I must do it justice: it was a complete system, full of coherence and consistency; well digested and well composed in all its parts . . . It is a thing humiliating enough that we are doubtful of the effect of the medicines we compound. We are sure of our poisons.[14]

It was imperative and urgent that Catholics should now be enfranchised. 'No nation in the world has ever been known to exclude so great a body of men (not born slaves) from the civil state and all the benefits of the constitution.' As for *which* Catholics, and how many of them, that was a matter for the prudence and discretion of parliament:

The whole being at discretion, I beg leave just to suggest some matters for your consideration – whether the government in church and state is likely to be more secure by continuing causes of grounded discontent, to a very great number (say two millions) of the subjects? Or whether the constitution, combined and balanced as it is, will be rendered more solid by depriving so large a part of the people of all concern, or interest, or share, in its representation, actual or *virtual* . . . Virtual representation is that in which there is a communion of interests, and a sympathy in feelings and desires, between those who act in the name of any description of people and the people in whose name they act . . . Such a representation I think to be in many cases even better than the actual.[15]

'The several descriptions of people', he wrote, 'will not be kept so much apart as they now are, as if they were not only separate nations, but separate species':

> Sure I am, that there have been thousands in Ireland who have never conversed with a Roman Catholic in their whole lives, unless they happened to talk to their gardener's workmen, or to ask their way when they had lost it . . . or at best had known them only as footmen, or other domestics . . . I well remember a great, and in many respects a good, man who advertised for a blacksmith; but at the same time added, he must be a Protestant. It is impossible that such a state of things . . . must not produce alienation on one side, and pride and insolence on the other.
>
> Reduced to a question of discretion, and that discretion exercised solely upon what will appear best for the conservation of the state on its present basis, I should recommend it to your serious thoughts, whether the narrowing of the foundation is always the best way to secure the building? The body of disfranchised men will not be perfectly satisfied to remain always in that state. If they are not satisfied, you have two millions* of subjects in your bosom, full of uneasiness . . . because you will not suffer them to enjoy the ancient, fundamental, tried advantages of a British constitution.[16]

He looked at the dangers immediately facing Ireland, including the possible merging of Catholic and dissenting Protestant discontent:

> Reflect seriously on the possible consequences of keeping, in the heart of your country, a bank of discontent, every hour accumulating, upon which every description of seditious men may draw at pleasure . . .
>
> Suppose the people of Ireland divided into three parts; of these . . . two are Catholic. Of the remaining third, one half is composed of dissenters. There is no natural union between those descriptions. It may be produced. If the two parts Catholic be driven into a close confederacy with half the third part of Protestants, with a view to a change in the constitution in church or state, or both; and you rest the whole of their security on a handful of gentlemen, clergy, and their dependants: compute the strength *you have in Ireland*, to oppose to grounded discontent, to capricious innovation, to blind popular fury, and to ambitious, turbulent intrigue.[17]

---

*His estimates of the Irish Catholic population vary between two and three millions.

Naturally, the language he employed in writing privately to his son was still freer. Of Chief Secretary Hobart, for instance: 'treachery beyond the practice even of Irish secretaries'. Of the archbishop of Cassel: 'a jackanapes in lawn sleeves'. Of the whole 'abominable system' of exclusive Church of Ireland dominance:

> I can never persuade myself that anything in our thirty nine articles, which differs from their [Catholic] articles, is worth making three millions of people slaves, to secure its teaching at the publick expence; and I think he must be a strange man, a strange Christian, and a strange Englishman, who would not rather see Ireland a free, flourishing, happy, *Catholick* country, though not one Protestant existed in it, than an enslaved, beggard, insulted, degraded Catholick country as it is – with some Protestants here and there scattered thro' it for the purpose not of instructing the people but of rendering them miserable . . . A religion which has for one of its dogmas the servitude of all mankind that do not belong to it – it is a vile heresy.[18]

(It was moreover, he throws in, one of the worst heresies also of 'that Protestant sect called Mahometanism'.)

Richard Burke's Irish mission of 1792 achieved no immediately apparent success. Westmorland and Hobart, who looked upon him as a troublemaker, had their way at least for the time being. Their tactic was to encourage the schism within the Catholic Committee for which Richard was agent, and then, after the Kenmare group (largely of landed gentry) seceded, to ignore the 'unrepresentative' remainder. Richard's eloquent petition to the Irish House of Commons on their behalf, very much in tune with his father's ideas and arguments, was never presented. Instead, the Committee chose to present an alternative, briefer version, which was duly rejected. With 2000 guineas, Richard was well paid for his services as agent, but was retained, in very ambiguous terms, only as unpaid non-resident adviser, being asked to report from London 'such information as your time and other avocations may admit'.[19]

Despite this setback, which he refused to accept as dismissal, he was back in Ireland for much of the autumn of 1792, and by letter kept up persuasive pressure, via Dundas, on the government in London, urging the Catholic cause. John Keogh and others from the Catholic Committee, including the future republican rebel and martyr Wolfe Tone, had by this time little more use for Richard Burke than had Westmorland and Hobart. Oddly enough, Keogh seems to have regarded him as a spy for Dundas. Equally strangely, Richard appears never to have let his father know the extent of the hostility he was experiencing from the Catholic Committee (Burke for a time was kindly host to Keogh's three sons at Beaconsfield), though he had already told Dundas that there were 'intrigues' against him by those who thought him 'too much attached to the principles and causes of Government'. Wolfe Tone ridiculed Richard's claim to act as spokesman for the Catholics even after he had been 'given his congé: He will be agent for the Catholics whether they will or not . . . His impudence is beyond what I could have imagined, and his vanity greater'.[20]

Again – this is the sort of verdict upon Richard that we commonly meet with. However, if his influence as official spokesman for the Catholics came to nothing, perhaps the flood of advice he poured out as informed commentator on the Irish scene – who carried additional weight as Burke's son and mouthpiece – did not go quite unregarded at Westminster. In the following year 1793 the government of Pitt and Dundas did finally give the vote to Irish Catholics on the same terms as those enjoyed by Protestants, although the right to *sit* in parliament was to be denied to Catholics for another thirty-six years.

Irish religious injustices and French revolutionary savageries did not entirely monopolise Burke's unresting mind during this critical year. From Beaconsfield on 'Easter Monday night 1792' he sent off a carefully considered and typically pragmatical letter on a difficult and complex subject which was again about to come before parliament: the African slave trade and the practicability of its abolition. Along with the letter went a 'Sketch of a Negro Code' in 42 paragraphs[21] – 'my old African code'; he had written it four years earlier and had recently promised to show it to Dundas. The 'sketch' proposed reform and regulation only, as an immediately practicable objective: but, as he told Dundas, he would now prefer 'utter abolition', *if only the African trade could be considered in isolation*. But it could not. The complete abolition of the African slave *trade* could not be achieved without the abolition of West Indian *slavery*. The true origin of the trade was not in the place it was begun at, but at the place of its final destination:

> I therefore was, and still am, of opinion that the whole work ought to be taken up together; and that a gradual abolition of slavery in the West Indies ought to go hand in hand with anything which should be done with regard to its supply from the coast of Africa . . . I am very apprehensive that so long as the slavery continues some means for its supply will be found. If so, I am persuaded that it is better to allow the evil, in order to correct it, than by endeavouring to forbid what we cannot be able wholly to prevent, to leave it under an illegal, and therefore an unreformed, existence. It is not that my plan does not lead to the extinction of the slave trade; but it is through a very slow progress . . . When a state of slavery is that upon which we are to work, the very means which lead to liberty must partake of compulsion . . . Hence it is that regulations must be multiplied. The planter you must at once restrain and support; and you must control, at the same time that you ease, the servant. This necessarily makes the work a matter of care, labour, and expense . . . But I think neither the object impracticable nor the expense intolerable; and I am fully convinced that the cause of humanity would be far more benefited by the continuance of the trade and servitude, regulated and reformed, than by the total destruction of both or either . . .[22]

Later that month Dundas brought forward the government's proposals for regulating the trade until the year 1800, when he envisaged its abolition. A Commons decision to bring forward to 1796 the operative date for abolition then met with delaying tactics in the House of Lords, and it was not until 1806 that British law made the trade illegal. But as Burke had expected, the task of finally *stopping* it until slavery itself was abolished in the West Indies was to prove long and difficult. Slavery in the British Empire lingered on until 1833; but it is noteworthy that in 1822 Wilberforce, planning for the great goal ahead, was on record as thinking that Burke's 'Sketch of the Negro Code', written thirty-nine years earlier, still provided useful guide-lines, or stepping stones, towards emancipation.[23]

Two of Burke's oldest close friends, Richard Shackleton and Joshua Reynolds, died in 1792. Shackleton he had continued to see, infrequently but regularly, since he had habitually come to London for the annual meeting of the Society of Friends; and now, to Shackleton's daughter Mary, recently become Mrs Lead-beater, Burke wrote movingly, 'penetrated' as he said 'by a very sincere affliction'. Her father 'had kept up the fervour of youthful affections, and his innocent vivacity and cheerfulness, which made his early days so pleasant, continued the same to the last . . . His talents were great, strong, and various.'[24] Reynolds's death, from cancer, had been long expected, but its impact on Burke was none the smaller for that. Financially as well as personally: under the terms of the will he had a bond for a £2000 loan cancelled (money borrowed earlier, probably to help William Burke) and was bequeathed a further £2000. The will also appointed him as one of the three executors, and as guardian of Reynolds's niece and favourite Mary Palmer. Inheriting from her uncle almost all of his very large fortune and now in her early forties, she almost immediately married (as his second wife) Burke's fellow Irishman, fellow Whig, Buckinghamshire neighbour, and good friend the Earl of Inchiquin. First as executor of the will and then as trustee of the marriage settlement, Burke here had a good deal of private business to add to his commitments to public causes. Inchiquin was deep in debt when he married his heiress, and one of the tasks facing Reynolds's executors was the rescue of Inchiquin's estate at Cliveden from creditors.

This was in the summer of 1792. Back in March, the Reynolds funeral, 'greatly attended' at St Paul's, had been an impressive occasion, full of 'melancholy pomp'.[25] The expense had been borne by the Royal Academy, but its management was entrusted to Burke: and when, after the ceremony, he rose as spokesman for the Reynolds family to thank the academicians, the tide of emotion that not infrequently mastered him in public again proved too powerful. He was obliged to sit down with his speech unspoken.

He and those near him had benefited from Reynolds's bequests (including Richard, junior, who had been left a Samuel Cooper miniature of Oliver Cromwell). The occasion seemed proper to him therefore to remember some neglected old family connections, particularly two of his now ageing and poverty-stricken Irish cousins, the daughters of his well-loved uncle, Patrick Nagle. 'I have long been uneasy in my mind', he wrote to Richard, who was then in Ireland, 'when I consider the early obligations, strong as debts, and stronger than some debts, to some of my own family':

> Mrs Crotty is daughter of Patrick Nagle, to whom (the father) I cannot tell you all I owe; she has had me a child in her arms and must be, I dare say, 74 years old at least, I wish her much to have some relief. So do I to Katty Courtnay [Ellen Crotty's sister]. Now my dearest Richard – I have destined, if you like it, a twentieth of what is lately fallen to us, to these two poor women, fifty to each; and I have *many and strong reasons* that it should be wholly *your* act (as indeed the money is yours) without any other reference to me than that you know how much I loved them . . . I always suppose that you consent it should be done at all. God knows how little we can spare it.[26]

Richard must at least have obeyed his father's injunctions regarding anonymity, for when Ellen Crotty wrote thanking Burke on behalf of herself and her sister, she expressed 'concern' that she was not allowed to say whom the money came from.

It was Richard also to whom, in his role as Burke family lawyer, it fell to act on behalf of William Burke in a settlement – at last – of his debt to Lord Verney. In fact for some years before Verney's death in 1791 Richard had been unsuccessfully labouring to arrive at an agreed composition, with Verney holding out to the end for the full £20,000 plus interest. Verney's niece and heir, however, Lady Fermanagh, proved more ready to compromise, accepting an immediate payment of 5000 guineas, with the somewhat shadowy promise of £5000 more to come in four years' time – shadowy, since she agreed, if only informally, that failing the second payment she would not 'arrest or otherwise molest him' – or as Richard put it, 'she promised to hear reason'.[27] Probably the Reynolds benefactions had played their part in making the settlement practicable.

William Burke's own correspondence of this period has not survived, but a joint letter to him from Edmund and Jane has. This sends 'a thousand thousand thanks' for 'all your letters'; gives all the latest political and personal news; and expresses the hope that William may now be able to return home 'safely' – meaning presumably free from danger of arrest. 'My ever dear old friend', Burke writes, 'God bring you safely to us. May we have one cheerful winters evening at the close of our short day, before we go to bed. You are in my heart to its last beat.' Then he ends his, the major, share of this letter with an extra trivial-sounding item of information: Jane had been ill 'by mistake of a medicine', but was now recovered. Jane then appends confirmation: 'I am my dear friend perfectly well on this third of September 1792. I wish in God we were assured of your being so well. But I hope and trust we shall hear soon that your health at least, whatever your finances may be is good . . . God preserve you and send you safe and well to us . . .'[28]

The mistake in the medicine had been far from trivial. Burke in fact had come near to killing his wife by giving her an overdose of opiates. She had been ill; and 'not choosing to trust to their most attached domestics',[29] he had in error administered 'a two-ounce phial of laudanum'. (Was this through short-sightedness? – contemporary cartoonists never tired of depicting him peering through his spectacles.) Then, realising in understandable panic what he had done, and first sending for the local apothecary, he dispatched a servant post-haste to Windsor to summon the eminent Dr James Lind. Expecting it is said to find his patient dead on arrival, Dr Lind nevertheless complied promptly but, fortunately, violent vomitings 'almost without intermission for five hours' had saved her. Two or three days later, reporting to Dr Lind in detail on her condition – happily recovering, 'I bless God for it', and 'very composed and cheerful' – Burke writes, 'You will be so good as to give your directions. You are to judge whether it be necessary for you to ride over.' Within a week or so, Jane was able to take the Buckinghamshire air in her carriage for a few days before travelling with her husband to Bath. There, though not exactly ill, and with the waters 'sitting well on her stomach', she took rather a long time to regain her strength.[30]

Very soon however she was active among a group of charitable ladies, which included Mrs Crewe and Hannah More, helping to raise funds for the many near-destitute French refugee priests in England. Burke himself became heavily engaged in this good cause and its organisation, devoting to it many careful hours and indignant pages of his ever-voluminous correspondence, and publishing in the *Evening Mail* an appeal on behalf of 'the suffering clergy of France' persecuted by 'a faction of atheists, infidels, and other persons of evil principles and dispositions, calling themselves philosophers'.[31]

The third of September, when Jane Burke after her dangerous mishap was assuring William that she was 'perfectly well', was the day after the capture of Verdun by the Prussians invading France. This prompted panicky alarms in Paris, where the Commune issued a proclamation, calling the populace to arms: 'The enemy is at the gates!' The tocsin was sounded, and there were fears of a prison break-out. For the ensuing five days, in Paris itself and in some provincial towns, the mob was in control. Many hundreds of prisoners, male and female, were butchered, most of them common-law criminals, though in Paris alone some 300 priests or political prisoners were among the victims. Altogether in Paris during those five days there were between 1100 and 1400 killings.

These September massacres had followed hard on the heels of one of the most significant, and to Burke horrifying, days of revolution – or series of revolutions, as it was fast becoming. On 10 August the Breton and Marseillais *fédérés* had marched on the royal palace of the Tuileries, obliging the King and his family to flee to the shelter of the Assembly, itself now approaching its death throes. In the fighting of 10 August 373 *fédérés* were killed, and about 800 of the nobility and Swiss guard. To Fitzwilliam, still his friend and patron despite their differences, Burke wrote immediately after these sombre events:

> The very place of refuge to this miserable King and his family, when he fled from one phalanx of disciplined assassins, was in the midst of another and the very leaders and instigators of the first. He entered as your Lordship sees amidst the ferocious cries of these cannibals,* and staid . . . at the Bar to hear all the barbarous eloquence of their bloody declamations against him preparatory to the sentence of formal deprivation which they passed against him in the presence of his wife, his sister, and his children. This late master of seven magnificent palaces lying in a little chamber of retreat, without table, chair, or bed for three days with his whole family of children all huddled together under the disgusting necessities of nature . . . are circumstances almost lost in the horrour of the scenes that passed in the Assembly. Add to this the dreadful massacre of all those who adhered to them, and which will run like fire from one end of France to the other – surely all this will be enough to satiate even Mr Fox [to whom Fitzwilliam was still
>
> *The London papers reported some actual cannibalism.

committed] and Mr Sheridan, or Dr Priestley – or whoever carries these triumphs the farthest . . .[32]

Such 'horrours' would not, could not, be contained within France. 'As long', he wrote, 'as the desperate situation which prevails in France can maintain itself, we shall always find some eruption or other here. The fire is constantly at work . . . The whole aedifice of antient Europe is shaken by the earthquake caused by that fire.' The whole of Europe, he told Grenville, faced 'the most important crisis that ever existed in the world'.[33]

Everything now depended on the Duke of Brunswick and his invading Prussian army; but then came, in September, the check to the Prussians at Valmy; the consequent negotiations – 'treason without parallel in history'[34] – between Brunswick and the French general Dumouriez; and Brunswick's unhampered retreat which allowed Dumouriez to attack the Austrian Netherlands. The centrifugal momentum, long to be irresistible, of French revolutionary conquest had from here its starting point.

Worse was very soon to follow. 'The Prussian and Austrian combined forces', Burke wrote in October to his son in Ireland, 'have fled before a troop of strolling players with a buffoon [Dumouriez] at their head. Savoy, Nice, etc., are occupied without a blow – Whilst the Duke of Brunswick flies out of France, the whole course of the Rhine is ravaged. The [Austrian] Empire is left exposed . . . The Netherlands are not much better off internally or externally. Their mountains will not protect the Swiss. A French fleet . . . will domineer in the Mediterranean without resistance.' These calamitous events would '*be fatal to this age and to a long posterity*'. 'I would expect to hear every day almost to a certainty of a sacking of Rome, worse than it has ever been sacked by the Goths or Vandals.' Sardinia, Naples, and Sicily were alike threatened. And when Spain looked likely to be the next object of French aggression, Burke expressed strongly to Fitzwilliam the view that she should be treated 'politically, commercially, financially' – Spaniards might well have hoped it could have been put with greater tact – 'as a member of the British Empire, and as much entitled to our protection as if nominally it was so'. If the French fleet intercepted Spain's fleet and took possession of her colonial commerce and treasure, Britain would be forced into war 'whether we will or not', and by that later time at a serious disadvantage: 'no time ought to be lost'. Fitzwilliam,

Burke's benefactor still, was still also, however shakily, attached to Fox and the anti-war Whigs; and it caused both men, Burke and Fitzwilliam, honest men both, genuine sadness that their political positions had fallen apart. 'Adieu my dearest Lord', Burke closed his letter: 'my mind is much oppressed but I keep it up by every resourse I can find.'[35]

When in November, after his victory at Jemappes, Dumouriez proceeded to overrun the Austrian Netherlands, the prospect of Britain entering the war became much more immediate. Burke continued hammering away at Fitzwilliam and at the urgent need for patriotic Whigs to join forces with Pitt's government. There must be 'an extinction', he wrote, 'or at least a suspension' of parties.[36] During the summer there had indeed been abortive negotiations for a coalition, even at one stage for Pitt and Fox to become joint Secretaries of State, with a neutral First Lord at the Treasury – an improbable-sounding arrangement which in any case the King would probably not have accepted. Among the Whigs it was Loughborough who with Elliot and Windham now stood nearest to Burke's political position; and Loughborough several times came near to being offered – and then was offered and came near to accepting – the important post of Lord Chancellor. The Duke of Portland, still nominally leader of the Whigs and still, as Burke complained, 'in Fox's power', managed for a long time to dissuade him; but after the French overran the Austrian Netherlands and Pitt himself saw that war had become both necessary and unavoidable, Loughborough's accession to the government, with Burke's strong approval, became equally unpreventable. He finally took the Chancellorship in January 1793, just three days before war was declared.

For some time yet, however, Loughborough was to be the only Whig to join Pitt. Burke despaired of Portland, for whom indecision seemed to have become a way of life. As Elliot once put it, 'the Duke of Portland will look at his nails and raise his spectacles from his nose to his forehead for a fortnight or so before he answers me'.[37] But to do the Duke justice, he was no longer quite so firmly bound to Fox as Burke had supposed. Fox's mind and disposition, so Portland told Fitzwilliam in November 1792, had recently become 'more warped'. In conversation with Portland, Fox had gone so far as to express *pleasure* at the failure of the Prussian and Austrian armies. He seemed, so Portland reported, insensible to the lust for domination shown by the French; was unafraid of the 'inundation of levelling doctrines'; and perhaps, hater of kings that he was, was ready to welcome a republican form of government for Britain.[38]

However, Portland still refused to criticise Fox openly and, together with Fitzwilliam, supported a Whig Club resolution 'confirming, strengthening, and increasing' its attachment to him – whereupon the Burkes, father and son, Windham, Elliot, and some forty others withdrew their membership. Burke then, 'with pain, and with a heart full of grief', set about writing (but delayed publication until autumn 1793 to give time, he said, to confirm the 'justice of hastily penned opinions') his *Observations of Parliament; addressed to the Duke of Portland and Lord Fitzwilliam.*[39] Sending a copy to Portland ('my account of my conduct to my private friends'), he asked him to put it away immediately, unread; 'and when a day of compulsory reflexion comes, then be pleased to turn to it'. 'I have just now read it over', he writes, 'very coolly and deliberately.' He had been accused of alarmism. Very well: 'that alarm in my mind is by no means quieted'. He cites the activities of 'Jacobins' at home, and criticises opinions hostile to the war expressed by the Whig Lord Lauderdale, for instance, and by Thomas Coke of Holkham, who appeared to be 'spreading disaffection through Norfolk':

> It is truly alarming to see so large a part of the aristocratick interest engaged in the cause of the new species of democracy which is openly attacking or secretly undermining the system of property by which mankind has hitherto been governed. But we are not to delude ourselves.

What he was now writing in his covering letter to Portland was 'in the manner of an apology':

> I have given it that form, as being the most respectful; but I do not stand in need of any apology from my principles, my sentiments, or my conduct. I wish the paper I lay before your Grace to be considered as my most deliberate, solemn, and even testamentary protest against the proceedings and doctrines which have hitherto produced so much mischief in the world, and which will infallibly produce more, and possibly greater.

'A general war against Jacobins and Jacobinism', he insisted, offered 'the only chance of saving Europe (and England as included in Europe) from a truly frightful revolution.'[40]

Portland's reply went some way towards echoing Burke's horror of Jacobinism, and repeated once more his admiration and affection. But, as he said, 'my imagination, my feelings, my judgement, my conclusions do not and cannot keep pace with yours – I have not the same sensibility, I have not the same fears'.[41] Three months later, however, Portland and Fitzwilliam at last steeled themselves to break publicly with Fox and declare themselves willing to give general support to Pitt's government and the prosecution of the war. Even then they were to hold back for another six months, until July 1794, from accepting *office* in coalition with Pitt.

Burke's anxiety to demonstrate how real the dangers of revolution were led him once, immediately before the declaration of war, to stage a piece of parliamentary theatre which his enemies were quick to ridicule. The occasion was the Commons debate on the government's Aliens Bill, and the point at issue was the making and storing of swords and daggers which (it was alleged) were perhaps for export to France, perhaps for a more sinister purpose such as insurrection in Britain. Burke had learned of a big Birmingham order for daggers, and knew that the government had contrived to secure samples. He accordingly sent Dundas, Home Secretary, a brief note asking for a 'pattern dagger' to be sent to him 'wrapped up in something which may not present it to observation in the street'.[42] Actually it was Bland Burges, Foreign Under-Secretary, not Dundas, who obliged Burke by complying with this strange request. Burke then kept the dagger concealed under his clothing until almost the end of his speech on the Aliens Bill when, brandishing it aloft, he cried to the astonished members that *that* was what they would get if they offered friendship to revolutionary France. Reports vary; the more adventurous or imaginative asserted that he hurled the dagger to the floor of the House; and the Foxite *Morning Post*, perhaps more predictably than reliably, went on to suggest that the only effect of so melodramatic and eccentric a gesture was to hold up proceedings while the House recovered its seriousness.[43]

In London and in the big provincial towns radical and anti-radical feelings were both running strongly. While loyalist demonstrations burned effigies of Tom Paine, radical clubs and Painite demonstrations execrated Pitt and the government – and naturally also Burke. At Dronfield, for instance, outside

Sheffield, an effigy of Burke, hanging from a gibbet, was ceremonially burned 'amidst the acclamations of the people', and a toast was drunk to the Swinish Multitude, with the rider: 'May they hold in contempt the man who first gave that appelation to free Britons'.[44] (He did no such thing of course; it was for the bloodthirsty Parisian mob that he had found that notorious phrase.) Just three days after Burke's effigy was being burned on its Yorkshire gibbet, the people of France, or rather 'that enormous aggregate of crime and madness' called the *government* of France,[45] were sending their King to the guillotine. 'The catastrophe of the tragedy of France has been compleated', Burke wrote to Loughborough. 'It was the necessary result of all the preceeding parts of the monstrous drama.' Nine months later the epilogue to the drama, with the guillotining of the Queen of France whose earlier plight had in Burke's *Reflections* elicited the most celebrated of all his impassioned outbursts, left him almost drained of words. Disgust by then even outweighed horror. 'Oh God!', he wrote to Windham; 'the charge! and the last article particularly!' – for Marie Antoinette had there been accused of committing unnameable indecencies with her own son.[46]

Even before Britain's entry into the war, Pitt and Dundas had sometimes held consultations with Burke. With war declared, these continued. In March 1793, for example, with the main group of the Portland Whigs still in opposition, Burke, Windham, and Elliot were received by Pitt and Dundas, and briefed on the state of military and naval preparations. According to Elliot's account of this meeting, Burke gave Pitt 'a little political instruction, in a very respectful and cordial way, but with the authority of an old and most informed statesman; and although nobody ever takes the whole of Burke's advice, yet he often, or rather always, furnishes very important and useful matter, *some part* of which sticks and does good. Pitt took it all patiently and cordially.'[47]

Pitt however had none of Burke's crusading temper, none of his longing to see 'the British sword leap from its scabbard' and plunge into the unclean body of the Revolution. If France could be denied the Netherlands coastline and the great anchorages of the Scheldt, if her cause could be damaged and her claws cut, a negotiated peace favouring British interests with suitable 'indemnity' (probably Martinique), might satisfy Pitt. His war policy, echoing his father's brilliant successes of the 1750s but signally failing to repeat them, meant that the main thrust of British activity should be colonial and naval, while the chief burden of the European war fell upon the shoulders of an Anglo-continental coalition assisted by British subsidies. Thus between 1793 and 1796 men and money were poured into the West Indies, where the British soon found themselves facing, in addition to the French army, an uprising of slaves, and where eventually the casualties from yellow fever proved for the troops horrendous, and for the campaign fatal. (Major Haviland, husband to Burke's niece Mary, was one of those dying from fever in Martinique.) As his father had, Pitt envisaged limited interventions on the continent of Europe, aimed at Toulon or points on the Brittany or Biscay coast (seats of royalist counter-revolution) or at Dunkirk and its Flanders hinterland. It was in this last area, during the winter of 1794–5, that British forces under the King's son Frederick, Duke of York, failing to gain satisfactory co-operation from their Prussian and Austrian allies, were driven northwards through the Netherlands to be evacuated – such frozen, half-starved remnants as survived – from Bremen by the Navy.

Toulon for a time offered lively hopes. 'This is a great thing, this of Toulon', Burke wrote to Charles Burney in September 1793. (Burney was helping with relief work for the French refugee clergy.) Toulon had declared itself loyal to Louis XVI's infant successor – 'Louis XVII' – and welcomed into its harbour the British Mediterranean Squadron commanded by Admiral Hood, who then issued a proclamation supporting the royalists and promising the eventual return of Toulon to the French monarchy. Only a few months later, however, Toulon fell to republican forces under the command of a young Corsican named Bonaparte, and Hood withdrew. It was worse than a calamity, Burke said to Windham; it was a disgrace.[48]

For a time western France, particularly Poitou and the Vendée coastal area south of the Loire, seemed to present better opportunity. Here a 'Royal and Catholic Army' had been assembled and had gained good initial successes against republican troops. Burke begged Dundas – still his best avenue of approach to the government – to consider: 'this [in Poitou and La Vendée] is a war directly against Jacobinism and its principle. It strikes at the enemy at his weakest and most vulnerable part. At La Vendée with infinitely less charge [than that expended in trying to take Martinique] we may make an impression likely to be decisive.' But at that stage the British government would only promise to send the Vendée royalists equipment, some *émigré* troops, and arms – and those only if they could first secure a port. British troops could not be spared.[49] The Vendéans did manage for a few months to hold, not a port of any consequence, but the offshore island of Noirmoutier, but had lost it before any help (which would probably have been limited only) could reach them there. Eight battalions of British infantry did attempt, unsuccessfully, in December 1793 to make contact with other royalist rebels further north besieging Granville in the Gulf of St Malo. They were obliged to withdraw to the shelter of Guernsey.

This virtual collapse of Vendéan resistance afflicted Burke 'beyond all measure . . . I have no words to express my sorrow for it', he wrote; 'but there is still a God; and that is a consolation'.[50]

'AN ILIAD OF WOE'

SUDDENLY IN April 1793 William Burke arrived back in England unheralded, and resumed as it were his old associate-membership of the Burke family. All too soon it became clear that the safety from pursuing creditors of which the younger Richard seems to have assured him was no safety at all. It was not only Lord Verney's niece Lady Fermanagh who had claims against him and was already thinking better of her earlier generous, though informal, promise not to 'arrest or molest' him failing payment of the agreed outstanding £5000. There was also a threat persisting from earlier money quarrels and litigation with his old deputy-paymaster in Madras. In the two years or so following his return, he was arrested for debt on both of these counts, being each time however soon rescued and released, though not without difficulties for his rescuers. His situation remained 'ruined', and his health no less so. At Bath for treatment six months after his return, he was soon sending out alarm signals, requesting remittances to be sent on to him from Burke's London bankers. 'Poor Will'; 'our worthy and unfortunate friend' – at least the second of Burke's adjectives fits the bill. But it was not only he who found William worthy and loved him so well. Young Richard and Jane Burke were both genuinely devoted to him.

So too they were to the elder Richard, the failed West Indian adventurer, the lawyer who became Recorder of Bristol, the occasional politician who twice was Secretary to the Treasury, the friend of Reynolds, the man (at least by Edmund's testimony) whom strangely Fox once rated 'superior in abilities' to his famous brother.[1] He had been ill several times latterly, and now, one night at his chambers in Lincoln's Inn, he was seized 'with a fit of coughing by which he was suffocated'. He was buried at Beaconsfield on 10 February 1794. The brothers had always been devotedly intimate, and Edmund was sufficiently grieved by Richard's death to talk once again of retiring from all public business, even of leaving the trial of Warren Hastings to the care of others.[2]

Through the previous six years, notwithstanding regency crisis, revolution in France, Whig party dissension, and now the war, Burke had toiled away at the Hastings impeachment, to ever-declining interest from public and parliament. He had said more than once that it was only his determination to fight the cause to its close – he could hardly now hope to win it – which kept him from resigning his seat, since of course it was only as spokesman for the House of Commons that he and the Committee of Managers could act. The Lords still sat on twenty-eight occasions in 1794 on impeachment business but, as Burke complained, only 'a miserable remnant' of a few dozen usually attended. Many of them moreover showed clear sympathy for Hastings and, Burke grumbled, pleaded his cause 'as if they had been his feed counsel'. At last, in June 1794, the Managers' case was concluded, although the verdict – acquittal, as long expected – was not given until the following year.

Burke had further reason for contemplating retirement from the Commons. He was confident that Earl Fitzwilliam, his patron at Malton, would allow him to nominate a successor there, and he *hoped* that that successor would be his son, who for four years now had been employed as Fitzwilliam's agent. If it were not to be Richard, perhaps it might be his close friend (and Burke's too) the young lawyer French Laurence, or perhaps William Elliot, a distant cousin of that other stout Burkian, Sir Gilbert. The doubts about Richard's chances arose basically from the political differences which had recently separated Burke from Fitzwilliam, although, with Portland and Fitzwilliam finally breaking with Fox, these were now largely repaired.

Richard, with his undoubted talent for ruffling feathers, had not helped his cause by the tone he had adopted in 1793, when (for the second time) he had seen a chance of being offered another of the Fitzwilliam seats, vacant at Higham Ferrers.

Fitzwilliam had declined then to nominate him, on the grounds that Burke – and by implication his son also – had deserted the Whig cause. Burke, he said, had 'deliver'd himself over into the hands of Pitt, formally and professedly, last November . . . How then can I bring you into Parliament?'[3] Richard's letter to Fitzwilliam, expressing his 'surprise' and, indeed, pique on learning of his rejection, runs fully to fourteen self-justifying and father-justifying pages.[4] Fitzwilliam thought it worth showing to Portland, calling it 'a very extraordinary peformance', and considered that it fully confirmed his decision not to nominate Richard. However, some of the language used by Fitzwilliam in these exchanges apparently brought him 'a severe remonstrance' from Richard's father, which affected Fitzwilliam 'so much that he was actually ill for some days' – so at least it was reported to Gilbert Elliot. 'When Burke heard this', wrote Elliot, 'he was so much hurt in his turn that he went to Lord Fitzwilliam, and the whole affair was completely made up.'[5] It was to Elliot that Burke was complaining at this time 'with something approaching to indignation', that Richard, 'qualified in every way, is set aside for every thing abroad and at home for the sins of his father'. The 'abroad' here relates probably to a request for an appointment Burke had made through Dundas, though without Richard's knowledge; it was refused.

Burke approaching his retirement in 1794 still *expected* Fitzwilliam to offer the Malton seat to Richard; and friends brought the fact home to Fitzwilliam, who proceeded formally to invite Richard to accept nomination. Thanking Fitzwilliam in an emotional letter for his 'great goodness to my son – by far the greatest goodness which could possibly be conferred on me' – Richard, he wrote, had been 'too good a son to be much known in the world'. He had devoted himself to his father and mother to a degree which had made his worth and talent inconspicuous to others. 'Without a tincture of parental partiality', he could assure Fitzwilliam and the borough of Malton that they would never need to be ashamed of their new member.[6] All seemed to be well. Fitzwilliam was delighted that Burke was delighted; surprised too that Burke had derived such obviously acute pleasure from his little note expressing appreciation for services past, directly he knew positively that Burke had applied for the Chiltern Hundreds. He had not thought there was much in his little letter of thanks: 'it was simply complimentary and kind, but he has found something in it which has pleased his affectionate heart – the young one seems exceedingly pleas'd too, . . . not a word of what pass'd before'.[7]

On 18 July the bailiff and burgesses of Malton formally elected Richard Burke, who was present with his father, to be member of Parliament for their borough. A fortnight later he was dead.

His health for the past several years had not been good, and we read more than once of visits to spas or the sea-coast, for 'the waters' or the sea-bathing, or of his being prescribed asses' milk. When Fitzwilliam learned of his death, his comment was that although he had not 'looked for a long life' and thought he saw signs of 'irreparable mischief', the suddenness of Richard's death took him by surprise. French Laurence said that for a year or so he had been fearing the worst. Yet although Burke and Jane had both worried constantly for their son and his well-being, there is no indication that they had at any time foreseen the closeness of this tragic blow.

It was to Burke's niece Mary, his sister Juliana's daughter now living at Beaconsfield, that French Laurence wrote on the day before Richard's death:

> The disaster is a consumption, which has however not yet actu-
> ally reached the substance of the lungs, but has spread to the
> lower part of the trachea*. . . The family are with poor Richard
> in country lodgings a little beyond Brompton. It is a house of
> mourning indeed, a scene of affliction, Dr Brocklesby says,
> almost too much for him, who as a physician is enured to these
> sights . . .[8]

Then, three days later to Mary Haviland again, thanking God that Richard's 'father and mother did not seriously feel his danger till the last week of his life' and that they had not been doomed, as the physicians had expected, to watch him 'dying by inches' over the long months, Laurence recounted the grievous story of Richard's end: how he had sunk back to his death literally 'in his parent's arms'; how afterwards Edmund had alternated between

*There is some mystery in Dr Brocklesby's diagnosis, at least as reported by Laurence. A 'consumption' – pulmonary tuberculosis that is – which has not reached 'the substance of the lungs' seems to carry some self-contradiction. Might the surprising extreme suddenness of the fatality suggest perhaps something other than consumption, possibly some acutely virulent infection, as the 'actual' cause of death?

fits of uncontrolled 'truly terrible' grief and calm periods for making necessary arrangements; how Mrs Burke after 'fits of violent weeping' sometimes showed serener composure than her husband; how, when in an accidental fall she sprained her wrist, 'she only lamented it had not been her neck'.[9]

Richard was buried, as his uncle had so recently been, at Beaconsfield. Among the pall-bearers were Burke's physician and benefactor Dr Brocklesby; French Laurence; Windham, Lord Inchiquin; and both the Duke of Portland and his son Lord Titchfield. Fitzwilliam's heart failed him when he tried to write his condolences, knowing the emptiness of words at such times – but then enclosed his letter of sympathy in a covering note to Walker King, leaving it to King's discretion to deliver it or not. Burke's reply – 'Oh your letter affected me to the bottom of my soul' – may perhaps be forgiven its surely extravagant eulogy of his son. 'May *your* son', he added to Fitzwilliam, 'grow up like him . . . and may not you receive, as I have done from my son, his last breath. Adieu! and may you be happy – and may I learn to be patiently and submissively miserable!'[10]

Richard to a large extent had been manager of the Burke family's financial affairs for some years, and he died at a time when they were, as usual, in some turmoil. Quite apart from William's, Burke's own complicated debts, including the mortgages on the Beaconsfield property and about £6000, including arrears of interest, still owed to the Garrick estate, may well have amounted in all to £30,000 – though, as Richard pointed out, this sum was covered, or more than covered, by the steadily rising value of the Beaconsfield estate. To have had to sell it would, however, have been for Burke a dire misfortune.

For the past nine or ten months he had known that the Pitt administration and the King both favoured the grant of a pension to him, perhaps with a peerage too, upon his coming resignation from the Commons, and several of his friends had been lobbying on his behalf. Burke himself had no great ambition for the peerage, though Windham, for one, was pressing Pitt to request it of the King. What mattered to Burke, said Fitzwilliam (whose own further generosity, after their political differences, Burke had for a time hesitated, and perhaps declined, to accept), was that he should know where he stood, so that 'he may square his expences with his means, be they ever so small'.[11] It was less than a month after Richard's death that Pitt signified to Burke the King's intention to make 'an immediate grant out of the Civil List of £1,200 per annum (being the largest sum which his Majesty is able to fix)' for the joint lives of Edmund and Jane Burke, or either survivor. But since the King considered this a reward not adequately proportioned to Burke's 'public merit', he wished parliament in the next session to confer a more substantial annuity. In the event, a year passed before Burke was awarded annuities totalling £2500 for three lives from the Crown's 'reserved revenue', which was not subject to the restrictions imposed by the Civil List Act of 1782. George III had not of course forgotten who had been chiefly responsible for that act, and thought that perhaps Burke now understood that he might earlier have been mistaken. When Pitt sent him Burke's letter acknowledging with thanks the award of the first (Civil List) pension, the King commented:

> Misfortunes are the greatest softeners of the human mind: and have in the instance of this distressed man made him own what his warmth of temper would not have allowed under other circumstances, viz, that he may have erred. One quality I take him to be very susceptible of, that is gratitude, which covers many failings, and makes me therefore happy at being able to relieve him.[12]

Knowing that his pension was now firmly promised, Burke was ready to welcome Fitzwilliam's renewed offer of a loan. 'I accept your Lordship's most generous offer', he wrote, 'giving my bond for these sums; for now my bond may be worth something.'[13]

French Laurence told Mrs Crewe that on first learning of the award of his Civil List pension at the end of August 1794, Burke seemed 'contented'. But at first it 'renewed his affliction, as his son's name was originally to have been included in the arrangement. "Alas", he cried, "this is but watering old withered stumps, the fresh young shoot which should have drawn nourishment from the dew of the bounty is torn away".' And to Walker King Burke wrote, 'Oh my dear dear friend, how many pangs attend this satisfaction! that he for whom I lived did not live to see this, and to dispose of money so justly his. Oh pray for my pardon.'[14]

For a long time after his son's death, nearly everything that Burke wrote, whether on political or private matters – and his

257

correspondence continued as busily, voluminously, and often passionately as ever – contains reference to the catastrophe which he and his wife had been stricken by. And by now his own grief and misery were inextricably mingled with his fear – more than just a fear, a conviction – that civilisation was at a point of crisis from which it might never recover. England and all Europe were in acute peril of being 'Jacobinized': and this was true of Ireland (where his attention was now once again intensively focused) no less than the rest of the continent. The war, thus for him a war to avert the destruction of European civilisation, was going badly; and some in the government, including he feared Pitt, were looking for a way out of it in some compromise arrangement with France – what to Burke would be an infamous 'regicide peace'. In much that he said and wrote during these latter years of his threescore and eight, there is a heavy weight of despair, public as well as private, a sense of looming apocalypse.

There was 'an Iliad of woe approaching', as he warned Windham, now Secretary at War. And again to Windham, a little more than two months after Richard's death, he wrote:

> I have been obliged to go into the open air from time to time to refresh myself, and thus the time went away. This is dreadful! dreadful beyond the loss of a general battle. I now despair completely. I begin to think that God, who must surely regard the least of his creatures as well as the greatest, took what was dearest to me to himself in good time.[15]

Still to Windham, 'I am almost literally a dying man. In several senses and to many purposes, I am dead.' 'I am tost by publick upon private grief.' 'I am in a state of mind as near compleat despair as a man can be in . . . Adieu, adieu, Ever yours, E. Burke, or what remains of him and his.' He hated going up to London, he told the Chancellor, Lord Loughborough – it meant showing 'to the world the face of a man marked by the hand of God'. To Mrs Crewe ('our incomparable Mrs Crewe', he called her; moreover he wished her and her husband to know how grateful he was for their kindness to him when he was 'expelled' from the party)[16] he wrote: 'Nothing but gloom covers any part of the horizon. All is alike, at home and abroad – a complete failure of counsels, in arms and in laws. The race of *men* seems to be lost – all are either miserable drivellers or ferocious savages.' Of course he exaggerated – hyperbole and the excited over-statement had always come naturally to him – so perhaps we need not follow him too literally when he writes to thank Lord Auckland (William Eden) for his kindness in turning part of his attention 'towards a dejected old man, buried in the anticipated grave of a feeble old age, forgetting and forgotten in an obscure and melancholy retreat'. More resiliently he said elsewhere at this time, 'Sloth ill deserves to merit the name of tranquillity . . . When I see my labourers work to seventy eight years old and assuage their afflictions with their toil, as I have seen one of them the other day expire in a manner with the flail in his hand, I see no bad example . . .'[17]

He had in fact little need for such examples. There was, with his son's death, no break in his energetic participation in public affairs, whether concerning high politics (the critical state of Ireland, the war, the *threat* of peace) or matters of lesser but still important concern, such as the welfare of the French refugee clergy, the education of the children of *émigrés* at a school at Penn in Buckinghamshire near his home, a controversy over the appointment of a new Provost at his old college, Trinity, Dublin – fury here at more Dublin Castle 'jobbery' – and the project to establish a seminary, St Patrick's College, Maynooth, for Irish Catholic priests.[18]

It used to be said that he and Mrs Burke 'did not dine out of their own house for two years after Richard's death'. Together and in the company of others, that may be strictly true; Burke himself affirms it.[19] Nevertheless he continued to be not infrequently in London where, since he no longer had a house of his own, he usually, and Jane too sometimes, stayed at Nerot's Hotel in St James's Square. It was from there for instance that in March 1795 (still protesting that his situation was 'not very remote from a man not existing in this life') he is to be found writing a note to Thomas Grenville – brother to the Foreign Secretary, William, Lord Grenville – begging the favour to be told at what hour that morning they might meet: 'I wish to say a word to one of the most sensible men I know'. Burke in fact was entirely incapable of altogether retiring from politics or of burying himself 'forgotten in an obscure and melancholy retreat'. There ought to be no belittling of the severity of his private affliction or the honesty of his public despair; but the very letter in which he used that dejected phrase was in acknowledgment of receiving a newly published pamphlet by Auckland which became the trigger to fire him off on the biggest project of his last two or three years, his *Letters on a Regicide Peace*. Auckland let Pitt see Burke's observations accompanying his letter of acknowledgment, eloquent and gloomy; and Pitt's dismissive comment is interesting. He found them 'like other rhapsodies from the same pen, in which there is much to admire, and nothing to agree with'.[20]

When Pitt reconstructed his cabinet to include the Portland Whigs, Portland himself had taken the post of Home Secretary, which embraced Irish affairs, and it was indicated to Fitzwilliam that he would be appointed Lord Lieutenant of Ireland as soon as a suitably prestigious post could be found for the existing Lord Lieutenant, Westmorland. This last matter brought some difficulty and delay, for it was a long time before Westmorland consented to take anything below cabinet office and, as time went on, Pitt appeared to be having second thoughts about appointing Fitzwilliam at all – or, as he preferred to put it, 'allowing the Duke of Portland' to nominate him.[21] The question then was, ought Portland and Fitzwilliam to resign? No, Burke advised, it would be better to sit tight and wait to be dismissed. He worked hard, however, and with at least temporary success, to heal the threatening breach; but although, by the time Fitzwilliam took up his post in Dublin, Pitt's cabinet *thought* it had an agreed policy on Ireland, events there were soon to show that Fitzwilliam's version of it was crucially divergent.

Fitzwilliam made no secret that he intended to act as a new broom when he arrived in Ireland; and already by October 1794, three months before going, had indicated that the first obstacle he wished to see swept out of his way was the Irish Lord Chancellor, Fitzgibbon (later Earl of Clare, a friend of Pitt). Between them, Portland and Fitzwilliam were confidently looking forward to introducing a new reforming spirit in Dublin; and Burke, his domestic sorrows notwithstanding, was stimulated by the prospect. Ireland perhaps might be saved from what he most feared, the Jacobin infection to which an alienated Catholic population was vulnerable. 'With every possible sentiment of love and gratitude', he wrote in November 1794 to Fitzwilliam:

> If anything could tend to make me lay down my sorrowing gray hairs in the grave with peace, it would be to see an anti-Jacobin administration [in Ireland] firmly united and solidly

settled; and to see my native land under a government of the best and wisest men that either country possesses.[22]

He was convinced and many times insisted that 'the Dublin Castle gang', 'the Junto' – Westmorland and his advisers, Fitzgibbon, Beresford, and the rest – 'by their innumerable corruptions, frauds, oppressions, and follies', were opening 'a back door to Jacobinism to rush in upon us and take us in the rear', since above all it was they, the 'Junto', the 'click', this collection of 'worm-eaten furniture', who were provoking the Catholic population into 'the phrensy of that malignant fever', the Jacobin disease. And the folly of it was that (changing his metaphor in a letter to his Irish friend Langrishe) the Catholics were the very people whose religious principles, church polity, and habitual discipline 'might make them an invincible dyke against that inundation'.[23]

Fitzwilliam crossed to Ireland at a moment when agitation by the Catholics for the removal of their remaining disabilities was pressing. Only a few weeks after his arrival in Dublin, the Irish government of Henry Grattan was proposing a measure to grant, among a number of important concessions, the one seen as the most important of all, the right of Catholics to sit in the Irish parliament. His speech introducing the bill on 12 February 1795 was perfectly and eloquently in line with Burke's position, including as it did loyal sentiments, further measures to support the war, and a harsh attack on Jacobinism. French 'liberty', he declared, meant death and bedlam. Burke passionately wished the bill well, although as he more than once pointed out, it would make little practical difference, given existing franchise qualifications, to the *composition* of the Dublin parliament. 'Three, or at the utmost four, Catholicks' would he thought be elected;[24] and this, he considered, should provide some reassurance. However 'pro-Catholic' he sometimes seemed to suspicious Englishmen, he was far from wanting to see an Ireland dominated by the Catholic Church. He was as far removed from idealising Roman Catholicism as he was from worshipping democracy. Although he considered the Protestant ascendancy 'generally corrupt and jobbish', the Catholics, he wrote, although 'uncorrupt, at least as yet, . . . are light, frivolous, and inconstant – in short they are *the people*'.[25]

Fitzwilliam, recognising the strength of Catholic pressure,

proceeded almost immediately on arrival to get rid of, not Fitzgibbon (he had promised not to), but five other pieces of Burke's 'worm-eaten furniture': the Chief Commissioner of Revenue, John Beresford; the Attorney General; the Solicitor General; and two Under Secretaries. Then, within a fortnight of coming to Dublin, he coolly informed Portland that, unless he received 'very peremptory directions to the contrary', he intended to give the necessary approval to Grattan's bill. The cabinet in London first warned him to go more carefully, to avoid committing himself; then, when he seemed to be ignoring ministerial advice, *instructed* him to block the bill. It was the hapless Portland's misfortune, as Home Secretary, to be the conveyor of this undeniably 'peremptory' message, and indeed of advice that Fitzwilliam should resign his lord-lieutenancy. Less than three months after arriving in Ireland, he left it an embittered man, proceeding very soon to write two memorials to the King in defence of his conduct, one short and duly presented, the other long but never presented, both with corrections and emendations from the pen of Burke. He was also very shortly *almost* involved in a duel with the John Beresford whom he had earlier dismissed for maladministration and alleged malversation of funds, and who now accused him of slander. Bloodshed was avoided only by the timely arrival of some police officers, who 'secured them, and told them they must submit to be taken into custody, unless they would give their honour that nothing further should pass: which they did . . .'[26]

Burke knew that Fitzwilliam in his Irish dealings had been impetuous and tactically maladroit. Still, he was indignant, indignant and depressed, at what had happened. He thought that Portland had somewhat let Fitzwilliam down; not fought his corner strongly enough in cabinet. He was convinced too that both the Archbishop of Canterbury and the King had played a part in the vetoing of Grattan's bill; and in the King's case at least he was certainly not wrong. George III's refusal to consider the possibility of Catholics being eligible for parliament was to be rigidly consistent, as Pitt himself would find to his cost a few years later. On 3 March 1795, at the time of Fitzwilliam's recall, he had indeed told Pitt of his alarm at his viceroy's 'subversive' and 'unwarrantable' behaviour. The King's mind, declared Burke, had been 'poisond about Ireland'.[27]

By the summer of 1795, still with only the Civil List portion of his expected pension settlement agreed, Burke's finances had reached a point of such 'critical exigence' – he was seriously contemplating flight abroad to escape his creditors[28] – that Walker King, acting for him, approached Pitt with an account of the severity of the crisis. Two sets of creditors, he explained, one of these being Garrick's executors, were being 'with great difficulty staved off from day to day'; a year's interest was due on the Beaconsfield mortgages; and there were 'very troublesome tradesmen's bills unsettled' for over £1000. Also, there was money owed, at least in theory, to Lord John Cavendish, that 'English nobleman of the old stamp' for whom Burke had immense respect and, as it turned out, cause for gratitude. By the terms of his will, dated 28 May 1794, he left 'to the Mr Burkes the money they are indebted to me and I give to Mr Edmund Burke the sum of £1000'. Pitt wasted no time, and the considerable intricacies involved in the remaining Treasury grants were quickly settled. By 2 August, a much relieved Burke was in a position to write, both to Pitt and the King, expressing his gratitude. The time was exactly the first anniversary of his son's death, and as it happened the moment also when news of further tragedy arrived – the death in the West Indies of Major Haviland, the husband of Burke's niece Mary, who was eight months pregnant with their child. 'Sorrow and suffering are our lot', wrote Burke; but at least one accumulation of trouble was now cleared away. For the first time for many years he could look forward to a *financially* secure future. But fear of a broader general insecurity crept into his letter of thanks to Pitt for making 'the remnant' of his existence 'calm and comfortable . . . As things are it is highly flattering to me that I should owe the future ease of my life to the person to whose wisdom and courage Europe must, under God, look for the existence of the moral and social order itself.'[29]

CHAPTER
19

NOBLE LORDS, PENSIONS, AND THE POOR

A FEW MONTHS later Burke published what Somerset Maugham once called 'the finest piece of invective in the English language'.[1] In the well-established manner, it came in the form of a letter[2] – some forty pages long – ostensibly to 'a noble lord' (unnamed, a conventional fiction merely), but actually to the British public at large, attacking two other noble lords, the young Foxites Bedford and Lauderdale, who in the Upper House had spoken against the grant of a pension to him; and also – inevitably, since the author was the Burke of the 1790s – broadening the scope to include his fears for European civilisation, his contempt for Jacobins and their British friends, an apologia for his own public life and career (with a side-glance at his recent personal tragedy), and another great paean of praise for the glorious British constitution:

. . . As long as our sovereign lord the king, and his faithful subjects, the Lords and Commons of this realm – the triple cord which no man can break; the solemn, sworn, constitutional frank-pledge of this nation; the firm guarantee of each other's being and each other's rights; the joint and several securities, each in its place and order, for every kind and every quality, of property and of dignity – as long as these endure, so long the Duke of Bedford is safe, and we are all safe together – the high from the blights of envy and the spoliations of rapacity; the low from the iron hand of oppression and the insolent spurn of contempt. Amen! and so be it . . .

But if the rude inroad of Gallic tumult, with its sophistical rights of man to falsify the account, and its sword as a make-weight to throw in the scale, shall be introduced into our city

264

by a misguided populace, set on by proud great men, themselves blinded and intoxicated by a frantic ambition, we shall
all of us perish and be overwhelmed in a common ruin.[3]

The letter, swift in its changing moods, begins in the urbanest of
irony:

My Lord,

I could hardly flatter myself with the hope that so very early
in the session I should have to acknowledge obligations to the
Duke of Bedford and to the Earl of Lauderdale . . . To be ill
spoken of, in whatever language they speak, by the zealots of
the new sect in philosophy and politics . . . is no matter of
uneasiness or surprise . . . I have laboured hard to earn what
the noble lords are generous enough to pay . . . It is well! It is
perfectly well! . . . I have to thank the Bedfords and Lauder-
dales for having so faithfully and so fully acquitted towards me
whatever arrear of debt was left undischarged by the Priestleys
and the Paines.[4]

He proceeds to a defence of his political career, referring in particular to two aspects of it. First, his work thirteen years before
for economical reform: 'I do not say I saved my country; I am
sure I did my country important service'. Second, India. If he
were to call for a reward, *which he had never done*, it would be for
those services in which, for fourteen years without intermission,
he had shown the most industry and had the least success.

'I was not, like his Grace of Bedford, swaddled, and rocked,
and dandled into a legislator . . . At every step of my progress in
life (for in every step was I traversed and opposed) and at every
turnpike I met, I was obliged to show my passport . . .' Even so,
with only his native abilities and 'many arts' (as he claimed) to
guide him, he had always seen virtue and political health in a
basically aristocratic polity, buttressed and fortified by 'the
people'.[5] What caused him now as much rage as grief was to
witness that same 'natural aristocracy' which he had always
championed betrayed from within:

His Grace may think as meanly as he will of my deserts . . .
But there is one merit of mine which he, of all men living,
ought to be the last to call in question. I have supported with
great zeal, and I am told with some degree of success, those
opinions, or if his Grace likes another expression better, those
old prejudices, which buoy up the ponderous mass of his
nobility, wealth, and titles . . . I have strained every nerve to

keep the Duke of Bedford in that situation which alone makes him my superior . . .[6]

He had been at pains to discover the details of the original grants sold by Henry VIII to the Russell family, at the head of which stood the Dukes of Bedford. He found them to have been 'so enormous as not only to outrage economy, but even to stagger credibility':

> The Duke of Bedford is the leviathan among all the creatures of the Crown. He tumbles about his unwieldy bulk; he plays and frolics in the ocean of the royal bounty . . . His ribs, his fins, his whalebone, his blubber, the very spiracles through which he spouts a torrent of brine against his origin and covers me all over with the spray – everything of him and about him is from the throne. Is it for *him* to question the dispensation of the royal favour?
>
> . . . It is his ancestor, the original pensioner, that has laid up this inexhaustible fund of merit which makes his Grace so very delicate and exceptious about the merit of all other grantees of the Crown. Had he permitted me to remain in quiet, I should have said, 'tis his estate; that's enough. It is his by law; what have I to do with it or its history? He would naturally have said on his side, 'tis this man's fortune – He is as good now as my ancestor was two hundred and fifty years ago. I am a young man with very old pensions; he is an old man with very young pensions, – that's all.
>
> Why will his Grace, by attacking me, force me reluctantly to compare my little merit with that which obtained from the Crown those prodigies of profuse donation . . . ?[7]

Then, rather with relish than 'reluctantly', he examines the circumstances of those rich grants made to 'a Mr Russell . . . a minion of Henry the Eighth'; the first being of lands confiscated from the nobility, the second from the plunder of monastic property – 'possessions voluntarily surrendered by the lawful proprietors, with the gibbet at their door'. The Duke of Bedford

> is secure, and long may he be secure . . . whether he performs any services or not. But let him take care how he endangers the safety of that constitution which secures his own utility or his own insignificance; or how he discourages those who take up even puny arms to defend an order of things which, like the sun of heaven, shines alike on the useful and the worthless. His grants are ingrafted on the public law of Europe, covered with the awful hoar of innumerable ages.

They are guarded by the sacred rules of prescription, found in that full treasury of jurisprudence from which the jejuneness and penury of our municipal law has by degrees been enriched and strengthened.[8]

A flame of serious anger runs through this most accomplished and often eloquent *Letter to a Noble Lord*; so too does a deeply felt fear of lurking civil disaster; but the mood of elevated rhetoric is constantly set off by contrasting passages of suave irony and teasing ridicule, making excellent mischief. The whole thing is brilliantly brought off – like the *Reflections*, it became an immediate best-seller – and more emphatically than any of Burke's previous books and pamphlets declares itself the work of a literary master. The ridicule is generously spread – for the young Duke himself, and his dangerous naivety (Lauderdale, his companion in the dock, is soon forgotten and ignored); for 'the Frenchified faction' with opinions in tune with the Duke's; and of course for those old recipients of Burke's scorn and hatred, the new religionists of the 'rights of man', the speculative revolutionists, the 'cannibal philosophers', and brave new 'constitution-venders' busy on both sides of the Channel.

Among the constitution-vendors he naturally allows pride of place to Abbé Sieyès, the revolutionary theoretician now best remembered for his *Quèst-ce que le Tiers Etat?* Surely the Duke of Bedford must know that the Abbé had an ideal new constitution waiting for all that extensive territory 'monopolised' by the house of Russell?

Abbé Sieyès has whole nests of pigeon-holes full of constitutions ready made, ticketed, sorted, and numbered; suited to every season and every fancy; some with the top of the pattern at the bottom, and some with the bottom at the top; some plain, some flowered, some distinguished for their simplicity, others for their complexity; some with councils of elders, and councils of youngsters; some without any council at all. Some where the electors choose the representatives; others where the representatives choose the electors. Some in long coats, and some in short cloaks; some with pantaloons; some without breeches . . . So that no constitution-fancier may go unsuited from his shop, provided he lives a pattern of pillage, oppression, arbitrary imprisonment, confiscation, exile, revolutionary judgment, and legalized premeditated murder . . . What a pity it is, that the progress of experimental philosophy should be checked by his Grace's monopoly![9]

Surely too the Duke's rolling acres presented an open invitation to an *agrarian* experiment? 'They are a downright insult upon the rights of man . . . They are more extensive than the territory of many of the Grecian republics . . . There is scope for seven philosophers to proceed in their analytical experiments, upon Harrington's seven different forms of republics, in the acres of this one duke. Hitherto they have been wholly unproductive to speculation; fitted for nothing but to fatten bullocks, and to produce grain for beer . . .' Then, Burke having come across a report (which reads incredibly, but he actually quotes from it) from a French revolutionary committee seriously investigating the possibilities of obtaining much-needed saltpetre – to promote gunpowder production – from the fabric of destroyed *châteaux*, Burke adopts this revolutionary fantasy with enthusiastic irony:

> [The French] geographers and geometricians have been some time out of practice. It is some time since they divided their country into squares [the *départements*] . . . They want new lands for new trials . . . The chemists have bespoken him [Bedford] after the geometricians have done with him. As the first set have an eye on his Grace's lands, the chemists are not less taken with his buildings . . . They have calculated what quantity of matter convertible into nitre is to be found in Bedford House, in Woburn Abbey, and in what his Grace and his trustees have still suffered to stand of that foolish royalist Inigo Jones, in Covent Garden. Churches, play-houses, coffee-houses, all alike are destined to be mingled, and equalized, and blended into one common rubbish; and, well sifted and lixiviated, to crystallize into true, democratic, explosive, insurrectionary nitre.[10]

If only this deluded young Duke could be brought to perceive that the butcher's knife was already half out of its sheath for him and the likes of him, however radical their views, or generous their intentions, whether their coat was 'long or short, whether the colour be purple or blue and buff' –

> Is it not a singular phenomenon, that whilst the sansculotte carcass-butchers, and the philosophers of the shambles, are pricking their dotted lines upon his hide, and, like the print of the poor ox that we see in the shop-windows at Charing Cross, alive as he is, and thinking no harm in the world, he is divided into rumps, and sirloins, and briskets, and into all sorts of

pieces for roasting, boiling, and stewing, that all the while they are measuring *him, his Grace is measuring me*; is invidiously comparing the bounty of the Crown with the deserts of the defender of his order, and in the same moment fawning on those who have the knife half out of the sheath – poor innocent!

This brief masterpiece, running swiftly through its moods of anger, eloquence, irony, invective, ridicule, even manages to incorporate – and without a sense of intrusion or irrelevance – a moving account of his own desolation at the death of his son and the consequent destruction of his own ambition to 'found a family' no less worthy than Bedford's:

Had it pleased God to continue to me the hopes of succession, I should have been according to my mediocrity and the mediocrity of the age I live in, a sort of founder of a family. I should have left a son who . . . in every liberal sentiment, and every liberal accomplishment, would not have shown himself inferior to the Duke of Bedford, or to any of those whom he traces in his line . . . But a Disposer whose power we are little able to resist, and whose wisdom it behoves us not at all to dispute, has ordained it in another manner . . . The storm has gone over me; and I lie like one of those old oaks which the late hurricane has scattered about me. I am stripped of all my honours, I am torn up by the roots, and lie prostrate on the earth! There, and prostrate there, I most unfeignedly recognise the Divine justice, and in some degree submit to it. But whilst I humble myself before God, I do not know that it is forbidden to repel the attacks of unjust and inconsiderate men . . . I am alone. I have none to meet my enemies in the gate. Indeed, my Lord, I greatly deceive myself, if in this hard season I would give a peck of refuse wheat for all that is called fame and honour in the world . . . I live in an inverted order. They who ought to have succeeded me are gone before me. They who should have been to me as posterity are in the place of ancestors. I owe to the dearest relation . . . that act of piety which he would have performed to me; I owe it to him to show that he was not descended, as the Duke of Bedford would have it, from an unworthy parent.[11]

At much the same time as *A Letter to a Noble Lord*, Burke wrote his *Thoughts and Details on Scarcity*.[12] The title of this short essay continues, *Originally presented to the Right Honourable William Pitt, in the month of November, 1795*; but it was published only posthumously, in 1800. This sets out Burke's views, as a practising farmer, on the rural economy, and on the part which government, either at national or local level, ought – and particularly ought not – to play in its regulation. In that month of November 1795 there had been noisy demonstrations and some bread rioting; the harvest had been poor; someone in a protesting mob had hurled a stone through the window of the King's coach as he drove to open the new parliamentary session. It was the year to which can be traced the practice, later widely adopted in southern England, of relieving rural poverty by supplementing wages, at the discretion of local magistrates, from the rates – the so-called 'Speenhamland system'. Even so, Burke insisted that, despite current hardships, farm labourers and their families in 1795 fared 'better than in seasons of common plenty fifty or sixty years ago', either out of their 'direct gains' or from charity. It was now proposed, he protested, that farmers should be taxed – *arbitrarily* taxed by justices of the peace – to prop up labourers' wages, 'My opinion', he wrote, 'is against an over-doing of any sort of administration, and more especially against this most momentous of all meddling on the part of authority; the meddling with the subsistence of the people.'[13]

'To provide for us in our necessities', Burke considered, 'is not in the power of the government.'

It would be a vain presumption in statesmen to think they can do it. The people maintain them, and not they the people . . . All the classes and descriptions of the rich . . . are the pensioners of the poor, and are maintained by their superfluity . . . The labouring people are only poor because they are numerous. Numbers in their nature imply poverty . . . That class of dependent pensioners called the rich is so extremely small that if all their throats were cut, and a distribution made of all they consume in a year, it would not give a bit of bread and cheese for one night's supper to those who labour, and who in reality feed both the pensioners and themselves. [Compulsory equalizations] pull down what is above. They never raise what is below; and they depress high and low together beneath the level of what was originally the lowest.[14]

It was still a predominantly rural Britain of which Burke was writing. The trouble as he saw it was that the policies being advocated for the countryside and the rural poor were coming from *townsmen* – tradesmen, manufacturers, shop-keepers; the last people to tolerate interference in their own concerns. Such men should be listened to only 'upon matters within their own province'. Farming ought to be allowed its own commercial freedom, its free market, which would ultimately operate to the benefit not only of farmers but of everybody.

Labour was a commodity, an article of trade. It must therefore be subject to the laws and principles of trade. If in times of low profits and hence low wages, the farmer was to be further burdened with taxation, a 'perfect equality' would indeed be produced, 'that is to say, equal want, equal wretchedness, equal beggary'. A farmer needed profits – and the higher the better. 'But if the farmer is excessively avaricious? – why, so much the better – the more he desires to increase his gain, the more interested is he in the good conditions of those upon whose labour his gains must principally depend.'[15]

Faced with the difficult question, what is to happen to the farm labourer where 'the rate of hire . . . comes short of his necessary subsistence, and the calamity of the time is so great as to threaten actual famine?' Burke's answer sounds bleakly to the modern ear. The man, the family, so situated would then be obliged to come within the province of charity, 'the jurisdiction of mercy'. In that province, Burke considered, 'the magistrate has nothing at all to do: his interference is a violation of the property which it is his office to protect'. Once again we are faced with the sovereign rights of property, a *sine qua non* of all Burke's belief in liberty and justice.

To accept poverty as ineradicable was nothing out of the way; it represented a conviction generally held. Burke's attitude to poverty was almost identical with that of his great contemporary Wesley, and perhaps of most thoughtful and humane men of his day: the true, just 'reward' for the very poor must be looked for only in a future existence. It was however the duty of governments, of the state, to do as little as possible to *worsen* the human conditions; 'it is in the power of government to prevent much evil; it can do very little positive good':[16]

Nothing, certainly, can be laid down on the subject that will not admit of exceptions, many permanent, some occasional. But the clearest line of distinction which I could draw, whilst I had my chalk to draw any line, was this; that the state ought to confine itself to . . . the exterior establishment of its religion;

its magistracy; its revenue; its military force by sea and land; the corporations that owe their existence to its fiat; in a word, to everything that is *truly and properly public* . . . In its preventive police it ought to be sparing in its efforts, and to employ means rather few, infrequent, and strong, than many and frequent . . . [Wise statesmen will] proceed in this the superior orb and first mover of their duty steadily, vigilantly, severely, courageously: whatever remains will, in a manner, provide for itself. But as they descend from the state to a province, from a province to a parish, and from a parish to a private house, they go on accelerated in their fall. They *cannot* do the lower duty; and, in proportion as they try it, they will certainly fail in the higher. They ought to know the different departments of things; what belongs to laws, and what manners alone can regulate.[17]

CHAPTER
20

LAST DAYS, AND AFTERWARDS

IT WAS hardly possible for one such as Burke to 'retire'. Distanced from Westminster politics he might be but, even there, he could not fail to be without some influence while he lived and while his restless intelligence still commanded that untiring pen of his. He possessed too the allegiance, more than ever necessary to him after his son's death, of that small group of devoted friends and admirers who between them acted for him in an assortment of roles – editorial assistant, copyist, proof-reader, political contact, legal or financial adviser – a kind of loosely associated unofficial Burke secretariat or composite 'man of business': the lawyer French Laurence (now, thanks to Fitz-william and indirectly Burke, M.P. for Peterborough); Major William Cuppage, a cousin of Will Burke's; the brothers Walker King (the future bishop of Rochester) and John King, who was currently Under Secretary to Portland at the Home Office; their brother-in-law Thomas Venables, who contrived to secure for the ever-unfortunate Will Burke, by now 'broken in mind, body, and fortune' (he had recently suffered two strokes), a haven in the Isle of Man from his still pursuing creditors*; Edward Nagle, a distant relative of Burke's, and Captain E. J. A. Woodforde,

---

*William Burke died in the Isle of Man in 1798. He has never had a good press, yet clearly he was a man who, despite his failings and shortcomings, could inspire sincere affection. Obviously so with Burke and all his family, but far from exclusively so. He left £350 in his will to pay for the return home to India of the servant he had brought with him on his coming back to England in 1793; but the man claimed indifference to India and, Burke was told, 'wishes to lay his bones as near his good master's as he can, and anxiously begs that a cast iron railing should be allowed to inclose the stone'.

these last two usefully placed as subordinates of Windham at the War Office. Windham himself was the one member of Pitt's cabinet personally close to Burke and wholly in sympathy with his views on the war and the Jacobin menace. He was, said Burke, the one 'gentleman in office' who sometimes visited him 'as an old and infirm friend', but with whom he avoided 'talk on public business'.[1] Specially valuable among this group of friends and assistants, during these last three years or so of his physical decline, were Walker King, Edward Nagle, and French Laurence. Both King and Laurence had been contemporaries and friends of his son, and now they became almost son-substitutes. Burke learned not only to rely on their business efficiency but to trust and love them for themselves. 'My dearest Walker', he writes to him, *meaning* it. And Laurence, newly member for Peterborough, became during the 1796–97 parliamentary session practically Burke's representative and spokesman. It was fitting that he and Walker King should eventually become editors of the first collection of Burke's writings.

A matter which absorbed Burke's energies during 1796 almost as vitally as the fate of European civilisation itself was the establishment and subsequent welfare of a school for the sons of French refugees, or (more usually) the refugee sons of dead French royalists. This essentially was *his* school. It was he who persuaded the government to make available an empty War Office building at Penn in Buckinghamshire, three miles away from Beaconsfield; and it was he who managed to extract from them an initial grant of £1000 to launch the project, together with a promise of future financial support. Among those associated with him in the enterprise were Lord Buckingham, the ever-admirable Mrs Crewe, and the Bishop of St-Pol-de-Léon, an *émigré* from Brittany; but Burke soon found that the Bishop's intentions for the school were very different from his own. For one thing, the Bishop wanted the staff to be French and the instruction to be entirely in the French language – in fact, according to the exasperated Burke, for the whole establishment to be 'run on the principles of a seminary of monks'.[2] Burke wished the teaching to be 'at least one good half, if not three parts' in English, if only to avoid condemning the boys 'to an universal exile'. However, despite difficulties and vexations, the school at Penn gave him a field of activity where he could see

results and be happy with them. He spent some of his own
money in helping to get things started, and we find him during
1796 busy with such unaccustomed tasks as stocking up the
school kitchen, procuring supplies of clothes and of beds and
bedding, and appointing a school housekeeper, as well as giving
himself the occasional pleasure of entertaining new arrivals at his
own house.

'The wastecoats and trowsers will be very acceptable', he tells
Lord Buckingham in June 1796. 'As yet we can make no great
use of the cravats. The boys in all the schools hereabouts have
their necks open . . . Government has given me hopes of reim-
bursement and support early this month. Otherwise I truly
touch the bottom of my resources.' He dressed his pupils in a blue
uniform; and their hats bore a white cockade inscribed *Vive le
Roi*.[3] The boys 'wear out their cloaths fast', he discovered, 'and
the first cloth I bought was not of a good quality'; they needed to
be 'compleatly new-clad'. James Prior, in his *Edmund Burke* (1826)
tells how Burke once ran into trouble with his long-established
Beaconsfield housekeeper, Mrs Webster, when he tried to spirit
away, for school consumption, a haunch of venison earmarked
by her for his own dinner table when important guests were expected: '"Sir, Sir", she cried out, fastening upon the article in
question – "I cannot part with my haunch – I cannot indeed"';
and part with it she would not and did not.[4]

There were only some twenty-odd boys at the start. 'I see them
almost every day', he told his fellow trustee Lord Buckingham,
'and at almost all hours, as well at their play as at their studies
and exercise . . . A set of finer lads, for their age and standing,
will not be seen in Europe.' With their teachers, especially during
the first months, he was not so happy. He refused to accept the
first two sent by the Bishop of St Pol (they spoke no English at
all), and the man recommended by the Bishop to be the principal
master Burke declared to be 'a poor obstinate ignorant clown
neither more nor less'. Although eventually, by what he described
as a judicious mixture of firmness and conciliation, he thought
he had brought this man 'into reasonable good humour', he still
considered that he had made 'a great error in the beginning' by
not putting an Englishman in charge. The number of boys at the
school swelled in time to sixty, with a staff of four, and it survived
until 1820.[5]

A visitor to Beaconsfield in May of the year 1796 was Burke's old farming acquaintance Arthur Young, who had by now become Secretary to the Board of Agriculture. Young, author of the *Travels in France during 1787, 1788, 1789*, had earlier thought Burke's all-out assault on the French revolutionaries over-harsh; but their extremism and violence had shocked him, and by 1793 he had published *The Example of France, a Warning to Britain*, which Burke commended as 'incomparably well done' and 'bottomd upon practical principle'.[6] Young wanted to learn at first-hand the views on regulating agricultural wates of the man he considered to be the 'greatest and most brilliant' figure of the day, whose name would 'without question descend to the latest posterity'.[7]

The two men spent five hours strolling round Burke's farm. The talk later, over dinner, interesting enough, would have become still more so (Young thought) if Mrs Crewe, who was among the guests, had not been so full of plans 'for ladies' subscriptions for the emigrants' and for extracting money from 'the fangs of the Bishop of St Pol de Leon'. This celebrated lady's powers of conversation Young reckoned brilliant; but they were

> not sufficient to raise the drooping spirits of Mr Burke; it hurt me to see the languid manner in which he lounged rather than sat at table, his dress entirely neglected, and his manner quite dejected . . . He gave more attention to her account of Charles Fox than to any other part of her conversation . . . To behold so great a genius so depressed with melancholy, stooping with infirmity of body, feeling the anguish of a lacerated mind and sinking to the grave under accumulated misery; to see all this in a character I venerate . . . wounded every feeling of my soul.[8]

No doubt Young had come to Beaconsfield on one of Burke's poorer days, of which he was beginning to have all too many. The cancer which was to kill him in rather more than a year's time (the 'vice in my stomach') already had a punishing hold. But not every visitor to Beaconsfield took away as depressing an image as Young's. James Mackintosh, whose *Vindiciae Gallicae*, five years before, had been next to Paine's the most substantial reply to Burke's *Reflections*, had read and very warmly praised in the *Monthly Review* the newly published *Two Letters on a Regicide Peace*. Mackintosh still considered Burke's view of 'the present politics of Europe' mistaken, but he had come round, somewhat as Arthur Young had, to approve of 'the general principles' of one whom he held in 'the most affectionate veneration'. Would Burke (he now wrote to ask) allow him the honour of a few minutes' visit in town in order that he might *tell him so* in person? Burke, although suspicious of Mackintosh's 'supposed conversion', replied that he was seldom well enough to be much in town, but would Mackintosh care to come instead to Beaconsfield? – which he did, and stayed not for a few minutes but for a few days, shortly after Christmas 1796.

Forty years later, his *Memoirs* recalled 'the astonishing effusions' of Burke's conversation, 'pouring out . . . the sublimest images mingled with the most wretched puns'; entering with 'cordial glee' into the children's games, even 'rolling about with them on the carpet'; and speaking of his approaching death 'with due solemnity but perfect composure'. It was to Mackintosh during this visit that Burke commented of Fox, *with a deep sigh*, that he was a man 'made to be loved'.[9]

For some months before this Burke had acknowledged that his stomach was 'irrecoverably ruin'd'. He and Jane, herself a semi-invalid now, went that August to Bath for 'the waters', but during their first fortnight there he became suddenly and seriously worse, losing much flesh and strength. Then he had briefly benefited from a remission – 'it seems', he said, 'as if Providence had intended me for some short reprieve' – remaining however very weak and afflicted. Though the flow of his correspondence and political writing continues to the end uninterrupted and unabated, for much the great part of it he now had to rely on dictation, the amanuensis most frequently employed being his friend and kinsman Edward Nagle.

When Mrs Crewe at the end of August had learned from Burke's Bath physician Dr Caleb Parry, misleadingly as it turned out, that his patient was 'in a state of progressive amendment', she was so pleased and relieved that she wrote off immediately to Fitzwilliam, to set his mind also at rest. What she went on to express in that letter, heartfelt plainly, is the handsomest possible testimonial to a very long friendship which had healthily survived all the latterday Whig ructions. She 'had no scruple to assert', she said, that Mr and Mrs Burke were 'the best friends I ever had out of my own family for above three and thirty years': Mr Burke had been 'ever *more* to me than a *real* parent'.[10]

By mid-September Burke and his wife were back at home. Bath would have been 'a terrible place in winter', he decided; 'no air – no exercise; colds perpetually caught. Here I have air – every convenience and accommodation – my old habits – and the consolation, such as it is, of not being far from what was dearest to me, and which I wish . . . to be my place of rest'.[11] Despite days when pain and discomfort made work impossible, even dictating to Nagle, he continued busily with his letters on the threatened, so-called 'regicide peace'. With their controlled indignation exploding from time to time in angry eloquence, they rank among the finest of his writings.

He was engaged on the third of these extended 'letters' (which he urgently instructed his new publishers, Rivington, to advertise but which failed to appear until after his death) at a time towards the end of 1796 when it really did seem possible that, to his high-principled disgust, peace between Britain and France might soon be arranged. Lord Malmesbury had been sent to Paris by the British government to negotiate the preliminaries. Malmesbury, however, in Burke's view fortunately, was 'kicked out of Paris' just before Christmas, or as Burke felt free to put it privately to his friend and ally Windham, 'this mongrel has been whipped back to his kennel yelping and with his tail between his legs'.[12] Negotiations had broken down, broadly because France would not relinquish the Austrian Netherlands and Britain refused to surrender Ceylon and the Cape of Good Hope. This failure could at least afford Burke a measure of *schadenfreude*, but the King's 'declaration' to parliament relating to it provoked from him just the sort of private outburst of *un*controlled indignation which he was always too good a writer to have passed for public scrutiny: it was 'a dreadful, shameful, scandalous act of incurable phrensy'.[13]

He did sometimes volunteer mild self-reproof for such intemperate outbursts, or offer a toning-down of the ungenerous name-calling and extravagant censure which the correspondence to his closest friends sometimes displays. He could for instance accuse Pitt – this in a letter to Fitzwilliam – of shabbiness, selfishness, and a mean desire to hang on to office at all costs, 'under the sufferance of France'. But shortly afterwards – this to

Mrs Crewe – he concedes, 'If I have written with any personal asperity towards Mr Pitt, it was very unwise and very unbecoming'.[14] His private correspondence might sometimes run wild, as once or twice in the Commons his speeches had in earlier days, but self-criticism and literary judgment ensured that his published writing very seldom slipped the leash.

At Beaconsfield his doctor was still his old friend and Trinity Dublin contemporary Richard Brocklesby, but in January 1797 he was persuaded to seek 'second opinions' in London, of which in the course of a few days he collected no fewer than four. Before the month was out, however, he was writing to tell his old doctor at Bath, the highly regarded Caleb Parry, that in view of the acceleration as he put it of his 'decline and fall', he proposed coming again to Bath. It was from there that he wrote to Windham, 'I can read upon my back and dictate as I do now, whilst all the great hunters are driving their spears into a dead boar'. Opiates were prescribed, which dulled the gastric symptoms but produced such giddiness that he became scarcely able to stand upright. 'They have taken the town', he told Laurence, 'and are now attacking the citadel.' The opiates therefore were abandoned. He continued to lose flesh, and thought in March that he would not be able to leave Bath even if he wanted to, being so feeble that he could not walk more than a few steps without assistance.[15]

At the end of May, however, he did go back to Beaconsfield. He knew of course that he was dying, and he had already directed in his will, made immediately after his son's death in 1794, that he should be buried, with as little 'noise' as possible, at Beaconsfield. He decided therefore that he might as well return home alive rather than as a corpse.

All around him he saw 'difficulty and disaster'. There were even naval mutinies in Spithead and the Thames estuary; and he suggested, no doubt not *quite* seriously, that they might soon see 'a French army convoyed by a British navy to an attack upon this kingdom'. Pitt's conduct of the war seemed to him passive and unenterprising, at least in European terms. 'What has an enemy to fear', he asked, 'from a nation who confines herself to an inert, passive, domestic defence?'[16] This was not as things had been in the days of Marlborough, or even of Pitt's father. And in these last months of his life he returned constantly, and ever more dispiritedly, to the problems of his native Ireland.

His hatred of the Protestant 'junto' at the seat of executive power in Dublin Castle was violent and unceasing, and they it was whom he held chiefly responsible for the dangerous alienation both of the Catholic majority and of the Presbyterian radicals. 'English government', he wrote, 'has farmed out Ireland . . . to the little narrow faction that domineers there.'[17] In general, he was much less inclined to blame the English for the woes of Ireland than the Irish themselves, particularly of course 'persons of power' there.

> Contrary to all reason, experience, and observation, many persons in Ireland [he told John Keogh] have taken it into their heads that the influence of the Government here has been the cause of the misdemeanours of persons in power in that country – I must speak the truth – I must say that all the evils of Ireland originate within itself . . . England has hardly any thing to do with Irish government. I heartily wish it were otherwise . . .[18]

And he reminded Keogh that his Catholic movement carried some dangerous luggage. There was Wolfe Tone for instance, professedly a Church of Ireland man, yet at the same time secretary to the Irish Catholic delegations in London and implicated with 'certain Protestant conspirators and traitors' who were acting 'in direct connexion with the enemies of all government and all religion'. Then there were the alarmingly radical 'United Irishmen'. Worst of all, the Irish Whigs (as he reminded Fitzwilliam, 'your Lordship's friends, and let me add my friends') had he claimed 'gone the full length of Jacobinism' and were doing all they could to 'pull up the land-marks of private property and public safety, and to disunite the two kingdoms'.[19] As usual in his private letters, he was somewhat exaggerating – they had *not* 'gone the full length of Jacobinism' – but it was true that they had of late parted company with Burke's opinions on three main issues. In addition to complete Catholic emancipation (where of course Burke agreed with them), they wanted a substantial measure of parliamentary reform, anathema to Burke; a tax on absentee landlords – he had always argued against one; and peace with France. Grattan, their chief and eloquent spokesman, claimed that their policies were aimed at *preventing* the spread of democratic principles, but Burke was sure they would have the opposite effect – on an Ireland already on the edge of a revolutionary precipice. The colours of the Irish Grattanites, he judged, were now hardly to be distinguished from the English Foxites.

He did not live quite long enough to see, and mourn for, the Irish rebellion of 1798; but already, at the time of his death, his native land was tearing itself apart in civil and religious unrest and violence. He could see for it only a bitter future, and to the end it caused him angry grief.

Shortly before his death, peacefully, on 9 July 1797, Jane Burke received a letter from Fox, suggesting the possibility of a visit; but there was to be no deathbed reconciliation. 'Made to be loved' Fox may well have been, but not to be forgiven in what might seem a show of putting past personal friendship above present public principle. 'Mrs Burke presents her compliments to Mr Fox', ran her stiff reply, 'and by his desire has to inform Mr Fox that it has cost Mr Burke the most heart-felt pain to obey the stern voice of his duty in rending asunder a long friendship, but that he deemed this sacrifice necessary; that his principles remain the same . . . and that these principles can be enforced only by the general persuasion of his sincerity. For herself Mrs Burke has again to express her gratitude to Mr Fox for his inquiries.'[20]

As he directed, he was buried in Beaconsfield church in the same grave as his son and brother. Seventy members of the 'benefit society' he had patronised walked in the procession to the church ahead of the coffin, which was borne on the shoulders of the Dukes of Portland and of Devonshire, of Earl Fitzwilliam and the Earl of Inchiquin, of Lord Chancellor Loughborough, Mr Speaker Addington, William Windham, and Sir Gilbert Elliot. Mrs Crewe supervised the funeral arrangements.* Jane Burke lived on at Beaconsfield with her husband's niece Mary Haviland for nearly fifteen years longer. Shortly before her death in April 1812 she had sold the estate to a Buckinghamshire neighbour, retaining only the right to the house and grounds for the rest of her days – a sale which incidentally extinguished the

---

*The account of the burial must carry the following rather macabre footnote. Papers among the Additional Manuscripts in the British Museum declare: 'Burke buried in a wooden coffin. Afraid the French should find his body; his bones moved from that coffin to a leaden one later.' See Thomas W. Copeland, *Edmund Burke, Six Essays* (1950), pp. 90–1.

last remnants of Burke's debts. A year after Jane's death the house died too, being completely destroyed by fire.

Burke's parliamentary career and his short post-parliamentary career after 1794, when he was still seeking to influence national policy, had been for the most part a record of failure. He never had office higher than the Paymastership, and never quite breached the defences protecting the exclusive circle of the governing class. He found what he thought would be the road of reconciliation with his fellow countrymen in America blocked by government, by the King, by the obstacles of nature, and (what to him was most galling) by popular opinion. The energies which he expended through half a lifetime to persuade Englishmen to treat his native Ireland, and particularly its Catholic majority, with more imagination and toleration, more generosity, more justice, ran into unending frustrations; and his disappointment here was made greater from his growing conviction that, in the end, it was the Irish who were their own worst enemies. The pro-secution of misgovernment in India, and especially the impeach-ment of Hastings, into which he poured fourteen years of con-scientious and strenuous effort, ended in defeat and bitterness. The Whig party which he had done more than anyone to build up fell apart at the first impact from the French Revolution, and he thenceforth regarded himself as expelled from it.

But from the ashes of all this failure arose a remarkable phoenix of achievement and repute. First, from a sifting of his assertions, declarations, insights, ruminations, fulminations, prejudices, digressions, and parentheses may be assembled a historic intellectual basis for politico-philosophical conservatism. For nearly two centuries now, with necessary reservations, qualifi-cations and adaptations, conservative thinkers and statesmen of Britain and the English-speaking, British-influenced world have been able to claim Burke as one, and perhaps the foremost, of their founding fathers. Paradoxically, he came for a long time to be seen also as one of the forefathers of nineteenth-century British Liberalism, though Fox usually remained the Liberals' preferred hero. (The paradox is perhaps superficial merely, since the Vic-torian Liberal party was itself partly the creation of liberal-minded ex-Conservatives such as Gladstone.) Whatever their sadness at his to them eccentric rejection of parliamentary reform and his anti-radical extremism, Victorian and Edwardian

Liberals could always admire Burke for his devotion to civil and religious liberty, his attacks on court influence and corruption, his campaign for clean government in India and better justice for Ireland.

Indeed, probably the best of all the short lives of Burke came from the Gladstonian Liberal and man of letters, John Morley. His assessment of Burke's stature is not without a few strong words of condemnation, particularly concerning the *Letters on a Regicide Peace*, which Morley reckoned to be 'deplorable' and even 'repulsive', with their 'gulfs of empty words, reckless phrases, and senseless vituperations'. He condemned the *Regicide Peace* not so much because in it Burke uncompromisingly urged a prosecution of the war (though Morley we may remember was the member of Asquith's cabinet who made his opposition to war in 1914 a resigning matter) as because in these last writings he deserted his own precepts of practicality and flexibility in the face of changed circumstances – the rulers of France after the end of the Terror, Morley thought, being incomparably better men than the earlier revolutionaries.[21]

Then there is Burke the writer. It is his double role, political and literary, which sets one looking for parallels or rivals. More or Bacon, perhaps, Sidney or Ralegh, Clarendon or Bolingbroke, in earlier times? Disraeli, Churchill in later ? Even among such remarkable company Burke must stand high. From the beginning, the best literary opinion accepted him as one of the great prose stylists; and as Hazlitt put it – excepting he thought only Jeremy Taylor – of all English writers the one whose prose was nearest to poetry. De Quincey, making *no* exception, called him simply 'the supreme writer of his century'.* Morley, reminding us that Burke's mind was 'full of the matter of great truths', gave him 'a magnificence and elevation of expression that places him among the highest masters of literature . . . And we do not dissent', he adds, 'when Macaulay, after reading Burke's work

---

*It is interesting to discover that Wordsworth and Coleridge – both at first friendly and later hostile to French revolutionary ideas – looked to Burke less as a writer than as a politician, and even in Coleridge's case as a sage and prophet. Wordsworth's Tory election pamphlet of 1818, addressed to the freeholders of Westmorland, rates Burke as 'the most sagacious politician of his age'. Coleridge's *Biographia Literaria* of the previous year praises him, however illogically or mistakenly, as 'a *scientific* statesman, and therefore a seer'.

over again, exclaims "How admirable! The greatest man since Milton!"' Matthew Arnold, again without qualification, called him 'our greatest English prose-writer'; and Leslie Stephen agreed: 'Considered simply as a master of English prose, Burke has not, in my judgment, been surpassed in any period of our literature'.[22] He was also of course a considerable orator, a practising farmer, and in his early days a writer on aesthetics and history. From an age now when politicians' contributions to literature and the arts amount usually to the publication during their retirement of volumes of self-justifying memoirs, Burke's protean activity and versatile excellence command all the more respect – even when we recall that he was himself never above publishing works whose principal object was self-vindication.

Some latterday historians have had dismissive or sharply critical things to say of him, and I remember Sir Herbert Butterfield severely chiding a leading member of the Namier school for presuming, as he said, to 'take a rise' out of Edmund Burke. But then Namier and his associates always rather downgraded the importance of ideas in eighteenth-century politics, concentrating instead on its 'structure' and minutiae, its mechanics and established practices. Richard Pares too, in his brilliant *George III and the Politicians*, of 1953, perhaps overstepped the mark when he wrote Burke down as 'the theorist and high priest of snobbery'.[23] But such writers of recent years, pointing as they do, often justly enough, to Burke's failings and mistakes, his misconceptions and excesses, seldom omit to grant him *genius*, even if only to palliate or excuse, or even if – as with Pares – the accolade is relegated to a footnote.[24]

Karl Marx, also in a footnote, once (in *Das Kapital*) dismissed Burke as a hireling, first, of the American colonists and then, during the French Revolution, of the English oligarchy. And Marxists subsequently have not failed to discover in Burke the 'essential bourgeois'. Surprising variations on this theme, however, and even inversions of it, may emerge, with Marxism and Freudianism engagingly mingled. Thus we are able to learn that Burke was a *conscious* anti-bourgeois who was troubled by *subconscious* bourgeois longings within himself, 'just as he was troubled by a divided sexuality'. The traveller down this byway off the highroad of modern enlightenment may explore further: Burke, it seems, hated the Jacobins because he *subconsciously identified them with the suppressed parts of his own sexuality.*[25]

Burke's massive correspondence reveals a man intimately and tirelessly engaged, not only with the great issues of the day, but with the details also of countless minor matters and ephemeral controversies public and personal. But in the major concerns of the day he rarely failed to penetrate beneath the surface of events to the foundations of principle below. Thus Burke the statesman becomes Burke the political philosopher, a change of description with which he would not have been altogether happy. Yet it is this constant resort to fundamentals which gives him a degree of relevance to the problems and controversies of succeeding ages. In a twentieth century that has had much experience of revolutions for export, his *Reflections on the Revolution in France*, with the various subsequent writings that may be regarded as its codas or appendices, possess perhaps a special resonance; and his objections to egalitarianism, his fears of 'levelling down' – it is the very modern-sounding phrase he sometimes uses – have a particularly contemporary ring. It is certainly tempting to picture some modern Burke – a Burke, with his literary powers, transposed through two centuries – responding for instance to the currently stock reaction to 'élitism', or to the now obligatory genuflection before the name of democracy, or to the present condition of Ireland. However, it may well be a mistake to search too particularly to discover Burke's relevance to modern problems and controversies, except in the most general manner, since at the centre of his political thought lay the conviction that every matter considered, every solution proposed, must be judged strictly in its contemporary context. The great and basic principles of justice and equity ought always to have as their guide, and must often need as their limitation, the hardly less important principles of practicality and prudence. Indeed he once declared prudence to be the most important of all.

Of course objections to Burke's fundamentals may be fundamental too. His idealisation of a 'natural' aristocracy for example, and the rigidity of his claims for 'prescriptive' rights of property, cannot hope for total assent today; but here too a sense of history (one of Burke's own greatest strengths) ought to rescue us from facile anachronisms. His view of society was no *more* aristocratic than that of almost all his parliamentary colleagues including even perhaps Fox, that inescapably aristocratic 'man of the people' whose interpretation of 'people' was no less limiting than Burke's own.

Burke's fierce hatred of atheism is intelligible enough; but when he observes no distinction between atheism and the fashionable 'deism' of his day, or what might now be called merely scepticism or agnosticism, a charge of intolerance (in many ways the weakest to be levelled against him) is not easy to dismiss. His repeated declarations that church and state must be component parts of an integrated unity may indeed be 'relevant' to modern controversies here and abroad, but they can hardly gain general acceptance in a largely secularised western world. Burke however saw himself as the defender of Christian civilisation. Christendom was a concept still alive to him, and to see Christendom menaced – perhaps wounded mortally – by 'atheists' and nostrum-mongers and the false philosophers of upheaval was intolerable to him; his critics said, not always unreasonably, drove him mad. To such criticism his reply would consistently echo the tone and spirit of the biblical verses which his memory spontaneously prompted when the Foxite pack in May 1791, 'the little dogs and all', were baying and yapping at him from the Commons benches. Turning aside amid the hubbub towards the chairman of the proceedings, he offered him the words of Paul[26] answering the Roman Procurator of Judaea, who had said that much learning had made Paul mad: 'I am not mad, most noble Festus, but speak forth the words of truth and soberness'.

CHRONOLOGY

1728	William Burke born.
1729	Edmund Burke born (Dublin, 12 January (New Style)).
1733	E.B.'s brother Richard born.
c.1735–c.1740	E.B. lives with relatives of his mother in Ballyduff, County Cork.
1741–44	E.B. at Abraham Shackleton's boarding school at Ballitore; Richard Burke also there later.
1744–49	E.B. at Trinity College, Dublin.
1748	Montesquieu's *De l'Esprit des Lois*.
1750	E.B. begins study for the bar at Middle Temple, London; abandoned by 1755; interests largely literary. Friendship with William Burke.
1756	E.B.'s *A Vindication of Natural Society*.
1757	E.B. marries Jane Mary Nugent (1734–1812), daughter of Irish Catholic doctor; publishes *Origin of our Ideas of the Sublime and the Beautiful*; contracts to write *An Abridgement of English History* (published posthumously). The elder Pitt Secretary of State.
1758	E.B. contracts to edit the *Annual Register*; birth of his sons Richard (February 1758–1794) and Christopher (December, died in infancy).
1759–64	E.B. private secretary to William Hamilton who, as Irish Chief Secretary, twice employs E.B. in Ireland (1761–2, 1763–4).
1760	Accession of George III.
1762	Rousseau's *Du Contrat Social*.
1762–65	Ministries of Lord Bute and George Grenville; the Stamp Act, 1765.
1763	E.B.'s brother Richard appointed Collector and Receiver General in Grenada, West Indies. Treaty of Paris ends 'Seven Years' ('French and Indian') War.
1764	E.B. joins Reynolds, Johnson, and others in founding 'The Club'. Wilkes expelled from Commons; riots in London. E.B. breaks with Hamilton.
1765	E.B. private secretary to Marquis of Rockingham; M.P. for Wendover (re-elected 1768). First Rockingham ministry (1765–6); Stamp Act repealed; Declaratory Act 'declares' British *right* to tax colonies.
1766–68	Elder Pitt (Lord Chatham) chief minister, but collapses; Townshend duties on tea, glass, paper, etc., 1767. E.B. receives Freedom of City of Dublin.
1768	E.B. borrows money to buy estate at Beaconsfield ('Gregories', 'Butler's Court'). Further Wilkes riots.
1769	E.B. indirectly but damagingly involved, with his brother Richard, William Burke, and Lord Verney in heavy losses in East India stock. *Letters* of 'Junius'.
1770	E.B. publishes *Thoughts on the Cause of the Present Discontents*. Richard

	Burke ordered back to Grenada. E.B. becomes Agent to the General Assembly of New York.
1772	Warren Hastings becomes Governor of Bengal.
1773	E.B. visits France with his son. Lord North's (East India) Regulating Act opposed by E.B. and the Rockingham Whigs. Boston Tea Party, followed by so-called 'Intolerable Acts' in Massachusetts.
1774	E.B.'s *Speech on American Taxation*. First Continental Congress in America. E.B. elected at Bristol. Warren Hastings Governor General in India. Accession of Louis XVI.
1775	E.B.'s *Speech on Conciliation with America*.
1776	American Declaration of Independence.
1777	William Burke goes to India as agent for the Raja of Tanjore. British surrender at Saratoga.
1778	France enters War of American Independence.
1779	Irish 'volunteers' active; North makes concessions to Irish Catholics and trade interests; E.B. in trouble with his Bristol constituents.
1780	E.B.'s *Speech on Economical Reform*. He declines the poll at Bristol; returned for Malton. Invasion of the Carnatic by Haidar Ali. Affair of the Begams of Oudh.
1781	E.B. becomes leading member of Commons Select Committee on Indian Affairs. British surrender at Yorktown signals early end of American war.
1782	E.B. Paymaster General in second Rockingham ministry which lasts only three months. Richard Burke (senior) Secretary to the Treasury, Richard Burke (junior) Deputy Paymaster, William Burke Deputy Paymaster in India. Legislative independence ceded to Dublin parliament. E.B.'s Civil Establishment Act. Death of Rockingham; Shelburne Prime Minister; E.B. resigns with Fox and Fox's followers.
1783	*Ninth Select Committee Report* on Indian affairs. Shelburne defeated; Fox–North coalition; E.B. again Paymaster; appointments of his 'family' similarly restored or confirmed. E.B. elected Rector of Glasgow University. Plays major part in steering Fox's India Bill through House of Commons. Loses office with its defeat in House of Lords and government's dismissal. Secures minor sinecure for his son Richard.
1784	General election confirms defeat of Whigs. The Younger Pitt prime minister for the rest of E.B.'s life, and beyond. Death of Johnson.
1785	E.B.'s *Speech on the Nabob of Arcot's Debts*. Select Committee publishes *Eleventh Report*.
1787	Constitution of United States of America drafted; ratified 1788. House of Commons votes to impeach Warren Hastings. Meeting of the Notables in France; fall of Calonne.
1788	E.B. opens Hastings impeachment proceedings in Westminster Hall.

1788–89　Illness and temporary madness of George III. E.B. at odds with his party during Regency crisis.

1789　French States General meets (May); becomes National Assembly (June); Bastille stormed (July); decrees abolishing feudal rights (August); the 'October Days'; Church property secularised (November). E.B. begins his 'Paris letter' to Depont.

1790　Civil Constitution of the Clergy in France (July). E.B. publishes *Reflections on the Revolution in France*.

1791　E.B. breaks publicly with Fox and a majority of the Whigs (May). French royal family's abortive flight to Varennes (June). E.B.'s son represents him on a mission to the émigré Princes at Coblenz. Tom Paine replies to E.B.'s *Reflections* in *The Rights of Man* (1791-2). E.B. publishes *Appeal from the New to the Old Whigs*.

1792　Death of Reynolds. France at war with Austria (April). Attack on Tuileries (August). French armies overrun Belgium, Rhineland, Nice, Savoy. September massacres in Paris. Richard Burke jr. goes to Ireland as agent for the Catholic Committee. E.B. active on behalf of French refugee clergy in England.

1793　Execution of Louis XVI (January) and of Marie Antoinette (October). Britain at war with France (February). Revolt in la Vendée. Reign of Terror in France (1793-4). Voting rights extended to Irish Catholics.

1794　E.B.'s final speech in the Hastings impeachment. Deaths of his brother and his son.

1795　Hastings acquitted. E.B. begins *Letters on a Regicide Peace*. Rule of the Directory begins in France (November).

1796　E.B. publishes *Letter to a Noble Lord, Thoughts on Scarcity*, and two *Letters on a Regicide Peace*. Founds school for émigré boys at Penn.

1797　E.B. dies (9 July); buried at Beaconsfield.

1798　Death of William Burke.

1812　Death of Jane Burke.

References

INTRODUCTION

1. Hazlitt, *Works*, vii.301–13
2. Works, iii.16
3. Ibid., vi.114
4. Corr., vi.303–4
5. Ibid., v.342
6. Works, ii.335
7. Ibid., 265
8. Works, ii.356
9. Ibid., 368
10. Ibid., 138

1. CHILDHOOD AND YOUTH, 1–9

1. Poem in letter to Shackleton, 9 June 1744
2. Samuels, 9
3. *Leadbeater Papers*, i.27; Samuels, 12
4. Samuels, 94
5. *London Evening Post*, April 14–17, 1770
6. Corr., i.3; Samuels, 23n.
7. Corr., i.15; Samuels,40
8. Corr., i.33–4; Samuels, 56–7
9. Corr.
10. Samuels, 96
11. Ibid., 83–4
12. Ibid., 84
13. Ibid., 99
14. Ibid., 214
15. Ibid., 162–3
16. Corr., i.101
17. Ibid., 102
18. Samuels, 364
19. Ibid., 197

2. EARLY YEARS IN LONDON, 10–22

1. Works, i.407
2. Corr., i.111
3. Dilke, *Papers of a Critic*, ii.368–70
4. *Memoirs of Sir Philip Francis*, ii.103
5. Corr., i.112
6. Ibid., 112–13
7. Ibid., 115–18
8. Ibid., 119–20
9. Ibid., 141
10. Ibid., 190n.
11. Magnus, *Edmund Burke*, 331–2
12. Copeland, *Edmund Burke, Six Essays*; Bryant, 289–97

13. Corr., i.129-30
14. Ibid., 133
15. Walpole to Montagu, 22 July 1761
16. *Leadbeater Papers*, i.47-8
17. Corr., i.147-8
18. Ibid., 161-2
19. Walpole to Montagu, 15 November 1763
20. Corr., i.178-81, 192-3, 197
21. Ibid., 166-7, 173-4
22. Wraxall, *Memoirs*, ii.28n.
23. Corr., i.215
24. Ibid., 206-8
25. *Grenville Papers*, iii.188-93, 212-13; Fortescue, i.139
26. Corr., i.208

3. WESTMINSTER AND BEACONSFIELD, 23-38

1. Corr., ii.xi
2. Burke to Markham, November-December 1771
3. Macleane to Wilkes, 24 December 1765
4. Corr., i.225
5. Ibid., 233
6. Ibid., 241
7. Blunt, *Mrs Montagu*, i.139
8. T. W. Copeland, in *Statesmen, Scholars, and Merchants*, 302n.
9. Copeland, op. cit., 299-300
10. Boswell, *Johnson*, ii.450
11. Northcote, *Reynolds*, ii.211
12. Boswell, *Johnson*, ii.450
13. Corr., i.250
14. Ibid., 252
15. Newcastle Papers, quoted Corr., i.252n.
16. Corr., ii.509, iii.186, iv.79
17. Works, i.412
18. Namier and Brooke, iii.93-4
19. Barry, *Works*, i.53-5
20. Ibid., 86-90
21. Corr., i.269; Namier and Brooke, ii.155
22. Corr., i.302
23. Walpole, *Memoirs of Reign of George III*, iii.16
24. Wecter, 38-9; Namier and Brooke, ii.156; Corr., ii.334n.
25. Corr., i.351
26. Boswell, *Johnson*, iii.310
27. Wecter, 26-39
28. Namier and Brooke, ii.156, iii.94
29. Corr., ii.252-86
30. Ibid., 31, 438, 443
31. Ibid., 58, 85, 140
32. Young, *Eastern Tour*, Letter 31
33. Corr., ii.165-7, 180, 212, 223, 231-3, 237, 240, 247, 316-19

4. COURT, ARISTOCRACY AND 'PRESENT DISCONTENTS', 39–54

1. Corr., i.352. ii.70
2. Corr., ii.96
3. Works, i.354
4. Corr., ii.78–9
5. Ibid., 80n.
6. O'Gorman, *Rise of Party*, 258–61
7. Albemarle, *Rockingham*, ii.144–5
8. Works, i.313–16
9. Ibid., 346
10. Ibid., 323, 335–7
11. *On a Regicide Peace*, Works, v.189–90
12. Works, i.367
13. Corr., vii.52–3
14. Pares, *George III and the Politicians* (1967 edn., 6)
15. Corr., ii.150
16. Works, i.365
17. Ibid., 367–8
18. Ibid., 372
19. Ibid., 375–8
20. Cavendish, *Debates*, i.15
21. G. Rudé, *Wilkes and Liberty*, 159
22. Corr., ii.336, 483
23. Ibid., 124–5, 127
24. Parl. Hist., xvi, 919–21, 923–4
25. Corr., ii.133–4
26. Ibid., 135–6
27. Shackleton to his wife, 25 May 1780
28. Corr., iii.181

5. 'THE LITTLE CIRCLE OF MY FAMILY', 55–62

1. Walpole to Lady Ossory, 11 March 1773
2. Works, ii.348
3. Corr., i.212
4. Quoted Wecter, 49–50
5. Corr., ii.109–110
6. Ibid., 149
7. Wecter, 57
8. Ibid., 60
9. Corr., ii.461
10. Corr., iii.285
11. Wecter, 64–5
12. Corr., iii.146, 453
13. Wecter, 66–8
14. Ibid., 69–71

6. INDIA, IRELAND, AND AMERICA 1770–1774, 63–74

1. Corr., ii.474–81
2. Ibid., 499
3. Walpole to Mann, 27 March 1772

4. Corr., ii.407
5. Ibid., 399
6. Ibid., 523
7. Hickey, *Memoirs*, i.284–5
8. Corr., ii.203–4
9. Ibid., 390
10. Ibid., 362, 365
11. O'Gorman, *Rise of Party*, 320
12. Burke to Rockingham, 9 September 1769
13. Walpole, *Last Journals*, i.494
14. Corr., ii.532
15. P. Langford, in *Statesmen, Scholars, and Merchants*, 135–52
16. L. Stephen, *English Thought in the Eighteenth Century*, ii.219
17. *Speech on American Taxation*, Works, i.382–437; Parl. Hist., xvii.1215–69

7.   BRISTOL AND AMERICA 1774–1779, 75–89

1. Corr., iii.33
2. Ibid., 48
3. Ibid., 53; Namier and Brooke, ii.156
4. Dilke, *Papers of a Critic*, ii.341
5. Corr., iii.375
6. H. Owen, *Ceramic Art in Bristol*, quoted Corr., iii.119n.
7. Works, ii.1–42
8. Corr., iii.191–5
9. Works, ii.1–42
10. Corr., ii.528–9
11. *Speech on Conciliation with America*, Works, i.450–509
12. Corr., iii.139
13. Ibid., 181–2
14. Burke to O'Hara, 17 August 1775
15. Corr., iii.179–80
16. Quoted ibid., 175
17. Ibid., 89
18. Ibid., 185–6
19. Ibid., 170
20. Burke to Rockingham, ibid., 88–9
21. Ibid., 107
22. Ibid., 192–3
23. *Morning Chronicle*, 16 October 1775
24. Parl. Hist., xvii.963–92
25. Corr., iii.218, 244–5
26. Burke to Shackleton, 11 August 1776, ibid., 286–7
27. Walpole, *Last Journals*, ii.104
28. Corr., iii.427
29. P. Langford, in *The Prime Ministers*, i.129–37
30. Corr., iv.126
31. Ibid., 142
32. Ibid., 43
33. Ibid., 169
34. Burke to Portland, 16 October 1779, ibid., 154–5

8. BRISTOL, IRISH TRADE, AND THE CATHOLICS, 90–101

1. Works, iii.301
2. Corr., iii.387
3. Ibid.
4. *Letter to Thomas Burgh*, Works, v.509
5. Span to Burke, 13 April 1778, Corr., iii.429
6. Corr., iii.430
7. Ibid., 439
8. Ibid., 433
9. Ibid., 442–3
10. Ibid., 438
11. Works, v.491–510
12. Ibid., 504
13. *The Popery Laws*, Works, vi.26
14. Works, vi.67
15. *Speech Previous to the Election*, Works, ii.165
16. Warren Hastings Speech, 15 February 1788
17. Corr., iii.112
18. *The Popery Laws*, Works, vi.32–3
19. Corr., iv.7
20. Works, vi.115
21. Corr., iv.245–7
22. Works, ii.127–68
23. Ibid., 138
24. Ibid., 137
25. Ibid., 145
26. Ibid., 142
27. Corr., iv.266–81
28. Ibid., 278, 293
29. To Joseph Harford, Corr., iv.296
30. Corr., iv.287n., 293

9. ECONOMICAL REFORM, TANJORE, 102–117

1. Corr., iv. 227
2. Ibid., 298
3. Crewe, *Table-Talk*, 52
4. Christie, *Myth and Reality*, 309–10
5. Corr., iii.348
6. *Annual Register* 1777, 97
7. J. D. Gurney, in *Statesmen, Scholars, and Merchants*, 220–41
8. *Writings and Speeches*, v.4–16
9. Ibid., 120–1
10. Fortescue, v.3019
11. *Parl. Hist.*, xxii.705
12. Corr., iv.423
13. O'Gorman, *Rise of Party*, 448
14. Corr., iv.424
15. Ibid., 437–8
16. Ibid., 315
17. Ibid., 304–5

18. Ibid., 430
19. Corr., v.70
20. *Parl. Hist.*, xxi.19
21. Ibid., 33–4
22. *Speech on Economical Reform*, 11 February 1780
23. *Parl. Hist.*, xxi.233
24. Brooke, *King George III*, 229
25. Grafton, *Autobiography*, 338
26. Russell, *Fox Memorials and Correspondence*, ii.322

10. SHELBURNE, COALITION, AND INDIA BILL, 118–133

1. Corr., v.8n.
2. H.M.C., Carlisle, 632–3
3. *Parl. Reg.*, vii.312–15
4. Walpole, *Last Journals*, ii.453
5. Boswell, *Private Papers*, xv.234
6. Corr., v.13–14
7. Walpole, *Last Journals*, ii.456
8. L. Sutherland, in Corr., ii. Appendix, 548–51
9. Corr., v.56, 72
10. Ibid., 86
11. Ibid., 87–9
12. *Parl. Hist.*, xxiii.803
13. Corr., v.911, 920
14. Ibid., 170–1
15. P.J. Marshall, in *Writings and Speeches*, 2–3
16. *Public Advertiser*, 21 January 1781
17. Corr., v.254
18. *Writings and Speeches*, v.196–333
19. *Parl. Hist.*, xxiii.800
20. Sutherland, *East India Company*, 391
21. Ibid., 397
22. Quoted Sutherland, op. cit., 401
23. Minto MSS, quoted Cannon, *Fox-North Coalition*, 112
24. *Writings and Speeches*, v.449
25. Ibid., 386
26. Ibid., 391
27. Ibid., 402
28. *Parl. Reg.*, xii.430
29. Fortescue, vi.4546

11. AWAY FROM POLITICS, 134–160

1. Minto, ii.136 (May 1793)
2. More, *Memoirs*, i.450
3. Boswell, *Journal*, 3 May 1781, 14 April 1788
4. Boswell, *Private Papers*, xvi.115–16
5. Bryant, *Edmund Burke and his Literary Friends*, 117
6. Quoted Bryant, 271
7. *Thraliana*, quoted Bryant, 272

8. Crewe, 12
9. Ibid., 33
10. Ibid., 42–3
11. Ibid., 39
12. Ibid., 22–3
13. Ibid., Corr., ii.544
14. Crewe, 13
15. Ibid., 29
16. Ibid., 56
17. Bryant, 2
18. Ibid., 289–97
19. D'Arblay, *Diary and Letters*, i.60
20. Corr., v.25
21. Ibid., viii.462
22. Ibid., 26
23. D'Arblay, op. cit., i.550
24. More, *Memoirs*, i.204, 235–6
25. Corr., iii.236–7
26. Boswell, *Johnson*, iv.276
27. Walpole, *Memoirs of . . . George III*, quoted Bryant, 276
28. Bryant, 196–7
29. *Farington Diary*, 103
30. Ibid., 136
31. Boswell, *Johnson*, iv.280
32. More, *Memoirs*, i.283
33. Boswell, *Johnson*, v.76
34. Bryant, 107
35. Boswell to Temple, 12 August 1775
36. Boswell, *Private Papers*, ix.156
37. Ibid., xvii.50–1
38. Corr., iv.444–5
39. Ibid., v.34–5
40. Boswell, *Private Papers*, xvi.49; Corr., v.138–9
41. Corr., v.248–50
42. Boswell, *Private Papers*, xvii.93–100; Bryant, 127–9
43. Crabbe, *Life*, 187
44. Quoted ibid., 90
45. Ibid., 95
46. Corr., iv.358–9; Bryant, 182
47. Corr., iv.454
48. Speech on parliamentary reform, 7 May 1782
49. Quoted Bryant, 223
50. Gibbon, *Autobiographies*, 320–1
51. Leslie and Taylor, *Reynolds*, ii.137
52. Gibbon, op. cit., 342n.
53. Ibid.
54. Leslie and Taylor, op. cit., i.319
55. Sir William Beechey, quoted Bryant, 58
56. Boswell, *Private Papers*, xv.202
57. Leslie and Taylor, op. cit., i.291
58. Hazlitt, *Works*, ed. Howe, xi.220

59. Corr., vii.41
60. Ibid., v.200
61. Ibid., 200–1, 261–2
62. Ibid., 50

12. THE CAUSE OF INDIA, 161–181

1. Corr., v.154
2. Ibid., 155
3. *Speech on East India Bill*, Works, ii.197
4. *Ninth Report of Select Committee*, Works, iv.29
5. *Writings and Speeches*, v.531
6. J.D. Gurney, in *Statesmen, Scholars and Merchants*, 220–41; P.J. Marshall, in *Writings and Speeches*, v.478–80; L. Sutherland, *East India Company*, 342n.
7. Book 3, lines 391–2
8. *Writings and Speeches*, v.550
9. Ibid., 531
10. Ibid., 506–7
11. Ibid., 532, 536
12. Ibid., 519–21
13. Ibid., 543
14. *Parl. Hist.*, xxiv.1352–62
15. Wecter, 87–9
16. Corr., v.297
17. Ibid., 214–15, 218, 296–8, 301–2
18. Ibid., 214, 255, 260
19. Ibid., 159
20. *Writings and Speeches*, v.460–78
21. Marshall, *Impeachment*, 33
22. Ibid., 35
23. Corr., v.241, 243
24. Ibid., 252–7
25. Prior, *Memoir*, ii.176
26. Corr., v.289, 300
27. Leadbeater, *Diary*, 23–24 October 1786
28. Quoted Marshall, in *Statesmen, Scholars, and Merchants*, 255
29. *Parl. Hist.*, xxvi.89
30. Ibid., 101–13
31. Corr., vi.197
32. Ibid., v.370–1
33. Minto, i.177–9
34. Speech, 27 May 1789
35. Speech, 27 May 1790
36. Marshall, op. cit., 85
37. D'Arblay, *Diary and Letters*, ii.479–80
38. Ibid., 509
39. Ibid., 516
40. Quoted Marshall, op. cit., 78
41. Corr., v.408–9
42. Ibid., 406
43. Ibid., 419–20

13. THE REGENCY CRISIS AND THE CONSTITUTION, 182–192

1. See I.R. Christie, in *History*, vol.71 (1986), 207–8
2. Burke to Charlemont, 9 August 1789
3. Minto, i.263
4. *Parl. Hist.*, xxvii.715
5. Corr., v.437
6. *Parl. Hist.*, xvii.822
7. Ibid., 819
8. Ibid., 820
9. Ibid., 881
10. *The Times*, 19 January 1789, quoted Derry, *Regency Crisis*, 136
11. Corr., v.437
12. Ibid., 436–45
13. D'Arblay, *Diary and Letters*, iii.149–56
14. *Parl. Hist.*, xxvii.1167–79, 1196–9, 1213–15, 1246–8
15. Ibid., 1248
16. Corr., v.461
17. Sheridan, *Letters*, ed. Price, i.211–12; Corr., v.453–4, 457
18. G.M. Trevelyan, *Lord Grey of the Reform Bill*, 25–6
19. Marshall, *Impeachment* . . . , 79
20. Corr., v.468

14. REVOLUTIONISTS, DISSENTERS, AND THE 'PARIS LETTER', 193–202

1. Corr., vi.10
2. Ibid., 25
3. Ibid., 30
4. Ibid., 39–46
5. Ibid., 47–8
6. Ibid., 49
7. Corr., vii.56–7
8. Corr., v.469–71, vi.82–5, 100–04
9. Corr., vi.94–5
10. Works, ii.348
11. Corr., vi.85–7, 151
12. Ibid., 89
13. Ibid., 91
14. E. Jerningham to Burke, Corr., vi.203–4

15. 'REFLECTIONS ON THE REVOLUTION IN FRANCE', 203–214

1. Works, ii.285–6
2. Ibid., 486
3. Ibid., 284
4. Ibid., 426
5. Ibid., 296–8
6. Ibid., 301
7. Ibid., 303
8. Ibid., 304–5

9. Ibid., 295
10. Ibid., 308–9, 312, 354–5
11. Ibid., 319
12. Ibid., 322–5
13. Ibid., 410
14. Ibid., 334–5
15. Ibid., 325, 396–7
16. Ibid., 328–9, 457–8
17. Ibid., 358–60, 362–3, 371
18. Ibid., 429–31
19. Ibid., 419–21
20. Ibid., 438–40
21. Ibid., 412–13

16. 'SEE, THEY BARK AT ME!', 215–228

1. Corr., vi.238–9
2. *Farington Diary*, iv.22
3. Corr., vii.58
4. Corr., vi.129
5. *Speeches of C. J. Fox*, ed. Wright, iv.194
6. Portland to Fitzwilliam, 21 April 1791
7. *Parl. Hist.*, xxix.377
8. Ibid., 380–1
9. Ibid., 387–8
10. Ibid., 394
11. Ibid., 397
12. Quoted Copeland, *Edmund Burke, Six Essays*, 80
13. Corr., vi.292, 300, 331
14. Ibid., 291
15. Works, iii.24
16. Ibid., 82, 85
17. Ibid., 86–7
18. Ibid., 109–11
19. Ibid., 111, 115
20. Charles Grey, quoted Mitchell, 179
21. *Morning Herald*, 8 May 1792
22. Windham, *Diary*, 213
23. Sir G. to Lady Elliot, Minto, ii.6–9
24. Corr., iv.310–311
25. Ibid., vi.271n.
26. Ibid., 271–6
27. Ibid., 313–14
28. Ibid., 449

17. FRANCE AND IRELAND 1791–1793, 229–251

1. Corr., vi.418–22
2. Ibid., 315, 347
3. Ibid., 340n.
4. Ibid., 349–52

5. Ibid., 441–5, 446–8
6. H.M.C., Fortescue, ii.190–1
7. Corr., vi.436–8
8. R. Therry, quoted ibid., intro. xvii
9. Corr., vi.132–5
10. Ibid., 398
11. Ibid., vii.268
12. Works, iii.298–344
13. Corr., vii.81
14. Works, iii.343
15. Ibid., 344
16. Ibid., 335–6
17. Ibid., 336–7
18. Corr., vii.118
19. Ibid., 166
20. Wolfe Tone, *Diary*, 16 October 1792
21. Works, v.521–44
22. Corr., vii.122–5
23. R.I. and S. Wilberforce, *Life of Wilberforce*, v.157
24. Corr., vii.189–200
25. Ibid., 93
26. Ibid., 106
27. Ibid., 141
28. Ibid., 189–96
29. *Memoirs of William Hickey*, ed. Spencer, iv.81
30. Corr., vii.184–5, 203–4, 213
31. Ibid., 207, 214, 216, 219–27, 230, 232, 280
32. Ibid., 171–2
33. Ibid., 191, 218
34. Ibid., 284
35. Ibid., 271–2, 277–8, 284
36. Ibid.; ibid., 307
37. Minto, ii.325–6
38. Portland to Fitzwilliam, 30 November 1792
39. Works, iii.467–510
40. Corr. vii.436–8
41. Ibid., 446–7
42. Ibid., 328
43. *Morning Post*, 29 December 1792, quoted Corr., vii.328
44. *Sheffield Register*, 18 January 1793, quoted Corr., vii.340
45. Corr., vii.304
46. Ibid., 344, 461
47. Minto, ii.121–2
48. Corr., vii.423, 514
49. Ibid., 445, 450n.
50. Ibid., 523

18. 'AN ILIAD OF WOE', 252–263

1. Corr., vii.596
2. H.M.C., Charlemont, ii.230

3. Corr., vii.418
4. Ibid., 396–410
5. Minto, ii.8
6. Corr., vii.558
7. Fitzwilliam MSS, quoted ibid., 559
8. Corr., vii.562–3
9. Ibid., 563–6
10. Ibid., 566–9
11. Fitzwilliam to Portland, quoted Corr., vii.562n.
12. J.H. Rose, *Pitt and Napoleon*, 228; Aspinall, *Later Corr.*, ii.238, 244–5
13. Corr., vii.578
14. Ibid., 575, 579
15. Corr., viii.35
16. Ibid., 325, 401
17. Ibid., 42, 52, 64, 70, 334, 347, 364
18. Copeland, *Edmund Burke, Six Essays*, 83; Corr., x.30
19. Corr., viii.183
20. Auckland, iii.320
21. Corr., viii.57
22. Ibid., 75
23. Ibid., 34–5, 136, 137, 255
24. Ibid., 133
25. Ibid., 207
26. Lord J. Cavendish to Burke, 28 June 1795
27. Corr., viii.192–3; Aspinall, *Later Corr.*, ii.336–40
28. Corr., viii.280
29. Ibid., 284, 290–2, 294

19. NOBLE LORDS, PENSIONS, AND THE POOR, 264–272

1. *Cornhill* magazine (Winter 1950), 49
2. 'A Letter . . . to a Noble Lord', Works, v.110–51
3. Ibid., 137–8
4. Ibid., 110–11
5. Ibid., 124–5
6. Ibid., 127
7. Ibid., 129–30
8. Ibid., 131, 136–7
9. Ibid., 142–3
10. Ibid., 143–4
11. Ibid., 135–6
12. *Thoughts and Details on Scarcity*, ibid., 83–109
13. Ibid., 109
14. Ibid., 84, 90
15. Ibid., 89
16. Ibid., 83
17. Ibid., 107–8

20. LAST DAYS, AND AFTERWARDS, 273–286

1.   Corr., ix.278
2.   Ibid., 21
3.   Prior, ii.356
4.   Ibid., 357–8
5.   Ibid., 17, 20, 40
6.   Corr., vii.356
7.   Young, *Autobiography*, 260
8.   Ibid., 260–1
9.   Mackintosh, *Memoirs*, i.91–2; Prior, ii.364–6; Corr., ix.192–6, 204
10. Corr., ix.76–7
11. Ibid., 139
12. Ibid., 203, 205, 211
13. To Windham, ibid., 211
14. Ibid., 79, 129
15. Ibid., 234–6, 241, 283
16. Ibid., 268, 333, 338
17. Ibid., 165
18. Ibid., 114
19. Ibid., 283
20. Prior, ii.397
21. Morley, *Burke*, 210–4
22. Stephen, *English Thought in the Eighteenth Century*, ii.222
23. Pares, *George III and the Politicians* (1967 edn.), 13
24. Ibid., 84n.
25. For this, and other modern 'interpretations' of Burke, see F.P. Lock, *Burke's Reflections*, 190–9
26. *Acts*, xxvi, 24–5

BIBLIOGRAPHY

THERE ARE numerous editions of the works of Edmund Burke. References in the text are to the six-volume Bohn edition of 1855-6. In this, among other miscellaneous writings,

Volume 1 includes On the Sublime and the Beautiful, Thoughts on the Present Discontents, Speeches on America.

Volume 2 includes Bristol Speeches, Speech on Economical Reform, Reflections on the Revolution in France.

Volume 3 includes Speech on the Nawab of Arcot's Debts, Letters on Irish Catholics, Appeal from the New to the Old Whigs.

Volume 4 includes Ninth and Eleventh Reports of Committee on Indian Affairs, Charges Against Warren Hastings.

Volume 5 includes Further Charges Against Warren Hastings, Thoughts on Scarcity, Letter to a Noble Lord, Letters on a Regicide Peace.

Volume 6 includes Further Letters and Tracts on Irish Affairs, An Abridgement of English History.

The standard American edition is *The Works of Edmund Burke* (Little, Brown; 12 volumes, Boston, 1865-7).

In progress is a complete edition from the Clarendon Press, Oxford of *The Writing and Speeches of Edmund Burke* (general editor, P. Langford). So far published are:

Volume 2: Party, Parliament, and the American Crisis, 1766-1774 (ed. P. Langford, 1981)

Volume 5: India, Madras, and Bengal, 1774-1785 (ed. P.J. Marshall, 1981)

The Correspondence of Edmund Burke (general editor, Thomas W. Copeland) is published by the Cambridge University Press and the University of Chicago Press, in 10 volumes:

Volume 1 (to 1768), ed. T.W. Copeland (1958)
Volume 2 (1768-1774), ed. L.S. Sutherland (1960)
Volume 3 (1774-1778), ed. G.H. Guttridge (1961)
Volume 4 (1778-1782), ed. J.A. Woods (1963)
Volume 5 (1782-1789), eds. H. Furber and P.J. Marshall
Volume 6 (1789-1791), eds. A. Cobban and R.A. Smith (1967)
Volume 7 (1792-1794), eds. P.J. Marshall and J.A. Woods (1968)
Volume 8 (1794-1796), ed. R.B. McDowell (1969)
Volume 9 (1796-1797), eds. R.B. McDowell and J.A. Woods (1970)
Volume 10 (index), by B. Lowe, P.J. Marshall and J.A. Woods (1978)

The most nearly up-to-date comprehensive Burke bibliography is by W.B. Todd, *A Bibliography of Edmund Burke* (1964)

Contemporary Sources

ALBEMARLE, Earl of: *Memoirs of the Marquis of Rockingham* (2 vols, 1852)
ASPINALL, A. (ed.): *The Correspondence of George Prince of Wales* (8 vols, 1963-71)
— *The Later Correspondence of George III* (vols 1 and 2, 1963)

AUCKLAND, Lord: *Journal and Correspondence* (4 vols, 1861–2)

BARRY, J.: *Works* (2 vols, 1809)

BOSWELL, J.: *Life of Johnson*, ed. G.B. Hill, rev. L.F. Powell (6 vols, 1934–64)

— *Private Papers*, eds. G. Scott and F. Pottle (New York, 1928–34)

CAVENDISH, Sir H.: *Debates of the House of Commons*, ed. J. Wright (2 vols, 1841–3)

CREWE, Mrs F.: 'Extracts from Mr Burke's Table Talk', in *Miscellanies of the Philobiblon Society*, vol.7 (1862–3)

D'ARBLAY, F. (Fanny Burney): *Diary and Letters*, ed. C. Barrett (4 vols, 1876)

FARINGTON, J.: *Diary*, ed. J. Greig (8 vols, 1922–28)

FORTESCUE, Sir J.: (ed.) *Correspondence of King George III, 1760–1783* (6 vols, 1927–8)

FOX, C.J.: *Speeches in the House of Commons*, ed. J. Wright (1815)

— *Memorials and Correspondence*, ed. Lord J. Russell (4 vols, 1853–7)

FRANCIS, Sir P.: *Memoirs*, eds. J. Parkes and H. Merivale (2 vols, 1867)

GARRICK, David: *Letters*, eds. D.M. Little and G.M. Kahrl (3 vols, 1963)

GIBBON, Edward: *The Autobiographies*, ed. John Murray (2nd edn., 1897)

Grenville Papers, ed. W.J. Smith (vol. 3, 1853)

HAZLITT, William: *Works*, ed. P.P. Howe, vol. 8 ('The Character of Mr Burke')

HICKEY, William: *Memoirs*, ed. A. Spencer (4 vols, New York, 1923–5)

Historical Manuscripts Commission: 15th report Appendix, Part 3 (Fortescue MSS) (1892); and Part 6 (Carlisle MSS) (1892); 12th report, Part 10, and 13th report, Part 8 (Charlemont MSS) (1891–4)

HOLLAND, Lord: *Memoirs of the Whig Party* (2 vols, 1852)

JOHNSON, Samuel: *Taxation no Tyranny* (1775)

LEADBEATER, Mrs M.: *Leadbeater Papers* (2 vols, 1862)

Leinster, Correspondence of Emily, Duchess of, ed. B. Fitzgerald (3 vols, Dublin 1949–57)

MACKINTOSH, Sir J.: *Vindiciae Gallicae* (1791)

— *Memoirs* (2 vols, 1835)

MINTO, Earl of: *Life and Letters*, ed. Countess of Minto (3 vols, 1874)

NORTHCOTE, J.: *Life of Sir Joshua Reynolds* (2 vols, 1818)

PAINE, Thomas: *The Rights of Man* (1791–2)

Parliamentary History of England, ed. W. Cobbett (1806–20), vols 16–31

Parliamentary Register, ed. J. Debrett (1780–96)

RUSSELL, Lord J.: *Memorials and Correspondence of Charles James Fox* (2 vols, 1852)

THRALE, H.: *Thraliana, the Diary of Mrs Hester Lynch Thrale*, ed. K.C. Balderston (2 vols, 1942)

WALPOLE, Horace: *Letters* (various editions)

— *Memoirs of the Reign of George III*, ed. G.F.R. Barker (4 vols, 1894)

— *Last Journals*, ed. A.F. Steuart (2 vols, 1910)

WINDHAM, William: *Diary*, ed. Mrs H. Baring (1866)

WRAXALL, Sir N.W.: *Historical and Posthumous Memoirs*, ed. H.B. Wheatley (5 vols, 1884)

YOUNG, Arthur: *Autobiography*, ed. M. Betham-Edwards (1898)

— *Travels in France during the years 1787, 1788, 1789*, ed. M. Betham-Edwards (1913)

Secondary Sources

ASPINALL, A.: *Politics and the Press, 1780–1850* (1949)
AYLING, S.: *George the Third* (1972)
— *The Elder Pitt* (1976)
— *A Portrait of Sheridan* (1985)
BARKER, E.: *Burke and Bristol*
BLUNT, R.: *Mrs Montagu 'Queen of the Blues'* (2 vols, 1932)
BROOKE, J.: *King George III* (1972)
— *The Chatham Administration, 1766–1768* (1956)
    (see also Namier)
BRYANT, D.C.: *Edmund Burke and his Literary Friends* (St Louis, 1939)
BUTTERFIELD, Sir H.: *George III, Lord North, and the People* (1949)
— *George III and the Historians* (1957)
CANNON, J.A.: *The Fox–North Coalition* (1969)
— *Aristocratic Century: the Peerage of Eighteenth Century England* (1984)
CHAPMAN, G.W.: *Edmund Burke, the Practical Imagination* (Harvard, 1967)
CHRISTIE, I.R.: *Crisis of Empire: Great Britain and the American Colonies, 1754–1783*
    (1966)
— *The End of North's Ministry, 1780–1782* (1958)
— *Myth and Reality in late Eighteenth Century Politics* (1970)
— *Stress and Stability in late Eighteenth Century Britain* (1984)
— 'George III and the Historians, Thirty Years On' (in *History*, vol. 71, 1986)
CLIMENSON, E.J.: *Elizabeth Montagu, Queen of the Bluestockings* (2 vols, 1906)
COBBAN, A.: *A History of Modern France* (vol. 1, 1957)
— *Edmund Burke and the Revolt against the Eighteenth Century* (2nd edn., 1960)
CONE, C.B.: *Burke and the Nature of Politics* (Kentucky, 2 vols, 1957–64)
COPELAND, T.W.: *Edmund Burke, Six Essays* (1950)
COURTNEY, C.P. *Montesquieu and Burke* (1963)
CRABBE, G.: *Life of the Rev. George Crabbe* (1834)
DERRY, J.W.: *Charles James Fox* (1972)
— *The Regency Crisis and the Whigs* (1963)
DICKINSON, H.T.: *British Radicalism and the French Revolution* (1985)
— *Liberty and Property, Political Ideology in Eighteenth-Century Britain* (1977)
DILKE, C.W.: *Papers of a Critic* (vol. 2, 1875)
EHRMAN, J.: *The Younger Pitt*, vols 1 and 2 (1969, 1983)
FOORD, A.S.: 'The Waning of the Influence of the Crown', in *English History Review*, vol. 62 (1947)
FREEMAN, M.: *Edmund Burke and the Critique of Political Radicalism* (1980)
GANDY, C.I. and STANLIS, P.J.: *Edmund Burke: a Bibliography of Secondary Studies to 1982* (New York, 1983)
GUTTRIDGE, G.H.: *English Whiggism and the American Revolution* (Berkeley and Los Angeles, 1963)
HEMLOW, J.: *The History of Fanny Burney* (1958)
HIBBERT, C.: *King Mob* (1958)
HUDSON, D.: *Sir Joshua Reynolds* (1958)
LANGFORD, P.: *The First Rockingham Ministry, 1765–1766* (1973)

LASKI, H.J.: *Political Thought in England from Locke to Bentham* (1920)

LESLIE, C.R. and TAYLOR, T.: *Life and Times of Sir Joshua Reynolds* (2 vols, 1865)

LOCK, F.P.: *Burke's Reflections on the Revolution in France* (1985)

MAGNUS, P.: *Edmund Burke* (1939)

MAUGHAM, W.S.: 'After Reading Burke', in *Cornhill* magazine (1950)

MARSHALL, P.J.: *The Impeachment of Warren Hastings* (1965)

MAXWELL, C.: *Dublin under the Georges* (1946)

MITCHELL, L.: *Charles James Fox and the Disintegration of the Whig Party, 1782–1794* (1971)

MORLEY, John: *Burke* (1887)

NAMIER, Sir L.: *England in the Age of the American Revolution* (2nd edn., 1961)

— (and) BROOKE, J.: *The History of Parliament: The House of Commons, 1754–1790* (3 vols, 1964)

O'BRIEN, G.: *Anglo-Irish Politics in the Age of Grattan and Pitt* (Dublin, 1988)

O'GORMAN, F.: *The Whig Party and the French Revolution* (1967)

— *Edmund Burke, his Political Philosophy* (1973)

— *The Rise of Party in England: the Rockingham Whigs* (1975)

PARES, R.: *King George III and the Politicians* (1953)

PARKIN, C.W.: *The Moral Basis of Burke's Political Thought* (1956)

PRIOR, J.: *Memoir of the Life of Edmund Burke* (2nd edn., 2 vols, 1826)

RUDÉ, G.: *Wilkes and Liberty* (1962)

SAMUELS, A.P.I.: *Early Life, Correspondence, and Writings of Edmund Burke* (1923)

SMITH, E.A.: *Whig Principles and Party Politics* (1975)

SMITH, V.A. and EDWARDES, S.M. (eds.), *The Oxford History of India* (2nd edn., 1923)

STANLIS, P.J. (ed.): *Edmund Burke: the Enlightenment and the Modern World* (Detroit, 1967)

— *The Relevance of Edmund Burke* (New York, 1964)

STEPHEN, Sir L.: *History of English Thought in the Eighteenth Century* (vol. 2, 1876)

SUTHERLAND, L.S.: *The East India Company in Eighteenth-Century Politics* (1952)

— 'Edmund Burke and the first Rockingham Ministry', in the *English Historical Review*, vol. 47 (1932)

THAL, H. van (ed.): *The Prime Ministers* (vol. 1, 1974)

WECTER, D.: *Edmund Burke and his Kinsmen* (Boulder, Colorado, 1939)

WHITEMAN, A., BROMLEY, J.S., and DICKSON, P.G.M.: *Statesmen, Scholars, and Merchants* (1973)

INDEX